FROM DEVELOPMENT TO DEMOCRACY

From Development to Democracy

THE TRANSFORMATIONS OF MODERN ASIA

DAN SLATER

JOSEPH WONG

PRINCETON UNIVERSITY PRESS
PRINCETON & OXFORD

Published by Princeton University Press
41 William Street, Princeton, New Jersey 08540
99 Banbury Road, Oxford OX2 6JX

press.princeton.edu

All Rights Reserved

First paperback printing, 2024
Paper ISBN 9780691231082
Cloth ISBN 9780691167602
ISBN (e-book) 9780691231075

Library of Congress Control Number: 2022931391

British Library Cataloging-in-Publication Data is available

Editorial: Bridget Flannery-McCoy, Alena Chekanov
Jacket/Cover Design: Karl Spurzem
Production: Erin Suydam
Publicity: James Schneider, Kathryn Stevens

This book has been composed in Arno

CONTENTS

Economic development is strongly associated with democracy, but economic development does not necessarily lead to democracy. This much we already know. *From Development to Democracy* does not assert otherwise; there is no inevitable or automatic historical trajectory whereby richer countries become more democratic ones. But our book's title sheds light on what the reader will encounter in at least three helpful ways.

First, "from development to democracy" speaks to our book's *scope*. In every empirical chapter, we begin by exploring the remarkable histories of economic development that have swept across Asia in the modern era. We see this as the necessary foundation for analyzing virtually any imaginable outcome in the region we call "developmental Asia." In this book, the outcome we seek to explain is developmental Asia's uneven record of democratization. We hope to persuade the reader that beginning with an understanding of the region's varied types of economic development goes a long way toward comprehending why some Asian authoritarian regimes have experimented successfully with democratic reforms, others have experimented unsuccessfully with democracy, and still others have not braved the risks of democratization at all.

Second, "from development to democracy" addresses a shared historical *sequence*. Nowhere in developmental Asia have political elites experimented with democracy before devoting decades to promoting rapid economic development. Democracy has sometimes followed development, and other times it has not. But the question of democracy cannot be ignored forever, and pressures for political reform cannot be forestalled forever in the face of a modernizing, increasingly demanding society.

In all twelve Asian cases we explore in this book, authoritarian rulers have faced the dilemma of whether to respond to the social changes attending rapid economic development with major democratizing reforms, or not. Unlike most conventional takes on democratic prospects, we do not presume that democracy emerges only from the ashes of a collapsed authoritarian regime (i.e., democracy through weakness). Rather, we contend and demonstrate that surprisingly stable and substantive democracies can evolve from strong authoritarian regimes that promote economic development and then concede democratic reforms, even without conceding defeat (i.e., democracy through strength).

Our theory offers an explanation for why some countries in developmental Asia have indeed moved "from development to democracy" while others have kept this sequence—a sequence long predicted by modernization theory—at bay. In a significant number of instances, incumbent authoritarian elites choose democracy because they see democratizing through strength as an optimal outcome when it comes on the heels of economic development.

In this important way, our theory of democracy through strength is an ode to the structural features of the classic modernization approach to development and democratization. But we nonetheless augment modernization theory: first, by exploring how different types of development shape differing prospects for democratization through Asia's diverse "developmental clusters"; and second, by stressing the decision among elites to democratize, and how profoundly elite confidence (i.e., victory confidence and stability confidence) shapes that decision. Democracy doesn't "just happen" as a matter of course with a society's modernization; rather, real people need to make risky decisions that have vital implications for democracy's fate.

Third and finally, "from development to democracy" says something about our own personal and professional *stories*. When we both began studying Asian politics as undergraduates in the early to mid-1990s, there was really no question of which aspect of Asian politics to study. Asian politics meant Asian political economy; Asia meant development. It was the part of the world where development was happening, and everybody who was interested in development wanted to learn from it. The Asian financial crisis of 1997–98 was not yet visible on the horizon. So when we both started looking at Asia as scholars, development was what we were looking at; development was what we were looking for. Our first research and writings as graduate students focused almost exclusively on topics related to economic developmental trajectories in East and Southeast Asia.

Democratic transition in Asia was seen as a side issue rather than a pattern of transformation that demanded systematic study. The fact that East Asia's giant, China, and Southeast Asia's richest country, Singapore, remained steadfastly authoritarian drew our scholarly attention away from the region's democratic prospects, energies, and successes. But when we both started looking more closely, we found a lot more democracy—and found that democracy mattered a lot more in developmental Asia—than we had come to expect.

For both of us, this reorientation in perspective—from trying to explain Asian development to trying to understand both Asian development and democracy, together, somehow—began in the same unlikely setting: Madison, Wisconsin. There, on the oft-icy slopes of Bascom Hill, Edward Friedman helped us both to see the world in entirely new ways. He made us think in a more rigorous, less blinkered, and more impassioned fashion about the problems of poverty and autocracy in Asia. He showed us by example that we could study universal principles and specific places at the same time, without sacrificing our dedication to either. Ed challenged us to think about democracy not as a fixed and final destination but rather as an imperfect experiment that requires continual tinkering and adaptation. Just as autocracies bear the stamp of individual dictators, democracies are crafted by individual political reformers. Democracy is possible anywhere, Ed taught us, but nowhere is it inevitable.

This is why we dedicate *From Development to Democracy* to Edward Friedman, our friend and mentor. Truth be told, our desire to write the kind of book that we could dedicate to Ed was a big reason we undertook this project in the first place.

Our personal and professional debts run much wider and deeper, of course. They begin with our partners, Jennifer DiDomenico-Wong and Tracey Lockaby. Watching Jen and Tracey become friends has been one of the highlights of working together so closely over the past decade, a highlight rivaled only by the opportunity to befriend and witness the blossoming talents of each other's teenage offspring (Ria, now 19; Kai, 17; and Oliver, 15)—from theater to music to basketball. It would be the understatement of all understatements to say that this book would never have been possible without Jen and Tracey's loving support and willing sacrifices. We thank them for the former and beg forgiveness for the latter, from the bottom of our hearts.

We are also grateful for the support we have received from our home departments and colleagues at our respective institutions. At the University of Toronto, much appreciation to many colleagues and friends in political science, with a special shout-out to Jacques Bertrand, Dan Breznitz, Vic Falkenheim, Diana Fu, Seva Gunitsky, Jeffrey Kopstein, Lynette Ong, Louis Pauly, Ed Schatz, Janice Stein, and Lucan Way. Colleagues at the U of T's Asian Institute and Munk School of Global Affairs and Public Policy have provided an extraordinary community of support, intellectual inspiration, and academic rigor. From shared time at the University of Chicago, special thanks and affection go to Mike Albertus, Kathy Anderson, Lis Clemens, Cathy Cohen, Bernard Harcourt, Will Howell, Ben Lessing, Stan Markus, John Mearsheimer, Monika Nalepa, Tianna Paschel, Paul Poast, Alberto Simpser, Paul Staniland, Jenny Trinitapoli, Lisa Wedeen, and innumerable incomparable graduate students. At the University of Michigan, much heartfelt appreciation to Nancy Burns, Christian Davenport, Mary Gallagher, Derek Groom, Allen Hicken, Pauline Jones, Gitta Kohler, Marysia Ostafin, all the incredible postdoctoral fellows at the Weiser Center for Emerging Democracies, and most of all to Rob Mickey (and all the McTraig clan) for support that has been as much personal as professional. Adam Casey deserves special accolades for the remarkable research assistance and research management he provided, working with whip-smart researchers Bill Achariyasoonthorn, Wilson Liu, and Max Shpilband during the book's final stages.

Beyond our home institutions, it is hard to know even where to begin. And once we begin, it is hard to imagine where we would ever end. But our greatest debts and appreciation for treasured friendship and brilliant advice go to Aries Arugay, Tun-Jen Cheng, Bruce Dickson, Iza Ding, Richard Doner, Alexandra Filindra, Edward Friedman, Anna Grzymala-Busse, Stephan Haggard, Mohamad Hanafi, Walter Hatch, Jeffrey Javed, Adrienne LeBas, Steve Levitsky, Rachel Riedl, Shelley Rigger, James Scott, Victor Shih, Ben Smith, Tariq Thachil, Kai Thaler, Kathy Thelen, Kellee Tsai, Maya Tudor, Tuong Vu, and Daniel Ziblatt. Rachel and Daniel deserve special mention and thanks for collaborating with us on an article in the *Annual Review of Political Science* that brought our shared lessons on authoritarian-led democratization together in one place.

Working on a book for this long means you get to share it with colleagues and present it to audiences, *a lot*. Over the past decade, we have benefited beyond measure from important insights and feedback from colleagues including Ben Ansell, Nancy Bermeo, Yun-Han Chu, Larry Diamond, Dafydd Fell, Douglas Fuller, Chang-Ling Huang, William Hurst, Bruce Jacobs, Cedric Jourde, Robert Kaufman, Byung-Kook Kim, Erik Kuhonta, Jih-Wen Lin, Chunrong Liu, James Loxton, Scott Mainwaring, Eddy Malesky, Marcus Mietzner, T. J. Pempel, Liz Perry, David Rueda, Paul Schuler, Jonathan Sullivan, Netina Tan, Shiping Tang and Steve Tsang. We have also benefited mightily from constructive and critical feedback on presentations at the Australian National University, East China University of Political Science and Law, Fudan University, Harvard University, Hong Kong University, Hong Kong University of Science and Technology, Institute for Southeast Asian Studies, Juan March Institute, King's College London, Korea University, McGill University, McMaster University, Monash University's Malaysia campus, Murdoch University, National Chengchi University, National Taiwan University, National University of Singapore, Northern Illinois University, Nottingham University's Malaysia campus, Royal Military College, School of Area and International Studies (SAIS), School of Oriental and African Studies (SOAS), Seoul National University, Singapore Management University, Stanford University, Stellenbosch University, Taiwan Foundation for Democracy, Tsinghua University, UC Berkeley, UC Irvine, UCLA, University of British Columbia, University of Cambridge, University of Chicago's Beijing Center, University of Helsinki, University of Hokkaido, University of Illinois-Chicago, University of Michigan, University of Notre Dame, University of Oregon, University of Oxford, University of South Carolina, University of Sydney, University of Tokyo, University of Toronto, University of Washington, Yale University, Yangon School of Political Science, and Yonsei University, and at the annual conferences of the American Political Science Association and Midwest Political Science Association.

The lengthy life span of this project also meant prevailing upon the patience of our friends and collaborators at Princeton University Press. It was Eric Crahan's "victory confidence" in our ability to successfully tackle a historical study of twelve Asian cases that truly got us started. And it was the savvy advice and assistance of Bridget Flannery-McCoy, as well as the superb editing of Elizabeth Byrd, Kate Gibson, and John Donohue, that helped propel us across the finish line.

Finally, we want to thank the many academics, activists, dissidents, government officials, and political leaders whom we have met and interviewed over the past three decades, and whose insights have deeply influenced this book. Democracy is never a risk-free proposition, either for the ruling elites who choose to accept it or the citizens who decide to demand it. We applaud the courage of everyone who has ever made these risky choices.

FROM DEVELOPMENT TO DEMOCRACY

1

Democracy through Strength

Starting with Development

Economic development is Asia's inescapable fact. Imagine a seasoned Asia traveler from the early 1970s being catapulted fifty years forward in time to any Asian city in the present day.[1] Whether they touched ground in Tokyo, Seoul, Hong Kong, Singapore, Shanghai, Taipei, or even Hanoi, Jakarta, Bangkok, or Kuala Lumpur, there is simply no question what transformation would strike them first. One of the world's poorest regions has become one of its richest.

We call this region "developmental Asia." It is a region defined by political economy, not just physical geography. All of its burgeoning economies lie along the Pacific Rim of Asia, so geography is hardly irrelevant. But not all countries in Northeast and Southeast Asia qualify. Developmental Asia is a region you have to "join" by pursuing particular developmental policies and accruing developmental successes. Specifically, the region's twelve cases[2] have all pursued national catch-up development through the political prioritization of rapid economic growth, grounded in a developmental model that prizes exports, uses state sponsorship to encourage industrialization, and treats private firms as a cornerstone of national economic advancement.

Economic growth across developmental Asia has been nothing short of spectacular. Yet it has also been undeniably uneven. Within each society, the fruits of economic growth have been very unevenly shared. Hundreds of millions have escaped poverty, but tens of millions still have not. Across cases, some began developing much earlier and have attained far greater levels of wealth than others. Japan, South Korea, Taiwan, Hong Kong, and Singapore have boasted high-income status for decades. Malaysia, Thailand, and Indonesia started later and have reached less lofty developmental heights. Meanwhile, among the four inward-looking laggards who did not "join"

1

developmental Asia by pursuing rapid export-led, state-sponsored capitalist growth until after the Cold War ended—China, Vietnam, Cambodia, and, most belatedly, Myanmar—China has skyrocketed past all the rest, while still not catching up to its developmental Asian predecessors in terms of per capita income.

The Patterns

Our core purpose in this book is not to explain developmental Asia's economic transformation, however. It is to explain a pattern that is far less obvious. For all of developmental Asia's remarkable economic modernization, only about half of the region has moved from authoritarianism toward democracy, even as the entire region has moved—albeit unevenly, both within countries and across them—from poverty toward wealth.[3]

This uneven pattern of democratization is nearly as striking and puzzling as Asia's impressive economic development. Because if economic development is Asia's inescapable fact, the connection between economic development and democratization is the modern world's inescapable correlation. There are obvious and important exceptions, of course: the occasional poor democracy in Africa, the handful of rich dictatorships in the Middle East. Yet the overall global pattern remains both clear and enduring, as modernization theory long ago identified: richer countries tend to be more democratic countries. This is especially true when, as in developmental Asia, economic development is driven by capitalist markets and accompanied by enormous class transformations.

We adopt a comparative and historical perspective to examine and explain developmental Asia's uneven democratization experience. Critically, *the region's unevenness in democratization does not map directly onto its unevenness in development.* Levels of economic development are not clearly correlated with levels of democracy in developmental Asia. If they were, Asia's democratization story would be a pure modernization story—but it plainly is not. Most strikingly, Singapore and Hong Kong are extremely wealthy but not democratic; China is getting no closer to democracy even as it grows phenomenally richer; Indonesia became a democracy and has remained a democracy for over two decades despite its modest middle-income status; and even Myanmar took substantial steps toward democratization in the 2010s, while remaining developmental Asia's poorest country, before a military coup reversed those tenuous yet tangible democratic gains in 2021.

One of the central propositions of our book is that democratization across developmental Asia has not merely been *uneven*; it has been *clustered*. That is, only certain *types* of political economies in developmental Asia have experimented with democratic reforms and, in some cases, completed and consolidated their democratic transitions. Other types have not. Explaining developmental Asia's clustered pattern of authoritarianism and democratization requires a fundamental rethinking of Asian geography itself.

It also requires a rethinking of how development shapes democratization. Economic development has profoundly shaped developmental Asia's patterns of democratization, as one would generally expect. But this is only because different types of *economic* development have been associated with different types of *political* development. Authoritarian regimes across developmental Asia built up considerable political strengths—but different types of political strength—while they were building up their national economies.

Of particular importance, different developmental patterns have been accompanied by the rise to positions of prominence and dominance of very different political organizations and actors: bureaucracies, conservative parties, socialist parties, and militaries. They have also positioned developmental Asia's twelve cases quite differently in the global economy, fostering different patterns of historical dependency on major powers such as China, Great Britain, Japan, and the United States. It is in this powerful yet indirect fashion that a shared overarching pattern of economic development had divided Asia by the early twenty-first century, almost evenly, into authoritarian and democratic halves.

The Argument

We argue that developmental Asia's most common pathway to democracy has been unusual but not unique. This pathway is *democracy through strength*.[4] It might seem like a truism to say that democracy can only emerge once an authoritarian regime has become too weak to endure. Yet developmental Asia's historical democratization experience consistently shows otherwise. From Japan after America's post–World War II occupation to Myanmar in the 2010s, and with Taiwan, South Korea, Indonesia, and Thailand in between, incumbent authoritarian regimes in developmental Asia have repeatedly conceded democracy without conceding defeat. They have opened themselves up to freer and fairer electoral competition, not as a way of exiting power and transferring power to their opponents but as a way of shoring up their own power in a democratic game.

The defining feature of democracy through strength in developmental Asia has been regime confidence, not regime collapse. Specifically, we see authoritarian regimes embarking on democratic reforms when their historically accumulated strengths give them two distinctive kinds of confidence. The first is *victory confidence*. This is the expectation among incumbent authoritarian elites that they can fare well, or even continue to dominate outright, in democratic elections. The second is *stability confidence*. This is their expectation that political stability—and with it, economic development—will persist under democratic conditions.

As we will discuss at length, the greatest source of stability confidence and victory confidence lies in political organizations, especially political parties and the bureaucratic state. Yet economic development itself contributes as well to both the victory confidence and stability confidence necessary for authoritarian regimes to democratize through strength.

In the barest possible terms, figure 1.1 displays our basic logic. With an impressive developmental track record, authoritarian rulers can generate a measure of performance legitimacy—a credible retrospective record of developmental achievement—to help them win free and fair elections moving forward.[5] And to the extent that economic development reduces poverty and expands the middle class, it softens the anticipated pressures for downward redistribution that often frighten the well-off away from embracing democratization.[6]

When authoritarian leaders in developmental Asia have lacked victory confidence and stability confidence, they have not pursued democratic reforms, no matter how much pressure to democratize they confronted. Rather, when they have democratized, they have done so not to surrender their power but to stabilize it on more solid footing.

This argument contrasts sharply with the conventional notion that dictators only give way under the most extreme, even existential pressures. As Plato concluded in *The Republic*, "Yes, that is how a democracy comes to be established, whether by force of arms or because the other party is terrorized into giving way." Much more recently, one of the most influential books on democratization of the twenty-first century thus far, Daron Acemoglu and James Robinson's *Economic Origins of Dictatorship and Democracy*, is built around the premise that authoritarian rulers only accept democracy as a way to prevent an imminent violent popular overthrow. In contrast, our argument centers not on *revolutionary threats* but on *stability expectations*.

This is not to say that expectations of stability are ever absolute or unequivocal. Conceding democracy with confidence is not without risk and

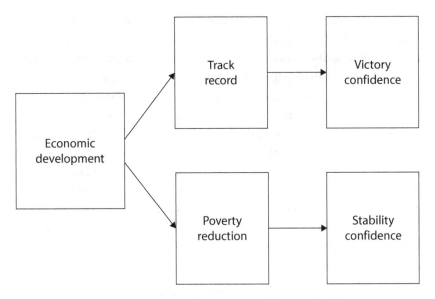

FIGURE 1.1. Authoritarian Development and Regime Confidence

uncertainty. We do not argue that strong authoritarian regimes ever possess perfect foresight and can predict precisely how well or poorly they would fare after conceding democratic reforms. Confidence is never omniscience. Democracy through strength is not intelligent design. It is a *reversible experiment*. Confidence must be considerable for democracy through strength to be commenced; it must be confirmed by experience throughout the reform experiment for democracy through strength to be completed.[7]

Our emphasis on stability expectations does not imply that pressures for democratization are unimportant, however. They are absolutely vital. Frederick Douglass was not mistaken when he famously claimed, "Power concedes nothing without a demand." When strong authoritarian regimes confront no pressure for change, they are highly unlikely to change course. Autocrats are extremely unlikely to embrace democratic reforms in the absence of political challenges.

Pressures for democratization can come from outside, as when Japan and Taiwan democratized, in part as a way of ensuring ongoing American security support. They can also come from below, such as when massive democratization protests helped accelerate regime change in South Korea in the late 1980s. And pressures for democratization can come from the economy, like when Indonesia's calamitous crash during the Asian financial crisis of the late 1990s made the exhaustion of the Suharto regime's development strategy painfully obvious.

The more such pressures dictatorships face, the more likely they are to de-mocratize. Yet it is essential to conceptually distinguish, and to empirically appraise in separate fashion, *the pressures regimes suddenly confront from the strengths they enduringly possess*. The considerable political strengths that au-thoritarian regimes in developmental Asia accrued while they were building up their economies came first and grew gradually; pressures for political change came later and emerged more suddenly, presenting fundamentally strong authoritarian regimes with new challenges, but also with new choices.

In sum, the key to democratic reform in our theory of democracy through strength is not authoritarian elites' perception of an imminent revolutionary threat and the regime's coming collapse. It is their well-founded expectation of continued stability and even continued outright victory after democ-ratization takes place.[8]

An Illustrative Comparison

Before spelling out our theory in greater detail, consider a real-world illustra-tion. No case of Asian democratization gained greater global attention than the People Power movement that toppled Ferdinand Marcos in 1986 in the Philippines. A discredited dictator, Marcos was chased out of office, and out of the country, by massive protests that paralyzed Manila and made his hold on power unsustainable. The protests themselves were prompted by a military coup against Marcos and by a dramatic plea by the archbishop of Manila, Car-dinal Jaime Sin, for the public to gather in the streets and force Marcos to step down. The military was too split to defend the Marcos presidency after he had brazenly stolen national elections. The aging dictator's American backers also made it clear they would not be helping him stay in power either.

This was a paradigmatic example of *democracy through weakness*. It is the most commonly understood way that democratization occurs, both to schol-ars who study democratization and to the wider public that has dramatic tele-vised images like those from Manila's People Power movement seared in their memory. Democratization through weakness means unmanageable, unrelent-ing, and sometimes violent crowds of urban protesters. It means a dictator flying off into exile, recognizing they have no path to holding power any longer. It means a triumphant replacement of the disgraced with the inspirational, as seen when the slight and humble figure of Corazon Aquino took the oath of office amid a throng of cameras and cheering onlookers, becoming the Philip-pines' democratically elected president in February 1986.

Almost two years to the day after Aquino was sworn in as president of the Philippines, in February 1988, a very different presidential oath of office would take place in nearby South Korea. Dressed in an impeccable business suit rather than military dress, former general Roh Tae-woo raised his right hand and swore to uphold South Korea's newborn electoral democracy. Despite his military pedigree, Roh was not assuming the presidency as a military leader or as an authoritarian ruler of any kind. He had been democratically elected a few months earlier in 1987 as leader of the Democratic Justice Party, which had ruled South Korea in authoritarian fashion under General Chun Doo-hwan. Democratic elections had not been forced by a revolutionary urban threat that toppled the ancien régime, by a divided and disloyal military, or by the abandonment of American backers. Rather, they were a strategic concession made by South Korea's authoritarian military and party leaders, with the relatively confident expectation that free and fair elections would let them stay in power rather than concede outright defeat or, worse yet, their own obsolescence. This confidence was fulfilled, and South Korea remains a highly functioning democracy to the present day.

Unlike the Philippines, South Korea experienced *democracy through strength*. We will elaborate all that this means, conceptually and theoretically, in the following sections. But a few observations about these two specific Asian cases are worth making before doing so, to illustrate some larger points. First, the Philippines has never been part of developmental Asia, and therefore it is not the kind of case we consider in this book. The fact that the Philippines democratized through weakness is consistent with a wide variety of existing theories of democratization in political science. It is also unsurprising insofar as the Philippines has not loosened its postcolonial political and economic ties to the United States in a manner that would allow it to pursue rapid state-led national economic development, as many of its Southeast Asian neighbors have done.[9] Countries like the Philippines that fail to build either authoritarian strength or developmental strength simply never have the option of democratizing through strength.

South Korea is the type of case we explore in this book. It tells a much less familiar story of how democratization happens. And yet in developmental Asia, it is the most important story to know. Authoritarian regimes can democratize from a position of strength, and those authoritarian elites can maintain much of their strength in a new democratic form. In the examples of democracy through strength that we examine in this book, former authoritarian elites can become successful democratic elites. Crucially, this does not mean that the democracy resulting from authoritarian concessions is less meaningfully democratic than one arising through authoritarian collapse. In fact, South Korea remains a far healthier democracy than the Philippines today, even though its democratic transition did not come with the immediate emotional catharsis of a dictator's ignominious departure, broadcast live on global airwaves.

Strength versus Weakness

Democracy through strength is not the typical scenario through which democracy is expected to arise. In this section, we contrast our historically underexamined democracy-through-strength scenario to the more familiar pathway of democratization through authoritarian weakness. To be sure, every authoritarian regime possesses a mix of strengths and weaknesses, and neither strengths nor weaknesses can be ignored in any real-world case of democratization. Yet there are striking differences between cases in which regime strength predominates in the democratization process and those in which authoritarian weakness is the key factor propelling regime change.

In the canonical understanding of how authoritarianism ends and democracy begins, which we call *democracy through weakness*, the story goes something like this: Ruling elites are deeply divided. They confront an increasingly imminent prospect of violent overthrow if they do not give way. They thus either sit down with opposition leaders to negotiate a peaceful exit from power or simply flee the scene and leave a collapsed regime in their wake. Democratization arises as the last resort of authoritarian leaders. In these scenarios, the regime's collapse is relatively sudden, and its legitimacy is entirely relinquished as an entirely new ruling group rises to power. The regime becomes opposition, if it survives the transition at all, and the opposition becomes the regime. Simply put, the regime collapses, conceding defeat. The demise of the Marcos regime in the Philippines in 1986 is a classic example.

In all of these aforementioned respects, democracy through strength looks different from democracy through weakness. Instead of being divided at the start of the democratization process, ruling elites are relatively unified. Although pressures for democratization may be growing, there is no imminent threat of the incumbent authoritarian regime being toppled. Instead of a revolutionary threat confronting the regime and giving it *little choice* but to give in, expectations of stability and even continued victory after democratization put the regime in a situation of relatively *little risk*. The incumbent authoritarian regime thus preemptively and unilaterally establishes new rules and a substantially leveled playing field, without being forced to negotiate the details with its opponents. This often takes the form of sequential concessions of gradual democratizing reforms. The authoritarian regime's political legitimacy gets redefined, not relinquished. Instead of being forced aside or stepping aside to make way for their opponents, ruling elites often continue ruling, or at least share power in a ruling coalition, despite the regime change. South Korea's democratic transition looked much more like this strength scenario than the weakness scenario that unfolded in the Philippines, almost simultaneously and amid much greater global fanfare.

An additional way in which democracy through strength differs from common understandings is worth underscoring. In much the same way that scholars of international relations believe countries tend to bungle their way into war, scholars of comparative politics increasingly claim that democratization happens by accident as well, rather than by design.[10] Some kind of miscalculation sets an authoritarian regime on a slippery slope toward democratization.

Our perspective is not diametrically opposed to this interpretation of how democracy sequentially unfolds, but it is different nonetheless. We do not argue that autocrats have perfect information. They cannot concede democracy with prescience. Rather, we see democracy through strength as a process of *reversible experimentation*. When strong authoritarian regimes begin liberalizing, they do not know for certain where the reform process will lead. They have a highly informed expectation of continued stability and success; but politics being politics, things might always go much worse and less smoothly than expected. If so, the liberalizing dictatorship can pull the plug and at least attempt to return to the authoritarian status quo ante. They can reverse the experiment.[11]

In fact, a virtue for incumbent authoritarian leaders of democratizing preemptively and from a position of strength is that they are far more able to guide the transition process to their own liking, maintaining the capacity to shift gears if and when surprises erupt. The stronger the regime is when it commences the experiment, the better its chances of controlling the transition. If the regime waits too long, by contrast, and squanders its window of opportunity to transform itself and the political system on its own terms, it is far more likely to lose control of the process entirely. This is what unfolded over the course of the 2010s in Malaysia, Cambodia, and Hong Kong, and what could potentially transpire in the very near future in China, Singapore, and Vietnam.

For strong authoritarian regimes like those that predominate in developmental Asia, the biggest miscalculation when it comes to democratization is waiting too long to attempt it. Regimes that transition through strength should do so before their "best before" date expires. Every authoritarian regime reaches its historical apex, and the trick to democracy through strength is pursuing it when that apex is still historically recent rather than distant. The closer the regime is to its apex of power, the more likely it can successfully concede democracy through strength. The opportunities to democratize through strength are almost certainly not inexhaustible because authoritarian strengths are almost certainly not inexhaustible. This makes the path of democracy through strength, we contend, a rational choice for strong authoritarian regimes.

A Region of Clusters

Developmental Asia is characterized by substantial but not equivalent strengths across its twelve cases. In the cluster that encompasses the world's exemplary "developmental states" of Japan, South Korea, and Taiwan, these strengths have been remarkable.[12] In the cluster comprising Southeast Asian military regimes—namely, Indonesia, Myanmar, and Thailand—these political strengths have been far less impressive.[13] Yet across this eclectic range of six Asian countries, the core story remains the same: *democratic reforms commenced when authoritarian elites felt considerable victory confidence and stability confidence, and not when they were in a death spiral of political crisis and imminent collapse.*[14] Moreover, the more strength these authoritarian regimes possessed before democratization, the more their confidence would be fulfilled after democratization. We demonstrate that these authoritarian regimes can be arrayed across a spectrum of *strength* before democratization that would then be reflected in their spectrum of democratic *success* afterward.

It is thus no accident that democratization went quite smoothly for strong incumbent conservative parties in postwar Japan, South Korea, and Taiwan, while military-led regimes in Indonesia, Thailand, and Myanmar experienced much rockier and reversible transitions from authoritarianism to democracy.[15] What is clear in hindsight was not entirely clear at the time, to be sure. Yet the relative "settledness" or "unsettledness"[16] of these six regimes' liberalization processes can be very well explained by the levels of authoritarian strength from which these parallel processes began. Postwar Japan, Taiwan, and South Korea—what we group together as the "developmental statist" cluster—were the strongest authoritarian regimes and became the strongest, most enduring democracies in Asia. We explore these cases and their journeys from development to democratization at length in chapters 3 through 5. Democratic experiments in the "developmental militarist" cluster of Thailand, Myanmar, and Indonesia (chapter 7), in comparison, have been far less certain and far more prone to authoritarian reversals.

In the case of Thailand, the experiment with democracy through strength that commenced in the early 1980s would be reversed entirely, though it took decades for the democratic collapse to occur. Myanmar's democratization experiment of the 2010s arguably stalled short of actually establishing democracy and was then reversed entirely, as in Thailand, in the 2021 military coup. Only in Indonesia has a military-led regime gone from initial democratic concessions to eventual democratic consolidation without authoritarian reversal. This relative success, we contend, reflects Indonesia's antecedent authoritarian strength, and especially the greater role played by a deeply rooted conservative ruling party during Indonesia's authoritarian period, which Thailand and Myanmar both sorely (and fatally for democracy) lacked.

The primary empirical focus of our book is to explore the different ways that democracy through strength has unfolded in these six developmental Asian countries. Yet our argument that spectrums of authoritarian strength predictably translate into spectrums of democratic success also has important implications for the six cases in developmental Asia that have not pursued democracy through strength. Unlike our aforementioned developmental statist cluster (Japan, South Korea, and Taiwan) and developmental militarist cluster (Indonesia, Myanmar, and Thailand), these six Asian political economies have pursued *democracy avoidance* rather than democratic concessions from their positions of authoritarian strength. But like the six instances of democratic concessions, the cases of democracy avoidance belong in two clusters of their own: "developmental Britannia" (Singapore, Malaysia, and Hong Kong) and "developmental socialism" (China, Vietnam, and Cambodia).

The final empirical chapters of our book (chapters 8 and 9) tackle the question of whether democracy through strength is as feasible in these latter two clusters of countries as in other parts of developmental Asia. Of particular interest are the developmental Asian behemoth, China, and Lilliputian, Singapore, which capture so much global attention for their durable authoritarianism despite spectacularly expanding national wealth.

Table 1.1 summarizes the entire region's developmental and democratic clustering. Along the left side of the table, *italicized*, we see the two clusters of "concession cases" that have, at one time or another, pursued democracy from positions of relative strength. The two CAPITALIZED cases, Thailand and Myanmar, are the "reversal cases" that have seen coups undo those democratic

TABLE 1.1. Developmental Clusters and Democratization Patterns

High Strength

Developmental Statism	Developmental Britannia
1. *Japan*	1. **Singapore**
2. *Taiwan*	2. <u>Malaysia</u>
3. *South Korea*	3. <u>Hong Kong</u>

Intermediate Strength

Developmental Militarism	Developmental Socialism
1. *Indonesia*	1. **China**
2. THAILAND	2. **Vietnam**
3. MYANMAR	3. <u>Cambodia</u>

Note: italicized type indicates concession cases (6); unitalicized type indicates avoidance cases (6); **bold** type indicates candidate cases (3); <u>underlined</u> type indicates embittered cases (3); CAPITALIZED type indicates reversal cases (2).

concessions. On the right side, unitalicized, are the two clusters of cases that have avoided making such concessions, despite enjoying sufficient authoritarian strength to do so.

Of these six "avoidance cases" on the right side of table 1.1, all developed enough authoritarian strength to concede democracy and thrive; but none has. Some—namely, China, Singapore, and Vietnam—remain strong enough to do so. We use **bold** to identify them as "candidate cases" because they could still democratize through strength if their authoritarian leaderships so choose.

By contrast, our three other avoidance cases have all allowed themselves to weaken to the point that they could only democratize through weakness, not strength. Formerly but no longer strong candidate cases, Malaysia, Cambodia, and Hong Kong are <u>underlined</u> as what we call, for reasons that will become clearer later in this chapter, "embittered cases." They have all missed their best window of opportunity to concede democracy without conceding immediate defeat. Incumbent regimes chose to hang on far past their authoritarian apex, relying on increasingly repressive means to stay in power, such that democracy through strength ceased to be a viable option.

Only time will tell if developmental Asia's three "candidate cases" (China, Singapore, and Vietnam) will eventually become "embittered cases" (like Cambodia, Hong Kong, and Malaysia)—that is, strong authoritarian cases that refuse to democratize through strength until they become too weak to do so—or not.

Table 1.1 should be read vertically as well as horizontally. The wealthier an authoritarian regime was when confronting pressures to democratize, the higher it sits in the table. Most broadly, six higher-income cases (the relatively wealthy statist and Britannia clusters) stand above six cases with more intermediate national income levels (the growing but lagging militarist and socialist clusters). For the basic reasons elaborated earlier in figure 1.1, these levels of wealth are very strongly if not perfectly associated with authoritarian strength and confidence. Richer regimes tend to have better development track records and enjoy deeper wells of performance legitimacy that enhance their victory confidence, including greater poverty reduction and expansion in the size of the middle class to bolster their stability confidence.[17]

Table 1.1's vertical dimension thus broadly displays levels of strength as well as wealth. Herein lies a critical point to our argument: although authoritarian strength is a prerequisite for democracy through strength, levels of strength are not an explanation for which countries pursue it and which do not. Paradoxically, *democracy through strength is not explained by strength itself*; strong regimes do not necessarily democratize. Rather, the likelihood of a democracy-through-strength scenario unfolding is most efficiently explained by the developmental cluster in which the case built up its strength. Every single developmental statist and militarist case conceded democratizing reform, at least for a time; every single Britannia and socialist case has avoided democratic reforms, steadfastly refusing to concede.

Why do developmental clusters shape democratization patterns so profoundly, and even precisely? As we will detail below, it is because clusters help determine the kinds of *signals and strategies* that, when combined with strength itself, best determine whether a democracy-through-strength transition is likely to occur.[18] Signals increase the likelihood of democratic reform when they convey either that sustaining authoritarianism is no panacea for whatever current governance ills face the regime (what we call "ominous signals") or that calling free and fair elections should not usher in a disastrous result for authoritarian incumbents (what we call "reassuring signals").

In the final analysis, democracy through strength is always a choice. More specifically, it is always a strategic choice made by incumbent authoritarian leaders contemplating the mix and balance of the strengths they have accumulated and possess versus the types and strength of signals they confront. It is not always the choice authoritarian leaders make, however, no matter how strong they might be.

Before laying out that entire argument in more detail, we define the key building blocks in our theory: democracy, strength, and confidence.

What Is Democracy?

Democracy is a form of government in which opposition parties and politicians are given the unimpeded opportunity to compete for popular support, and thus for power, in national elections. This is not all that democracy means, but democracy cannot exist without it. This book is squarely focused on the question of how authoritarian regimes that substantially impede their opponents from competing for popular support and national power come to remove those substantial impediments. In the fortuitous metaphor of Steven Levitsky and Lucan Way, democracy requires a level playing field.[19] This book explores and explains why some authoritarian regimes level the playing field on which they compete with their opponents, while others do not.

There is a great deal to democratic development that this focus sets aside. A fully healthy democracy respects the rights of minorities, imposes constraints on the political executive and the state's coercive organizations, fosters widespread political participation, allows significant transparency into the inner workings of government, and minimizes the outsize influence that the very wealthiest citizens tend to have over the electoral process. Nothing in our book explains why some countries fare better on these vitally important democratic virtues than others. As long as authoritarian regimes concede free and fair elections and respect the outcome of those elections, they have made a substantial democratic concession, even if they still fall very far short of establishing a high-quality democracy, with all that it entails.

Although merely leveling the playing field may seem like a modest change, it nonetheless requires substantive and substantial transformation of the political system and its rules of the game. Leveling the playing field is not trivial. Of particular importance are the liberties that must precede and accompany a free and fair electoral process. Political parties must be freely allowed to form, mobilize, and communicate; the press must be free from censorship; voters must be able to make choices on the basis of free-flowing information rather than coercion and intimidation. When elected governments fail to meet these standards, we tend to call them "electoral authoritarian," and thus no longer even minimally democratic.[20]

Of less importance in our analysis are the liberties that we hope and believe must follow democratic elections. Chief executives may run roughshod over parliament; the police may be given license to kill suspected criminals without due process; ethnic majorities might physically attack religious minorities with impunity and without government intervention; and so on. Tellingly, such acts tend to be described as "illiberal democracy." As awful as these government actions and inactions may be, they do not mean that a country has lost its core democratic substance: the unimpeded opportunity for people outside government to compete in democratic elections for power inside government.[21]

In sum, electoral competition without substantial impediments may not be the most important or desirable aspect of democracy. But it is a central aspect of democracy, and it is the one we focus on in this book. As a democratic achievement, it is significant enough to be worthy of explanation.

What Is Strength?

Having offered our approach to the question of democracy, how do we approach the question of authoritarian strength? Authoritarian strength in our framework is primarily absolute rather than relative. In other words, *an incumbent authoritarian regime's strength does not automatically decline as opposition strength increases.* A stronger opposition means pressures on an authoritarian regime are on the rise. Yet it tells us nothing about how much strength the regime has, and has accumulated over decades of development, to confront that rising challenge. In fact, activists who oppose authoritarianism may come to support the "authoritarian successor party" after democratization because of its developmental track record, and hence its appeal to voters who wish to see the decades of development continue.[22] This is demonstrated most clearly in the case of Taiwan's Kuomintang.

The strength of any authoritarian regime is a moving and difficult target to measure. We focus on the institutions and coalitions that underpin the regime over time. Institutions are the heart of authoritarian strength. By this, we primarily mean organizations rather than rules. Rules matter less under autocracy than under democracy since it is easier for an authoritarian leadership than a democratic government to change them on the fly. Yet political organizations often endure in authoritarian settings, and dominate.[23] For instance, the "rule" in China that presidents could only serve two terms had for decades been considered a cornerstone of the Chinese Communist Party (CCP) regime's institutionalization. Xi Jinping had this "institution" discarded in 2018, allowing him to rule in perpetuity—at least in principle. His rule can only continue so long as he leads the CCP itself. In the past, in the present, and for the foreseeable future, the CCP is the most important institution in China.

The essence of institutions is that they structure political interactions over time, such that even when the current generation of leaders leaves the scene, we can expect established patterns of interaction and the lasting underpinnings of domination more or less to continue. In authoritarian settings, it is organizations more than rules that give the regime a sense of continuity and predictability over time. They are the locus of repeated interactions, even when authoritarian leaders alter the rules of interaction within and between these organizations dramatically. These authoritarian organizations range from incredibly strong to pathetically weak. In developmental Asia, they have tended to be exceptionally strong and capable, although the spectrum running from our strongest cases, such as Taiwan, Singapore, and Japan, to our weakest cases, such as Cambodia, Thailand, and Myanmar, is quite vast.

The most important organization in any authoritarian setting is the state apparatus.[24] While leaders and regimes come and go, the "iron cage" of the state—with its many bureaucratic agencies as the individual bars that uphold it—remains. When the state recruits its personnel in meritocratic ways, affords those personnel some measure of autonomy from day-to-day interference by political leadership, and invests those personnel with financial resources and organizational infrastructure necessary to implement national policy goals, the state is quite strong.

States with these characteristics have generally been dubbed Weberian or bureaucratic. By contrast, when state personnel are recruited on personalistic rather than meritocratic grounds and denied the autonomy, resources, and infrastructure necessary to govern society effectively, the state is weak. Such weak states are often described as patrimonial.

The developmental implications of state strength versus weakness are enormous. Only Weberian states can be developmental states, while patrimonial states more often deteriorate into predatory forms of rule. While real-world states typically combine bureaucratic and patrimonial features, exhibiting intermediate strength as a result, the distinction remains informative and analytically useful.[25]

On average, developmental Asian states are more Weberian and less patrimonial than their contemporary counterparts across the postcolonial world. Yet the spectrum of bureaucratic strength across the region is expansively wide. Within the developmental statist cluster of Japan, South Korea, and Taiwan, bureaucracies have long been among the world's very strongest and most effective. China since the late 1970s also stands out within the developmental socialist cluster for the relative meritocracy, autonomy, and resourcefulness of its bureaucracy, at least compared with the other cases in the developmental socialist cluster, Vietnam and Cambodia. Bureaucratic strength is also remarkably high in Singapore, and compares favorably with its neighbor and fellow former British colony Malaysia, which has long combined Weberian and patrimonial features. Finally, in the developmental militarist cluster, Myanmar stands apart for the relative weakness of its bureaucratic organizations, while Thailand's bureaucracy, and specifically its economic bureaucracy, has a far more impressive history of capacity and autonomy. Indonesia lies somewhere in between, with an initial colonial legacy of a strong bureaucracy, followed by highly patrimonial patterns of authoritarian rule. State strength not only varies across countries but over time within countries as well.

States do not only rule populations through the bureaucracy, however. Especially in authoritarian settings, they also coerce them through the state's security apparatus, including policing organizations, intelligence bodies, and ultimately the military. Just as with bureaucratic organizations, strength for these coercive organizations depends on available resources and an expansively built infrastructure for rule. Yet it does not depend on Weberian characteristics. To the contrary, a police, intelligence, or military apparatus that enjoys substantial autonomy to ignore political pressures from above is not the kind of coercive machine an authoritarian leadership typically wants. Hence, when it comes to coercive organizations, authoritarian strength depends not so much on the Weberian characteristics that underpin a strong bureaucracy, as it hinges on the political cohesion of those who command and deploy force.[26]

On this front, we see far less variation in the political cohesion of coercive organizations in developmental Asia's authoritarian regimes than we see in the Weberian capacity of their bureaucratic organizations. Virtually nowhere in developmental Asia has disloyalty or factionalism been a major impediment preventing authoritarian regimes from relying on their coercive organizations to stifle and repress dissent. Coercive sources of strength have been impressive almost entirely across the board.

This is a major reason why democratization has not unfolded in developmental Asia through authoritarian collapse. Autocrats in the region have not liberalized because they doubted their military and police's capacity to defend them against popular threats. They have done so because they had very good reason to expect the incumbent regime's most important political and economic organizations to endure and even flourish under newly democratic conditions. When democracy is pursued from a position of strength, democracy offers bureaucracies, militaries, and police forces a new lease on life rather than sounding a death knell. Democratization can also prove perfectly consistent with the interests of the authoritarian regime's most important leaders and followers, as we now explore.

What Is Confidence?

For our argument, at the end of the day, *strength matters because confidence matters.* The two concepts are related but distinct. In some cases, an authoritarian regime might lack strength but be overconfident in its capacity to thrive after making democratic concessions. This accords with the argument that democratization is usually a miscalculation by autocrats who expect democracy to serve their interests better than it ultimately does.[27] Alternatively, a regime might possess imposing strength yet lack confidence that those strengths could readily transfer into continued dominance and stability under democracy. This is most evident in China and Singapore, strong states and dominant regimes that have steadfastly avoided democracy. Like a currency that must be converted before it is spent, strength must be translated into confidence if democracy through strength is to occur.

If authoritarian regimes are not confident that they can continue to thrive after democratization, they will not concede democracy from a position of strength. State strength as just discussed is especially important because it increases *stability confidence*: the expectation that democratic concessions will not undermine either political stability or economic development. Yet stability confidence is only half of our story. The other half is *victory confidence*. If stability confidence mostly comes from strong state organizations, because they can be expected to persist even if the regime type changes, where does victory confidence primarily come from? Our answer is strong authoritarian ruling parties, underpinned by broad support coalitions and impressive developmental track records.[28]

At one level, the strength of any political party is a purely organizational matter. Like Weberian states, strong parties are professionalized organizations that draw clear boundaries between members and nonmembers, ascribing to members formal roles in which they are expected to follow predictable rules. Strong parties boast loyal members and experienced leaders. They are built as organizational pyramids, starting off broad at the bottom and gradually narrowing near the top, as loyal and competent cadres get rewarded with promotions and outsiders are prevented from parachuting into the organization at high levels.

Yet a strong and confident authoritarian ruling party cannot be determined merely from an organizational chart. We need to look at a party's history of interactions, both within the party itself and between the party and society, to gauge its strength and likely confidence in a democratic concession scenario. One way party cadres can gain experience and exhibit loyalty in an authoritarian setting is by competing and prevailing in authoritarian elections. These are typically meaningful, if skewed, exercises. If a ruling party has an impressive history of winning elections that generally capture the will of the voters, it stands to reason the party should have more confidence that it can carry that popularity over to a fairer, democratic electoral arena. Competitive authoritarian elections provide an especially important gauge of a regime's incumbent strength and its victory confidence in democracy.

Strong ruling parties also gain internal coherence in large measure by promoting a consistent ideology that appeals across class and ethnic divides. They are not "cleavage" parties, attracting a specific segment of the electorate like a single economic class or an ethnic community, but "catch-all" parties, striving to generate support and popularity among the entire national body politic. In developmental Asia, they promise economic development as a means of expanding national strength, pragmatically leveraging state intervention and unleashing market forces as needed, rather than rigidly favoring one over the other. In other words, no ideology matters more than national development.

A history of economic development is a source of party strength. These strong, developmentally oriented authoritarian ruling parties are also often bound tightly together by a shared sense of historical heroism and purpose, frequently grounded in the experience of winning a revolution, expelling imperialists, or rebuilding peace and stability from the detritus of civil war. In China and Vietnam, in fact, long-ruling communist parties credibly claim historical credit for all three of these achievements.

Finally, and again resembling strong states, strong ruling parties construct an encompassing national infrastructure over time, at the most local levels and in the most remote corners of national territory. Strong parties are national parties. This party machinery can be converted and deployed in democratic electoral competition after authoritarian controls are lifted. Although democratic concessions always entail risks, the robustness of a built ruling-party infrastructure mitigates those risks. Individual party members might defect to other parties or run as independents under democracy; but the party is virtually certain to live on as an authoritarian successor party when democracy is conceded by an authoritarian regime that is still strong.

To be the kind of strong organization that lends authoritarian elites victory confidence when contemplating democratic reforms, a ruling party must be strong on the outside as much as on the inside. In other words, it needs a dependable support coalition that is both wide enough to win national elections and tight enough to generate a loyal set of core voters and followers. To some degree, and in some cases more than others, this is a product of the consistent ideology mentioned earlier. Voters and followers, after all, are motivated by ideological appeals and historical mythology as much as, if not more than, party members themselves, who enjoy selective benefits from membership that nonmembers lack. However, strong party coalitions are also the result of lasting links between the party and social organizations like labor unions, business associations, peasant leagues, and religious communities. This societal infrastructure, standing alongside the internal infrastructure of the party itself, gives party leaders the capacity to mobilize a nationwide network of supporters, and the confidence that it can keep doing so after democratization.

These state, party, and coalitional strengths are the bedrock of victory confidence and stability confidence for authoritarian regimes. They are the strengths that make democracy through strength possible. But just because authoritarian leaders can reasonably expect to thrive under democracy does not fully explain why they actually ever preemptively democratize. Paradoxically, *any authoritarian regime strong enough to thrive under democracy is strong enough to retain its authoritarian power in the near term if it so chooses*. In the following section we offer an explanation for such choices, and why some strong authoritarian regimes concede democratic reforms while others—surely most, in fact—do not.

Why Democratize from Strength?

Our core argument in this book is that in developmental Asia, the modal path to democratization has been through strength. "Through strength" does not mean "because of strength," however. Of the twelve cases we consider in developmental Asia, all of which have exhibited substantial authoritarian strength, exactly half have pursued democracy through strength at some time or another, and half have not.

The difference between the two halves is not their levels of authoritarian strength, as we demonstrated visually in figure 1.1. At first glance, the key difference between those authoritarian regimes that democratized through strength and those that chose not to is simply the developmental cluster in which the country is located. The three developmental statist cases (Japan, South Korea, and Taiwan) and developmental militarist cases (Indonesia, Myanmar, and Thailand) have all conceded democracy from a position of strength. By contrast, the three developmental Britannia cases (Singapore, Malaysia, and Hong Kong) and three developmental socialist cases (China, Vietnam, and Cambodia) all have not. We call the first set of cases our six "concession cases" because they have at some point conceded democracy; we call the second set our six "avoidance cases" because we argue that they have at some point exhibited enough strength to concede democracy without conceding defeat, yet all have avoided taking the leap.

In the next chapter, we consider the variety of reasons why developmental clustering has shaped democratic clustering. At its core, our causal story is far simpler. Put most starkly, we argue that democracy through strength results from a combination of strengths, signals, and strategies.

Developmental clusters matter for democratization in many ways, as we will shortly detail. But they matter most significantly because of how they shape these three core ingredients in the causal recipe of democracy through strength. We have already discussed how economic development and the strong states, parties, and coalitions that tend to accompany it generate victory confidence and stability confidence. But these strengths alone, to reiterate, do not explain why some strong authoritarian regimes choose to preemptively democratize, while others do not. What shapes this fateful choice? To understand this variation, we turn our attention to signals and strategies.

As a matter of political survival, authoritarian regimes are constantly seeking and receiving signals of their shifting strength. By driving economic development and modernization, they generate new bases of support, but also new cleavages and citizen demands.[29] Thus, the common phrase "authoritarian status quo" is a misnomer. This is especially so in a region like developmental Asia, where authoritarian regimes' dogged commitment to pursuing breakneck economic growth and development means that the background conditions against which regime maintenance takes place are flowing like rapids, not frozen like a glacier. Even for extremely strong authoritarian regimes, stability requires consistent adaptation to shifting signals, not "standing pat" to preserve some elusive and even illusionary status quo. Even two of the most stable and seemingly durable authoritarian regimes in the world, China and Singapore, have evolved to look very different—and to offer their citizens far more benefits in exchange for accepting authoritarian controls—from how they looked before the turn of the twenty-first century. Their adaptations reflect their changing societies, their evolving political economies, and the developmentally oriented states driving them.

We divide the kinds of signals authoritarian regimes can receive into four types: electoral, contentious, economic, and geopolitical. These signals vary in their clarity and strength. Harking back to our earlier distinction between enduring strengths and emerging pressures, what is critical to our argument is that these signals often (but do not always) assume the form of pressures on the regime to consider experimenting with democratic reforms.

Of the four, electoral signals are the *clearest* signals. When an electoral authoritarian regime experiences rising or falling electoral fortunes, it is as clear a signal of shifting regime strength as it can possibly receive. The second kind of signals, contentious signals, are the *strongest* signals. When thousands (and sometimes tens and hundreds of thousands) of citizens pour into the streets to demand the reform or even removal of an authoritarian regime, it is impossible for authoritarian leaders to ignore. We pay particularly close attention to electoral and contentious signals in our empirical chapters. They are the most vivid forms of opposition pressure to democratize that an authoritarian regime can confront.

The third and fourth types of signals, economic and geopolitical, tend to lack both the extreme clarity of electoral signals and the thundering strength of contentious signals. Yet they prove quite important in particular developmental clusters.[30] For instance, the geopolitical signal of shifting and waning American support was vital to democratic prospects in the developmental statist cluster. In Taiwan, Washington's decision to withdraw diplomatic recognition in favor of mainland China provided powerful pressure for new thinking by the Kuomintang on democratic reform. In South Korea, American diplomatic pressure became more strident during the spring and summer of 1987, changing the political calculations of Seoul's authoritarian elite and nudging them toward a concession strategy. In Japan, America's "reverse course" in its policy in 1947 signaled its support for conservative-led democratization. Analogously, economic signals have proved especially consequential in the developmental militarist cluster, particularly Indonesia, where the 1997–98 Asian financial crisis strongly signaled that the Suharto regime's days of rapid growth and social stability had evaporated.[31]

How do signals increase the chances that a strong regime will democratize through strength? Our causal logic is that signals must help shatter one of two illusions: (1) that authoritarian repression is a panacea or (2) that democratization would be a disaster for the incumbent authoritarian regime. We call the first kind of signals *ominous* signals, and the second type *reassuring* signals.

Which kind of signal is more conducive to democratic reform depends on the strength of the regime. If the regime is extremely strong (e.g., Singapore), it is unlikely to reform unless it receives ominous signals. If the regime is only somewhat strong (e.g., Vietnam), it is more important for it to receive reassuring signals if it is to take the risk of democratic concessions. Returning to our theory's core moving parts: signals matter because they affect authoritarian regimes' stability confidence and victory confidence.

Democracy through strength becomes especially likely when a fortuitous mix of ominous and reassuring signals shifts relatively strong authoritarian regimes into what we call the "bittersweet spot."[32] *This is the zone where an authoritarian regime expects neither that continuing or raising levels of repression will restore political stability nor that leveling the playing field with its opponents will lead to its imminent defeat.* When new signals—electoral, contentious, economic, or geopolitical—show that conditions have fundamentally changed, repression cannot look like a panacea, and democratization cannot look like a catastrophe, if democracy through strength is to emerge. Signals of shifting regime strength and support can neither be so reassuring that nothing *needs* to be done nor be so ominous that there is nothing *left* to be done.[33]

This zone is "bitter" for authoritarian regimes because it always includes a significant dose of bad tidings. Ominous signals are indicating that there is no longer any restful and enduringly stable "authoritarian status quo." Something must be done. Yet it is still a "sweet spot" because it contains significant hope for the regime's democratic renewal. There is still something left to be done, for the polity in general and the incumbent ruling party specifically. Reassuring signals suggest democratization would mean a soft landing, not suicide.

If the incumbent regime fails to reform during this moment of opportunity, however, it could miss it entirely, hurtling through the bittersweet spot and weakening too far to pursue democracy through strength. This is exactly what happened in Malaysia, as we discuss at length in chapter 8. There, one of Asia's strongest authoritarian regimes as of the mid-1990s resisted democratization through strength in the wake of the Asian financial crisis. This commenced a two-decade decline that culminated in the ruling National Front's outright landslide defeat—despite its substantial remaining authoritarian controls—in the elections of 2018. Malaysia's authoritarian regime missed its window of opportunity to concede with strength.

Hurtling through and missing the bittersweet spot has also been the fate of Cambodia. A regime popular and successfully developmental enough to have won free and fair elections in the first decade of the 2000s effectively overstayed its welcome by the 2010s. Hun Sen's Cambodian People's Party (CPP) now can only stay in power by shedding its electoral character, doubling down on authoritarian controls, and becoming effectively a single-party regime, mimicking its developmental socialist neighbors China and Vietnam.

The most dramatic instance of missing the bittersweet spot in developmental Asia has recently unfolded in Hong Kong. Ever since the island's handover from British to Chinese control in 1997, competitive elections delivered predictably strong results to conservative, pro-Beijing parties and candidates. Yet protests over the slowness and reversals of democratic reforms still erupted periodically, signaling the dangers to Hong Kong's ruling conservatives and their backers in Beijing of waiting too long to address local reform demands. In large measure because Hong Kong's fate is ultimately determined in China, however, democracy avoidance instead of democratic concessions remained the order of the day. By 2019, mass protests had exploded to a scale at which Hong Kong became ungovernable, and local elections produced a shocking, unprecedented victory for the anti-Beijing, democratic opposition. As in Cambodia and Malaysia, the foundations for victory and stability confidence that conservatives in Hong Kong enjoyed during the early 2000s had eroded by the end of the 2010s. By then, the local administration had hurtled through the bittersweet spot. Any remaining prospect of democratic experimentation had evaporated. "Candidate cases" had become "embittered cases."

The examples of Malaysia, Hong Kong, and Cambodia vividly illustrate a vital lesson of our argument: *democracy through strength always begins with strength, but it also always requires a choice—a choice that authoritarian leaders can simply refuse to make.* But this refusal comes with a risk of its own: the risk that a narrow window of opportunity to concede democracy in a stabilizing fashion may be frittered away. This is why we have to take the strategies of incumbent regime leaders seriously as the final link in the causal chain running from regime strength, which builds up over a long period of time, to democratic concessions through strength, which can be unveiled in virtually an instant.

There can be no possible single explanation for why some of the most powerful people in the world—authoritarian rulers in strong regimes—choose the strategies they do. Democracy through strength is never anything close to inevitable. Nor is it ever structurally foreclosed for strong rulers who wish to pursue it, even when no ominous or reassuring signals arise to prompt it. We simply see democratic concessions as extraordinarily unlikely in the absence of the kind of signals we have described, and increasingly likely as such signals gain in strength and clarity.

In the end, it ultimately comes down to leaders' strategies. We argue that *it is primarily from new legitimation strategies that democracy through strength finally arises.* It is not crucial that a single leader have overwhelming decision-making power; although such power might well describe Taiwan's Chiang Ching-kuo, it most certainly did not apply to Indonesia's weak president B. J. Habibie. What does seem to be essential, however, is that leaders and their core followers come to perceive that old authoritarian legitimation formulas, such as economic performance alone, have run their course, and that preemptive democratization offers these power holders a new lease on political life.

As an observational matter, we can never be sure what leaders think. We can know, however, what they do and what they say. In politics, actions and words matter, especially when they are used to justify major changes of direction. In the chapters that follow, we expect to see democracy from strength commencing when leaders claim that "the end of an era" has been reached and that, having delivered development and stability to the nation, democratization will be the authoritarian regime's next great gift. When it comes to democracy through strength, the goal is not to exit the national stage and hand over power to a regime's opponents, but quite the opposite: to keep competing for power, and ideally continuing to win power outright, but to do so in a democracy rather than a dictatorship.

The Book to Follow

The primary goal of this introductory chapter has been to lay out our argument, including the concepts on which it is based and the geographical terrain on which it will play out.

Chapter 2 has much more to say about that terrain: developmental Asia and the four distinctive clusters it encompasses. Chapters 3–5 detail how developmental statism paved the way for an especially stabilizing form of democracy through strength in postwar Japan, Taiwan, and South Korea. Though all three cases demonstrate democracy through strength, we also highlight variations in strength among the incumbent regimes and how these shaped their respective democratic transitions.

Chapter 6 shows that China had not accumulated strengths comparable to those of its developmental statist neighbors in Northeast Asia by the time of the 1989 crisis in Tiananmen Square, leading to a crackdown from a position of weakness rather than concessions from a position of strength. Departing from the standard view that the CCP was *much stronger* than its socialist brethren in the Soviet bloc, and hence did not collapse, we show how the CCP as of 1989 was also *much weaker* than its neighbors in the developmental statist cluster of Japan, Taiwan, and South Korea, and hence could not confidently concede democracy from a position of strength. The CCP in 1989 was too strong to collapse, but not yet strong enough to concede democracy through strength.

Chapter 7 shifts our attention to the developmental militarist cluster of Indonesia, Thailand, and Myanmar. Here, more intermediate levels of developmental and authoritarian strength have yielded far shakier and reversible experiments with preemptive democratic reforms than in Japan, Taiwan, and South Korea. We turn our attention in chapter 8 to the developmental Britannia cluster of Singapore, Malaysia, and Hong Kong, where, puzzlingly for modernization theory, truly spectacular levels of economic development have been accompanied by democracy avoidance instead of democratic concessions. Chapter 9 returns our focus to China as the behemoth of the developmental socialist cluster, arguing that the CCP's impressive strength has not been accompanied by the requisite signals that democratic reforms are either pertinent or pressing enough to meet the growing governance challenges China faces. In other words, China today has the strength to stably concede democracy, but it lacks the signals. Vietnam and Cambodia persist with democracy avoidance within the developmental socialist cluster as well, as we more briefly detail.

We conclude the book with a wider theoretical discussion of the fraught relationship between democracy and stability. Democracy may not be the world's ultimate value, we readily concede, but it remains a universal value. Wherever democracy cannot solve problems of peace and prosperity, it will be eternally vulnerable. Clarifying the multiple ways in which democracy can prove compatible with political stability will be vital if democracy is to have a future equal to its past.

2

Shaping Developmental Asia

ASIA AND AUTHORITARIANISM are tightly linked in popular imaginations of global politics. Ask virtually anyone to assign a single cardinal direction to democracy, and the answer would almost certainly be "Western." Recent challenges to the health of democracies in Europe and the United States have justifiably raised doubts that democracy is somehow the natural, inevitable regime type in the Atlantic world. Yet just because democracy is no longer seen as safe in "the West" does not mean that it has ceased to be perceived as more of a Western phenomenon than an Eastern one. The notion that "the West" has a democratic advantage and "the East" a democratic disadvantage persists.

Rather than simply blaming old-fashioned Orientalism, we acknowledge that the persistence of such perceptions has empirical grounding. The stubborn belief that Asia and authoritarianism go together is being sustained, more than anything else, by the stubborn stability of one huge authoritarian regime and one tiny yet very rich one. On the large side, China's enduring dictatorship naturally looms large whenever eyes are cast toward Asia, especially when democracy-watchers fret that Asia's many Davids are increasingly falling under the influence of the authoritarian Goliath in Beijing. On the small side, Singapore's extraordinary combination of extreme wealth and modernity with strict political controls understandably lends a hint of "otherness" and even inscrutability to Asian politics. This supposed otherness is reinforced when the tiny island state's leaders have long proudly touted "Asian values" as a bona fide authoritarian alternative to the liberal and democratic—but decadent—"West."

The common conflation of Asian politics with authoritarian politics is not only a product of cultural bias but of selection bias. China and Singapore stand out as authoritarian exemplars; Japan and Indonesia, on the other hand, are treated like democratic outliers. Yet when we look across the full breadth of developmental Asia, as we do in this book, we quickly see that the scales are much more even than one might initially believe. Six of the region's twelve countries have pursued democratic reforms in the post–World War II era, while another six have not. When half the cases pursue democratic reform, they cannot be outliers; rather, they beg for explanation.

Any satisfactory accounting of democracy and dictatorship in developmental Asia will need to transcend the question of why Asia and authoritarianism go together and ask, first, why democratic reforms have been pursued in one half of the region but not the other; and second, why some of these six democratic experimenters have experienced a smooth democratization path, while others have suffered regime instability and even outright democratic reversals.

Any explanation for Asia's democratic diversity must begin with an appreciation of its developmental diversity. Across the region, high growth rates through state-sponsored industrialization have reduced poverty levels, expanded the middle class, and produced massive fortunes for business entrepreneurs who are as likely to see authoritarian rulers as a grabbing hand that could expropriate them as a helpful hand needed for their ongoing prosperity. Commonalities and diffusion across the region in terms of economic policies, developmental orientations, and class transformations are unmistakable.

This is why, for all their many differences, all twelve cases considered in this book are part of what we call "developmental Asia." In the following sections of this chapter, we first argue that these cases bear enough of a family resemblance to be considered a single world region. Our emphasis thus begins with similarities. But we then argue that there is so much radical variation within this single region that we can identify altogether different types of political economies.[1]

While this variation is radical, it is not random. This variation in types yields four different developmental clusters, each populated by three cases. Furthermore, we insist that within each of these four clusters, the three cases can be characterized by their substantially varying levels of strength in their authoritarian institutions and coalitions. This is what we call the spectrum of strength.

In sum, developmental Asia is a single region that can be divided into four clusters of cases. These clusters differ by type, not just by aggregate strength. Within each cluster, furthermore, the three cases can then be arrayed along a spectrum of strength in authoritarian governing capacity and developmental success.

This exercise in clustering is not merely descriptive. As we will show, it can hardly be a coincidence that all six cases in developmental Asia that have at some time pursued transformative democratic reforms can be located in the "developmental statist" (Japan, South Korea, and Taiwan) and "developmental militarist" (Indonesia, Myanmar, and Thailand) clusters. Meanwhile the other six cases, all of which have consistently resisted field-leveling democratic reforms, are all located in the "developmental Britannia" (Singapore, Malaysia, and Hong Kong) and "developmental socialist" (China, Vietnam, and Cambodia) clusters. Correlation may not always be causal, but perfect correlation across such a large handful of cases is unlikely to be purely coincidental. Somehow, *developmental clustering has fostered democratic clustering* in Asia. It is one of our core purposes to figure out why and how.

To foreshadow: membership in a particular developmental cluster strongly determines the overall likelihood of preemptive democratic reforms. Meanwhile, the spectrum of authoritarian strength both across and within clusters profoundly shapes the smoothness of democratization. It also largely determines the success that formerly authoritarian elites enjoy under newly democratic conditions.

This smoothness during democratization and success after democratization are intrinsically linked. It is precisely because old authoritarians at the higher end of the spectrum of strength can translate their considerable accumulated capacities into a successful life in a new democracy that regime openings in these cases face fewer obstacles, downturns, and reversals. Stronger incumbent authoritarian regimes are more likely to experience smoother transitions if they choose to democratize through strength.

By contrast, democratic reforms that have unfolded in cases with less impressive levels of authoritarian strength have proved—predictably, we argue— to be far rockier and frequently reversible pathways. In the future, there is every reason to believe that the relative smoothness or rockiness of democratic transitions in developmental socialist cases like China as well as developmental Britannia cases such as Singapore would be shaped by the stock of accumulated strengths those authoritarian regimes have built up over the decades.

Outlines and Origins of a Region

The typical way to carve up Asian geography is into cardinal directions. "South Asia" means the subcontinent, with India at its center and Pakistan, Bangladesh, Nepal, Bhutan, and Sri Lanka radiating outward from it. "Southeast Asia" typically denotes the dozen or so countries lying east of the Indian subcontinent, south of China, and northwest of Australia. This includes "mainland" cases like Myanmar, Thailand, and Cambodia, as well as "island" Southeast Asian cases like Indonesia, Malaysia, and the Philippines. "Northeast Asia," or simply "East Asia," radiates from China like South Asia radiates from India. The two Koreas, Japan, Taiwan, Hong Kong, and Mongolia are all commonly located here. "Russia's 'Far East'" is usually not, since its capital is located in Eastern Europe rather than East Asia. "Central Asia" primarily means the former Soviet central Asian republics (e.g., Kazakhstan, Uzbekistan), with Afghanistan sometimes thrown in for good measure. Meanwhile the term "West Asia" appears to have fallen out of fashion, leaving countries like Iran, Lebanon, and Yemen continentally adrift, in "the Middle East" rather than any region of "Asia" per se.

This purely directional approach to Asia's geography does not work for our purposes. As even a rudimentary look at these cardinally defined regions will show, they all contain tremendous internal diversity. Location within any of these "directional Asias" tells us precious little about a country's economy, political system, or developmental trajectory.

To understand what developmental Asia is, it makes sense first to discuss how developmental Asia began. It has its deepest origins in Meiji Japan's revolutionary economic reforms of the late nineteenth century.[2] Through the uneven, gradual, and sequential spread of Japan's developmental-state model along the Pacific Rim after World War II, an identifiably new world region emerged. Through the collision of Japan-inspired developmentalism with a wide assortment of different polities—some dominated by British imperialists, others by highly politicized militaries, and others by long-lasting communist parties—developmental Asia assumed not just a *common* character but a *clustered* character. The upshot was not twelve cases that looked strikingly alike, but four distinctive developmental clusters containing three cases each.

Before addressing the region's clustering, however, we need to establish that developmental Asia is a single region in any meaningful sense in the first place. Contrary to regnant, contemporary visions of Asia as a region long shaped and dominated by China, it was in fact Japan that began forging a modern region in its own developmental image, spreading all the way across Southeast Asia, brushing along the eastern borders of the Indian subcontinent. In the process of securing its sovereignty from encroaching imperialism in the mid-nineteenth century, Japan built new political and economic institutions that allowed the country to industrialize rapidly and integrate itself fully into growing global markets as a major economic power.

No country in Asia had ever attempted anything similar. And no Asian country that sought to "catch up" in Japan's footsteps would ever do so in a way other than through the same combination of state-sponsored industrialization and export-oriented growth that Japan had introduced to the rest of the region.

Japan's rise turned the world upside down, starting with Asia itself. Fifteen years after America's "black ships" humiliatingly forced Japan to open two treaty ports to foreign trade in 1853, the Meiji Restoration of 1868 commenced history's greatest "revolution from above" by renovating the state apparatus and transforming society's feudal institutions. Parallel to developments in newly unified Germany at the time—and learning adroitly from the German model, among others—Japan built one of the world's first developmental states, centered on a mighty economic bureaucracy, directed toward the national goal of *fukoku kyohei* (rich country, strong army).[3]

By 1895, Japan had announced its arrival on the world stage by winning the Sino-Japanese War and joining the ranks of imperial powers by seizing Taiwan from China. By 1905, at the very apex of global European imperialism and domination, Japan shocked the world to its core by trouncing Russia in the Russo-Japanese War.

The inspirational effects of Japan's geopolitical rise are hard to fathom in retrospect. It was widely considered unthinkable before 1905 that white Europeans could be defeated by nonwhite non-Europeans in an all-out international war. Japan became an inspiration for anybody suffering under European imperialism, especially in Asia. The very idea of national catch-up first took root outside Europe in Japan. Although models of economic development varied considerably throughout the twentieth century, Japan-inspired developmentalism—the patriotic impulse to bring one's nation into the same league as the world's richest, strongest powers—would leave a deep imprint among Japan's Asian neighbors that remains plainly visible to the present day.

It is this shared, steadfast orientation toward rapid national economic development, grounded in similar but not identical economic policies and political institutions to implement them, that makes developmental Asia an identifiable region. The political prioritization of rapid economic growth—motored by a capitalist developmental model that prizes exports and integration into the international economy and unhesitatingly uses state sponsorship to encourage industrialization, while still treating private firms as the cornerstone of national economic advancement—marks developmental Asia as distinctive from the rest of the world. Nowhere else, ever, has a set of countries in the same geographic region shown such a shared political commitment to this highly transformative economic model.

Imperialism and Developmentalism

There was a long interlude, however, between Japan's rise as Asia's first developmental state in the late nineteenth century and the emergence of a full-blown developmental region in the latter half of the twentieth. This was as much a reflection of just how pioneering Japan's revolution from above truly was as it was of the region's lateness in catching up. For nearly a full century, developmental Asia was nothing more than developmental Japan. Japan remained Asia's only export-oriented industrial power until the so-called Four Tigers or Four Dragons—South Korea, Taiwan, Hong Kong, and Singapore—began experiencing rapid economic growth and industrialization in the 1960s and 1970s.

The reasons for this lengthy delay in the emulation and spread of export-led industrialization from Japan to its neighbors were many. Most important was imperialism. So long as Asian countries lacked national sovereignty, they could not pursue national industrialization policies. The second main factor was Japan's devastating military defeat in World War II. It would only be when Japan rebuilt its state-led export economy in the 1950s and 1960s, and not when it first built it during the Meiji Restoration, that Japanese-style developmentalism blossomed into a wider phenomenon of Asian developmentalism. Back in the Meiji era, it was said that Japan was "leaving Asia"; during the Cold War, Asia began following Japan.

Japan could not shape all of Asia in its own image under its own leadership because it was blocked by external powers. The two powers doing the most to block it were the United States and Great Britain. These two hegemonic powers shaped Asia in ways that would endure until the present day, and thereby help mold developmental Asia's distinctive clusters. British influence came first, starting in the first half of the nineteenth century and accelerating greatly in its second half. After assuming control of Singapore in the wake of the Napoleonic Wars in 1815, Britain enjoyed an outpost from which to push for an "open economy" in Asia that would supply it with desired resources in exchange for British exports. The First Opium War, from 1839 to 1842, saw Britain bring this battering ram to China, gaining control over Hong Kong for over 150 years.

The United States followed closely behind. When its "black ships" arrived on the shores of Japan in the 1850s, America assumed a major if unwelcome role in inspiring Japan's internal political and economic reforms of the Meiji era. By 1900, America had formally joined the imperial game in Asia, assuming control over the Philippines. Yet Japan was still the more transformative regional power. Quite importantly for our story to come, Japan became not merely an industrialized nation and an inspirational force but an imperial power in its own right in the face of external pressures, colonizing Taiwan in 1895 and Korea in 1910.

The upshot by the eve of World War II was a highly internationalized but thoroughly imperial regional political economy. The United States, Great Britain, and Japan were its leading powers. World War II's devastating effects would leave the United States as the only superpower left standing in Asia throughout the Cold War era. The Soviet Union may have had proxies in Asia—which would eventually help constitute the developmental socialist cluster of China, Vietnam, and Cambodia—but nothing approximating the overwhelming power and ubiquitous presence of the Americans.

Japan's remarkable economic recovery after World War II is a story for the following chapter. For present purposes, the key point is that American domination in Asia set the stage for developmental Asia to emerge as a full-blown region in two main ways. First, the United States oversaw a general if gradual dismantling of formal empire in Asia. As a latecomer to the imperial game, America had long resented the strongholds that European powers had entrenched over resource-rich colonies like British Malaya (Malaysia), the Dutch East Indies (Indonesia), and French Indochina (Vietnam and Cambodia). The postwar United States stood to benefit immensely as the world's leading economy from a global trading system devoid of imperial controls.

America would not need formal imperialism to ensure its own domination in the region. The Philippines were granted national independence as soon as World War II was over, and America's occupation of Japan ended peacefully once a friendly government was firmly established. American troops remained in the Philippines and Japan in large numbers, however, just as they did in South Korea after the Korean War ended in a stalemate, and in South Vietnam before it was routed by the communist North. The key point is that American troops did not keep their boots on Asian soil to stifle the growth of a robust and globally oriented Asian economy, but to stimulate it.

Herein lies the second way in which American postwar hegemony set the stage on which the key actors in our drama—Asians themselves—would create developmental Asia. Driven by desires to outperform and contain the Soviet Union, keep a newly pacified Japan in the pro-American camp, and leverage its enormous postwar economic advantages to the utmost, the United States oversaw the birth of an open trading system across the Pacific Ocean that benefited the Asia region and the United States in tandem. *Developmental Asia would be export-led Asia.*

This was only possible in the decades following World War II if the United States was willing to do the bulk of the importing. Exports to America from Japan began booming in the 1950s and 1960s, then skyrocketing in the 1970s and 1980s. And it was not just Japan. During the earliest postwar period, Taiwan and South Korea benefited immensely from Japan's international capitalist developmentalism. Decades before America pressured Japan to let its currency appreciate in the Plaza Accord of 1985, and thus reduce Japan's ballooning trade surplus with the United States, the aforementioned Four Tigers—South Korea, Taiwan, Hong Kong, and Singapore—had already become major exporters to the United States as well.

Focused as it was on strengthening the Japanese yen, the Plaza Accord did not seal America off from the flood of Asian exports as intended, but spread the range of Asian economies from which American imports would flow. With its currency boosted in value, Japan began investing furiously across Asia, moving the finishing stages of its high-tech manufacturing to countries where both currencies and workers were far cheaper. In the 1980s and early 1990s, this mostly meant Indonesia, Malaysia, and Thailand. By the late 1990s and 2000s, China became the largest beneficiary.[4] Not to be left out, Vietnam, Cambodia, and Myanmar increasingly joined the race for inward investment and export production opportunities as well. At the center of this emergent region was Japan, followed by its former colonies and most apt developmental pupils: South Korea and Taiwan.

Thus developmental Asia as a region was born. American markets and Japanese investments may have served as the key engines of growth, but it was the political will of developmentally focused governments across most of East and Southeast Asia to keep pace with Asia's economic leaders that would provide the most important raw material for building a new world region. The combination of a state-led yet market-oriented developmental model exemplified by Japan, ready access to the American export market as well as Japanese foreign direct investment, deep embroilment in Cold War rivalries, and a nationalist ethos of developmental catch-up spread across Northeast and Southeast Asia. It made all twelve cases that we explore in this book strikingly different from Asian neighbors such as Bangladesh, India, Laos, Mongolia, Pakistan, the Philippines, and North Korea. Developmental Asia would spread to encompass most of the countries reached by the Japanese Empire during World War II, but no further.

Four Clusters: Developmental Statism, Developmental Britannia, Developmental Militarism, and Developmental Socialism

To say that developmental Asia is an identifiable region is not to deny its internal heterogeneity, but rather to set the stage for appreciating and apprehending it. Within this broad developmental Asian family, we witness both "horizontal" variation in type across developmental clusters and "vertical" variation between and within clusters in terms of institutional capacity (recall table 1.1). After explicating all four clusters, we explain the spectrum of strength that characterizes each one.

At the most granular level, developmental Asia's twelve cases represent twelve different political economies. Every economy is, of course, ultimately unique. Yet striking patterns across the cases are nevertheless discernible, and the heterogeneity across types that they represent cannot be ignored for purposes of comparison. Indeed, sorting developmental Asia into clusters is necessarily a prior task to assessing each case's institutional strength.

This is because like needs to be compared with like: an especially strong case in the developmental socialist cluster such as China, for instance, cannot have its strength directly compared with that of a case from the developmental Britannia cluster such as Malaysia. China's strength, and the developmental resources that contribute to that strength, should be compared with the strength of fellow developmental socialist travelers like Vietnam and Cambodia. Malaysia should be directly compared with "siblings" Hong Kong and Singapore because it allows us to hold the type of political and economic institutions largely constant, or at least more plausibly comparable than juxtapositions across clusters rather than within them.

Developmental clusters make democratic clusters, as it turns out. This is the striking pattern we see in developmental Asia's descriptive statistics. Only by looking closely at the developmental clusters from which these twelve cases come can we move beyond the standard modernization account that levels of development straightforwardly predict levels of democracy. A clustered analysis helps us recognize that it is *types* of development, and not simply levels of development, that have led to regime types in developmental Asia.

Developmental Statism

Developmental Asia began with developmental Japan. Japan's developmental turn was both a consequence of foreign empire and the cause of its own eventual empire. Responding to American and European encroachments, Japan began to build an empire of its own, extending its core developmental institutions through formal imperialism into Korea and Taiwan during the first half of the twentieth century. Although World War II decimated Japan and broke its empire apart, the seeds of our first developmental cluster—the *developmental statist* cluster encompassing Japan, South Korea, and Taiwan—were sown in this prewar period of growth, empire, institutional transfer, and eventual emulation.

What makes this cluster distinctive within developmental Asia is its shared success at state-led industrial and technological upgrading and eventual rise to global leadership in high-tech manufactured exports. This economic prowess was built on a foundation of political institutions that bear a strong family resemblance across the developmental statist cluster.

Most fundamental is a competent and bureaucratic state that has been closely allied with, but never subservient to or captured by, leading business exporters. State strength allowed Japan, South Korea, and Taiwan to become global economic leaders through eventual indigenous technological advances, more than relying solely and perpetually on inward foreign direct investment (FDI) and technology transfer. All three states were governed consistently by conservative political parties throughout the postwar era as well, while militaries remained relatively professional and the landed elite was politically marginalized through sweeping land reforms. In geopolitical terms, all three cases similarly benefited throughout the Cold War period from America's security umbrella and commitment to relatively open transpacific trade. Unlike their relatively resource-dependent, FDI-dependent, and location-dependent neighbors, all three cases in Asia's developmental statist cluster leveraged their considerable institutional strengths to achieve developed-country status as bona fide national manufacturing and technological powerhouses.

The economic fruits of this common developmental strategy are hard to exaggerate and impossible to miss. As figure 2.1 shows, Japan, South Korea, and Taiwan followed a common trajectory after World War II from developing to developed economy status. Japan, naturally, went first. Its level of development in 1960 was not reached in South Korea until 1980. Nonetheless, the shared upward trajectory is unmistakable. Although Japan's development trajectory flattened out in the 2000s, allowing both South Korea and Taiwan to

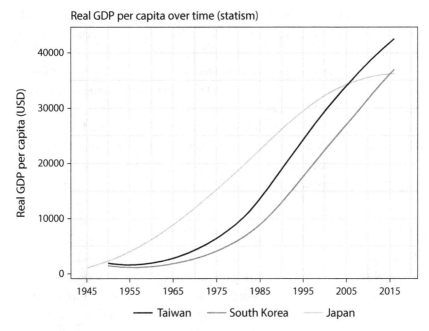

FIGURE 2.1. Economic Development in the Statist Cluster

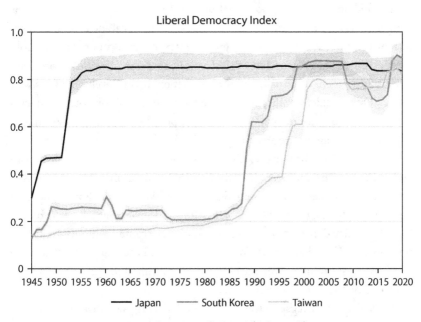

FIGURE 2.2. Democracy Scores in the Statist Cluster

surpass it on a per capita basis, it remains one of the richest countries on Earth, with annual gross domestic product (GDP) per capita comfortably clearing US$30,000.

Nowhere is the correspondence between developmental cluster and democratic cluster clearer than in the statist cluster. Built on powerful bureaucratic states, popular and broad-based incumbent conservative parties, and enviable economic track records, Japan, South Korea, and Taiwan would all democratize from positions of considerable strength. As figure 2.2 shows, the result in all three cases has been stable, enduring, high-quality democracy. The cardinal direction for democracy is not only West; it is also East.

Developmental Britannia

Developmental Asia's second cluster has its roots in empire as well. The British imperial advance across Asia during the nineteenth century brought hundreds of millions of Asian subjects under the Union Jack. The vast majority, however, were in the Indian subcontinent, in the territories that would become the demographic colossi of India, Pakistan, and Bangladesh, as well as smaller Sri Lanka. Distant as these countries were from both American consumers and Japanese investors, they would not join developmental Asia.[5]

It would only be in Singapore, Malaysia, and Hong Kong—tiny Lilliputians compared with South Asia's giants—where British political and economic institutions would mix with the rapidly growing transpacific economy of the Cold War and post–Cold War periods. British rule bequeathed powerful institutions, but subtly different types of institutions from those in the developmental statist cluster. Of particular significance was the greater emphasis on courts and legal institutions in developmental Britannia, as opposed to the bureaucratic autonomy and discretion that loomed larger in the developmental statist cluster.[6]

Also critical was Britain's relatively low level of economic interventionism and protectionism, consistent with the British emphasis on legal institutions as bulwarks for market development. Singapore, Malaysia, and Hong Kong were already deeply integrated into global trading and investment markets by the time the British departed. They also lacked the active interventionist industrial policies that Japan had practiced for a century and transferred to its Korean and Taiwanese colonies over decades of imperial rule, and that had then been emulated by their developmental states.

These distinctive legacies were compounded by the fact that Britain left all three colonies through negotiations involving conservative local allies, rather than through a sharp rupture in which rising radicals displaced an old collaborationist guard. Negotiated exits allowed the British to install their favored Westminster electoral system, particularly in Malaysia and Singapore, inadvertently giving the dominant parties of the time extra strength with which to consolidate electoral authoritarian rule from the 1960s onward.

Despite its many differences in type from the statist cluster, the Britannia cluster has witnessed similarly impressive upward trajectories of economic development. As figure 2.3 shows, all three Britannia cases are phenomenal economic success stories. This is especially true of Singapore and Hong Kong, purely urban economies whose lack of a sizable rural sector helped them both reach and eventually even surpass levels of industrial and economic development seen across the statist cluster of Japan, Taiwan, and South Korea. Malaysia is a definite laggard within the Britannia cluster but still easily the second-richest capitalist economy in Southeast Asia. Like Japan, Hong Kong has experienced a flattening of its growth trajectory since the late 1990s, when it shifted from British to mainland Chinese control. Yet its overall developmental record remains nothing short of spectacular.

Once again, the developmental cluster predicts the democratic cluster. While all three developmental statist cases pursued democracy through strength during the Cold War, none of developmental Britannia's three cases followed suit, even decades after the Cold War ended. There is no single story for this shared pattern of democracy avoidance. The absence of democratic reform pursued by conservative incumbents in all three cases, captured strikingly by the extraordinarily flat trajectories of electoral-authoritarian persistence in figure 2.4, arises from very different political tales, as we discuss in chapter 8. Yet the perfect correspondence between membership in developmental Britannia and failure to democratize through strength has at least some identifiable roots in their shared British colonial experience, which we have introduced here and will dive into deeper detail on in chapter 8.

Before concluding our discussion of the developmental statist and Britannia clusters, it is vital to appreciate how much they both stand apart from the developmental militarism and socialism clusters in economic terms. As figure 2.5 vividly shows, developmental statism and Britannia share the status of being wealthy regions, with only Malaysia skirting the edges of middle-income status. The militarist and socialist clusters, to be discussed momentarily, are substantially poorer clusters overall. Of the six countries in these latter two clusters, only China and Thailand have come close to transcending middle-income status. However, neither country is yet even as wealthy on a per capita

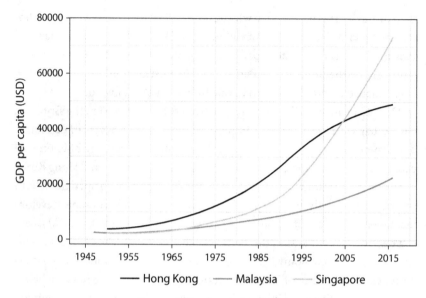

FIGURE 2.3. Economic Development in the Britannia Cluster

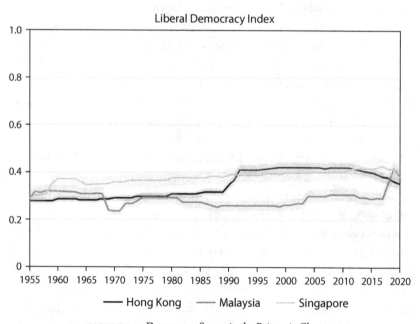

FIGURE 2.4. Democracy Scores in the Britannia Cluster

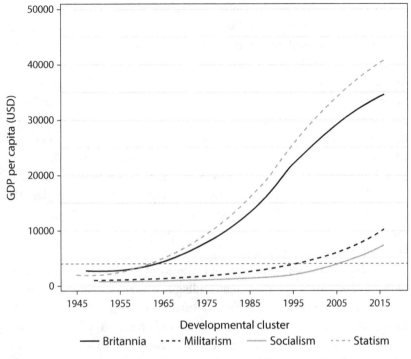

FIGURE 2.5. Two High-Income and Two Middle-Income Clusters

basis as Malaysia, which is far less developed than any other economy in either the statist or Britannia clusters.

As we move away from the clusters of developmental statism and developmental Britannia, we move into cases where authoritarian regimes have developed substantially lower, though not insubstantial, institutional capacity.

Developmental Militarism

In Indonesia, Thailand, and Burma (renamed Myanmar in 1990), authoritarian power during the Cold War primarily resided in a ruling military, rather than the dominant party and bureaucratic organizations characteristic of the two previous clusters. However, this did not prevent all three militarist cases from joining developmental Asia with export-oriented growth policies and considerable state intervention, beginning with Indonesia and Thailand joining by the 1970s and Myanmar by the 2000s. They did so as developmental Asia's economic laggards rather than leaders.

None of the developmental militarist cases were defined by imperial legacies, unlike the developmental statist and developmental Britannia cases. Rather, political development in all three militarist cases was emphatically anticolonial in its orientation. In Thailand, colonialism was resisted so successfully that the country remained formally independent. The Thai military assumed the leading position in national politics when it toppled Thailand's absolutist monarchy in 1932. In Indonesia and Burma, colonialism was deeply disruptive and traumatic, and militaries emerged to expel European imperialists trying to return after being sidelined by Japanese invasions during World War II. Indeed, the Burmese and Indonesian armies were both Japanese creations. They were built to fight off returning imperial forces and replace the collaborationist armies those European rulers had formed. As it turned out, they were also built to fight domestic regional separatists after independence was won, and ultimately to rule.

Developmental Asia's military-led regimes did not preside over similarly impressive economic growth and upgrading as witnessed in the previous developmental statist and developmental Britannia clusters (see figure 2.6). Although all three countries eventually embraced an export-led strategy, they were overwhelmingly dependent on natural resources and low-skilled, low-value-added production. This dependency was sufficient to support decades of very rapid growth in Indonesia and Thailand, which were ready to embrace the deluge of Japanese investment as it swelled throughout the 1970s and 1980s. Burma, on the other hand, was far less prepared, still hewing to an autarkic and socialist growth strategy until 1988, and suffering global pariah status thereafter for having cracked down violently on the country's democracy movement. For all these differences, which we devote significant attention to in chapter 7, Burma can still be considered a final entrant to developmental Asia as part of the developmental militarist cluster.

Having achieved much less economic development, this cluster also attained much less stable democratization than its developmental statist counterparts, as the jagged peaks and valleys (and at times, even missing data) in figure 2.7 attest. When militaries stepped aside from direct rule, they did so knowing outright electoral victory for their conservative party allies was not in the cards. Yet they preserved enough safeguards in their constitutions and enjoyed enough civilian support to feel confident that they could engage in, at the very least, a power-sharing "cohabitation" arrangement with elected politicians after democratization. It is only in Indonesia where the experiment

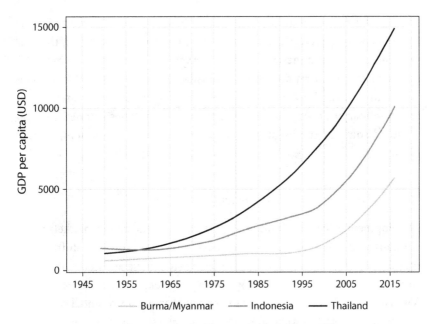

FIGURE 2.6. Economic Development in the Militarist Cluster

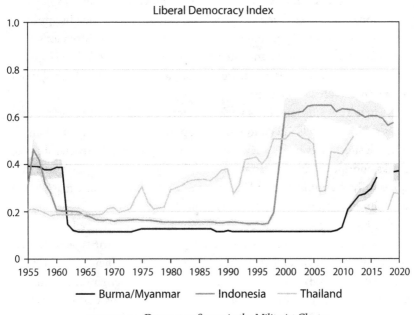

FIGURE 2.7. Democracy Scores in the Militarist Cluster

of democratizing from strength has thus far brought the lasting fruit of stable democracy, as figure 2.7 clearly shows. As we explore in chapter 7, this was precisely because Indonesia's military-led regime built stronger and more durable conservative party organizations, analogous if not equivalent to the ones we see in postwar Taiwan and South Korea, than either Burma or Thailand under military rule. At its core a military regime, Indonesia nonetheless resembled some of the institutional features of the developmental statist cluster.

Developmental Socialism

Developmental Asia was built on export markets, and export markets mean capitalism. It was thus an enormous occasion and profound shift for the world's largest communist regime—China—to pursue economic liberalization and embark on an export-led growth strategy beginning in the early 1980s. Vietnam has followed a broadly similar track of externally oriented economic reform, albeit with less stupendous developmental success. Even further down the spectrum of economic success lies Cambodia, the country Vietnam invaded and imposed its regime type on in the late 1970s.

We refer to all three of these cases as developmental socialist despite these differences, however, because they have all combined socialist political institutions—most importantly a ruling single party—with strenuous if belated efforts to industrialize and integrate into the regional and global capitalist economy. They may be laggards rather than leaders, but they have "joined" developmental Asia nonetheless.

As figure 2.8 indicates, the socialist cluster resembles the militarist cluster in its middling levels of economic development on average. More than any other cluster, however, the average level of development in the socialist cluster cloaks enormous internal variation. Specifically, China has grown so stratospherically in comparison to Vietnam and Cambodia that one may wonder whether they belong in the same cluster at all.

Getting richer, however, does not automatically change a political economy's type. Recall that our clustering strategy is based on the type of political economy rather than level of political economic development. China is by far the most successful developmental socialist case, and Vietnam and Cambodia aspire to follow in its footsteps. China clearly shares certain "techno-nationalist" characteristics that are more famously and accurately associated

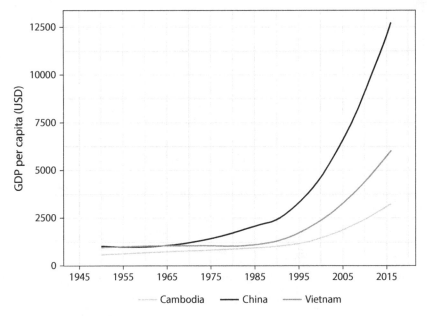

FIGURE 2.8. Economic Development in the Socialist Cluster

with Japan and South Korea. Yet one must keep in mind that the nationalist ideology of catch-up is a common feature of the entire region of developmental Asia, not just the cluster of developmental statism. As we will see in chapters 6 and 9, China has very different political and economic institutions from those in the statist, Britannia, and militarist clusters.

Several features make the developmental socialist cluster distinctive, with major implications for their prospects of democratization. For starters, socialist rule in China, Vietnam, and Cambodia was preceded and accompanied by truly astonishing levels of political violence. This makes stability confidence, or the lack thereof, loom especially large in ruling parties' calculations of risk when it comes to democratic reform and its potential consequences. Also vital is the fact that socialism is associated with single-party rule rather than electoral authoritarianism, although Cambodia defied this pattern for most of the post–Cold War period, due to United Nations intervention and external insistence on competitive multiparty politics. Single-party regimes lack the clear electoral signals multiparty regimes can more readily receive. Asia's developmental socialist cluster also naturally has the weakest historical connection with and dependence on the United States, making external democratizing

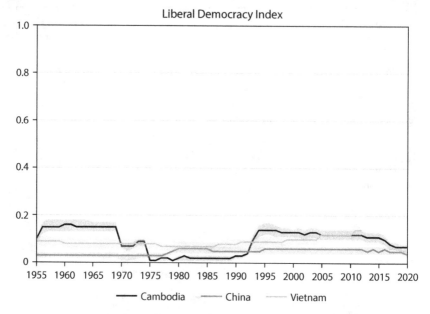

FIGURE 2.9. Democracy Scores in the Socialist Cluster

pressure not merely ineffective but counterproductive. The abject lack of democratic reforms in the developmental socialist cluster is eloquently expressed in the flat lines seen in figure 2.9.

These factors may speak to the *unwillingness* of developmental socialist regimes to pursue democracy through strength, but not to any *incapacity* to do so. Having annihilated organized opposition many decades ago in their rise to power, communist parties in China and Vietnam could open up the party system without immediately confronting any meaningful national rival. Decades of rapid economic growth and political stability have greatly expanded the urban middle class, especially in China, and gradually reoriented citizens' political expectations toward a growing economic pie rather than an unbreakable iron rice bowl.

Cambodia, to be sure, is a different story. A product of external imposition, the ruling Cambodian People's Party (CPP) regime did not command nationalist revolutionary forces like its Chinese and Vietnamese counterparts. Cambodia had a decades-long history of competitive elections before aging ruler Hun Sen undermined them in the 2010s, effectively making Cambodia a one-party system in the process. In this respect, Cambodia has recently become even more true to its developmental socialist cluster.

From Clusters to Spectrums

The troikas of cases that inhabit each Asian developmental cluster bear strong sibling resemblances, but they are not identical triplets. In all four clusters, the cases with the most and the least institutional strength during authoritarian times are relatively straightforward to establish. For instance, among our developmental statist cases, Taiwan's ruling party clearly enjoyed the most authoritarian strength. In South Korea, more institutional power rested in the military and bureaucracy than in the ruling party. China's powerful party-state is the obvious frontrunner in the developmental socialist cluster, with Vietnam and especially Cambodia lagging far behind. Singapore enjoys a level of institutional strength in the developmental Britannia cluster that Hong Kong and Malaysia rival in certain respects but can by no means match. And in the cluster where authoritarian institutional strength has been lowest overall—the developmental militarist cluster—Indonesia's relatively stout party institutions made it stand apart from both Burma and Thailand before democratization.

In the chapters to follow, we explore how clustered patterns of development foreshadowed democracy through strength in the statist and militarist clusters, but not the socialist and Britannia clusters. We also demonstrate that the differences in political and economic strength *within* each cluster—the spectrums of strength—shaped regime variation across developmental Asia quite profoundly. Taiwan's democratization was predictably smoother than South Korea's because of the Kuomintang regime's greater antecedent strengths; Indonesia's democratization was predictably smoother and more sustainable than Myanmar's for similar reasons based on antecedent strength. Extrapolating forward, we expect that democratization through strength in Singapore would be the smoothest trajectory in the Britannia cluster, while China's political institutions offer the ruling Chinese Communist Party (CCP) considerable capacity for a smooth democratization trajectory that its ruling-party counterparts in Vietnam and Cambodia cannot rival.

From Development to Democracy

Having both defined developmental Asia as a single region and differentiated it by its four clusters, we can now say more about how this developmental clustering has shaped democratic clustering. We have already shown some basic descriptive statistics from the Varieties of Democracy (V-Dem) Liberal Democracy Index for each cluster separately in the previous section. We now

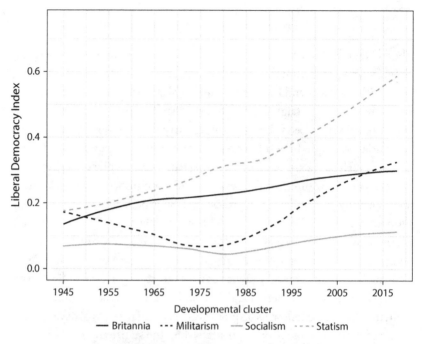

FIGURE 2.10. Democracy Scores across All Four Clusters

aggregate and compare the four clusters in figure 2.10, tracking the overall tra-jectories of the four clusters from the end of World War II until the present.[7]

Several aggregate patterns leap out. First, the region that would eventually become developmental Asia had no democratic cases when the postwar era began. Second, the only cluster to experience relatively smooth democratic development throughout the postwar era is the statist cluster (Japan, Taiwan, and South Korea). And third, the only cluster lacking significant multiparty electoral experience is the socialist cluster (China, Vietnam, and Cambodia).

As always, cluster averages mask important exceptions. South Korea was deeply authoritarian in the 1970s and early 1980s for the statist cluster, while Cambodia trended unusually democratic for the socialist cluster in the 1990s and 2000s. But the overall picture—that developmental statism has been associ-ated with gradual, smooth democratic development, while developmental socialism presents an aggregate image of persistently closed authoritarianism—serves as an important starting point.

The clusters of developmental Britannia and militarism lie in between. The fact that developmental Asia's former British colonies have always retained multiparty electoral competition and Westminster systems bequeathed by their shared imperial experience means that this cluster's aggregate democracy scores have always been higher than those of the developmental socialist cluster, where single-party rule has been the unbroken norm. What figure 2.10 captures so accurately is that all three cases in developmental Britannia moved toward a hybrid form of authoritarianism—electoral authoritarianism—during the postwar era and remained remarkably stable in that supposed "halfway house" between closed authoritarianism and fully competitive democracy.[8] At no point has any ruling party in developmental Britannia preemptively and voluntarily leveled the playing field with its opponents. The Britannia cluster has exhibited durable electoral authoritarianism through strength.

The militarist cluster has reached the present moment with a very similar aggregate democracy score to that of the Britannia cluster. Yet its regime types and regime trajectories have been dramatically different. Whereas the Britannia cluster's impressive economic and institutional strengths have parlayed into authoritarian stability, the militarist cluster's more modest economic and institutional strengths have meant far greater authoritarian instability.

At times of high stability confidence (e.g., Thailand in the 1980s, Indonesia in the 1990s, and Myanmar in the 2010s), military regimes in developmental Asia have pursued transformative democratic reforms. Yet the relative weakness of conservative political parties in the militarist cluster, especially when compared with the developmental statist cluster, has meant rockier and less stable democratic experiences and more reversible democratic experiments. And when militaries in power have lacked stability confidence, as in Myanmar during the 1990s and in Thailand today, no democratic reforms have been forthcoming. Although the militarist cluster's strength is only intermediate, its democratization experience has primarily unfolded through strength and concessions rather than weakness and collapse.

Before going further, it is worth eyeballing the similarities and differences between figure 2.5 (which measures development by cluster) and figure 2.10 (which does the same for democracy), and pondering their implications for modernization theory. The more the four lines follow similar trajectories in each figure, the better modernization theory looks. And indeed, the wealthy and democratic developmental statist cluster (the top line in each figure) makes modernization theory look good, as does the far poorer and fully autocratic developmental socialist cluster (the bottom line in each figure).

Asia is thus no graveyard for modernization theory, as one focused strictly on China's stratospheric growth and stubborn authoritarianism might think. Still, it certainly flies in the face of modernization theory that developmental

Britannia is so much richer yet also so much more resistant to democratic concessions than the developmental militarist cluster; the two lines are worlds apart on development in figure 2.5, but practically converge in their democracy scores in figure 2.10. Juxtaposing these two figures thus vividly displays that modernization theory gets us part of the way, but by no means the whole way, to understanding Asia's trajectories from development to democracy.

From Patterns to Mechanisms

Why do Asia's developmental clusters shape its democratic clusters? Answering this question requires that we consider the causal mechanisms through which they do so. We would be paying short shrift to a complicated and eclectic historical record to claim that development types have shaped regime types through a very small and consistent set of mechanisms that travel across all twelve of our cases. Many case-specific details on causal mechanisms are explored in the empirical chapters to follow. However, for present purposes, we can highlight several mechanisms of particular importance across the full set of cases and tie them to our theory of democracy through strength.

Recall the centrality of *confidence and signals* in our theory. Authoritarian regimes that enjoy considerable strength are most likely to democratize when they have both victory confidence and stability confidence and when they receive signals that their apex of authoritarian domination has recently passed them by.

These signals, which often take the form of sudden shocks to authoritarian systems, come in four types: electoral, contentious, economic, and geopolitical. Hence, if our theory is correct, developmental clustering matters because it somehow shapes how different authoritarian regimes receive, process, and respond to these four types of signals. Presumably there is something about the institutions of these clustered regimes that determines their vulnerability and receptivity to the four different types of signals. This should shape the victory confidence and stability confidence of these regimes in turn, making democratic concessions either more or less likely.

Let us begin with *electoral* signals. How do the differing political institutions of the different developmental clusters shape these regimes' vulnerability and receptivity to electoral signals of incipient yet irreversible regime decline? In China and Vietnam, both in the developmental socialist cluster, electoral signals are absent because competitive elections between multiple political parties are prohibited. This contrasts sharply with developmental Britannia cases such as Singapore and Malaysia, where dominant parties have long received regular signals of their rising and declining popularity through national elections. An intriguing implication, therefore, is that democracy through strength is more likely to unfold in the near future in a case like Singapore than one like China, because electoral results may clearly signal incipient decline to Singapore's People's Action Party (PAP) in a manner that China's CCP currently cannot receive.

Geopolitical signals also differ substantially across developmental Asia's four clusters. The contrast between the statist and socialist clusters is especially striking. Postwar Japan, South Korea, and Taiwan have all sheltered under the American security umbrella in the Asia-Pacific from the beginning of the Cold War until the present day. Signals of diminishing American tolerance for authoritarian rule during the 1980s, near the end of the Cold War, were received more clearly and strongly in the developmental statist cluster than anywhere else in the region.

The developmental socialist cluster, on the other hand, is a world apart when it comes to geopolitical signals. China has become America's primary geopolitical rival, as well as Cambodia's chief geopolitical sponsor. Hence, to the extent that American pressure was a factor facilitating and emboldening democratic experiments in different parts of developmental Asia, it makes sense that geopolitical signals would be received with greater clarity and urgency in some developmental clusters than others.

No signals that an authoritarian regime has passed its apex of power are more powerful than *contentious* signals. When massive cross-class protests erupt to challenge a regime's continued rule, some form of adaptation is virtually unavoidable. Adaptation can vary, however, with some dictatorships repressing brutally, others adapting in a more liberal direction, and some devising new and flexible mixes of repression and responsiveness.[9] Since all authoritarian regimes are potentially vulnerable to mass protests at certain times, and no authoritarian regime can simply ignore them, it is less likely that variation in contentious signals explains developmental Asia's clustered variation in democratization as much as electoral and geopolitical signals.

The same causal ambiguity is true of *economic* signals. Since developmental Asia is capitalist Asia, and capitalism comes everywhere with the risk of severe and sudden economic downturns, no authoritarian regime in the region is ever immune to the potential effects of economic crisis on authoritarian legitimacy. There is no particular reason to believe either that certain clusters are more vulnerable to economic signals of regime decline or that such signals, once received, would matter more in some developmental clusters than others.

In sum, of the four signals that drive our theory of democracy through strength, some are likely more influential in determining variation across developmental clusters than others. *Electoral and geopolitical signals are especially likely, and contentious and economic signals are least likely, to produce clustered effects.* Yet within specific countries, all four types of signals can produce major shifts in a regime's victory confidence and stability confidence, shaping prospects for preemptive democratic reforms as a result. The ensuing chapters delve deeply into these signals and mechanisms and how they interact in all twelve cases and all four clusters.

The Key Features of Clusters

These four types of signals by no means exhaust the many mechanisms through which developmental clustering might determine patterns of democratic clustering, however. The real world is always far more complicated than the theoretical toolkits we construct to make sense of it. Every cluster has a shared political history, with certain features that shape prospects for smooth democratization, a rocky transition, or the persistent absence of democratic experimentation altogether. Although we address these case-specific and cluster-specific features in greater detail in the following chapters, it behooves us to introduce a few especially prominent examples for each cluster.

For starters, the developmental statist cluster enjoys several democratic advantages beyond its wealth and the remarkable strength of its political institutions. All three countries conducted extraordinarily sweeping land reform in the immediate aftermath of World War II.[10] This helped produce more egalitarian societies, which inoculated them somewhat from the kind of intractable redistributive conflicts that can derail or prevent the emergence of democracies. This was especially true in Taiwan, where the ethnic divide between mainlanders and native Taiwanese would have made redistributive conflict all the more explosive and destabilizing if economic inequality had been severe. It should be noted as well that in all three cases, postwar land reform was carried out by the ruling coalition that eventually initiated democratization. This illustrates how early economic reforms generated strength and nationwide support (including from the countryside) for developmentally oriented regimes in postwar Japan, South Korea, and Taiwan, ultimately setting the stage for democratic concession from positions of conservative strength.

Developmental Asia's statist cluster also benefited from the externalization of the communist threat during the Cold War. In all three cases, communism was a far greater danger from without than from within. This was especially true of Taiwan and South Korea, where civil wars left a literal political border between these anticommunist regimes and their communist rivals in China and North Korea. The relative mildness of the internal communist threat in all three cases meant conservative incumbent political forces enjoyed more stability confidence after opening up the system to full democracy than in most of their neighbors.

Several common features in the Britannia cluster are worthy of special mention at the outset as well. Sharing a British colonial legacy has meant that Singapore, Malaysia, and Hong Kong have shared both a Westminster-style electoral system and a highly developed legal system. Nowhere in the world do authoritarian conservatives have as much experience with competitive rule-based elections as in developmental Britannia. And nowhere have incumbents benefited more from the first-past-the-post electoral rules that gave ruling parties such as Malaysia's United Malays National Organization (UMNO) and Singapore's (PAP) supermajoritarian seat shares in their respective legislatures, even when their share of the popular vote declined.

Citizens of Singapore, Malaysia, and Hong Kong have generally been able to count on competitive elections as well as a reasonably effective and professional legal system as compensation for their systems' sometimes suffocating authoritarian controls. Owing to a stronger rule of law (or at least "rule by law")[11] in the Britannia cases, corruption, though far from absent, has been far more attenuated than in any of the other three clusters.

Consider also the distinctive geopolitical positioning of developmental Britannia. An underappreciated by-product of British colonial roots is that the cases in developmental Britannia are much less dependent on the United States than the developmental statist cases of Japan, Taiwan, and South Korea. Moreover, it is not the case that dependence on America is replaced by dependence on Britain. Given Britain's much weaker global standing, the regimes clustered in developmental Britannia have enjoyed a balanced set of global dependencies that prevent any single outside power from dominating them.

Balanced and dispersed dependencies also mean that geopolitical shocks are less likely to disrupt the authoritarian status quo. Japan, the European Union, and Australia all play major supportive roles in developmental Britannia, in addition to the generally heavier-handed interventionism of the global superpowers, the United States and China. Indeed, the increasingly tempestuous relationship between the people of Hong Kong and the Chinese government is the exception that proves this rule. Even after China gained literal sovereign control over Hong Kong, the island's British roots and balanced global dependencies have made it difficult for Beijing's CCP to bring it completely to heel, other than through increased repression.

Prominent shared features characterize developmental Asia's weaker two clusters as well. The developmental militarist cluster of Indonesia, Thailand, and Myanmar have all seen the military play an outsize role in national political affairs, making the assurance of stability confidence more decisive in prompting democratization than the regimes' victory confidence. The relative weakness of authoritarian parties in the militarist cluster is accompanied by relatively weak states that are prone to patrimonialism. Economic development has been heavily reliant on foreign direct investment and overwhelmingly dependent on natural resources. Corruption is severe in the militarist cluster. Nevertheless, it has been conservative incumbents in the militarist cluster and not in the Britannia cluster who have, at times, experimented with the risk of removing authoritarian controls and attempted to maintain their ruling status amid the hurly-burly uncertainty of free democratic competition.

Part of the reason lies in the distinctive historical patterns of violence experienced in the developmental militarist cluster. Recall that the primary violent threat to developmental statist cases (Japan, Taiwan, and South Korea) emanated *from outside*—from neighboring communist rivals. In the militarist cluster, by contrast, the main violent threat has come *from within*, in the form of regional rebellions. For most of their history as independent countries, Indonesia, Thailand, and Myanmar have faced a greater danger of dismemberment by armed internal separatists than conquest by either external rivals or center-seeking insurgents.

These threats have justified the military's continuous leading role in politics in Indonesia, Thailand, and Myanmar.[12] Yet they have also been more compatible with democratic reforms, in the sense that introducing free and fair elections never meant letting the organized forces those militaries feared most gain a shot at national power. Time and again in the developmental militarist cluster, democratization has gone hand in hand with growing stability confidence, particularly when a military retreat from national office has not threatened to tear the territorial nation-state asunder.

Finally, the developmental socialist cluster has key shared features that should be emphasized at the outset as well. The most obvious is socialist ideology. To be sure, China, Vietnam, and Cambodia all had to cast aside communist orthodoxy to pursue state-sponsored capitalism as a new pathway to national strength. Yet socialist ideology continues to affect these countries' antagonism to electoral democracy, even if statist capitalism has gradually been embraced. Specifically, socialism promises an alternative path to a different type of democracy from the liberal and electoral variety, stressing the delivery of universal social goods under the never-ending tutelage of a single ruling party, legitimized by its leading role in the nation's revolutionary ethos.

Although it is surely self-serving, it is not purely self-serving for leaders of socialist ruling parties in China, Vietnam, and Cambodia to proclaim that their countries are already building a better kind of democracy than what exists in the hostile West.[13] From an ideological perspective, one can argue that liberal multiparty democracy is incompatible with these countries' DNA, making an inquiry into their democratic prospects quixotic. Then again, capitalism was even more ideologically incompatible with socialism than democracy, so the adaptive capacities of these developmental socialist regimes should not be underestimated.

Of perhaps even greater importance, countries in the developmental socialist cluster share a history of revolutionary violence that has shaped prospects for democratization up until the present day. All three regimes were preceded by enormously destructive levels of political violence, including World War II and the civil war that followed it in China; wars of liberation in Vietnam against the French and Americans, plus a war for internal unification of North and South; and in Cambodia, the genocidal revolutionary rule of the Khmer Rouge, followed by Vietnam's invasion and imposition of the socialist ruling party that still rules more than four decades later.

One thus cannot gainsay the Hobbesian legitimacy all three Asian developmental socialist regimes have garnered simply from providing a modicum of political stability, even before considering the importance of economic growth. In addition, these violent histories mean that these regimes face weakly organized opposition forces and little in the way of contentious signals that might prompt democratic reforms—with the massive exception of the 1989 protests in Tiananmen Square. They have generally lacked both the clearest (electoral) and most powerful (contentious) signals of the regimes' incipient decline. Yet this also means they should have substantial victory confidence if multiple parties were ever allowed to form from scratch and compete for elected office against these established and durable socialist ruling parties.

From Propensities to Politics

This chapter has made the argument that developmental Asia is an identifiable world region, one that can be usefully divided into distinct developmental clusters. This clustering helps greatly in explaining why some countries in developmental Asia have had a greater propensity to democratize through strength than others. But *propensities are not politics; they simply set the stage on which the dramatis personae of politics act.* In the following chapters, we show how authoritarian regimes with certain impressive strengths received signals that the authoritarian status quo could not last forever. This prompted them to contemplate and carry out new self-interested political experiments that in some cases went as far as full democratization.

The bulk of our attention in this book is paid to the paradigmatic cluster for democracy through strength: the developmental statist cluster of Japan (chapter 3), Taiwan (chapter 4), and South Korea (chapter 5). It is these cases, especially Taiwan, that lay out the logic and display the dynamics of democracy through strength as we have theorized in the opening two chapters. These cases are then juxtaposed with China and the CCP up to 1989 (chapter 6), where a lack of accumulated developmental strength, we contend, meant the CCP confronted a choice between crackdown and collapse in the face of protesters in Tiananmen Square and around the country. The regime, of course, chose to crack down.

We then offer two comparative chapters that extend the causal logic from our theory's best cases to its borderline cases. First, we examine a developmental cluster that has seen preemptive democratic experiences from positions of far less strength than the statist cluster—namely, the developmental militarist cluster of Indonesia, Thailand, and Myanmar (chapter 7). We then analyze a cluster that has not seen such experimentation despite similarly impressive strength to that of the statist cluster: the developmental Britannia cluster of Singapore, Malaysia, and Hong Kong (chapter 8). Since the fate of democracy in the developmental socialist cluster hinges so overwhelmingly on China, and considering the enormous implications of Chinese democratization for both the largest population on earth and the entire world, we devote chapter 9 primarily to the Chinese case, before turning our attentions in more cursory fashion to Vietnam and Cambodia.

It is at this stage in the book that, in essence, political science begins taking a backseat to political history. Although we believe that our theory of democracy through strength offers greater insight into developmental Asia's patterns of democratization and authoritarianism than any other existing theory, we do not mean to suggest that our theory can possibly do justice to this complicated range of historical cases.

Our primary goal in the chapters to follow is to get the histories of development and democratization in these twelve cases right, and thereby to bring them into wider conversations about why democracy arises around the world more generally. Even if the reader finds little value added in the conjunctural theory we propose to make sense of democracy and authoritarianism in developmental Asia, there is much to learn in the histories we do our best to curate. Our theories of democratization will remain badly impoverished if we fail to take such complicated histories fully into account.

Our analysis begins with the biggest case of democratization in world history that political scientists have simply never seen fit to theorize, treating it as an uninteresting example of democracy forcibly imposed from the outside by American occupation forces: Japan.

3

Japan

ASIA'S FIRST DEMOCRATIC
DEVELOPMENTAL STATE

JAPAN OFFICIALLY BROUGHT World War II to the Pacific in 1941, when Japanese warplanes attacked the American naval base at Pearl Harbor. The Allied powers quickly turned their attention to fighting the Pacific War, in addition to their ongoing campaigns in Europe. The atomic bombing of Hiroshima and Nagasaki in early August 1945 prompted the Japanese emperor's unconditional surrender on August 15. At the war's end, over two million Japanese soldiers had been killed. Including civilian deaths, upwards of three million Japanese perished during the war.

Within weeks after Japan was defeated, the victors—the Allies led by the United States—installed an occupation administration that would last from 1945 to 1952. Chief among America's objectives in its postwar mission was to "demilitarize and democratize" Japan. Historian John Dower describes America's ambitions as a "remarkable display of arrogant idealism—both self-righteous and genuinely visionary." The occupation, under the iron-fisted rule of General Douglas MacArthur, set out not just to reform Japanese political institutions but to thoroughly transform Japanese society and its politics.[1]

In many ways, the occupation sought to re-create war-torn Japan in America's own democratic image. The promulgation of Japan's democratic constitution was as much a reflection of the United States' triumphal hubris as it was a consequence of its formidable military and economic power in that postwar moment. Picture it: Japan's postwar constitution took effect in May 1947 at a ceremony in front of the Imperial Palace as a Japanese orchestra performed "The Stars and Stripes Forever." Against this backdrop, one might see Japan's democracy—which has endured with remarkable stability until the present day—as nothing more complicated or puzzling than a foreign creation forced on a weak Japan. Simply put, Japan's was a democracy imposed.

We take no issue with the standard image of Japan after 1945 as utterly vanquished. World War II decimated the country. Millions of Japanese soldiers and citizens were killed during the war. The atomic bombs dropped on Hiroshima and Nagasaki unleashed massive destruction to the nation and its institutions. The government was in disarray. The war destroyed Japan's once-thriving economy. Industrial productivity in the wake of the war went back to pre-1930 levels. Reeling from both devastation and shame, the country's psyche was fragile. One might reasonably conclude, therefore, that because Japan was weak and vulnerable, it had little choice but to accept and adopt an externally imposed democratic transition by a powerful America. The Japanese case appears to be the consummate case of *democracy through weakness,* and out of step with a book on democracy through strength.

Japan did not democratize itself, according to this common narrative; the United States democratized Japan. As Mary Alice Haddad critically summarizes this overly simplistic, conventional account, "Japan lost the war in 1945. The United States gave it a democratic constitution. Japan became a democracy."[2] Like Haddad, we reject this standard, simplistic, and wholly externalist account, in which Japanese politicians played a minimal and inconsequential role in bringing about a stable and lasting democracy in Japan. Japan's democratic transition has remained woefully undertheorized, understood simply as a story of democracy through imposition.

This is our argument: Japan's conservative civilian elites, who accumulated sources of political power or "antecedent strengths" during the decades before the war, were by no means wiped out in the wake of World War II. Many of the collaborators in the fascist regime were indeed convicted of war crimes and out of the picture. Yet many among the conservative elite, who were initial supporters of Japan's early democratic experiments during the 1920s, were not prosecuted. Those conservative elites who managed to "pass through," as historian Andrew Gordon puts it, ended up playing an important role in crafting and solidifying Japan's democratic transition with the occupation leaders.[3] Postwar democracy in Japan was therefore in large part the creation of Japanese conservative politicians, who, like the Kuomintang in Taiwan, the dictators in South Korea, and even the authoritarian Golkar party in Indonesia, eventually saw democracy to be a way to regain and maintain political power.

Japan's conservative political elites, we contend, were not nearly as weak and powerless in 1945 as most presume; as they managed to emerge from the rubble of the war, so too did their antecedent sources of political and economic strength. While Japan itself was horribly weakened in absolute terms, the relative strength of civilian conservatives was dramatically heightened by the abolition of Japan's military and the diminution of the Japanese emperor after the war. Conservative politicians also retained deep ties to the state bureaucracy that had guided Japan's remarkable industrial and economic development beginning in the nineteenth century. They remained connected with prewar industry leaders, who were poised to resurrect Japan's industrial development. Most critically, the political elite revived conservative parties, which they had founded decades before but which fell to fascism in the 1930s. By resurrecting parties and the party system, conservative politicians were prepared to govern in a new democracy.

In other words, over the course of America's occupation from 1945 to 1952, conservatives became increasingly confident that the introduction of democracy would not undermine their political and economic power bases. They recognized that democratic competition, in which the conservative parties enjoyed significant advantages over their competitors on the left, would in fact help consolidate their hold on power, albeit on a more level playing field. The strength of the state bureaucracy, which remained intact after the war, assured conservative politicians of the political and economic stability needed to revive Japan's prewar developmental trajectory. In the language of our theory, conservative politicians possessed both victory confidence and stability confidence, based on the endurance of their sources of prewar strength. Democracy was therefore not simply imposed on Japan, as conventional wisdom suggests. Rather, *Japan's conservative elites conceded and eventually embraced democracy because they were confident it served their interests to do so.*

We do not seek to rewrite history in this chapter, falsely asserting that the American occupation was not a critical precondition for democracy to take root in postwar Japan. The occupation was unequivocally necessary for Japan's democratic transformation; without it, democracy would not have been so swiftly installed. However, American intervention by itself was not sufficient to fully explain Japan's postwar transition and eventual democratic consolidation over the longer term, nor could it explain its remarkable stability after the 1950s.

Japan did not become Asia's longest-running stable democracy simply because America desired and delivered it. As our account in this chapter shows, the conservative elite in Japan could have reversed the postwar democratic experiment many times, and especially once the American occupation ended, but chose not to because democracy was beneficial to conservatives.

While democracy served America's geopolitical interests, we contend, it also served the political and economic interests of Japan's elites, and specifically the conservative elite held over from the prewar period. As we will see in the case of South Korea in the 1960s (chapter 5), conservative incumbents in the "developmental statist" cluster were perfectly capable of reversing democratic experiments when they were under extreme duress, regardless of their strong ties to Washington.

In this chapter, we assert that Japan's conservative elites strategically conceded democracy to preserve their political and economic power, and that their antecedent strengths inherited from decades of development gave them the necessary victory and stability confidence to start and eventually stay the democratic course. Japan's postwar experience moving from development to democracy, while not the exemplar of democracy through strength—that mantle goes to Taiwan (explored in chapter 4)—provided the playbook for autocratic regimes in developmental Asia to strategically choose and thrive in democracy. Japan provided a positive example of combining development with democracy, and later democratizers in the developmental statist cluster—namely, Taiwan and South Korea—emulated the Japanese experience.

Modernizing Japan

Japan today is an economic powerhouse. As the world's third-largest economy, it is surely a postwar twentieth-century developmental miracle, the leader among developmental Asia's economic dynamos. Yet Japan in fact began its drive to modernity in the middle of the nineteenth century. The story of modern Japan begins before all of the other cases explored in this book. Its origins lie in the 1860s with the Meiji Restoration.

Japan first confronted the West and its superior technology in 1853, when the United States sent a fleet of warships into Edo Bay. This forced Japan, previously isolated from the world economy, to open its ports. The "black ships," as they were known to the Japanese, were a fearsome show of foreign modernity and military might. Japan's backwardness in the face of foreign power led to Japanese concessions and commercial treaties. American power pried open Japanese ports to international trade, which sparked Japan's efforts to rapidly modernize and catch up to the West.

Japan's confrontation with the West prompted internal reforms to modernize Japanese politics and society, as well as its economy. The Meiji Restoration was a "revolution from above," an elite-led revolutionary transformation rather than a popular uprising from below.[4] Beginning in 1868, Japanese rulers abandoned their feudal political system, dismantling the daimyo (feudal lords) class system and its shogunate (feudal warriors) protectorate.

In response to the black ships, Japan's military modernized as well. The Meiji regime created a national army, developed its naval capabilities, and introduced conscription. The conception of a Japanese "nation" took root during the Meiji Restoration, with the introduction of a standardized linguistic dialect and a national education system. In terms of political development, the imperial court promulgated the Meiji constitution in 1889, which led to the creation of a national legislative body, the Imperial Diet, in 1890.

The formation of a modern bureaucratic state apparatus accompanied the consolidation of administrative power in the Meiji regime. Previously, the daimyo lords managed matters of state as part of a feudal coterie of elites. Public administration before the Meiji Restoration served the interests of the landed gentry and preserved a balance among feudal warlords. The emergence of a modern state and strong bureaucracy, however, required a professional, technocratic, and, importantly, nationwide civil service.

In 1887, Meiji reformers introduced Japan's first national civil service exam. Meritocratic recruitment ensured state bureaucrats were selected from among the best and brightest, skilled with technocratic expertise. Meiji Japan's meritocratic bureaucracy was a key feature of the Asian developmental state model emulated in the postwar period by the other late developers in the developmental statist cluster, Taiwan and South Korea.[5]

Japan's modern bureaucracy focused on catch-up economic development and industrialization. Its confrontation with the West confirmed how far behind Japan's economy was in relation to other industrializing powers. Drawing on the technocratic expertise of those recruited into the developmental state, the Meiji regime fixed the government's fiscal system, and specifically its capacity to extract taxes and allocate public resources for national economic development.

With the ability to tax and spend, the Meiji state invested in hard infrastructure such as railroads, shipyards, and ports. Between the 1880s and 1900, for instance, the national rail line grew nearly three and a half times in length, accelerating Japan's ability to develop a nationally integrated and commerce-based economy. The government invested in soft infrastructure as well, notably with the introduction of public education and modern health care.

Government investments paid off. Overall, manufacturing production in Japan grew two and a half times between 1895 and 1915, outpacing growth in the

United States. The state did not invest indiscriminately into any and all industrial sectors, however. The developmental state employed a strategy of picking winners. It invested public resources into sectors identified by the bureaucracy to be of strategic importance to the Japanese economy, such as steel and shipbuilding in heavy industrial sectors, as well as in labor-intensive manufacturing industries. Production in mining, a strategic industry in Japan, grew sevenfold in the last quarter of the nineteenth century. Government and private-sector investment into textile mills increased silk production, which was critical to Japan's burgeoning export economy.

The developmental state also had a hand in nurturing and organizing industrial firms. The bureaucracy oversaw and actively encouraged investment in zaibatsu firms, Japan's massive industrial conglomerate companies. Large firms, rather than small enterprises, dominated Japan's industrial landscape. Zaibatsu firms such as Mitsubishi and Mitsui leveraged the economies of scale and integrated national supply chains to gain economic dominance domestically and a foothold into international trade. Japanese firms quickly climbed the technological ladder, catching up with the West and integrating into the global economy. In a relatively short time, Japan became a globally competitive industrial manufacturer.[6]

By the turn of the century, Japan was a modern industrial nation: self-sufficient, globally integrated, and militarily secure. It was a "rich nation" with a "strong army." Modern Japan caught up to the West and began to flex its muscle in the region. Japan defeated China in a war over control of the Korean peninsula in 1895. The resulting treaty ceded Taiwan to Japan, which it ruled as a colonial regime until the end of World War II. In 1910 Japan annexed Korea, and set the stage for Japan's imperialist and expansionist agenda in the 1930s.

Experimenting with Democracy

Modernization theory tells us that social, economic, and political modernization begets its own discontents and creates a more demanding society. Expectations for popular political participation soon emerged in modernizing Japan. Imperial "subjects" of the Meiji regime increasingly saw themselves as modern "citizens." Popular protest and mobilization for political reform, such as the Rights and Political Participation Movement, arose during the end of the nineteenth century and crystallized a political culture of dissent in Meiji Japan.

Japanese citizens began to challenge the absolutist power of the monarchy and the imperial court. They demanded greater voice and participation in how they were governed during the early 1900s. Political discontent spread across the nation. As Japan modernized, industrial workers organized and mobilized in the streets and on the shop floor. Worker riots, strikes, and popular protests became increasingly common. Citizens sought the more assertive legislative body that had been promised, but was unfulfilled, in the Meiji constitution. They demanded the government expand the right to vote, which it did gradually throughout the 1910s and 1920s, culminating in the Universal Suffrage Act of 1925. Simply put, as Japanese society and its economy modernized, citizens demanded and received more political democracy.

The Meiji regime, which was in many ways quite politically progressive, responded to popular demands for reform beginning at the turn of the century. During the 1910s, Japan started to open up its political system, experimenting with democratic forms of power sharing and institutions for more citizen-based participatory governance. Social relief and antipoverty policies were developed as well. This period of initial reform, spanning the 1910s through the 1930s, was known as the era of Taisho democracy, named after Emperor Taisho, who was at the helm of the imperial court at the time.

The main feature of Japan's early democratic experiment was the emergence of parties in the political arena. An influential newspaper, the *Osaka Asahi Shimbun*, ran an editorial in 1924 that stated, "Political parties should design national policies for citizens as a whole and ask citizens whether their policies are right or wrong." From early on, political parties in Japan were not only an institutional mechanism to organize and mobilize political power; they were viewed as legitimate political actors because they reflected and represented citizens' will and preferences. The editorial continued, "If its [party's] principles no longer agree with the will of the citizens, it should transfer the government to an opposition party."[7] The notion that political power ought to be shared and potentially transferred among contending parties reflected an understanding of democratic alternations in government as well as a commitment to electoral competition that was far more than cursory. Japanese citizens expected political parties to compete for power.

Basic democratic principles took root in prewar Japan. With the exception of the two years from 1922 to 1924, political parties formed all of the government cabinets between 1918 and 1932 during the era of Taisho democracy, Japan's first democratic experiment. The inaugural party-led cabinet was formed in 1918 by Prime Minister Hara Takeshi, who was the first leader selected from the elected legislature. Until the early 1930s, a popularly elected, party-led (as opposed to military- or authoritarian-led) cabinet was the most common form of government during this period of imperial democracy.

Taisho democracy was not, however, tantamount to the full democratization of Japan. After all, imperial democracy was a reversible experiment, foreshadowing other reversible experiments that emerged across developmental Asia—beginning with Japan itself—during the postwar period. The Meiji constitution reflected a mix of authoritarian rule with some characteristics of democratic participation and political power sharing. For example, the constitution empowered the emperor to be the ultimate political authority in imperial Japan, though it also allowed the functioning of participatory political institutions such as the National Diet, the elected legislature. Taisho democracy relied on a razor's-edge balance between authoritarian Meiji traditions and an incipient democratic trajectory.[8]

Still, there is no denying that Japan's early democratic experiment—referred to as "imperial democracy"—was built on a foundation of political power sharing between elected and nonelected actors. In the language of our chapter on developmental militarism, it was a kind of "cohabitation." Though citizens elected members of the legislature, the Diet's legislative powers were constrained by other nonelected actors in the complex political system. For example, the House of Peers, the upper house of the legislature, functioned as a check on the cabinet. The Privy Council, appointed directly by the emperor, had the power to veto legislation. To ensure the imperial court maintained a direct hand in governing Japan, the emperor appointed the Genro, a small corps of political elites loyal to the monarch who advised him on policy matters. The Genro had the power to appoint the prime minister, ensuring the imperial court had a say in who led the government. The modern military played a significant role in maintaining order and supporting the imperial regime when it came to quelling threats of popular uprising.

Thus, the concept of imperial democracy embodied a tension between a powerful and adored monarchy and a popularly elected civilian government. Many historians conclude that Taisho-era democracy was at best a shallow and deeply flawed democracy destined to collapse. The concepts "imperial" and "democracy" were contradictory, they point out, and difficult to reconcile in practice. "Imperial" implies the supremacy of the monarchy, which violates the liberal precondition of "government by the people" intrinsic to democracy.

Andrew Gordon, acknowledging these contradictions, nonetheless points out how so-called imperial democrats during this period were "pro-emperor,

pro-empire" and yet at the same time "committed to elusive notions of government and popular involvement in politics." Imperial democracy during the
Taisho era, according to Gordon, resolved its contradictions and endured for
a spell because the goals of the emperor, the military, the bureaucracy, and
democratic political parties "were logically related." In other words, these political actors coexisted—and indeed shared power—in Taisho-era Japan
because they were aligned and bound by a national aspiration to rapidly modernize Japan.[9]

This alignment did not last, however. After nearly a decade and a half of
party-led governments in Taisho-era Japan, the democratic experiment collapsed, replaced with a fascist military regime beyond 1932. Various economic
crises, accentuated by the devastating global depression after 1929, exposed
party-led governments for their inability to manage the economic turbulence.
Political blame had to be laid somewhere: political parties, and party-led governments specifically, bore the brunt.[10]

As early as 1927, the Japanese banking sector, saddled with massive quanti-
ties of nonperforming industrial loans, threatened an insolvency crisis, which
led to widespread panic. Japanese citizens criticized the party-led government
for its handling of the banking crisis, requiring the Privy Council to issue
emergency decrees to stem a financial meltdown. A few years later, when the
Great Depression spread in 1929, Japan's economy ground to a halt, as did
many other economies around the world. Again defying the wishes of the
government, the banks took advantage of the Depression by speculating on
the yen, profiting during the early 1930s while ordinary Japanese people suffered. Japan experienced an economic crisis as well as a governance crisis.

While speculative profiteers got rich during the Depression, wages declined
and union activity and political instability grew throughout Japan. The number
of labor disputes exploded from 282 in 1920 to 906 in 1930. Few were spared during the Depression. Commodity prices plummeted, which had a crippling effect
on Japan's agricultural sector. The average farming household income halved
almost overnight, from an average of 1,366 yen in 1929 to just 641 yen in 1931. The
number of tenant-landlord disputes increased more than sixfold during this
time, from 408 in 1920 to 2,478 in 1930, and increased again to over 6,800 in 1935.

Widespread political, economic, and social instability during the 1920s and
into the 1930s discredited the party system and party-led governments. Parties
were viewed as incapable of leading the country. What we call "stability confidence" was tumbling by the wayside. Meanwhile, chauvinistic nationalism
spread throughout Japan, a vision propagated among politicians across the

ideological spectrum, by right-wing fascists as well as left-leaning labor organizations that had abandoned class struggle in favor of nationalist populism. Amid the political economic crisis of the late 1920s and 1930s, the emperor lost confidence in the ability of political parties to govern Japan, exploding the contradictions of Japan's fledgling imperial democracy.[11]

The delegitimation of party-led government opened a window of opportunity for the military to wrest political power away from elected politicians and their parties. Democratic breakdown loomed on the horizon. The reversible democratic experiment was about to be reversed.

During the early 1930s, the military openly defied the civilian government. In 1931, for instance, the army invaded China and established a puppet regime in Manchuria, despite concerns within the party cabinet about Japan's growing expansionist ambitions. The infamous 1937 "rape of Nanking" was a particularly brutal episode. Hundreds of thousands of Chinese were slaughtered, including tens of thousands of women and girls raped and killed, as Japanese forces occupied the Chinese port city. At home, the government, increasingly penetrated by fascist and antidemocratic politicians who had cast their lot with the military, rounded up opposition activists. Hammering the final nail in Taisho democracy's coffin, right-wing factions of the Japanese military assassinated Prime Minister Inukai Tsuyoshi in 1932. He was Japan's last civilian head of government until the end of the war nearly a decade and a half later.[12]

Before closing the book on Japan's first attempt at what was a spectacularly failed democracy, however, it is important to acknowledge the lasting legacies of Taisho-era democracy and the Meiji modernization project, and their impact on Japan's postwar democratic transformation.

First, the Meiji constitution ensured that political power sharing was a key feature of Japan's modern political system, even if its practice ultimately succumbed to fascist militarism. It was also clear that so long as the military enjoyed overwhelming power, the political playing field could never be level, and thus the vision of Taisho-era imperial democracy was fundamentally flawed unless it could be more deeply reformed.

Second, the Meiji Restoration destroyed the vestiges of feudalism in imperial Japan. From this emerged a corps of political and economic elites who would eventually become Japan's champions for development and democracy after 1945.

Third, modernization efforts during the Meiji reform period created a modern national bureaucracy that managed to remain intact during the postwar transition. Bureaucratic continuity was a source of confidence that democratizing the postwar political system would not automatically lead to instability. Rather, state-led economic recovery could stabilize Japan, and the bureaucracy, if intact, was critical to this recovery.

Fourth, Japan's early democratic experiment introduced parties as a viable, if at the time weakened, political organization to mobilize citizens and generate popular legitimacy for the government. These legacies, which may have seemed inconsequential in the face of fascism, set the stage for Japan's eventual—and stunningly successful—democratic transformation.

Crafting Postwar Democracy

Emperor Hirohito offered Japan's surrender on August 15, 1945, days after America's atomic bombs leveled Hiroshima and Nagasaki. The devastation and destruction of the atomic bombs were too much to bear, and Japan's surrender was formally signed on September 2. Literally within days, the US-led occupation assumed administrative power, with the explicit aim of demilitarizing and democratizing Japan.

The Potsdam Declaration, the blueprint for Japan's surrender and postwar reconstruction, stipulated unequivocally that "freedom of speech, of religion, and of thought, as well as respect for fundamental human rights, shall be established." Section 10 of the declaration made clear that "the Japanese government shall remove all obstacles to the revival and strengthening of democratic tendencies among the Japanese people."

It was noteworthy that occupation leaders did not view democracy as an entirely new or foreign concept in Japan. Instead, they acknowledged the seeds of democratic experimentation that had been planted decades before and the positive legacies of Taisho democracy for postwar Japan. The occupation's goal was thus to revive and ultimately consolidate democracy in Japan, rather than inventing it anew.

General Douglas MacArthur headed up the US-led occupation. In his role as the Supreme Commander for the Allied Powers (SCAP), he immediately launched a democratic reform agenda. In charge of the occupation, MacArthur wielded tremendous political power and authority in Japan. He once quipped he was Japan's new political sovereign, even more powerful than the monarchy and the legislature. Japanese citizens referred to MacArthur as the shogun with blue eyes.

Importantly, the occupation administration did not rule directly over Japan. Instead, it governed "indirectly," choosing to cooperate with Japanese leaders to carry out reform. From a political standpoint, it was sensitive about appearing too heavy-handed in its approach to reforming Japan's political system. It did not want to be seen as imposing democracy through force or coercion. The occupation, for instance, deliberately framed the SCAP's democratic reform agenda as "the [Japanese] government's own recommendation" in order to cultivate domestic legitimacy.[13] As Japanese political scientist Sodei Rinjero contends, the success of the occupation's reform efforts was due in part to the "indigenous cooperation" the GHQ (General Headquarters) sought and received from Japanese politicians.[14]

The strategy of indirect rule, however, was not only motivated by politics. From a practical and administrative point of view, the occupation *needed* Japanese politicians to lead democratic reform. In the weeks after its surrender, the occupation looked to immediately appoint a prime minister to form an interim government that could faithfully implement democratic reform. Initially the SCAP selected a member of the imperial family to take on that role. MacArthur quickly dropped that plan as the first candidate proved uncooperative.

The occupation leadership required reliable and capable Japanese partners if it were to craft a new democracy. MacArthur turned to veteran politician and diplomat Kijuro Shidehara to cooperate with and carry out the occupation's reform plan. Before the war, Shidehara was foreign minister, a moderate conservative who championed party-led imperial democracy and who opposed Japan's expansionist policies of the 1930s. Sidelined by the wartime fascist regime, he continued to be a member of the upper House of Peers, but no longer part of the Japanese legislature or cabinet. Though he planned to retire from politics after the war, Shidehara was appointed interim prime minister by MacArthur in October 1945, and he immediately formed an interim cabinet. In late 1945, the conservative Shidehara government reformed the suffrage laws, expanding the right to vote to women and lowering the voting age, a harbinger of democratic reforms to come.

As in other cases of democracy through strength that we explore in this book, continuity in political leadership was a key feature of Japan's democratic transition. Though Japan was defeated in the war and subsequently occupied by a foreign power, the war did not wipe out Japan's political leadership class. As we noted earlier in this chapter, a critical legacy of Taisho-era democracy was the creation and endurance of a corps of conservative politicians who had been champions of imperial democracy.

These politicians were products of the Meiji Restoration. They held conservative and traditional views about the role of the monarchy, to be sure, but were nonetheless proponents of party-led, popularly elected government. Marginalized during the fascist regime of the 1930s, these politicians—such as interim prime minister Shidehara—managed to pass through the postwar transition. They not only survived the war; they remained politically relevant to Japanese citizens, an important vestige of Japan's early democratic experiments. With the military crippled and the monarchy constrained, these politicians had seen their relative strength in the Japanese system of rule substantially expanded.

Conservative politicians became important partners of the occupation in reforming Japan's political system. In this respect, the occupation empowered them to lead democratic reform in Japan. They cooperated with the occupation leaders, certainly, but these conservative politicians also helped to shape the course of democratic reform. They were not passive but instead active agents of political change in Japan.

How the democratic constitution came about is illustrative of this two-sided process. The acceptance of Japan's democratic constitution in the spring of 1946 and its enactment in 1947 was the centerpiece of the occupation's efforts to democratize Japan. The constitution created and strengthened democratic institutions, including the extension of rights and freedoms to all citizens. The National Diet was empowered as the primary institution for public policy making. The political playing field became more level. The role of the emperor was downgraded to a symbolic one. Most importantly, the military was severely constrained, limited in its size and its ability to procure arms. The democratic constitution was referred to as the "peace" constitution, to reflect the extent to which the military had been defanged.

The conventional wisdom is that because MacArthur's advisers drafted the constitution, the constitution-making process involved little to no input from the Japanese. It was as though, as Mary Alice Haddad puts it, the American-led occupation simply "gave" and imposed on Japan a democratic constitution. It is true that a small group of American experts appointed by the SCAP drafted the constitution ultimately accepted and enacted by Japan. It is also true the occupation's negotiators threatened to take the draft constitution to the public to put pressure on the interim Japanese government to accept the American version.

It is not true, however, that the Japanese side, and specifically the conservative politicians who had been anointed by the occupation to help lead democratic reform, had no voice or agency in the process. Beneath the conventional account of democracy through imposition was a deeper story of contestation, negotiation, and concession on both sides: the occupation, on the one hand, and Japan's conservative political leaders, including members of Shidehara's cabinet, on the other.[15]

Soon after the occupation began, the SCAP invited the Japanese government to draft a new constitution for Japan. Conservatives being conservatives, the interim Japanese government proposed a constitution that retained many of the authoritarian elements of the Meiji regime, notably a prominent political role for the emperor. Simply put, they sought to resuscitate imperial democracy, albeit without the overseas empire.

Japan's conservative political leaders were not about to succumb to the American vision of democracy without a fight. They believed, naively it turns out, the occupation might accept their constitutional draft, or at least consider it in negotiations. It was then that MacArthur, incredulous that the Japanese interim government had the audacity to propose such a constitution, appointed a small group within the GHQ to draft a new version. In other words, it was not until after Japan had had a crack at making its own constitution that the US-led occupation embarked on drafting a revised version.

The initial constitutional draft from the Japanese interim government made clear that the government was not going to accept a "foreign" constitution without first having a say in how Japan could be governed. Indeed, MacArthur, to his credit, did not ignore Japanese political realities. He recognized the importance of the emperor and the monarchy as a unifying force in Japan. The emperor could not be eliminated entirely, as distasteful as the concept of a monarchy was to the Americans and MacArthur himself. Democracy's prospects, MacArthur was forced to concede, rested in part on the emperor's role in forging national cohesion and stability in the wake of the war, as well as in legitimating a new constitution. MacArthur reluctantly admitted that a constitution acceptable to the Japanese needed to preserve the monarchy.

Thus, when US general Courtney Whitney visited senior Japanese leaders in February 1946 to discuss the constitution, he presented a draft that retained a symbolic role for the emperor and the monarchy, a strategic concession to Japan's conservative interim government. Despite MacArthur's concessions, the Japanese reaction was predictably hostile. The Japanese delegation, headed by foreign minister (and future prime minister) Shigeru Yoshida, argued the constitution was doomed to fail in Japan and "simply unacceptable." Prominent Japanese legal scholar Matsumoto Joji warned in the most dire of terms that "tyranny and misrule result when constitutions do not accord with national circumstances."[16] Many in the government and its conservative allies saw the constitution to be an affront and an attempt by the occupation to strong-arm Japan.

Several prominent voices within the conservative elite, however, engaged the constitution-making process with a strategic, and ultimately self-interested approach. These politicians reasoned that conceding the constitution would generate a political payoff for the incumbent conservative government. For instance, Ashida Hitoshi, a senior government leader, argued that opposing or rejecting the constitution could lead to conservative defeats in coming elections. He further argued that by conceding the constitutional draft presented by Whitney, conservative politicians, many of whom were incumbent seat holders in the legislature, could expect to do well in future elections, and specifically in the April 1946 Diet contest. Conservative politicians could win electoral support from prodemocracy voters. In other words, conceding the constitution increased the conservatives' confidence it could win a substantial base of popular support. Rejecting it, on the other hand, would create problems for incumbent politicians seeking to retain their seats in the Diet.

Others in the conservative camp took a more long-term but similarly strategic view. Some believed the interim government had little choice but to accept the occupation's constitutional draft at the time. The political pressures to do so, as noted previously, were simply too great to ignore. These same politicians also believed, however, that "at a later date, it would be possible to undo much of what had been done." Conceding the constitution did not preclude the government from amending it later, after the occupation had ended. Future prime minister Yoshida, who was present during the 1946 meeting with Whitney, admitted, "There was this idea at the back of my mind that whatever needed to be revised after we regained our independence could be revised then."[17] Conceding the constitution gave the interim government not only a potential boost at the polls in the coming Diet election but also the opportunity to eventually revise the constitution, and without American interference. Like other, later instances of democracy through strength in developmental Asia, Japan's initial democratic concessions were a reversible experiment.

Ultimately, the Japanese government conceded the democratic constitution out of a strategic logic of political self-preservation. American pressure certainly mattered, though Japanese conservative politicians also saw that by accepting the constitution, they stood the best chance of retaining their hold on power through democratic means: by winning votes. Politicians in the interim government may have conceded democracy, but they were not conceding defeat or political obsolescence. *Instead, they conceded democracy to win.* Conservative politicians revived the party system that had been in place during the 1910s and 1920s to mobilize the conservatives' electoral base. Prime Minister Shidehara's reform of the suffrage laws in late 1945 was similarly motivated by his belief that voters remained supportive of conservative politicians. Expanding the vote "would help the continuation of conservative forces," not defeat or even hamstring the incumbent government.[18]

The incumbents' concede-to-win strategy paid off quickly. In April 1946 Japan held its first postwar general election for the National Diet. The Liberal Party and the Progressive Party, Japan's two largest conservative political parties, mobilized their base and won a combined 258 of 464 seats, or 56 percent of the legislature. The two conservative parties evolved from their conservative predecessors, recruiting veterans and politicians from Taisho-era political parties to run in the 1946 election. The third-largest party in the Diet after the election, the Socialists, won just 96 legislative seats. The voter turnout rate for the 1946 contest was over 70 percent, further evidence of the conservatives' broad base of popular support.

Contrary to the conventional wisdom, conservative political forces in the immediate postwar period were not weak, and not at all a spent and irrelevant political force. The process by which the constitution came to pass in postwar Japan illustrates the extent to which the Japanese political elite—and specifically, the corps of conservative politicians who managed to pass through the postwar transition—exercised a good deal of strategic agency in crafting the constitutional terms of Japan's postwar democratic experiment. They conceded democracy to ensure their continued incumbency. The interim government and its conservative allies bet big on their inherited strengths—and in 1946, in Japan's first postwar election, they won.

Conceding with Confidence

Electoral uncertainty is a hallmark of democracy, as the democratic theorist Adam Przeworski reminds us.[19] Free and fair democratic contestation means that political outcomes can never be preordained or, worse yet, manipulated and fixed by corrupt, coercive political forces. Electoral uncertainty does not mean, however, that political actors cannot be confident that by conceding democracy they may in fact grow their political support and become more, not less, politically powerful. After all, democracy is not entirely uncertain, Przeworski argues, but rather a form of *"institutionalized* uncertainty" in which popular ruling parties can be confident that elections will be repeated and respected, and can redound to their recurring benefit.

In Japan, conceding from strength meant conceding with confidence that the introduction of democracy would serve incumbent political interests. Conservative politicians with their roots in the earlier era of Taisho democracy had many reasons to be confident not only that the postwar democratic constitution would contribute to a stable transition but also that the incumbent conservatives would maintain and potentially even grow their political power.

Despite their association with a failed democratic experiment in the prewar period, the conservative politicians who championed imperial democracy were able to demonstrate to voters that they had successfully delivered democracy in postwar Japan. This was due in part to the fact that conservative politicians were integrally involved in constitutional negotiations and could point to the new constitution as evidence of their commitment to democracy. Furthermore, the credibility of their claim to have delivered democracy was due to the occupation's inclusion of conservative politicians in the reform process, positioning them as partners, rather than adversaries or nondemocratic standpatters, in bringing about democratic reform.

Delivering democracy earned conservative politicians and the incumbent government democratic legitimacy and credibility. As we will see in subsequent chapters, the ability of an incumbent regime to portray itself as the party of reform and to take credit for democratic transformation generates important sources of political and electoral support. It has proved a winning political tactic, and not only in Japan. In Taiwan and South Korea, for example, initiating democratic transition and delivering democracy allowed the incumbent authoritarian ruling parties, to some degree, to neutralize the regime cleavage and siphon electoral support away from the prodemocratic opposition.

Democratic reformers in Japan not only revived the party system; they were confident the first-past-the-post electoral system, also inherited from the Taisho era, benefited the incumbent conservative parties. During the run-up to the 1946 general election, the smaller Socialist Party and Communist Party pushed to redesign the electoral rules of the game and implement a proportional representation (PR) electoral system. Such systems give advantages to smaller and more ideologically driven political parties. The Socialists' and Communists' preference for a PR system therefore was not surprising, as it ensured a greater voice for Japan's leftist parties in the legislature.

The conservatives, also not surprisingly, resisted this change. They sought to preserve the existing first-past-the-post system, which featured large electoral districts where voters selected from among various party candidates. In that system, the candidate with the most votes, a plurality and not necessarily a majority of support, won the district seat. Moreover, while the larger conservative parties were able to field a competitive slate of electoral candidates that spanned the entire country, smaller parties, such as the Socialist and Communist Parties, could not, as they tended to be more popular in the cities. The existing system thus gave the national conservative parties a sizable seat bonus in rural districts, where they had made significant inroads during the 1920s, and where the urban-based leftist parties had little support, putting them at a further disadvantage. Simply put, maintaining the electoral system, rather than reforming it, gave large national parties a significant advantage over the opposition.[20]

Though democratization entails free and *fairer* elections, the specific rules of the game almost invariably create advantages for some political parties over others. As we will see in the chapters on Taiwan and South Korea, the specific electoral system at the time of democratic transition figured critically in how democracy unfolded there as well. In both cases, the electoral rules of the game provided advantages for the incumbent regimes. A party that is more confident that democratic transition will not spell their electoral demise but instead improve their electoral fortunes is a party more likely to pursue a democratic option.

The conservative preference for the district-based, first-past-the-post system prevailed in Japan. As expected, the two conservative parties, the Liberal Party and the Progressive Party, delivered a strong showing in the 1946 general election, Japan's first postwar contest. The Liberal Party won a plurality of seats, making it the largest party in the Diet. The two conservative parties combined to win 45.7 percent of the popular vote with nationwide support from the cities and countryside alike. Because of the electoral rules and district apportionment, however, the conservative parties' 45.7 percent vote share translated into control of 56 percent of Diet seats, representing a 10 percent seat bonus. The opposition Socialist Party, meanwhile, gained a seat bonus of just 2 percent, reflecting the party's overrepresentation in urban areas and its lack of support in rural districts. The Communist Party won less than 4 percent of the vote, confirming conservative confidence.

Democratic transformation did not undermine or weaken the strong and capable bureaucracy that was at the core of Japan's prewar developmental state.[21] Despite the occupation's goal of transforming Japanese politics, remarkably, it left the bureaucracy untouched. The Americans were interested in stability, so they did not wish to dismantle the developmental state bureaucracy. The occupation instead viewed the bureaucracy through a Weberian lens, as a nonpolitical actor. A strong and capable state bureaucracy, in the minds of occupation leaders, was not a threat to democracy. Quite the opposite, in fact, the SCAP believed a strong and capable bureaucracy was necessary for implementing political reform and for reviving Japan's economy. The developmental state apparatus, first developed in Japan after the Meiji Restoration in the mid-nineteenth century, was instrumental for ensuring a stable transition in the mid-twentieth century.

As we argued earlier in this chapter, the prewar developmental state bureaucracy was critical for Japan's economic development, and Japan's swift postwar economic recovery was important for generating political support for the conservative government and for overall stability. Bureaucratic continuity also enabled the conservative parties to highlight their record of prewar development, or what Anna Grzymala-Busse calls a regime's "usable past."[22] In this respect, bureaucratic continuity and the endurance of a capable developmental state benefited the incumbent conservatives, bolstering their confidence that democratization would not threaten, and likely would even strengthen, the conservative grip on political power.

In contrast to postwar bureaucratic continuity, the military that destroyed Japan's early democratic experiment in the 1930s was sidelined after 1945. Section 6 of the Potsdam Declaration stated that "the authority and influence of those who have deceived and misled the people of Japan into embarking on world conquest" would be "eliminated for all time." Immediately after Japan's surrender, the SCAP disbanded various branches of the armed forces. Notably, the occupation eliminated the special police force, the internal security apparatus employed by the wartime fascist regime to repress its citizens. During the Tokyo Trials of 1946, thousands of military officers were tried and punished for their involvement in the war and Japan's imperialist expansion. The democratic constitution deliberately constrained Japan's ability to rearm its military.

The impact of the American occupation in removing Japanese democracy's greatest enemy, in its thoroughness and swiftness, cannot be overstated. Without American intervention, the introduction of democracy would not have been possible. The coercive power of the American-led occupation ensured the dismantling of the military and put what remained of the military firmly under civilian control. This, combined with the constitutional restraints imposed on the monarchy, resolved the contradictions of Taisho-era imperial democracy and ameliorated the fragile balance among the emperor, the military, and popularly elected political parties.

The removal of the military created the political space for the revitalization of parties and their role as the key organizational and institutional pillar of democracy. Before the political playing field could be leveled between incumbent parties and opposition parties, as democracy always requires by definition, democratization in Japan required a leveled playing field between elected politicians and unelected powerholders. The civilian-military "cohabitation" of prewar imperial democracy was not to be repeated in postwar Japan.

In sum, conservative politicians and their allies conceded democracy from a position of relative strength, not weakness, which gave them the confidence that the introduction of democracy would not spell their political demise or lead to instability. Democracy would instead strengthen the conservative hold on power, revive the developmental state, and launch Japan's economic recovery. The 1946 election outcome validated the conservative parties' victory confidence and stability confidence.

Staying in the Democratic Game

Soon after, Japan held another general election for the Diet, which dealt a surprising blow to the incumbent conservative coalition. The 1947 election ended up being a close three-way race, with the Liberal Party, the newly formed Democratic Party (the successor of the conservative Progressive Party), and the Socialist Party each winning just over 26 percent of the popular vote. The Socialist Party increased its vote share by 8 percent and grew its number of Diet seats from 96 to 144, a 48-seat swing. The Socialists ended up being the largest party in the Diet, with 31 percent of legislative seats. The Liberal and Democratic Parties each accounted for 28 percent of the legislature.

The 1947 general election marked a critical juncture in Japan's postwar transition to democracy. Though the two conservative parties together continued to comprise a majority of popular support in terms of electoral votes (53 percent) and Diet seats (56 percent), neither the Liberal Party nor the Democratic Party was the dominant party in the Diet in that neither controlled a plurality of seats, unlike after the 1946 election. Instead, a nonconservative party, the Socialist Party, controlled a plurality of Diet seats, allowing them to form a left-leaning coalition government. For one of the very few times in the electoral history of developmental Asia, the Left was more unified than the Right, at least for a brief moment.

Political infighting between the two conservative parties did not bode well for the conservative coalition to oppose a Socialist-led government. Many feared that conservative politicians might even defect from the democratic game, as some did when the going got tough for the conservative governments of the 1930s. Many also worried that the 1947 Diet elections, without a clear winner and with a Socialist Party plurality, might lead to political instability. Japan's democratic experiment was already on shaky ground.

In the end, conservative politicians remained loyal to democracy. Why? For one, the Socialist-led coalition was fragile and ultimately short-lived. The Socialists could not form a stable partnership with any of the other major political parties. After some delay, the Socialist Party was able to lure the progressive faction of the Democratic Party to join forces in a coalition. By then, however, it was too late. The coalition was doomed from the get-go. Rather than a show of decisive leadership by the Socialist Party, its patchwork coalition instead highlighted the enduring relevance of the conservative parties and the political power they continued to wield. Similar to Golkar in Indonesia (explored in detail in chapter 7), Japan's conservative parties, though no longer the singularly dominant parties in the Diet, were nonetheless "kingmakers" in determining the fate of the Socialist-led government.

Unable to govern, the government collapsed in the fall of 1948, only a few months after it was formed. Liberal Party leader Shigeru Yoshida was appointed interim prime minister, and he called a snap election for the Diet in January 1949. By staying in the democratic game, even after their electoral setback in 1947, the conservatives were able to instigate an election and the opportunity for conservative politicians to regain their political leadership through democratic means. Staying loyal to the democratic game, despite an early setback at the hands of the Socialist Party, worked out well for Japan's two main conservative parties. As we have argued, democracy served conservative political interests.

Importantly, conservative dominance also served the Allied occupation's interests. For geopolitical as well as ideological reasons, the US government preferred the conservatives to be in power in a democratic Japan, rather than the left-leaning Socialists or Communists. The emerging communist threat in the region prompted what the Japanese call the 1947 "reverse-course" policy in Washington. With the coming Cold War, the United States needed Japan's government to be robust and resilient, and for Japan to be a reliable ally and backstop to communist expansion in the region.[23]

The "Japan Crowd," an informal lobby group in Washington, began to push for a scaled-back, moderate, and ultimately less ambitious democratic reform plan in Japan. The pro-Japan lobbyists prioritized political and economic stability, and worried that the occupation's ambitious reform agenda might cause instability and leave Japan vulnerable to communist infiltration. The growing concern for communist containment in the region meant the US government and the occupation leadership in Japan placed less emphasis on the speed and scope of democratic political reform and prioritized political stability and economic recovery instead.

With a change in American policy back home, the occupation leadership encouraged the reconstruction of a national police force in Japan, remarkable given that it had disbanded the force only a few years earlier. Moreover, the Japanese government began to curtail workers' rights that were protected under the constitution, and with little opposition from the occupation leadership. In line with American Cold War policy, for instance, the SCAP refrained from interfering when the government began to crack down on the Communist Party and its supporters. Defeating the Socialist Party in Diet elections became a more explicit priority of the Americans after 1947.

The emerging Cold War context, the United States' geopolitical strategy in the region, and the so-called reverse-course policy politically strengthened the conservatives in Japan, contributing to a conservative resurgence soon after the Socialist coalition collapsed in 1948. As Jennifer Miller puts it, the "Americans relied on—and in turn helped empower—decisively right-wing and conservative parties, which quickly recognized a growing convergence with American visions."[24] There could not be a clearer and more reassuring signal that staying the democratic course endorsed by the Americans was the best option for the conservative parties.[25]

In the 1949 general elections, the Democratic Liberal Party (DLP), the new amalgam of the conservative Liberal Party and factions from the conservative Democratic Party, dominated the contest. The DLP won 44 percent of the popular vote and 58 percent of Diet seats, a 14 percent seat bonus and the largest margin of victory for any political party in the postwar period. The elections also marked the first time in the postwar period that a single political party controlled an outright majority (and not merely a plurality) of seats in the legislature. The Socialist Party suffered a massive defeat, winning just 13.5 percent of the popular vote and only forty-eight Diet seats (or 10 percent), a loss of ninety-six seats from 1947.

The conservatives' resurgence in the 1949 general election and their eventual dominance was not only the preferred outcome of Japan's conservative politicians and parties, obviously. It was also that of the US occupation and the US government. Sheltered under the American security umbrella, Japan—and specifically its conservative leaders—gained a powerful patron in Washington, affirming the DLP government's victory and stability confidence in democracy. The United States wanted democracy to work in Japan and specifically with its conservative allies at the helm.

For similar geopolitical reasons, the United States had an interest in ensuring Japan's postwar economy was strong. A revitalized, market-oriented, industrialized Japanese economy, one that was integrated into world markets, provided an important trading partner and economic ally for the United States. Just as democracy helped ensure the United States a political ally in Japan, an economically strong Japan also ensured an effective bulwark against communist expansion.

The DLP revived Japan's developmental state, and economic growth rates increased rapidly soon after. By the end of the 1950s, overall industrial productivity had returned to almost 80 percent of prewar levels. Mining and manufacturing, the two main engines of Japan's industrial economy, recovered to prewar levels by the middle of the 1950s. The Japanese government doubled down, instead of cracking down, on the zaibatsu firms, the prewar commercial conglomerates the occupation GHQ had initially tried to dismantle, to drive industrial growth. The developmental state, revived by the DLP-led government, created the powerful Ministry of International Trade and Industry (MITI) in 1949, strengthening the state's bureaucratic capacity to design and execute targeted industrial policies.

To be sure, American patronage contributed to Japan's economic recovery. Specifically, American trade and economic policies directly benefited Japan. The 1947 reverse-course policy compelled the United States to write off Japan's war reparations. Canceling the reparations gave the Japanese government a huge fiscal break and freed up resources for state-directed investments into the economy. Furthermore, at the encouragement of American trade officials, the Japanese government implemented a fixed and undervalued exchange rate in 1949, which increased Japanese exports, especially to American markets, a trade advantage the Japanese economy enjoyed well into the 1980s.

Perhaps the greatest benefit the Japanese economy—and by extension the conservative Japanese government—gained through US patronage came about with America's involvement in the Cold War conflict on the Korean peninsula. When the Korean War broke out in 1950, American demand for industrial goods supplied by Japanese manufacturers stimulated an economic boom. American procurements between 1951 and 1953 accounted for almost two-thirds of Japan's exports, jump-starting Japan's export-oriented strategy for rapid economic growth. The trade stimulus brought about by the Korean War accelerated Japan's economic recovery during the 1950s, which reflected American geopolitical priorities and domestic political interests among the ruling conservatives in Japan. As Japan's economy grew, so too did support for conservative party leadership, setting the stage for the consolidation of conservative dominance in Japan's postwar democracy.

Consolidating Conservative Dominance

The Liberal Party, the reincarnation of the DLP that formed for the 1949 election, handily won the 1952 general election again, controlling 52 percent of the seats in the Diet. The Socialist Party, meanwhile, splintered after its devastating defeat in 1949 and contested the 1952 election as two separate political parties. Even when combining the two socialist parties' votes, the parties on the left won just 23 percent of the popular vote and 25 percent of the legislature, a sizable rebound from the 1949 election though still well short of the leading, conservative DLP.

Despite the appearance of partisan stability, however, the party composition of the Diet portended a shift in the early 1950s. Though the two conservative parties continued to be in the political driver's seat, the party system was being shaken up. Fragmentation in the Liberal Party and the conservative camp more generally gradually ate away at their electoral dominance. The socialist parties on the left, in the meantime, were making another charge at the polls. The 1953 general election was particularly unsettling for the conservative parties, as the Liberal Party, under the leadership of Prime Minister Yoshida, lost forty Diet seats, while the two socialist parties gained twenty-two additional seats. The Liberal Party continued to be the sole dominant party in the Diet, as the largest single party by far in the legislature after 1953, though its hold on power had definitely been loosened.

In the watershed 1955 election, the governing Liberal Party polled just 27 percent of the popular vote, down from 40 percent in 1953, winning just 114 Diet seats. Meanwhile, the Democratic Party, the other conservative party that found its origins in the Taisho era and which reemerged just before the 1955 election, took 37 percent of the popular vote and 185 legislative seats. The two socialist parties, on the other end of the political spectrum, won a combined 29 percent of the vote and 156 legislative seats, or about one-third of the Diet.

In 1955 the political party system featured four main parties: the two socialist parties and the conservative Liberal and Democratic Parties. None of the four was electorally dominant. One interpretation of the 1955 election and the resulting four-party system portended a significant partisan breakdown in Japan's democratic politics, possibly toward more party system instability. However, another interpretation would have seen the conditions for partisan realignment. History shows the latter interpretation was correct.[26]

The 1955 election actually consolidated the party system in Japan. Despite partisan fragmentation on both the left and right, the overwhelming majority of Japanese voters cast their lot with the two conservative parties in 1955. The two major conservative parties, the Liberals and the Democrats, accounted for 64 percent of the seats in the legislature, while the socialist camp controlled 33 percent. In the wake of the 1955 general election, the two socialist parties merged to form the single Japan Socialist Party (JSP). The creation of the JSP, in turn, prompted the merger of the two conservative parties to form the Liberal Democratic Party (LDP). Known as the "1955 System," swift partisan realignment after the general election resulted in a two-party system featuring the JSP on the left against the conservative LDP. The 1955 realignment also resulted in a dominant-party system, in which the LDP controlled a commanding majority in the Diet and would continue to maintain control of the government for nearly four decades into the 1990s. The LDP set out to consolidate its conservative dominance in democracy.

After 1955, the ruling LDP assumed leadership of Japan's developmental state apparatus. Controlling nearly two-thirds of the Diet, the LDP presided over an efficient legislature, free from partisan wrangling about economic policy priorities and direction. To strengthen its own policy-making capacity, the LDP created the Policy Affairs Research Council, which developed the party's internal policy expertise and enabled the LDP to play a leadership role alongside and in tandem with the developmental state bureaucracy. Mirroring the developmental state, the council staffed the best and brightest technocrats to guide government policy, often recruiting from the meritocratic bureaucracy.

The LDP government also collaborated closely with Japanese industrialists. In a custom known as *amakudari*, retired government and party officials occupied leadership roles in key industrial firms. As Chalmers Johnson documents in *MITI and the Japanese Miracle*, powerful retired vice-ministers in the developmental state bureaucracy were appointed as vice presidents, presidents, and board chairs in Japan's zaibatsu firms.[27] The circulation of elites among the LDP, the developmental state bureaucracy, and leading industrial companies in Japan created a very tight-knit developmental alliance.

The LDP-led developmental state accelerated Japan's economic recovery and development after 1955. The LDP targeted Japan's infrastructure and heavy industries, allocating the vast majority of government investment to developing the electric power, shipbuilding, coal, and steel industries. The investments paid off quickly. Between 1955 and 1965, Japan's steel manufacturing output grew by more than four times, which in turn supported the development of other important infrastructure and heavy industrial sectors. Through government subsidies, targeted investments, and strategic industrial policies, the developmental state nurtured the reconsolidation of Japan's leading zaibatsu firms, especially in labor-intensive, export-oriented manufacturing sectors.

Overall, Japan's manufacturing industries increased their output nearly fourfold in the decade after the LDP took power. Economic growth in Japan averaged over 9 percent annually between 1955 and 1965. Much of its economic development was due to Japan's integration into international markets, as the LDP government encouraged an export-led growth strategy. Kick-started initially by the Korean War, the value of Japanese exports grew tenfold between 1950 and 1965. In 1965 Japan posted a trade surplus and positive balance of payments, a remarkable achievement considering the state of the Japanese economy immediately after World War II. Other fast-growing postwar economies in the region, notably Taiwan and South Korea, adopted the LDP's development strategies, including a push for export-oriented industrialization.

By the 1960s, Japan had reemerged as an economic powerhouse, one of the fastest-growing economies in the world and a model emulated in the Asian region. The LDP took credit for managing the economy and leading Japan's developmental state. Not surprisingly, Japanese citizens, who benefited from the economic recovery, consistently rewarded the incumbent ruling party at the polls. The LDP increased its political dominance throughout its first two decades as Japan's governing party, winning commanding legislative majorities in every election until 1976.

In addition to developing big business and targeting key industrial sectors to grow, the LDP government prioritized rapid *growth with equity*.[28] This deliberate strategy employed by the LDP expanded and solidified a broad base of electoral support. Despite its conservative origins, the ruling party recognized it needed to be a "catch-all" party if it was to continue to stave off the opposition Socialist Party. By incorporating social welfare policy initiatives, the leading conservative party cut into electoral support that would have gone to left-leaning political parties.

The ruling party successfully grew its appeal beyond its traditional conservative constituents. The LDP remained a political party for big business, but not exclusively. For instance, farmers in rural areas made up a key electoral constituency for the LDP and its conservative predecessors. Early on in the occupation period, the conservative interim government implemented land reform, similar to postwar Taiwan and South Korea. Land reform and the breakup of landlord control over land tenure encouraged the development of smaller-scale farming operations. Throughout the democratic 1950s and 1960s, the LDP disbursed more and more agricultural subsidies to farmers, a crude but effective strategy of doling out political pork aimed at winning rural votes. In the cities, meanwhile, the LDP government provided similar subsidies and credit to business owners and entrepreneurs to encourage the growth of small and medium-sized enterprises.

The LDP government implemented the Ikeda Plan in 1960, named after then–prime minister Hayato Ikeda. Growth with equity was central to the Ikeda Plan, and specifically the "income-doubling" program for urban workers. Through targeted economic policies to promote industrial growth and sectoral diversification, the income-doubling plan relied on a full-employment strategy to alleviate poverty, a strategy fueled by a growing international economy and favorable trade arrangements with importing countries such as the United States. By nurturing the export-oriented industrial sector, the Japanese economy grew the size of the labor market and created high-paying industrial jobs.

In an even more deliberate effort to expand its electoral base, the LDP legislated a slew of government-supported social welfare programs in the 1960s and 1970s. Japan was the first of the nonsocialist economies in developmental Asia to implement universal social insurance schemes for health, employment, and old-age income security. Taiwan and South Korea copied the Japanese model of social welfare policies decades later, once they became democracies in the 1980s and 1990s. Conservative dominant parties, such as the Kuomintang (KMT) in Taiwan, would eventually lead the way in social policy reform, not unlike the LDP in Japan.[29]

The economic and political payoffs from the growth-with-equity strategy proved massive for the LDP. State-led development posted extraordinary economic growth rates along with an equitable distribution of income. Japan's

Gini coefficient during the high-growth period of the 1960s and 1970s was in line with levels of income egalitarianism in the Nordic welfare states. Politically, the strategy of equitable growth broadened the LDP's appeal, winning the party electoral support from traditional conservative voters, as well as those who might otherwise have voted for parties on the left such as the beleaguered Socialist Party after 1955. Growth with equity consolidated the LDP's electoral dominance in democratic Japan, which lasted nearly four decades without interruption. Between 1955 and 1993, the LDP formed every elected government, with outright majorities in the Diet or as the leading partner in a coalition government elected in developmental's Asia's largest, most stable, and richest democracy.

The Japanese Playbook

One aim of this chapter is to add to and revise, not dismiss, the conventional wisdom about Japan's postwar democratic transition, and specifically the singularly decisive role the US occupation played in this transformation. The occupation was critical for democratic transition in Japan. The elimination of the military, for instance, was necessary for parties to be revived and flourish anew. That Japan adopted a constitution drafted by American experts is further evidence of America's influence in Japan's democratization. Political pressure by the occupation was instrumental to securing Japan's acceptance of the constitution.

That is also not the full story, however. In this chapter, we have shown how postwar Japan, a defeated nation, was not a tabula rasa on which an American vision of democracy could be easily imprinted and imposed. Japan's democratic transition was not the result of a discrete, single event, such as the installation of the US occupation, but rather that of a series of connected events and *continuities* from before and after the war.

Contrary to the conventional wisdom that democracy was introduced de novo and in toto after Japan's surrender in 1945, we contend instead that there was a democratic thread that emerged in Japan during the nineteenth century and that worked its way through various periods in Japan's modern development, contributing ultimately to democracy through strength. As would occur elsewhere in developmental Asia in the decades to come, democracy through strength in Japan was an extended process of reversible experimentation. Only when we recognize the importance of conservative strength in stabilizing democracy can we fully understand how Japan's postwar democracy survived the Cold War and endured to the present, and why its reversible democratic experiment was never in fact reversed.

As we recount in this chapter, a modern and capable bureaucracy emerged in Meiji Japan. The developmental state remained intact through the postwar period and enabled the conservative political leadership to revive Japan's wartorn economy. Likewise, the legacies of Taisho-era democracy of the 1920s proved critical to democratic transition after the war. Taisho democracy not only introduced political parties as an important democratic institution; it also created a foundation for party-led governments, political contestation, and alternation in power. It also gave rise to a large corps of conservative politicians, who were traditional monarchists but who were nonetheless supporters of representative government. Though the fascist regime of the 1930s marginalized and ultimately defeated these nascent democratic ideas and practices, they were resurrected, not invented de novo, in postwar Japan.

Continuities—rather than ruptures—in the state bureaucracy, parties, and the passing through of conservative politicians after the war provided the antecedent strength and confidence for Japanese politicians to accept the democratic constitution in 1946, to rejuvenate the developmental state and accelerate Japan's economic recovery soon after, and to consolidate the democratic party system. While Japan as a country was weak after the devastation of the war, political leadership, the state bureaucracy, and political parties, hobbled and sidelined by the war, were not. Despite the fascist period of the 1930s, these sources of antecedent strength endured. They provided victory and stability confidence to postwar incumbent politicians who conceded democracy, not as an act of defeat but with the expectation of stability and future electoral victories.

As we have suggested in this chapter, Japan's gradual democratization experience from 1946 to 1955 can be reconceived as a time of reversible experimentation. Japan's regime in those years resembled the "electoral authoritarian" regimes that pursued gradual electoral liberalization in cases such as Thailand and Taiwan, other key Asian examples of reversible democratic experiments. The success or failure of such reversible experiments hinged, however, on the continued victory and stability confidence of conservative parties and their elite allies. In Japan, the grounds for such confidence proved ample by the mid-1950s.

Though the Americans played a leading role in initiating this reversible democratic experiment in the 1940s, it was the calculations and accumulated successes of Japanese conservatives that were most crucial for completing

Japan's democratization during the 1950s. The American occupation was critical, though on its own not decisive, in determining Japan's democratic fate; after all, as we show in the subsequent chapters of this book, many other American-supported democratic experiments were unsuccessful.

Our analysis offers new insights into an underappreciated puzzle: why Japan's powerful bureaucratic state never descended into bureaucratic-authoritarian rule during the Cold War era. The Japanese case is not the best example of democracy through strength; the best example of that is the KMT in Taiwan. But as the first democracy to form in developmental Asia, the Japanese case provides important empirical and theoretical insights into how the rest of democratic developmental Asia eventually emerged.

In democratic developmental Asia, we observe that strong authoritarian parties concede democracy not to concede defeat but to preserve their hold on political power, and potentially consolidate their enduring dominance in democracy. They choose democracy when they are *confident* that inherited antecedent strengths give them an advantage over the opposition and that stability will ensue. The Japanese experience also supports the notion that democracy and development can go hand in hand, and that successful and enduring democratic experiments can strengthen a nation's developmental prospects over the long term.

As the rest of the chapters and case studies unfold in this book, we will see how the experiences of other late democratizers in the developmental statist cluster reflect the Japanese case. The parallels in the process of development and democracy in Japan with other later democratizers in the region are striking. Such parallels, we contend, are not coincidental: they are clustered.

4

Taiwan

THE EXEMPLAR OF DEMOCRACY
THROUGH STRENGTH

IF POSTWAR JAPAN was the first case of democracy through strength in developmental Asia, Taiwan is the paradigmatic case. Whereas the prewar conservative elite in Japan had an opportunity to rise from the rubble and ashes of World War II, the Kuomintang (KMT) in Taiwan initiated democratic reform from an enduringly strong position.

Taiwan had been under the KMT's authoritarian rule for almost forty years when, in 1986, opposition activists announced the formation of a new political party, the Democratic Progressive Party (DPP). Taiwan at the time was under martial law. The KMT ruled the island with an iron fist and prohibited the formation of opposition parties. The DPP was thus formed illegally and in defiance of the authoritarian regime. Most expected the KMT to crush the upstart opposition; after all, that is what powerful authoritarian regimes do.

Instead, the unexpected happened. President Chiang Ching-kuo, the leader of the KMT, decided to permit the formation of the opposition party. A year later, in 1987, the regime lifted martial law, started opening up the political arena for more opposition mobilization, and scaled back the most repressive parts of the authoritarian state. Opposition candidates contested a limited number of legislative seats in 1989. Party banners other than the KMT's were permitted for the first time. Three years after that, in 1992, Taiwan held its first fully free legislative elections, and in 1996 it held its first contested presidential election featuring candidates from the KMT and the DPP. The sequence of political concessions, starting with Chiang's initial decision not to crack down on the DPP in 1986, set off a chain of political events that eventually led to Taiwan's democratic transition.

What is peculiar about the Taiwan case—and why it is our paradigmatic case of democracy through strength—is that the KMT, when it initiated the process of democratization in the late 1980s, remained a very powerful political party. It was not a party in crisis in 1986, nor was Taiwan on the brink of collapse, economically or politically.

Taiwan's economy was strong, with no signs of slowing. Taiwan had undergone several decades of sustained economic growth with the KMT at the helm of the developmental state. The regime was politically stable during the 1980s as well. Protests erupted occasionally, but nothing the KMT regime could not handle, either through state-sponsored suppression or with selective economic payoffs. The *tangwai* opposition that emerged during the early 1980s, the precursor to the eventual opposition DPP, was essentially an elite political movement made up of local politicians and intellectual dissidents, not a mass-based revolutionary movement like we often see challenging other authoritarian regimes.

Moreover, limited elections during the 1970s and 1980s, which independent, non-KMT candidates contested, showed consistently healthy returns and popular support for the ruling party. Though electoral support for the KMT gradually declined over those two decades, the KMT still polled 67 percent of the popular vote in the 1986 election, retaining the ruling party's commanding, virtually unassailable control over the government. In other words, when the ruling regime began to liberalize and ultimately democratize the political system during the late 1980s, the KMT was hardly a party in a death spiral that presaged its impending collapse. Instead, the KMT, notwithstanding a gradual decline in its electoral support, remained a very strong party and the sole, dominant force in Taiwan's politics.

Hence the puzzling question: If democracy was not forced on the KMT regime during the 1980s, and indeed it remained a powerful, stabilizing, developmentally oriented party, why did it concede democracy, and why then? Put another way, why did the KMT concede democracy when it did not have to, when regime collapse was not even on the imaginable horizon? We contend that *the KMT conceded to embark on a democratic path in part because it remained such a strong political party*, confident that its incumbent strengths and bases of political support at the time would all but guarantee its dominance in the near term and the party's survival in democracy over the long term. The signals the regime received that its authoritative power was on the decline were as reassuring as they were ominous, in that the KMT's continued electoral appeal was virtually unbeatable. Simply put, it did not concede democracy to exit or relinquish power, but rather to restore its grip on power by democratic means—which it did rather easily throughout the 1990s.

The rest of this chapter tells the story of Taiwan's political and economic development in the postwar period, leading to the KMT's momentous decision to concede democracy through strength. More than any other chapter in this book, it narrates this history from the perspective of a single ruling party that guided the democratization process. As we have seen in the case of Japan, a powerful developmental bureaucracy can play a stabilizing role in democratization even before a strong party establishes its dominance. In this way, the developmental state bureaucracy mattered greatly in the story of Taiwan's democratic transition as well, though center stage belonged much more exclusively to the KMT. Hence, to understand Taiwan's political and economic development means understanding the KMT above all else.

Our story begins with the party's origins in China and how the KMT successfully reinvented itself in Taiwan after it was defeated by the Chinese communists in the 1940s. Thereafter, the KMT began a deliberate process of party-building and state-building in Taiwan, orchestrating Taiwan's economic miracle and fostering remarkable political stability, all the while earning the ruling party broad bases of political and economic support as an authoritarian regime. We also recount how the regime's developmental achievements sowed the seeds of a more demanding Taiwanese society, and how the KMT ultimately chose a democratic path to governing it—not because the KMT was a party in crisis, but instead to stave off future challengers to its hegemony and to reconsolidate its power by winning support through democratic elections. We explain how Taiwan transformed from a "one-party dictatorship [in]to a dominant party system" in which the KMT remained Taiwan's paramount power, even as the political system moved decisively from authoritarianism to democracy.[1]

The Origins and Exile of the KMT

Prior to the early twentieth century, China had been ruled by successive dynastic regimes, the last being the Qing dynasty. Anti-Qing movements emerged during the late nineteenth century, culminating in the abdication of the emperor in 1912 and the end of the last dynasty; in its place, republican Chinese forces formed a provisional government.

The KMT, which was officially formed in 1912, had its origins in the anti-Qing movements and soon took control. Yet the early KMT was not a strong political party, even after it formed the government in 1928. In the wake of the Qing collapse, China was not unified, and the KMT had to fight several wars with regional warlords in a failed effort to consolidate the Chinese nation-state. The KMT did not enjoy broad support and was internally corrupt and rife with factional conflicts. As a result, despite its anti-Qing bona fides and its claims to be the legitimate ruler of the newborn Republic of China (ROC), it was unable to unify and bring stability to modern China.

The KMT's inability to govern China opened the door for the rise of the Chinese Communist Party (CCP), led by Mao Zedong. Founded in Shanghai in 1921, the CCP mobilized support in the countryside, rallying peasants around a vision of agrarian socialism and a resilient, nationalist China that could stand up to foreign imperialism. The Chinese Communists, under Mao's charismatic leadership, resisted Japanese imperialism in the 1930s. Mao's peasant army also fought a civil war with the KMT to determine which vanguard party would rule China.

The KMT, under the leadership of Generalissimo Chiang Kai-shek, was eventually defeated by the Communists and forced to flee China's mainland during the late 1940s, retreating and reestablishing the ROC government in Taiwan, an island off the southeastern coast of the mainland that had, from 1895 until 1945, been under Japanese colonial rule. The KMT, though formally recognized as the legitimate government of the ROC, or "Free China," was essentially a broken party by the time it arrived in Taiwan, internally corrupt and in institutional decay, with no connection to the local Taiwanese society. Chiang remained the leader of the KMT and the president of the ROC government-in-exile.

Though the KMT was defeated and forced to retreat to Taiwan, Chiang did not intend for the KMT to be permanently based there. Nor did he anticipate the KMT would remain weak for long. He had grand ambitions to reinvigorate and rebuild the party in Taiwan. Its relegation to the island was to be temporary, and once the KMT had rejuvenated itself, Chiang reasoned, the party would retake China from the CCP to reclaim the ROC government on the mainland.

The KMT's retreat to Taiwan was not smooth. For one, Taiwan had been under Japanese colonial rule since 1895, when China ceded the island after its defeat in the Sino-Japanese War. Taiwan had not been governed by any Chinese authority since the end of the nineteenth century. When the KMT arrived during the late 1940s, therefore, local Taiwanese were not particularly welcoming of what some saw to be yet another colonial regime. The KMT made matters worse when, on February 28, 1947, Republican soldiers severely beat a Taiwanese woman, which in turn sparked massive riots, marking that day as the infamous "228 Incident." The consequences of the 228 Incident were not trivial for Taiwan's political development. A nascent "Taiwanese" identity began to form: an ethnic, and eventually political, identity that differentiated the majority Taiwanese locals from the minority mainlanders who had arrived with the émigré KMT regime.

One thing the party had going for it, however, was that the KMT was recognized by the international community as the legitimate government of the ROC, which nominally included the entire mainland. The Communists, meanwhile, were shunned internationally and regarded by most countries in the world as a renegade regime. The postwar logic of communist containment benefited the KMT, much as it also benefited the ruling parties in Japan and South Korea, by securing the United States as its superpower patron. As we will see, geopolitics played a significant role in the evolution of the KMT.

Strengthening the KMT

Consolidating the KMT's authority in Taiwan was, to say the least, no easy task, requiring the weakened party to strengthen itself internally and externally in its relations with local Taiwanese. Many leaders were purged from the party's highest internal body, the Central Standing Committee, including several who had been in Chiang's inner circle while in China. In May 1949 Chiang assembled ten high-ranking KMT officials, all loyal to him, to begin planning the party's internal reforms. Later that year, the leadership committee outlined guiding principles for the KMT's reorganization. What did not change, however, was the explicit expectation that the KMT would remain the sole paramount political authority in Taiwan, and that power was to be exercised through the party in authoritarian ways. The KMT was not about to democratize or lead a process of political liberalization on Taiwan; if anything, the reorganization campaign was intended to strengthen the authoritarian KMT.

The party's rebuilding campaign began in 1950 and was overseen by the KMT's Central Reorganization Commission. The commission comprised Chiang's hand-picked loyalists, all of whom had mainlander Chinese origins. The campaign had several aims. Most importantly, the KMT in Taiwan immediately set out to centralize power inside the party. Chiang felt the party had been weakened from within during the civil war, allowing corruption and clientelism to pervade throughout and ultimately to undermine the party's ability to rule.[2] The campaign aimed to eliminate intraparty factionalism, another perceived source of party weakness and a leading cause of the KMT's defeat to the Communists.

Another goal of the commission was to create new institutional mechanisms embedding the party within society. Upon reflection, the KMT conceded the CCP had done a better job of winning grassroots support among the Chinese peasantry, which proved decisive in mobilizing the Communists against the KMT. Chiang and the KMT leadership reasoned that if the KMT was to effectively govern and generate popular support on Taiwan—and eventually back in China—the party needed mechanisms that allowed it to exercise top-down authority while generating bottom-up feedback to the party.

It accomplished this in several ways. First, the KMT penetrated all government institutions through networks of party cells, small groups made up of party loyalists. By the end of the reorganization campaign in 1952, over 2,700 party cadres had been organized into nearly 300 party cells in various central government branches. The Presidential Office and executive branch had almost 1,500 party cadres operating in 155 cells. KMT politicians in the legislative branch were similarly organized into party cells. Administrative organs of the state, such as the Executive Yuan (the cabinet) and the Judicial Yuan, were penetrated by political "small groups" that were accountable to the party's Central Reorganization Commission. By the end of the reorganization campaign, the ratio of party members to nonmembers in the central government bureaucracy was five to one. Over one-third of local government bureaucrats were also party members.

Second, the ruling party established its firm control over the military. In April 1950 Chiang Kai-shek appointed his son, Chiang Ching-kuo, to head-up the General Political Work Department in the army. The younger Chiang reestablished the political commissar system, which had been abolished during the 1920s when the KMT was still on the mainland. Through the commissar system, the party established cells within the army's ranks and imposed strict party discipline among soldiers, specifically through political education programs. Suspected communists were dealt with as well, either purged or imprisoned. The commissar system served as "the party's eyes and ears in the military." In 1952 about 145,000 party members were enlisted in the military and security branches of the government. This figure grew rapidly over the next two years when over 95,000 new party members were recruited by the military. By 1954 over one-third of the armed forces were KMT members.[3]

Third, the KMT set out to build up its popular base within Taiwanese society, unleashing a mass membership drive. Civilian membership in the KMT in 1950 was just over 80,000 members; and two years later, it had more than doubled to approximately 170,000. Almost half of new party members in 1952 were farmers and workers, and not from the professional or middle classes, reflecting the party's deliberate strategy to broaden its base of support. New party members were also considerably younger, and a disproportionate number of them were born in Taiwan, an early indication of the KMT's strategy to localize or "Taiwanize" the party.

At the start of the party reorganization campaign, the ratio of party members to the general population was about one to one hundred, or just 1 percent; by 1952, this had increased to 3.5 percent; and five years later, the KMT boasted over a half million members, or 5.3 percent of the population. Civilian party members were organized into 30,000 work and residential cells, giving the authoritarian party a presence in both rural villages and urban centers. KMT cells and branches proliferated throughout public-sector institutions as well, from public schools to government agencies. Though the KMT at the time did not believe it was only going to rule Taiwan for long—the goal, after all, was for the party to return to China triumphantly—it successfully reorganized, internally and in connection with local society, which established a firm foundation for Taiwan's extraordinary development.[4]

The Developmental State and the KMT

The vertical organization of the developmental state apparatus reflected the authoritarian organization of the KMT. Bureaucratic ministries within the state, including powerful ones that oversaw Taiwan's economy, foreign affairs, and finance, were subsumed under and directed by the central Council for Economic Planning and Development, which was in turn led by senior KMT officials. Bureaucratic and political power was concentrated in the council, or what Chalmers Johnson calls a "pilot" organization, tasked with directing and shaping public policies, including Taiwan's economic policies.[5]

The developmental state, despite being centralized, was not rampant with corruption, unlike the KMT state in China. Though thoroughly penetrated by KMT members and party leadership, the state bureaucracy was organized along meritocratic lines rather than patron-client linkages. Technocrats staffing ministries, for instance, were selected from Taiwan's top universities and through a highly competitive civil service examination. Developmental bureaucrats tended to be trained in technical fields, predominantly in engineering. In other words, Taiwan's state apparatus was lean, effective, and staffed with the very best and brightest. Modeled after the Japanese experience, the developmental state in Taiwan was tasked with leading, from the top down, Taiwan's industrialization and economic development.[6]

Taiwan began accelerating its industrial growth in the 1950s, though a solid economic foundation had been laid before that with intensive land and agricultural reforms. During the late 1940s, when the KMT first arrived in Taiwan, more than half of the Taiwanese population were farmers, and the vast majority of them were tenant farmers working the land for landlords, a legacy of Japan's earlier colonization of Taiwan. The KMT, with assistance from American advisers, initiated a thorough land reform campaign starting in 1949. The first part of the campaign centered on rent reductions for tenant farmers as well as an outright land seizure by the state. During the early 1950s, land that had been seized from landlords was sold or transferred directly to landless farmers. In the land-to-tiller effort beginning in 1953, land was transferred from landlords to tillers, such that by the 1960s most of Taiwan's farmable land was owned by individual households.

By tilling their own land, farmers not only increased agricultural productivity and ensured food security for those living in the countryside but also generated surplus crops, such as rice, that were sold domestically and later exported to foreign markets. Taiwan's early foreign trade earnings were primarily from agricultural exports, which were in turn invested into jump-starting Taiwan's industrialization. In this respect, land reform primed Taiwan for its industrial takeoff.[7]

Importantly, early land reform in Taiwan politically reorganized the countryside so that large landholding elites would not become a barrier to democratization later, which we know stymied democratic transitions in other regions, notably in Latin America. By the time democratization began in the late 1980s, Taiwan's countryside would be ruled by KMT politicians who had cultivated their local bases of support, and not landed elites holding the peasantry in their coercive grip.

In the 1950s, local Taiwanese industrial firms entered into labor-intensive light manufacturing sectors. These firms, as expected, were not competitive in more technically sophisticated industrial sectors. What they had, however, was access to abundant and cheap labor, as in many developing economies. The KMT developmental state was effective in guiding economic development from the top down by nurturing the growth of new businesses. The Taiwanese government provided macroeconomic stability through mechanisms such as exchange rate management policies and fixed import pricing, along with a host of regulatory controls over the financial sector to provide loans and tax incentives for growing industries and firms.

The KMT also made it a priority to prevent the kind of runaway inflation that had been experienced on mainland China and that contributed to the party's downfall there. The KMT developmental state pursued a conservative monetary policy to mitigate inflationary pressures on consumer prices and industry inputs. Investment capital, such as loans and industrial credit, was strategically managed by the state-controlled finance and banking sector. Even the informal secondary lending market—the so-called curb market—was monitored closely by the state.

Taiwan's postwar industries were unique among Asia's developmental states in that most industrial firms were small and medium-sized enterprises (SMEs). Whereas huge firms in Korea and Japan—the chaebols in the former, and the zaibatsu in the latter—were husbanded by credit-generous banks that favored large firms and economies of scale, in Taiwan, the government chose an alternative investment strategy of leveraging fiscal (i.e., tax-based) incentives to seed and nurture small and agile firms. The KMT's SME growth strategy reflected the legacies of colonial Japan's regime in Taiwan, and specifically the development of rural, small-scale firms. From an ideological standpoint, the proliferation of SMEs also reflected the KMT's long-standing "anti big capitalist bias."[8] Politically, the SME strategy benefited the KMT by preventing the concentration of economic wealth in industrial sectors, which the regime feared could become a source of opposition power.

The SME strategy also made economic sense for Taiwan's industrialization. Small and agile firms plugged into global supply chains, which the government encouraged by strategically attracting foreign direct investment into targeted industrial sectors. The state focused specifically on labor-intensive manufacturing industries. It implemented import substitution industrialization policies to raise import tariffs in competitive sectors to protect Taiwan's infant industries and firms. Over time, as local firms matured to become competitive suppliers and assemblers of manufactured products, local SMEs were encouraged, again with fiscal incentives, to compete in global markets.

The shift to export-oriented industrialization accelerated in the 1960s. During the late 1950s, Taiwan's annual export growth rate was just under 3 percent; after 1960, export growth increased to 25 percent per year. Throughout the 1960s, exports grew between 33 and 55 percent annually, and Taiwan became a major trading economy in global markets.

The early 1970s was another significant turning point in Taiwan's economic miracle. Up to that point, Taiwan's industrial companies were mainly labor-intensive, light manufacturing firms. The KMT's economic planners felt Taiwan needed to diversify its industrial base and to concentrate on growing higher-value-added industries and firms, notably in the electronics sector. If Taiwan wanted to continue upskilling its workforce and to stay competitive in the global economy, its firms would have to climb the global value chain.

To facilitate this, the developmental state proposed a plan to cultivate "Ten Major Projects" starting in the early 1970s, a major government-led infrastructural investment campaign. The Ten Major Projects—which included infrastructure initiatives in energy production, ports and rails, steel production, and the growth of other heavy industries—were intended to strengthen Taiwan's export competitiveness and to support the growth of capital-intensive industrial sectors, in a deliberate move away from Taiwan's earlier reliance on lower-skilled, labor-intensive, and light manufacturing industries.

The Ten Major Projects plan was almost derailed, however, in November 1973 when the Organization of the Petroleum Exporting Countries (OPEC) energy crisis quadrupled the price of imported oil. Immediately Taiwan's economy was shocked into stagflation. The consumer price index went from 8 percent to nearly 50 percent between 1973 and 1974, and the wholesale price index nearly doubled from 23 percent to 41 percent. Economic growth stagnated and slowed to just 1 percent growth in 1974, and for the first time in a long time, Taiwan experienced a trade deficit.

In response, the government implemented a strict monetary program. The conservative monetary policy approach stabilized the economy and absorbed the inflationary pressures brought on by the price spike. The pain of adjustment was acute, to be sure, but ultimately short-lived, and the economy soon got back on track.[9]

In the wake of the OPEC crisis, the government again pushed ahead with the Ten Major Projects. The state doubled down on the development of non-energy-intensive sectors that would eventually become the foundation for Taiwan's turn to high-tech industrial sectors, which leveraged Taiwan's burgeoning science and technology capabilities. The KMT-led developmental state was critical in seeding and nurturing the growth of Taiwan's high-tech-intensive industries. In 1973 the government created the Industrial Technology Research Institute (ITRI) in Hsinchu, just outside Taipei, which today remains Taiwan's premier science and technology commercialization hub. The publicly funded research and development (R&D) center emphasized applied research and commercial development, with an initial focus on the electronics sector. Eventually ITRI concentrated its R&D and commercialization activities on more sophisticated information and communications technology (ICT).

The best example of how Taiwan's developmental state steered its industries toward the ICT sector was the growth of its manufacturing prowess in semiconductors and integrated circuits. In the early 1980s, ITRI was instrumental in creating the Taiwan Semiconductor Manufacturing Corporation (TSMC), which pioneered the pure-play foundry model in semiconductor manufacturing and chip-making. With its innovative production model, TSMC became a global industry and market leader in semiconductor and integrated circuit manufacturing, a vital and lucrative part of the high-tech ICT global value chain. The creation and success of TSMC was the result of publicly funded technology licensing (the original technology was in-licensed to ITRI from an American chipmaker) on the front end, and direct government investment into the creation of the firm downstream.

TSMC was not the only example of how Taiwan's developmental state mitigated the risks of high-tech industrial upgrading by picking and making industrial winners. Other high-tech industry successes for Taiwanese firms, in sectors such as photonics, computer hardware manufacturing, and even medical devices, followed a similar upgrading strategy, for which the developmental state led the way.[10]

The Apex of Authoritarian Dominance

In just three decades, Taiwan became a dynamic economic powerhouse. Not surprisingly, its postwar economic development and the role the KMT-led developmental state played in directing Taiwan's economic transformation won the authoritarian regime tremendous performance legitimacy. As in other authoritarian systems where citizens' civil and political rights are sacrificed on the altar of national economic development, performance legitimacy was an important source of political support for the KMT.

Under the KMT's authoritarian rule, Taiwan went from being one of the poorest economies in the world to becoming one of Asia's developmental front-runners. During the 1960s Taiwan's average economic growth rate reached nearly 11 percent a year. Through the 1970s and 1980s, when Taiwan's industries entered into high-tech manufacturing sectors, Taiwan's economy continued to post annual average growth rates of 8 percent. Putting this in

comparative perspective, in 1962 Taiwan ranked as one of the poorest economies in the developing world, alongside Zaire and other sub-Saharan countries. During the period from 1962 to 1986, Taiwan rose from eighty-fifth in the
world to thirty-eighth in terms of the size of its economy. In dollar terms, per
capita income in Taiwan went from US$50 in 1952 on the eve of Taiwan's eco-
nomic takeoff to nearly $5,000 in 1987, almost a hundredfold increase.

As Taiwan's economy became richer, people's lives changed as well, becoming more modern. Car ownership, one indicator of socioeconomic modernization, multiplied more than five times over the course of the 1970s. Access to
daily newspapers and magazines doubled during that decade, and telephone
connectivity increased fivefold. The structure of the economy was transformed. The percentage of those employed in manufacturing industries more
than doubled between 1953 and 1983, reaching almost half of the workforce.
Meanwhile the share of agricultural workers drastically declined from
55 percent to just 18 percent. Taiwanese society became increasingly urban and
middle class. At the same time, access to education expanded when the government universalized primary and secondary education in the 1960s.

Taiwan's modernization process was especially extraordinary given how
quickly it happened. To put its experience in comparative perspective, Hung-
mao Tien, in his book *The Great Transition*, notes that while "the modernization
of Europe and North America occurred over a period of two or more centuries,"
in Taiwan "that time span has been compressed into a few decades."[11]

Economic takeoff in Taiwan—sustained and transformative over three decades from the 1950s to the 1980s—was unsurprisingly critical to the KMT's
political fortunes. The political payoff in terms of the KMT's performance
legitimacy and political support for the regime, however, was not limited to just
the benefits of Taiwan's overall economic development. In addition to aggregate economic growth from the 1950s onward, the KMT-led developmental
state also took credit for promoting growth with socioeconomic equity. The
distribution of income in Taiwan actually became more egalitarian in the
1960s and 1970s during Taiwan's industrial takeoff, precisely the period when
we would expect higher, not lower, levels of inequality. In fact, until the late
1980s, Taiwan's Gini coefficient (a standard measure of the distribution of
income) hovered around 0.3, putting Taiwan in line with the most equitable
Scandinavian economies.

Facilitating growth with equity made good political sense with respect to
the authoritarian KMT's prospects for political survival, especially in the face
of rising ethnic tensions in Taiwan. Particularly worrisome for the KMT was

the emergence of an ethnic Taiwanese identity among the majority of people living in Taiwan. Specifically, the ruling party was anxious about simmering ethnic tensions, going back to the infamous 228 Incident between the mainland-born minority and local Taiwanese, who accounted for the majority of the population. When the KMT fled China and arrived in Taiwan in the late 1940s, the influx of Chinese mainlanders (who came with the KMT) accounted for just 13 percent of the island's population. Ensuring an equitable distribution of the fruits of growth paid political dividends to the authoritarian regime by preventing the concentration of economic wealth in mainlander hands. Growth with equity also preemptively deflected any criticisms of the regime for disadvantaging local Taiwanese in favor of Chinese mainlanders tied to the KMT government.

Recall that in Japan, growth with equity broadened the electoral base of the conservative Liberal Democratic Party (LDP) during the 1950s and consolidated its "catch-all" appeal. Similarly, equitable development in Taiwan shored up political support for the authoritarian KMT regime. As was the case in postwar Japan, growth with equity in Taiwan was the result of deliberate government policy choices. For instance, land reform during the early 1950s not only increased agricultural productivity; it also contributed to a more equitable distribution of land for farmers and economic opportunities by destroying the vestiges of the colonial-era landlord system. The strategy to promote SMEs, rather than large firms, lowered the entry barriers for local entrepreneurs, which in turn resulted in more socioeconomic mobility among Taiwanese. The introduction of universal education during the 1960s contributed to a more skilled labor force and higher-paying employment opportunities across the board. The KMT's efforts to mitigate massive inequality were also evident during crisis moments. As we described earlier, when the late 1973 OPEC price spikes threatened runaway inflation, the KMT-led government employed a strict and conservative monetary policy and allocated subsidies from state-owned firms to rein in consumer inflation, ensuring the gap between the haves and have-nots did not widen.

Though the KMT-led government took credit for facilitating economic growth with equity in postwar Taiwan, this did not mean that Taiwan's was what we would call a robust welfare state. Growth with equity was the result of macroeconomic policies aimed at growth, full employment, and labor upskilling. Whereas the LDP in democratic Japan created universal social welfare programs beginning in the 1960s, social policies and social protection programs in Taiwan were fragmented and managed by different parts of the bureaucracy. Social welfare programs were not integrated into a single, generous welfare state. The disparate social programs that existed were selective in their beneficiaries and were for the most part financed through contributory insurance schemes, rather than through government funds.

Nonetheless, social programs served a political purpose for the regime, in that they helped maintain the KMT's authoritarian dominance through the selective use of benefits to win over or maintain critical political bases of support. Selective welfare programs, such as the labor insurance program, were deliberately expanded during moments of political crisis for the regime. This was the KMT's way of buying off potential political opponents, a strategy of crisis and selective compensation. When social benefits were expanded by the government, they were extended first to political constituents of the KMT regime, such as military officers, soldiers, and civil servants. Workers in smaller firms, farmers, and their dependents were excluded from social policy schemes until the 1980s and 1990s when Taiwan democratized. Social policy schemes initially targeted those who were important for the authoritarian regime's survival.[12]

The decades after the 1950s were the golden age of the KMT's authoritarian dominance in Taiwan. But the party's strengths were not just a natural byproduct of the KMT's economic track record and performance legitimacy. KMT strength also had a lot to do with the party's deliberate efforts to consolidate its political base in Taiwan. During the 1970s, the KMT actively refashioned the membership and composition of both the party leadership and the government civil service. The party became younger in terms of membership after it created its Youth Commission. Economic growth with equity in Taiwan also prevented the concentration of wealth, which diffused the economic power of a potential political opposition.

Importantly, the KMT increasingly and actively recruited local-born Taiwanese into the party ranks and the government bureaucracy. By the end of the 1970s, significant portions of the government's leadership as well as that of the KMT included local Taiwanese officials. The KMT intentionally "localized" and "Taiwanized" the party to transform its image from that of a mainlander émigré party into a local party. Taiwanization broadened the KMT's base of political support. In other words, while the party employed authoritarian tactics to suppress its enemies, it also actively generated support among Taiwan's citizenry.[13]

This tactic of generating political support within Taiwan was especially clear in the KMT's efforts to legitimate its rule through local elections. In 1966 the KMT government amended the electoral rules to allow supplementary elections for legislative bodies, whereas previously elections were mere political window dressing for the KMT dictatorship. Reflecting the KMT's authoritarian nature, the supplemental elections were limited in scope, as opposition parties were banned under martial law. Still, independent (i.e., non-KMT) candidates could participate in supplementary electoral contests after 1966.

The electoral amendments initiated by the KMT should not be confused with genuine political liberalization, however. The 1966 changes were not a harbinger of political democratization. On the contrary, the limited elections were a tool used by the KMT to strengthen, not weaken, its monopoly on political power, in part by casting a positive halo effect of having "won" electoral contests. Given the rapid development of Taiwan's economy from the 1950s onward and the KMT's economic performance legitimacy, combined with the fact that opposition parties were banned, the likelihood of an independent, non-KMT lawmaker being elected in these supplemental elections was very low. The KMT won eight of eleven seats in the first supplementary election in 1969. It swept the 1972 and 1975 supplementary legislative elections handily as well, winning 73 percent and 78 percent of the popular vote, respectively, and winning almost all of the contested seats.

Supplementary legislative elections were not intended to be free and fair contests, but rather an opportunity for the KMT to consolidate its political power through the ballot. Limited but regular elections provided a clear signal of peoples' support for the regime. Local elections for magistrates and mayors also provided an institutionalized feedback mechanism for the regime, connecting the KMT with local communities and routinely activating its local party cells. Not surprisingly, the KMT developed a strong political machinery throughout the island because of these elections. It gained experience in contesting elections, from nurturing and nominating candidates to deepening clientelist ties. In other words, contesting regular elections gave the ruling party an overwhelming strategic and organizational advantage over the opposition, such that by the time a formal opposition party emerged in Taiwan during the 1980s, the KMT was a party already experienced and seasoned in winning elections.[14]

Demanding Society, Divided Polity

As we saw in Meiji Japan, modernization brings its discontents. From the 1950s through the 1970s, Taiwan's economy grew by leaps and bounds. At the same time the KMT's authoritarian dominance was flourishing, Taiwan's economic structure was becoming diversified. Taiwanese society became more modernized as well: literate and educated, urban, increasingly middle class, and industrialized. Developmental states do not necessarily spawn *democratic* citizens, but a modernizing society and a developing economy eventually sow the seeds of more politically *demanding* citizens.

The KMT's Taiwan was no exception. Interest groups formed during Taiwan's modernization. Agricultural associations started to politically mobilize during the 1960s. In the following decade, industrial, commercial, and professional workers' associations formed as well. More politically explicit groups, such as the Chinese Human Rights Association and the Taiwan Human Rights Association, emerged during the 1970s. These organizations occasionally mobilized against the KMT regime, but because political protests were concentrated in pockets around Taiwan, they were easily suppressed by the authoritarian regime. Sporadic protest movements did not pose serious threats to the KMT at the time, though they portended an increasingly demanding Taiwanese society, and one that could not be ruled in the same way as in the past.

The regime confronted a growing labor movement during the 1960s and 1970s, as Taiwan's economy became more industrialized and workers gained more voice and power. Though most industrial workers were co-opted into the government-subsidized Chinese Federation of Labor and independent unions were illegal, worker disruptions on the shop floor and protests in the streets grew steadily throughout the 1970s. In 1963 there were 20 labor disputes on record. Between 1971 and 1982, however, the government recorded nearly 6,400 labor disputes, and in 1981 alone, over 1,000 disputes involving around 7,000 workers took place. Workers were increasingly unhappy with their wages and work conditions. However, protests and worker disputes did not galvanize a large-scale labor movement. Taiwan's industrial structure, which was dominated by small-scale firms, meant that worker protests were generally contained within firms. The large SME sector also undermined efforts to foment larger-scale collective action. Unlike in South Korea, where thousands of employees in conglomerate firms made it easier to mobilize mass protests, worker unrest in Taiwan tended to be fragmented and diffuse.

The diffuse labor protests mirrored oppositional civil society more generally in authoritarian Taiwan. Though Taiwanese society was becoming increasingly restive during the 1970s and 1980s, and contentious politics was definitely on the rise, the scale and composition of protest did not pose a major threat to the regime's survival. According to data reported by Yun-han Chu, the number of recorded protest movements, as we would expect, increased dramatically from 1983 to 1988, though the actual number of such protests was actually quite small. In 1983 there were just 175 protests, of which only three were considered politically sensitive. The spike in social protest movements occurred in 1987 and 1988, after the KMT lifted martial law and loosened its authoritarian grip on power, when the number of protests jumped to 734 and 1,172, respectively. Still, the vast majority of social protests between 1983 and 1988 had fewer than one hundred participants. Only about one-quarter of protests targeted the central KMT government, while the majority focused their criticism on local authorities.[15]

Thus, while bottom-up mobilization signaled an increasingly demanding society in Taiwan, oppositional protest was not the strongest and most ominous signal that the regime was losing its grip on political power. The contrast between Taiwan and South Korea (the focus of chapter 5) in terms of the size and scope of contentious political mobilization was significant. Whereas hundreds of thousands of protesters took to the streets in Seoul in 1987 demanding an end to authoritarianism in South Korea, the KMT never faced such strong bottom-up mobilization.

Still, the KMT did receive strong signals that its once unassailable grip on authoritarian power was weakening. It experienced a clearer, potentially more ominous signal in the international sphere. The Sino-Soviet split of the early 1960s, which saw the CCP regime drift away from its Cold War alliance with the Soviet Union, provided an impetus for the United States and China to start a process of rapprochement. This was disastrous for the KMT regime in Taiwan. In 1971 the United Nations officially derecognized Taiwan as the legitimate government of so-called Free China. Over the next several years, relations between the United States and China gradually improved. In December 1978 the Carter administration reached out to forge diplomatic relations between the United States and the CCP-led People's Republic of China, reflecting a significant shift in America's Cold War containment strategies. These two events—the UN derecognition of the ROC and the normalization of relations between the United States and China—essentially delegitimated the KMT regime's claims to govern the whole of China.

The United States did not fully abandon Taiwan, however, even after formalizing its diplomatic relationship with communist China in January 1979. Congressional action ensured a continuing security guarantee when Congress passed the 1979 Taiwan Relations Act. Though the United States no longer officially recognized the KMT government in Taiwan, the Taiwan Relations Act signaled its continued indirect support of Taiwan. The implicit understanding was that America's security commitment to Taiwan hinged on it continuing to be the bastion of a "Free China," distinct from the communist regime on the Chinese mainland. In other words, while the United States could not place direct political pressure on the KMT to democratize, Taiwan's former superpower patron could—and eventually did—apply external indirect pressure on the regime to liberalize the political system.

Domestically, the normalization of diplomatic relations between the United States and China created political pressures for the KMT regime. The ROC's exclusion from the UN undermined the KMT's claim to be China's legitimate government, making the KMT regime essentially obsolete, without its raison d'être to be in Taiwan in the first place. The KMT was now really an outsider regime in Taiwan. Its diplomatic isolation reignited identity politics, deepening the ethnic and identity cleavage in Taiwan's political landscape. By the end of the 1970s, the connection between Taiwanese identity and democratic opposition among Taiwanese was politically explicit. Taiwanese activists increasingly focused their attacks on the authoritarian nature of the mainlander KMT.[16]

Identity politics posed a serious threat to the authoritarian regime, especially as the identity and regime cleavages became mutually reinforcing. In 1975, Taiwanese intellectuals published the first issue of the *Taiwan Political Review*. The *Review* was a forum for Taiwanese opposition voices, especially local critics of the KMT regime. It published articles and opinion pieces about Taiwanese ethnicity, reinforcing a distinctly Taiwanese political identity in opposition to the mainlander KMT regime. That the *Review* used "Taiwan" in the journal's title, rather than "Republic of China," was perceived by the KMT as an intentional smear of the ruling party's claims to govern all of China.

The *Review* lasted only five issues before government censors shut it down. Taiwanese intellectual activists nonetheless continued to mobilize. After local elections in 1977, non-KMT candidates accused the ruling party of electoral fraud. The election prompted protesters to take to the streets in the town of Chungli, culminating in a confrontation with the state security apparatus. The protesters were suppressed by the regime, and the Chungli Incident crystallized the formation of the opposition tangwai movement.

It is important to distinguish between what the tangwai was and was not. Tangwai, which literally means "outside the party," was a loose coalition of Taiwanese politicians and dissident intellectuals opposed to the authoritarian KMT regime. Tangwai politicians contested elections as independent non-KMT candidates but were not able to form a political party or alliance under martial law. Tangwai activists were not a mass movement, but rather an elite intellectual coterie. They were politically subversive but not the vanguard of large-scale protests.[17]

In August 1979 dissident tangwai activists launched the *Formosa* journal. Like the *Taiwan Political Review*, the magazine published anti-KMT articles and galvanized the regime's opposition among Taiwan's intellectual elites. *Formosa*, furthermore, explicitly linked identity and regime cleavages among activists; to be Taiwanese was to be anti-authoritarian, and thus anti-KMT. Similar to the *Review* before it, the name of the journal was chosen to reflect a politically subversive position. Formosa, which in Portuguese means "beautiful island," was actually the European colonial name for Taiwan, and tangwai activists appropriated it as a direct affront to the KMT regime. In December 1979 the *Formosa* office in the southern city of Kaohsiung organized a massive human rights rally. The police and protesters clashed on December 10. Many were injured and the protest leaders were jailed. Immediately after the confrontation, *Formosa* leaders were targeted, rounded up, and arrested. Some of them were severely beaten while in custody. Others were deported.

In 1980 a military court, which was controlled by the KMT regime, ruled that the defendants were guilty of attempting to overthrow the government, not unlike the *Taiwan Political Review* editors before them. Like the leaders of the *Review*, the *Formosa* leaders received harsh sentences, including life imprisonment for some. The Kaohsiung Incident reaffirmed the KMT's willingness to use violence as well as the courts to thwart any opposition to the ruling party. The incident became a potent symbol of Taiwanese resistance to the KMT regime, generating more momentum for tangwai politicians and dissidents.

Though the KMT enjoyed a golden age of political dominance through the early 1980s, the political bumps in the road on the domestic and international fronts foreshadowed a less secure political future. Signals that the party had begun to pass its apex of power became clearer during this period, and specifically in the electoral arena, where the KMT enjoyed significant advantages over the tangwai opposition. The first election after the Chungli Incident and the 1979 Kaohsiung roundup was the 1980 supplementary election for the Legislative Yuan, for which about one-quarter of the seats (97) were up for grabs. The KMT won 82 percent of the contested seats in the legislature with 72 percent of the popular vote. Non-KMT candidates fared surprisingly well, however, especially considering that independent candidates did not have the resources and organizational advantages enjoyed by incumbent KMT candidates.

A decisive victory for the ruling regime, the 1980 election was nonetheless troubling for the KMT. Particularly striking and troubling was that its share of the popular vote declined from 78 percent in 1975 to 72 percent in 1980. The 1980 election was a turning point in the KMT's electoral dominance, in fact. The ruling party's popularity continued to decline throughout the 1980s, dipping below 60 percent in 1989.

Local elections in the first half of the 1980s showed a similar pattern. While the KMT continued to poll very well in limited supplemental elections, electoral results for non-KMT candidates continued to improve as support for opposition tangwai candidates grew. In the 1981 local elections, KMT candidates won the majority of contested seats, though non-KMT candidates, and specifically those affiliated with the tangwai, fared better than they had in any previous contests. Notable tangwai leaders such as Chen Shui-bian (who would eventually be democratically elected as Taiwan's president in 2000) and other activists, many of whom became notable DPP politicians in the 1990s, successfully won elections for seats in the Taipei city council, for county executive positions, and for seats in the Provincial Assembly.

Tangwai candidates continued to improve their showing in subsequent contests. In the 1985 Provincial Assembly elections, more than half the tangwai candidates who ran won seats. That same year, all of the tangwai candidates who ran in the Taipei city council elections won their districts. In other words, though the KMT was still politically preponderant, with absolutely no immediate threat to its hold on power, the gradual and irreversible growth in support for tangwai candidates was worrisome for the ruling party. As we explained in the introductory chapters to this book, electoral signals delivered the clearest possible message that the incumbent ruling party had passed its apex of power and that the KMT would have to adapt if it was to continue to politically thrive.

Democratic Opening

Adapting to thrive was not new to the KMT. Since arriving in Taiwan in the late 1940s, it had proved to be a highly adaptive party and one for which continual reform and adaptation had been critical to its political survival over several decades. That said, old habits die hard, and even when it was increasingly clear the KMT had passed its apex of political power by the 1980s, the party did not, overnight, shed its authoritarian stripes. Predictably, it continued to draw from its repertoire of suppression tactics to stymie its opposition.

Activists and dissidents continued to be jailed regularly into the 1980s. Some were even killed. Most infamously, in October 1984, two years before the opposition DPP formed, in an outrageous demonstration of its disregard for the rule of law, the KMT ordered the assassination of Henry Liu, an American citizen and journalist who was critical of the regime. The authoritarian regime brazenly admitted the assassination, though the general who ordered it was only lightly punished. Opposition activists latched onto this extraordinary event as evidence of the KMT's brutal and unrelenting dictatorship.

Yet in the fall of 1986, just a couple of years after the Liu assassination, tangwai politicians were permitted to create the DPP. President Chiang Ching-kuo then lifted martial law in 1987, sparking Taiwan's transition to democracy. Why did the KMT, as Steve Tsang puts it, "dismantle" the authoritarian controls underpinning the party-state and begin experimenting with democratic reform?[18] And why suddenly then?

The DPP was founded on September 28, 1986. The week before, tangwai activists gathered in Taipei and decided that despite martial law, it was time for an opposition political party to form. Government-controlled media and party officials, within days, mounted a campaign to discredit the DPP. It looked as though the DPP was going to be short-lived. On September 30, two days after the announcement of the DPP's creation, then–vice president Lee Teng-hui reported to President Chiang on the recently formed opposition party. According to Lee's journals, Chiang reacted calmly. He proclaimed, "At this time it is not good to resort to anger and recklessly take aggressive action that might cause great disturbances in society."

Chiang's conciliatory reaction contrasted starkly with his earlier response to the rise of opposition activists in the 1970s, when he instructed KMT loyalists to "go out among the people and control them so that we can take aim at our enemies and defeat them." In the wake of the DPP's formation in 1986, however, Chiang instructed the same KMT loyalists to "take no retaliatory action against the DPP." The KMT conceded the formation of the DPP.[19]

Bruce Jacobs, a critical voice when it comes to the KMT's role in democratizing Taiwan, reminds us that while Chiang "did contribute to Taiwan's ultimate democratization," he himself was no democrat. There is scant concrete evidence that Chiang suddenly embraced democratic principles and commitments. Nonetheless, his political decisions were pivotal in putting Taiwan on a path toward democracy. There is plenty of evidence to suggest Chiang had already begun to change his mind about the KMT's authoritarian hold on power before the critical events of 1986. As Jacobs points out, Chiang made clear in 1985 that Taiwan would not be ruled by a family dynasty, and that the next president would be someone from outside the Chiang family.[20] Chiang, to the surprise of many, chose Lee Teng-hui, an ethnic Taiwanese politician, to be his vice president and successor.

Chiang noted to a foreign journalist in 1983, three years before the formation of the DPP, that "political opponents in our society serve to generate progress," a marked departure from his views in the 1970s and an indication of his willingness to tolerate opposition voices in a gradually liberalizing Taiwan.[21] Most remarkably, after the DPP formed in defiance of martial law, Chiang famously conceded that the "times have changed; events have changed; trends have changed. In response to these changes, the ruling party must adopt new ways to meet this democratic revolution and link up with this historical trend."[22] Shelley Rigger, a leading authority on Taiwan's political development, puts it this way: "Persecution and repression gave way to toleration and competition."[23]

Taiwan's democratic opening, created by the DPP's unexpected formation in 1986 and followed by the KMT regime's even more unexpected acquiescence, set in motion Taiwan's democratic transition. The authoritarian dominos soon began to fall as the regime conceded other democratic reforms. Supplementary elections for a limited number of seats were held in December 1989 for the Legislative Yuan, and for the first time, candidates were permitted to run under an opposition party banner. In that unprecedented election, DPP candidates won nearly 25 percent of the popular vote and took twelve of seventy-three of the contested seats. Subsequently, full legislative elections were held in 1992, followed by Taiwan's first presidential contest in 1996, both landmark events in Taiwan's democratization.

Taiwan's democratic opening was not just reflected in changes in the electoral arena. The KMT regime also opened up political space in civil society. After the formation of the DPP in 1986, DPP and opposition activists took to the streets and staged demonstrations against the authoritarian state. Political protests specifically, as opposed to economic or environmental activism, nearly doubled in number from 1986 to 1987, as did the size of social protests.[24]

The regime did not repress. Instead, the KMT responded by releasing some political prisoners who had been jailed for their opposition activities. Most remarkably, the authoritarian regime lifted martial law in July 1987, ending nearly four decades of repressive rule. Although this decisive and watershed move was preceded by months of intense debate within the KMT leadership, there was no open dissent or defections once it occurred. Democratic concessions that rolled out one after the other reflected a party that was impressively unified, not intractably divided.

The regime loosened its authoritarian grip in other ways as well. In late 1987 the government allowed Taiwanese residents to visit China for the first time since before the KMT arrived in the late 1940s, reflecting the ruling party's moderating stance on cross-strait relations. On January 1, 1988, just weeks before his death, President Chiang lifted media restrictions, specifically those that were imposed on independent news sources critical of the KMT regime. This led to the proliferation of new dailies, magazines, radio stations, and television news networks, many of which carried stories and published editorials that would have led to their closing and censorship in authoritarian Taiwan. Social protest activity increased significantly from 1987 onward, as the number and size of social protests grew rapidly, and the central KMT government became the target of opposition mobilization. Virtually overnight, it seemed, Taiwan's political system and Taiwanese society had opened up.

The KMT's political about-face was confounding for several reasons. For one, Taiwan democratized in economically good times.[25] Unlike in many democratizing societies in which democratic reforms are conceded during severe economic crisis, Taiwan's democratic opening occurred when the economy was humming along as it had before, and society, for the most part, was stable. Taiwan's economy was strong, and in fact getting stronger. Employment rates continued to be high. Taiwan's industries were climbing the global value chain, and workers and employers alike were getting richer. It was not as though the KMT was presiding over a failing or even a limping economy in the mid-1980s; rather, it presided over a developmental state that most people on the island continue to credit for Taiwan's economic miracle.

Politically speaking, the party was also not in crisis, nor was the regime on the verge of collapse. It was not a party in even the very beginnings of any death spiral to obsolescence. Social protests increased in 1987, though comparatively speaking, political protests in Taiwan were few and tiny compared with other authoritarian countries, notably South Korea and the *minjung* protests of the mid-1980s, which rallied hundreds of thousands of protesters in the streets. What transpired in Taiwan was definitely not an example of democracy through weakness, such as we saw in the Philippines a few years before as Ferdinand Marcos was chased out of the country and his overthrown regime left in tatters after the People Power movement.

Furthermore, there was no political party waiting in the wings in Taiwan, ready to replace the KMT. Despite impressive electoral gains by tangwai politicians and independent candidates during the late 1970s and early 1980s, the KMT remained the dominant political force in the Legislative Yuan and executive branch of the government. Though the party's popularity was clearly on the gradual decline, the downward curve was not steep. Even after the KMT violently crushed the Chungli and Kaohsiung protests during the 1970s, and the party took a hit in the polls, it continued to win more than two-thirds of the popular vote in legislative elections. In other words, the emerging opposition was in no position to seriously threaten the KMT and its hold on power. And yet, despite this—or as we argue, because of this—the KMT conceded democracy.

Conceding with Confidence

We contend that the KMT chose to concede democracy not because of any imminent threat to its hold on political power but precisely because there was no real threat to the party's political dominance, *even after full-blown democratization*. The KMT had passed its apex of power by the mid-1980s, but it was *just* past the apex. Hence conceding democracy at that time was not necessarily bad for the KMT, nor would it be calamitous for its political fortunes going forward.

As the paradigmatic case of democracy through strength, the KMT conceded democracy in large part *because of* its overwhelming strengths. Electoral signals were clear that the KMT faced an emergent opposition, but the signals were nonetheless reassuring to the incumbent regime that its hold on power—even in a democracy—would remain strong. In the first supplemental legislative elections in 1989, after the end of martial law and when the DPP participated as an official party, the KMT polled 59 percent of the popular vote and won 68 percent of the contested seats. The ruling party retained its supermajority in the Legislative Yuan.

As we stress in our theory of democracy through strength, when an authoritarian ruling party passes the apex of power, it finds itself in a "bittersweet" spot. This is the ideal time to consider a strategy of democracy through strength. It is "bitter" because the party has passed its apex of power, but nonetheless "sweet" because the incumbent party, in this case the KMT, retains a more than sufficiently broad coalition of support to make it likely the authoritarian-turned-democratic party would fare well in democracy. If the party is especially strong, like the KMT, then it may even continue to be dominant.

As we will see in the next chapter, the incumbent authoritarian regime in South Korea was also strong but not as strong as the KMT in Taiwan. The

South Korean regime's electoral popularity was much lower than the KMT's, and the Chun Doo-hwan regime confronted a much larger and sustained opposition movement. Simply put, the concession strategy in South Korea was much riskier for the incumbent regime. For the KMT, on the other hand, conceding democracy was quite clearly not tantamount to conceding defeat. As political scientist Bruce Dickson puts it, accepting democracy and initiating reform in Taiwan were the party's "best means to maintain their hold on power . . . and improve the KMT's reputation abroad."[26] Ironically, democracy through strength was not only good for Taiwan but also ultimately good for the KMT.

The KMT's greatest source of confidence regarding its prospects in democracy came from the party's credible claim to have directed Taiwan's postwar economic miracle. Starting with land reform in the early 1950s, followed by investments in education during the 1960s, the KMT-led developmental state put Taiwan's economy on a path to not only rapid growth but to equitable economic growth. The state's emphasis on nurturing the development of SMEs enabled most Taiwanese to benefit from economic modernization. Local industrial firms were supported by state policies—from targeted fiscal incentives to subsidies for high-tech R&D—that protected and incentivized Taiwan's infant companies to become globally competitive and to plug into global value chains. The KMT's developmental record, combined with a credible promise of continued growth into the future, won the KMT tremendous amounts of performance legitimacy. The ruling party was confident this legitimacy would translate into electoral support in democracy.

The KMT was confident about its prospects in democracy for several other, more proximate reasons as well. First, and perhaps most importantly, the KMT enjoyed a tremendous electoral advantage over the DPP. As the incumbent party—and until 1986, the *only* political party in Taiwan—the KMT had amassed a massive grassroots membership base as well as a top-down organizational structure that allowed the party to penetrate deep into society. Furthermore, as discussed earlier in this chapter, the KMT recruited local and ethnically Taiwanese officials into the party rank and file and for leadership roles in the government, anchoring the ruling party in Taiwanese political society and attempting to shed the image of the KMT as an émigré regime. The ruling party had also established a formidable political machinery at the time of Taiwan's democratic opening, in control of vast networks of party cells that could deliver votes in local electoral districts. Having initiated supplemental elections beginning in 1966, the KMT had gained experience in contesting elections, which ultimately helped it retain an electoral advantage in democracy.

As the incumbent ruling party, the KMT also possessed the power to lead Taiwan's political transition by shaping the rules of the democratic game. Similar to the conservative parties in postwar Japan, the KMT crafted rules that advantaged the incumbent party, while remaining consistent with democratic processes. Notably, the regime adopted a single nontransferable vote and multimember district electoral system, which heavily favored the KMT. The KMT, due to its size and vast party resources, was able to strategically nominate candidates and allocate votes within a single district. The DPP, meanwhile, possessed neither the candidate pool nor the resources to keep up with the incumbent party. In addition, the opposition DPP was deeply factionalized between moderate and radical wings, making it difficult for the party to coordinate candidate nominations in multimember electoral districts. The electoral map and the apportionment of electoral seats also gave the KMT, like the LDP in Japan, a disproportionate seat bonus in rural areas where the ruling party was particularly effective in winning votes, and where the opposition was notably weak. The DPP found its electoral strongholds in the cities among the educated Taiwanese elites.

In other words, while democratization in Taiwan introduced free and *fairer* elections, the electoral rules of the game, combined with the KMT's incumbent power, meant the KMT could be confident that it would thrive in democracy. Though the rules governing the political playing field were leveled, the massive disparity in the parties' antecedent strengths made it, at least early on in Taiwan's democratic experience, an unfair fight. This unfairness was a product of the KMT's inherited strengths, not any intrinsic unfairness or undemocratic character of the electoral rules the KMT insisted on.

Another proximate source of confidence for the KMT was that it could credibly claim to be the party of democratic reform. It was proactive in pursuing political reform, not a stand-pat party that resisted democracy until the bitter end. Even before the formation of the DPP in 1986, Chiang Ching-kuo had begun to coalesce the moderate faction within the KMT, paving the way for eventual party leader and vice president Lee Teng-hui to consolidate the reform-oriented "mainstream" faction inside the party. The moderate mainstream faction proved critical in marginalizing and exorcising the hard-line KMT faction, who were opponents of democracy. The consolidation of Lee's power and of the mainstream faction solidified the moderate wing of the party and legitimated its willingness to engage in democratic dialogue with the opposition.

As early as 1984, President Chiang had reached out to moderate opposition tangwai activists to start political dialogues about political reform. The discussions helped the KMT identify moderate leaders within its ranks and their counterparts in the opposition. Gathering moderates from the two sides reassured the KMT that the eventual formation of an opposition party would not lead to a radicalization and potential destabilization of politics. The pretransition dialogue allowed moderate factions in both parties to become familiar with one another as well, even before the official formation of the DPP.

By the time the writing was on the wall in the months leading up to the formation of the DPP in 1986, the KMT, again at Chiang's explicit orders, initiated dialogue "with the opposition to increase mutual understanding" between the two parties.[27] Moderates from both the KMT and the tangwai emphasized the need for political harmony, agreeing to, among other reforms, the need for a new constitution and the creation of the tangwai-affiliated Public Policy Research Association, the organizational precursor to the DPP.

Despite the KMT's dictatorial past, the ruling party was able to draw on its republican foundation and anticommunist bona fides to legitimate its democratic turn. Chiang referred to Sun Yat-sen's Three Principles to anchor the KMT's democratic republican heritage and legitimate the party's vision of a democratic future. Chiang asserted the party must "initiate democratic, constitutional government; do away with dictatorship and class warfare; really implement a way for our people to determine their destiny; return political power to the people; and make them entirely equal before the law."[28] That Chiang made this statement during the KMT's plenum meetings in March 1985, eighteen months before the formation of the DPP, gave further credibility to the moderate wing of the KMT leading democratic reform.

In the end, Taiwan's democratic transition was less rocky than most other democratic experiments in developmental Asia. Much of that stability could be attributed to efforts by both the KMT and the opposition to moderate their positions around a democratic blueprint, even before the transition process began. Moderation was important to the KMT's confidence that democratization would neither foment political instability nor threaten the ruling party's ability to retain political power, at least in the near term. From the opposition's point of view, the transition, even if the KMT's fingerprints were all over it, meant the DPP could legitimately contest democratic elections as a political party, and that it might, no matter how remote a possibility at the time, eventually defeat the KMT and become a democratically elected ruling party in Taiwan.[29] The opposition was also invested in Taiwan's democratic prospects.

Consolidating the KMT's Democratic Dominance

On the eve of Taiwan's democratic transition, the KMT was the strongest incumbent party among the dozen cases examined in this book, confident that democratization would threaten neither Taiwan's political and economic stability nor the KMT's hold on power. When the KMT initiated democratic reform beginning in the late 1980s, the ruling party continued to poll a majority of voters' popular support and presided over a booming economy. Social protest, while on the rise, was nowhere near the size and scale of political protest that we saw in South Korea during its transition to democracy. Geopolitically, conceding democracy was good for the KMT and Taiwan because it ensured continued American support, even though the superpower had normalized relations with China. In the spectrum of "concession cases" that pursued democracy through strength examined in this book, *the KMT was the strongest among incumbent authoritarian parties, the most confident that conceding democracy would be stable, and the most likely to continue as a democratic ruling party.*[30]

As we expect in our theory of democracy through strength, the strongest incumbent parties that choose to concede democracy will predictably prevail as the strongest political party *after* a democratic transition. Going from strength to strength, the KMT did indeed remain the dominant political force in Taiwan's young democracy.

In the 1992 legislature elections—Taiwan's first free elections for the entire legislative body—the KMT won 53 percent of the popular vote and took 63 percent of the legislature's seats. In the founding presidential elections of 1996, the KMT ticket of Lee Teng-hui and Lien Chan won easily, with 54 percent support from voters. Meanwhile, the DPP candidate, longtime dissident Peng Ming-min, won just 21 percent of the vote. The KMT's democratic gamble paid off; it conceded democracy not to hand over power to the opposition but to retain its political dominance.

The KMT's early electoral success ironically helped normalize democracy in Taiwan, rather than derail it or prompt a democratic backslide. It was not as though the KMT took its early election victories in 1992 and 1996 as a sign that Taiwanese voters wanted a return to KMT authoritarianism; that ship had sailed. The KMT instead saw its ongoing electoral success as an imperative to further reform and to transition the party into becoming a truly *democratic* and democratically dominant political party. *The KMT hastened democratic transition because of the confidence it had in its ability to fare well in democracy.* It is not the case that dominant democratic parties will necessarily spoil or roll back democracy at the first sign of political trouble. With respect to the KMT, the incumbent ruling party continued a reform trajectory precisely because the party was poised to thrive.

While the KMT ensured its own advantages in democracy, notably with the multimember district electoral system, the ruling party also exercised ongoing democratic restraint after Taiwan's democratic opening. Democratic restraint begot democratic deepening, which further leveled the political playing field for the opposition and imposed democratic safeguards within the KMT.

After Chiang died in 1988, his successor, Lee, convened the 1990 National Affairs Conference (NAC). The NAC brought together KMT and opposition leaders to build consensus around additional political reforms. In the run-up to the NAC, Lee successfully solidified the KMT's reform-oriented mainstream faction, fending off his authoritarian rivals in the party. The political moderation of the KMT, with Lee at the helm, enticed opposition DPP leaders to the negotiating table in 1990, just as Chiang's efforts to bolster the moderate camp in the KMT camp did in the mid-1980s. At the 1990 conference, leaders from the KMT and the DPP drew up a blueprint for democratic reform, including agreements on constitutional reform and the introduction of full legislative and presidential elections. The NAC forum was revitalized in several negotiating forums in the ensuing years, during which KMT leaders and their DPP counterparts laid out further democratic reforms.

Under the democratic rules of the game, the KMT could no longer maintain power through authoritarian means, such as suppressing dissent, but instead needed to win highly competitive elections. The incumbent party needed to broaden its electoral base of support. Taking a page from the LDP's playbook in Japan, the KMT grew its base of support by moderating its policy platforms and programs, focusing, for instance, on policies that explicitly promoted more economic redistribution to narrow the gap between the rich and poor.

Like the LDP, the KMT positioned itself as a catch-all party, crowding out the opposition on popular issues such as economic reform and social policy expansion. Beginning in the 1990s, the KMT introduced a flurry of new social and economic policies, much as the LDP did in Japan during the 1960s when the conservative ruling party consolidated its electoral power. The KMT government initiated significant social welfare policy reforms and expanded the scope of coverage and benefits in existing social programs, such as the government-managed labor insurance scheme as well as workplace benefits.

The logic of the KMT's political strategy was clearest in the example of healthcare reform. In 1988 the KMT announced a plan to introduce a universal national health insurance program in 1995, winning the KMT considerable support among urban workers and rural farmers on the eve of Taiwan's first legislative election. With pressure from President Lee, the government officially launched the national health insurance program just months before Taiwan's first presidential election in 1996. The implementation of the universal health insurance scheme was a significant social policy achievement and one that cut into the DPP's electoral base, especially its social democratic faction.

The ruling party employed a similar catch-all strategy in other elections. In local-level contests, KMT candidates introduced old-age income security programs to appeal to older voters, forcing the DPP to follow suit and make similar social policy promises. The key point is that the KMT's continued political dominance into the 1990s was not simply a holdover from its authoritarian past but rather due in part to its deliberate efforts to moderate its policies and platforms to appeal to more voters.[31] The KMT, in other words, was not merely "gaming democracy"[32] but "game for democracy,"[33] and it was figuring out ways to win at it.

Normalizing Democracy in Taiwan

Nothing is guaranteed in democracy. Indeed, democracy equals the institutionalization of political uncertainty, as Adam Przeworski reminds us. The KMT's electoral dominance could not be a foregone conclusion forever. The normalization of democracy requires at least the *possibility* of an alternation in power. Otherwise, the opposition might not see the value of democracy, and defect because the democratic institutions are perceived to be so shallow, and the political playing field so uneven or unfair, that they are mere window dressing for an authoritarian regime.

Opposition defection and democratic backsliding did not happen in Taiwan, however. The KMT's firm hold on power, once seemingly unassailable, gradually diminished as democracy became normalized. In 1993 the remnants of the hard-line faction within the KMT splintered off to form the New Party. The New Party was a fringe party at best, though it nonetheless cut into the KMT's seat share in the Legislative Yuan. In the 1995 legislative elections, as expected, the KMT won a smaller majority, with 52 percent of legislative seats, down from 59 percent in 1992.

Importantly, as democracy became more normalized in Taiwan, the opposition's prospects to unseat the KMT improved. Between the 1992 and 1995 Legislative Yuan elections, the DPP's seat share improved slightly, from 51 seats to 54. The DPP's share of the popular vote also increased slightly from 31 percent to 33 percent. The KMT, in the meantime, experienced a significant dip not only in its seat share in the legislature but also in the popular vote, declining from 53 percent of the vote in 1992 to 46 percent in 1995. This was due in part to the gains made by the New Party as well as the improved showing of the DPP over several elections. The DPP was clearly not a flash in the pan but rather a political party that was there to stay.

Taiwan's democracy experienced its first alternation in power in the 2000 presidential elections, when the DPP candidate Chen Shui-bian narrowly defeated the KMT slate with 39 percent of the vote. Chen won again in 2004, though by a smaller margin. The election of Chen to the presidency in 2000 marked a critical juncture for the KMT, and ultimately for the fate of Taiwan's democratization. Though the KMT continued to control a majority of seats in the legislature, the 2000 presidential election was the first time the KMT had lost an election in Taiwan—*any* election. It was unclear at the time how the KMT would react to its first defeat. Some speculated the KMT might roll back democratic reform and resuscitate the party's authoritarian past, and that it may become a democratic spoiler when it suffered its first defeat.[34]

Instead, the KMT regrouped. After suffering another, even narrower defeat in the presidential elections in 2004, the KMT chose then–Taipei mayor Ma Ying-jeou to become the new party leader. Ma was popular among voters and viewed by many at the time as a young, charismatic, and, importantly, moderate leader. The party also actively recast its image by implementing more democratic reforms within the party. Rather than choosing to become a democratic spoiler, as some might expect of a former authoritarian party whose electoral fortunes continued to decline, the KMT chose to double down on deepening its commitment to democracy and investing in the party's democratic competitiveness.

The KMT chose the path of normalizing democracy for several reasons, all of which stemmed from the party's strengths and confidence that it would continue to thrive in democracy, even as it suffered periodic electoral defeats. For one, the KMT continued to highlight its past developmental record, appealing to voters with the message that it was the party equipped to sustain

Taiwan's economic development. It continued to moderate its social and economic policy platforms, putting more emphasis on redistributive programs in an effort to broaden the catch-all party's base of support. The KMT claimed the DPP, on the other hand, was unproven in governing and narrowly focused on specific issues. Meanwhile, the KMT continued to enjoy a significant seat bonus in the countryside, meaning its declining popular vote share did not threaten its majority in the Legislative Yuan.

The KMT started the path toward democracy in Taiwan because of its confidence and its incumbent sources of strength, and it remained confident despite presidential election defeats in 2000 and 2004. To put things in perspective, those electoral setbacks were not especially devastating for the former ruling party. The defeats were by small margins, especially in the razor-thin 2004 contest. Despite having lost the presidency, the KMT continued to control a majority of seats in the Legislative Yuan throughout the 2000s. In other words, it retained the strengths and confidence it possessed when it conceded democracy in the first place.

Though the former ruling party was technically "in the woods" (i.e., no longer in power), the KMT also knew that it was not *that far* in the woods and that it was very unlikely it would permanently stay there. It was confident it would return to power in the not-so-distant future. It did in fact return to power when Ma easily won the 2008 presidential election and again in 2012. The KMT continued to dominate in the legislature, though it suffered a series of stinging defeats in subsequent presidential contests. Still, it chose not to be a democratic spoiler, because under democratic rules of the game it could compete again in future contests, and as a strong party with a deep reservoir of inherited strengths, it was confident it would be competitive again, and perennially so.[35]

5

South Korea

DEMOCRACY IN FITS AND STARTS

THE SUMMER OF 1987 in South Korea was a tumultuous one. Students, workers, and their middle-class allies took to the streets in Seoul to protest the authoritarian regime, which had ruled over South Korea in successive waves under different military dictators since the 1960s. Hundreds of thousands of protesters who mobilized across the entire country had had enough. They demanded political reform, and specifically that South Korea go the path toward liberal democracy.

Such political drama had played out before in postwar South Korea. However, this time the outcome was different. South Korea's outgoing president, General Chun Doo-hwan, identified his successor, Roh Tae-woo, that summer, in what many expected to be a smooth transition of authoritarian power from one dictator to the next. Under immense pressure from South Korean civil society and the US government, however, Roh "shocked the country" and conceded democratic reform, announcing in late June 1987 that a presidential election would be held in December, with free and fair legislative elections the following spring. In an abrupt about-face, South Korea started along a path toward what would become one of developmental Asia's most enduring democracies.[1]

South Korea's democratic triumph was not a foregone conclusion. In fact, the South Korean regime was widely expected to have become democratic much sooner, but it had failed many times to consolidate a lasting democracy. If we think of democratic transition as a reversible experiment in political reform, then South Korean democratization had been, until the late 1980s, a perennial series of failures.

In the immediate post–World War II period, the US military occupied the southern portion of the Korean peninsula, and the Soviet Union administered the North. The goal of the US-led occupation was to install democracy in South Korea, not unlike in postwar Japan. The South Korean occupation even had its own version of General Douglas MacArthur in Lieutenant General John Hodge. And yet, despite democratic success in Japan, as we described in chapter 3, prospects in South Korea quickly became bleak against the back-drop of the Korean War from 1950 to 1953 and the failure of South Korea's first democratic experiment, which ushered in a military regime in 1961.

Edward Wagner, considered the pioneer of Korean studies in America, pub-lished an article in *Foreign Affairs* in 1961 entitled "Failure in Korea."[2] The title of his essay says it all. His was a pessimistic take on the state of political and economic affairs in South Korea and the country's future. Wagner bitterly noted that "in South Korea today, 16 years after the United States set out to help instill the art of democratic self-government among its people, we find ourselves with an openly authoritarian regime."

If one looked only at Japan, one might believe America had the unrelenting power to "impose" a lasting democracy anywhere after World War II. South Korea's simultaneous historical experience, however, shows that America alone had no such power. *Democracy would only take root in developmental Asia where conservatives were strong enough to thrive under it.* This was not to be the case in immediate postwar South Korea.

In many ways, South Korea's path from economic development to eventual democratization would come to mirror Taiwan's experience, as parallel exem-plars of the developmental statist cluster of cases examined in this book. Similar to Taiwan, the South Korean developmental state facilitated industrialization, economic modernization, and societal transformation, sowing the seeds of a more politically demanding society. Also similar to the Kuomintang (KMT), the postwar authoritarian regime in South Korea was initially weak, corrupt, and internally fragmented, though successive dictatorships accumulated tre-mendous developmental capacity over time. Authoritarian consolidation in South Korea began during the 1960s. The once weak state and ruling regime became extremely powerful, sustained through a combination of economic performance legitimacy and the regime's brutal repressive power.

By the time Roh introduced democracy in 1987, the authoritarian regime had clearly passed its apex of power. As in Taiwan, performance legitimacy generated from economic development alone was no longer sufficient to keep

South Korea's increasingly demanding society at bay. Also as with the KMT, the South Korean regime was not politically out of touch but rather attuned to various signals of its weakening grip on power, from clearly devastating election results in 1985; to the mobilization of antiregime contentious politics; to waning support from the United States and even direct and public pressure from the US government on the regime to embrace democracy.

Under these conditions of quickly rising pressures and slowly shrinking dominance, incumbent leaders in South Korea gambled. They calculated that the regime retained enough power, if not preponderant power, as well as enough legitimacy born of its remarkable record of developmental success to survive a democratic transition, and potentially even thrive in democracy. Authoritarianism in South Korea did not collapse, nor was the regime overthrown, but rather the incumbent ruling party introduced and led the democratization process, much as we saw in chapter 4 on Taiwan. In this respect, South Korea is another example of democracy through strength.

However, as we point out, strong states and strong parties are not equally strong across cases and over time, and even highly effective developmental states, such as Taiwan's and South Korea's, are arrayed across *a spectrum of strength*. While the KMT maintained and increased its grip on authoritarian power over time, authoritarian rule in South Korea was less continuous, divided into eras and successive regimes, each one headed by a different dictator. The story of Taiwan could be told through the lens of the KMT, a single regime under a single ruling party. But for South Korea, the story is one of successive authoritarian regimes in which the name of the ruling party changed and the military played a much more forward role than in Taiwan. South Korea's political development vacillated, with moments of political opening and democratic experimentation followed by longer periods of authoritarian enclosure.[3]

By the time Roh conceded democratic reforms in 1987, the incumbent ruling party was still quite strong, but not nearly as politically dominant as the KMT was in Taiwan. Reflecting a weaker instance of authoritarian-led democratic transition, the South Korean case is nonetheless illustrative of democracy through strength—albeit a democracy that developed in fits and starts, with an uncertain fate for the incumbent authoritarian regime when it conceded democracy in 1987.

South Korea's First Failed Democracy

Korea was a victim of Japanese colonialism from 1910 to the end of World War II. Its colonial experience was especially brutal, and anti-Japanese sentiment was deeply implanted in the Korean national psyche. Economic extraction, military occupation, and human atrocities, such as the exploitation of Korean "comfort women," left postwar Korea in shambles, economically and politically. Japan's surrender in 1945 was a welcome restart for Korea, ushering in the possibility of Korean independence, self-reliant economic development, and democracy.

Immediately after the war, and with emerging Cold War tensions, the Korean peninsula was administratively divided, with the 38th parallel marking the Soviet jurisdiction in the North and the American occupation in the South. The US military occupation lasted from 1945 to the fall of 1948, a shorter period than its occupation of Japan. From Washington's point of view, there was much to do to rebuild Korea in the wake of World War II, and in a short amount of time. Chief among American objectives was to introduce democratic institutions, and specifically a democratic constitution, as in Japan. American leaders perceived a democratic impulse at the time in South Korea, as they did in Japan, and occupation leaders looked to grow that impulse into a full-fledged democracy. Unlike in Taiwan, which was not occupied by the Americans and where the KMT dictatorship was more or less tolerated by its American allies, US aspirations for democracy in South Korea were central to the occupation from the start.

The American occupation authorities, headed by Hodge, essentially copied MacArthur's playbook for transforming Japan. Between 1945 and 1948, occupation authorities consulted Korean elites and an emerging political leadership class about installing a democratic constitution. As in Japan, occupation leaders led this consultative process. Early on, Hodge outlined the "Proclamation on the Rights of the Korean People," a blueprint for political reform. Mirroring the Japanese experience, Hodge's proclamation ensured all South Koreans would be "equal before the law" and that their "personal liberty" would be "inviolable." As was the case in Japan, the American occupation sought to create a South Korean democracy in its own image. To the extent a democratic experiment was imposed on Japan, the same could be said of America's aspirations in South Korea.

The US proclamation inspired the content of the constitution, which the South Korean National Assembly formally adopted in the summer of 1948.

The constitution's general provisions stated that South Korea was to be a democratic republic, thereby establishing its sovereign independence and laying the groundwork for its democratic evolution. Democratic institutions were swiftly installed. The military was put under the authority of the civilian government. Executive, legislative, and judicial branches were created, providing democratic checks and balances on political power. Political parties were one of the bedrocks of democratic competition.

South Korean voters elected the National Assembly in 1948, and the legislature elected South Korea's first president, Syngman Rhee. American-educated and a staunch anticommunist, Rhee was considered an ally by the United States, even though the occupation leadership did not completely trust him. They saw Rhee as a political opportunist. His democratic bona fides were suspect because of his lack of a democratic activist résumé. Given the emerging Cold War context at the time, however, American authorities had little choice but to accept him as their man in Seoul.

It soon became clear the South Korean democratic constitution was vulnerable to authoritarian practices under Rhee.[4] Two articles (Articles 28 and 57) allowed the government and the president specifically to suspend and impose restrictions on citizens' rights in the interest of "public order" during "extraordinary times." These kinds of stipulations are common in constitutional democracies. The expectation, however, is that these extraordinary constitutional powers would be used only under the most extreme circumstances. This proved to be shortsighted in Rhee's South Korea. Prompted by mass protests and a government crackdown, the National Assembly passed the National Security Law in December 1948, which gave the president the coercive power to suppress the opposition. The National Security Law empowered the regime to prosecute and imprison "enemies of the state," including opponents to the Rhee regime.

Despite such extraordinary and repressive powers at his disposal, Rhee was actually a politically weak president. He did not have a strong power base in either his party or the military. One of the main contentions of this book is that party strength facilitates a stable transition from autocracy to democracy. In Taiwan, the party reorganization campaign of the early 1950s transformed not only the internal structure of the KMT but also its reach into society, specifically the penetration of party cells throughout the island. The KMT also initiated a mass membership campaign during this period to bolster the party's rank and file and strengthen its roots in Taiwan society. Likewise, in Japan, the importance of early democratic experiments and the legacy of Taisho-era parties provided the institutional and organizational foundation for the consolidation of the Liberal Democratic Party (LDP) in the postwar period. In South Korea, however, the transition from foreign occupation (both Japanese and American) yielded more paltry institutional fruit. As a result, democracy stumbled as it came out of the gate.

Rhee's party, the Liberal Party, lacked organizational capacity. Unlike the LDP and KMT, the South Korean Liberal Party did not grow its mass-based membership and was unable to mobilize its rank and file, leaving the party vulnerable to challenges from the opposition. During the 1950s, the Liberal Party never polled more than 45 percent of the popular vote, ceding more and more electoral ground to the opposition Democratic Party. Moreover, unlike the LDP and KMT, Rhee did not mount an organizational campaign to strengthen the ruling party's capacity to penetrate deeply in South Korean society. He in fact alienated other leaders within his own Liberal Party. Factionalism and corruption weakened the party from within.

Confirming the United States' worst fears about him, Rhee proved ultimately to be a fair-weather democrat at best, intent on maintaining power by intimidation through the police and the state's internal security apparatus rather than the consent of South Korean citizens. Early on in his reign, Rhee used the National Security Law several times to maintain political order. Starting in the late 1940s and through the 1950s, the government routinely and brutally suppressed protest movements, including the infamous Cheju Island uprising of 1948, during which thousands of protesters were violently repressed and arrested. This was followed by the 1949 Mungyeong massacre, when the police killed nearly a hundred unarmed civilians, including children.

In the meantime, Cold War tensions between the United States and the Soviet Union, and by proxy South and North Korea, continued to fracture the Korean peninsula. A "hot" war between the North and South was clearly on the horizon by the late 1940s. When the Korean War erupted in 1950, Rhee again invoked the National Security Law to clamp down on domestic opposition to his government. Fears of internal communist subversion ran rampant in South Korea in the late 1940s and 1950s, which justified the imposition of the state's draconian emergency powers.

Geopolitically, the Korean War deepened the codependency between Seoul and Washington, complicating an already fraught relationship. Given Rhee's anticommunist position and the strategic imperative for the United States to contain the threat of communist expansion in the region, Washington was forced to deepen its alliance with Rhee. To contain communist expansion in Asia required it to placate the Rhee regime with military, economic, and even tacit political support. Rhee, meanwhile, increasingly tightened the authoritarian screws. Estimates suggest that under the Rhee regime, hundreds of thousands of South Koreans were detained and prosecuted, and many killed, on suspicion of being communist sympathizers.

Aside from brute force and suppression, however, authoritarian regimes can depend on economic development and performance legitimacy to fend off challenges to their power. In Taiwan, the KMT's developmental state was effective in generating economic performance legitimacy, which, alongside the KMT's autocratic capacity, sustained the authoritarian regime for nearly four decades. In the next chapter, we will see how, a bit later in the Cold War period, rapid economic development shored up military-dominated regimes in Indonesia and Thailand. The South Korean economy, on the other hand, remained sluggish in the early postwar period under Rhee. His regime scored low on performance legitimacy, leaving him vulnerable to replacement by an authoritarian regime promising more effective developmental rule.

Historically, the southern portion of the peninsula was agricultural, and it stayed that way during the period of Japanese colonialism. The colonial regime invested in the North's industrial development while neglecting the South. When World War II ended, the southern part of the Korean peninsula remained largely agricultural. South Korea faced an energy shortage as well, making it unable to fuel its initial industrial takeoff. Unemployment rates skyrocketed, exacerbated by massive rates of inflation in the early part of the 1950s. Whereas Taiwan quickly got its economic fundamentals right relatively early on in the postwar period, South Korea lagged behind.

Despite American economic and military aid, South Korea remained economically underdeveloped, and with little reason for optimism. To make matters worse, the Korean War, which ended with the 1953 armistice, contributed to further devastation of South Korea's economy. The physical destruction from the war alone amounted to nearly two times the value of South Korea's entire economy in 1953. Rhee's corrupt regime siphoned millions of aid dollars that flowed to South Korea, padding his personal wealth and that of his cronies while impoverishing millions of South Koreans. Per capita gross national product in 1953 was US$67 and increased only marginally to $79 in 1960.

Without performance legitimacy to sustain the Rhee regime and without a plan to develop the economy, the government experienced a series of setbacks during the latter half of the 1950s. Opposition party support continued to grow as Rhee's Liberal Party failed to put together a winning majority in the National Assembly. Protesters were increasingly emboldened, calling out the Rhee administration for its corruption and economic mismanagement, culminating in the April 19 Uprising in 1960. Thousands of students and workers took to the streets. The security forces, sensing the impending demise of the Rhee regime, refused to fire on the protesters.[5]

Internal factionalism fractured Rhee's own Liberal Party. Some in the ruling party began to reach out quietly to opposition leaders to negotiate possible reforms and their own exit strategies. In the 1960 National Assembly elections, Rhee's Liberal Party won just two of 233 contested seats. Many Rhee supporters jumped ship when his party was thoroughly defeated, instead of sticking around to rebuild the party. Rhee's poor leadership of the Liberal Party drove it into oblivion. The president had no choice but to resign and step down from power. Though Rhee himself was a strong*man* ruler, he never controlled a strong political *party*. By the time his reign ended, his government on death's door, Rhee lacked any organizational power base to manage his political exit. He lived in exile, a despot discredited, until his death in 1965.

Shaky Interregnum

Rhee's exit sparked some hope for a democratic turnaround in South Korea. From the debris of Rhee's crumbled administration arose Chang Myon, who led the opposition Democratic Party to a decisive victory in the 1960 National Assembly elections. In the wake of the elections, the original 1948 constitution was promptly reformed, eliminating many of the powers that had been abused by Rhee. South Korean lawmakers also crafted a new constitution to strengthen parliamentary rather than presidential institutions. The role of the president, for instance, became ceremonial, and the prime minister gained executive powers over the cabinet. The National Assembly elected Chang prime minister in August 1960.

The Democratic Party had won a massive majority of seats in the National Assembly. Despite this, the new ruling party was organizationally weak, divided along irreconcilable factional lines between contending party elders. The party was not ideologically divided so much as it was fractured along personalist lines among the party's leaders. Chang led one faction, and he was unable to win the support of the other major factions. Unlike Lee Teng-hui in Taiwan, who deftly maneuvered to consolidate his support within the ruling KMT in the late 1980s, Prime Minister Chang was unable to cobble together a reform coalition inside the Democratic Party. South Korea's new governing party was paralyzed, unable to break legislative impasses and internal party deadlocks. This hindered South Korea's developmental restart. Despite efforts by the Chang faction to revitalize several economic initiatives, predictably they all failed. South Korea's economy grew just 1 percent in 1960.

Chang lacked other political power bases as well. Notably, he did little to win American support for his regime. A foreign-policy dove, he tried to choke off the military's resources, a move that irritated American decision makers. While the United States was keen to see Rhee go, it did not welcome Chang's attempt to demilitarize South Korea, which undermined America's Cold War efforts to contain communist expansion. Chang also defanged the internal security apparatus that Rhee had relied on to repress the opposition. He did not, however, pursue the prosecution of former president Rhee, even though the evidence overwhelmingly pointed to his corruption and perversion of South Korea's democratic constitution. While Chang attempted to undo many of the repressive institutions Rhee had put in place, South Korean society saw Chang to be weak on the former president, prompting hundreds of thousands of protesters to mobilize against the new government throughout 1960 and 1961. The Chang government was barely hanging on less than one year in.[6]

Whereas Rhee prolonged his regime through brutal, strongman tactics, despite having a weak party, Chang was a weak leader who inherited an internally divided ruling political party. He was not a strongman, nor did he have a strong organizational power base in his own political party. *The quickly fleeting experiment with democracy under Chang was thus an example of democracy through weakness, not strength.* The transitional interregnum was unstable and rocky from the start, and without a strong ruling party, democracy was unstable. South Korea had democratized through weakness rather than strength in 1960, yielding a democracy that was weak and unstable rather than strong and stable.

Not surprisingly, Chang's government ended as abruptly as it began, when General Park Chung-hee successfully launched a swift military coup in 1961. As South Korea's economy stagnated and its political institutions deteriorated under the corrupt Rhee regime, followed by the anemic Chang administration, Park formulated a new political and economic vision for a modern South Korea. As with others in the developmental statist cluster, nationalism and national self-reliance were central to Park's plan for South Korea's social, economic, and political development. Democracy, however, was not.

Developmental Authoritarianism

Before assessing the Park regime and how it transformed South Korea from weak to strong authoritarianism over the course of the 1960s and 1970s, it is worth underscoring how little democratic content South Korea's regime possessed before Park's 1961 coup. The regime had essentially been bogged down, in fits and starts, between democracy and authoritarianism throughout the 1950s. In this regard, beginning in the 1960s, the Park regime was not more authoritarian than its predecessors; it was not as though Park dismantled or reversed robust democracy in favor of authoritarianism. Rather, the critical point is that the Park regime was decisively more *developmental*.

Soon after the May 16, 1961, coup, Park hit the political restart button and established the Supreme Council for National Reconstruction, the political nerve center for his regime. As a career military man, Park ruled with the support of the military, a power base neither Rhee nor Chang was able to draw from during their administrations. Though Park enforced his rule with the backing of the military, he governed South Korea through the Democratic Republican Party (DRP). The ruling party was the organizational apparatus through which Park exercised political power. Other political parties were permitted to contest elections during the 1960s, though the electoral rules were highly skewed in favor of the ruling DRP, eliminating any chance the opposition had to win.

To be sure, Park did not hide his disdain for liberal democracy, which he described as an "abstract, useless concept." In his mind, South Korea could not achieve political modernization and democratic transition without economic development. He espoused the tenets of modernization theory, and specifically the sequencing of economic modernization before political transformation. He elaborated his theories of development in his famous essay *The Country, the Revolution and I*, asserting that underdeveloped countries, such as South Korea, "have to resort to undemocratic and extraordinary measures in order to improve the living conditions of the masses." Democracy would have to wait.[7]

From Park's point of view, so long as South Korea was poor and its economy underdeveloped, it was not in a position to experiment with political democratization; and South Korea was still very poor. At the start of Park's authoritarian reign, the economy had barely grown from the preceding decade. In the immediate postwar period, South Korea was one of the world's poorest countries, and it remained one of the least developed economies at the end of the 1950s.[8] Unlike Rhee and Chang, Park jump-started South Korea's industrialization and economic modernization. The state invested heavily in human capital development, most notably in education. Similar to Taiwan's developmental state, the South Korean government universalized primary schooling during the 1960s, and access to higher education expanded during the 1970s. As the World Bank notes, investments in education and human capital development were critical to upskilling South Korea's industrial labor force, ensuring industrializing firms had an ample supply of skilled workers in the domestic labor market.[9]

Similar to the developmental state in Taiwan and Japan, the Park regime employed strategic industrial policies and interventions to facilitate national industrial growth and economic development. Beginning in the early 1960s, the developmental state implemented a raft of import substitution tariffs to protect homegrown infant industries, specifically in labor-intensive manufacturing sectors, such as textiles, in which South Korean firms faced stiff competition from foreign companies. Buoyed by tariffs to artificially make imports more expensive, South Korean companies were able to develop their domestic manufacturing capabilities so that they could eventually compete in global markets.

Manufacturing firms rapidly developed during the 1960s under the Park regime. Similar to Japan and later Taiwan, the South Korean developmental state picked and helped make industrial winners. Benefiting from strategic import tariffs, promising companies were encouraged by the state to sell to international markets. The government employed various export incentives, such as financing credit and tax breaks, to promote export-oriented industrialization. Exports more than doubled from US$41 million in 1961 to $87 million in 1963, doubling again to $176 million in 1965. By 1970, a decade into the Park regime, the value of South Korean exports totaled $882 million, with an increasing share of export earnings coming from manufacturing industries.

The developmental state also nationalized the banking system during the 1960s, which allowed it to control the distribution of investment capital. Foreign aid dollars and investment were cycled through the state-controlled banking system, giving the state leverage in the allocation of industrial financing, rewarding winning export-oriented firms with credit and fiscal incentives.

Economic growth skyrocketed during the 1960s under the Park regime. Between 1961 and 1970, per capita income increased threefold, from US$82 to $243. South Korea's economy grew on average nearly 8.5 percent each year, and between 1965 and 1970 at an average rate of 10.4 percent annually. The state's investments in manufacturing industries paid off, as the share of the manufacturing sector in the economy grew from 13.6 percent in 1961 to 21 percent in 1970. As a sign of a modernizing economy, economic productivity in South Korea also became less dependent on agriculture, as agriculture's share of economic output declined from 39.1 percent in 1961 to just 26.6 percent in 1970. By the end of the 1960s, labor markets shifted toward urban industrial centers. Household incomes became more egalitarian as workers gained employment in urban, industrial, wage-earning occupations. South Korea's middle class grew.[10]

As in the developmental states of Japan and Taiwan, the power to direct and facilitate industrial transformation was concentrated within a strong state bureaucracy. The Economic Planning Board (EPB) was the pilot agency in the state apparatus. Similar to the Ministry of International Trade and Industry in Japan and the Council for Economic Planning and Development in the KMT's developmental state, South Korea's EPB possessed coordinative authority over the various line ministries. The bureaucracy was vertically organized, and the line ministries took their cues and orders from the EPB. As in other developmentally oriented states, the bureaucracy employed meritocratic recruitment practices, ensuring the best and brightest technocrats drawn from the country's top universities staffed its ministries.[11]

Again as in Japan and Taiwan, the bureaucratic apparatus in South Korea was firmly under the political control of the ruling regime. President Park met with the heads of ministries regularly and intervened in setting the agenda of the EPB. In this regard, the developmental state was as much a skilled and technocratic bureaucracy as it was an instrument of political power for Park and the ruling party.

The Park regime's monopoly over political power was not solely due to coercion. Park enjoyed performance legitimacy with much of South Korean society, fulfilling the promise of economic development to compensate for the absence of political reform. Recall that Park's view of democracy was that it could only arrive after a society was economically modernized. His hold on power during the 1960s was thus never in question. Despite the regime's disdain for democracy and the expansion of political rights, support for him and the ruling DRP continued to rise through the 1960s. The first decade of the Park regime was South Korea's apex of developmental authoritarianism.[12]

Authoritarian developmental states eventually sow the seeds of discontent and their own opposition, however. We saw this in Taiwan, when after decades of economic growth and social transformation, citizens started to mobilize for political change. We saw this earlier in prewar Japan as well, when citizens demanded greater political participation, leading to the Taisho democratic experiment during the 1920s. Developmental regimes eventually come under pressure because of what Alexis de Tocqueville characterizes as the revolution of heightened expectations. In short, successful development creates demanding societies.

A politically demanding society in South Korea arose at the start of the 1970s. After a decade of sustained economic development, opposition voices emerged, including the mobilization of opposition parties in elections. Park's DRP won fewer votes in the May 1971 National Assembly elections than before, and the opposition New Democratic Party (NDP) increased its popular vote share by nearly 12 percent. Though Park handily won the presidential election a month prior, the opposition NDP candidate polled just behind him. This cut it too close for the ruling regime. Park was reportedly "incensed" by the election results.[13]

Rebooting Authoritarianism

Park imposed the highly repressive Yushin constitution in 1972, centralizing political power in the president's hands. The dramatic move strengthened the regime and gave Park a firmer grip on political power and the instruments of state repression. Opposition activities were violently suppressed. The Korean CIA, Park's most trusted arm of the state security apparatus, was empowered to root out and punish opposition activists. What few citizens' rights existed in the 1960s were curtailed with the imposition of the Yushin constitution. Park accelerated the nationalist New Village Movement as well, unleashed in the spring of 1970, to generate mass political support in the countryside.

The Yushin constitution crushed any semblance of citizen political participation. Though elections during the 1960s were gerrymandered to favor the ruling party, they gave some modicum of political participation for South Koreans. From the point of view of the regime, elections also provided important societal feedback. They gave the ruling party and president at least the sheen of having been elected into power. The Yushin constitution changed all of that. Direct elections for the president were banned after 1972, and instead a newly created electoral college within the National Assembly selected the president. Furthermore, the constitution restricted opposition candidates from running in presidential contests. Park "won" the presidency unopposed in December 1972.

Though National Assembly elections were not canceled altogether in the 1970s, the ruling party changed the electoral rules to ensure it was essentially unbeatable in legislative contests. Under the Yushin constitution, the president allocated one-third of the assembly's seats to members of the ruling party. In the 1973 legislative elections, for instance, the ruling DRP won a 67 percent supermajority of seats in the assembly with only 39 percent of the vote, a 28 percent difference between the popular vote and apportionment of legislative seats.

Even the KMT in Taiwan, which benefited enormously from electoral rules that favored the incumbent regime, did not enjoy anywhere near the same magnitude in its seat bonus as the DRP did in South Korea. Between 1972 and 1989, the average difference between the popular vote and Legislative Yuan seats won by the KMT was 12 percent, compared with the 28 percent bonus that Park's DRP gained in 1973. Simply put, the DRP in South Korea was far weaker than the KMT in Taiwan, so it had to cheat and manipulate far more to generate similar results.

Gerrymandering in South Korea became even more blatant and egregious in the subsequent 1978 National Assembly election, when the opposition NDP polled the largest share of the popular vote but took only 26 percent of assembly seats. Meanwhile, Park's DRP polled fewer votes than the opposition, but because of the apportionment rules and the power of presidential seat allocation, the ruling party ended up controlling 63 percent of the National Assembly. In other words, the opposition won the popular vote but still lost the election.

The Yushin constitution was not just a political power play, but an effort to bolster the state's leadership role in directing economic development. With Park's unassailable grip on political power, the developmental state pushed harder and faster in South Korea's industrialization and economic development. During the early 1970s, Park unveiled the "big push" industrial policy, which steered the economy into heavy industries, such as steel and chemicals. These sectors were strategically chosen because they provided important industrial inputs into what Park envisioned to be a more diversified industrial economy.

South Korean firms continued to climb the global value chain, moving away from labor-intensive light manufacturing into higher-value-added sectors such as construction, shipbuilding, and eventually high-tech manufacturing industries like automobiles and electronics. Utilizing a mix of strategic tariffs, export incentives, government-subsidized research and development, and the state-controlled allocation of investment capital, the developmental state engineered continual industrial transformation.

Domestic companies increased in size and scale. South Korea's leading chaebol firms, such as Samsung and Hyundai—enormous, internally diversified but organizationally consolidated financial and industrial conglomerate firms—accounted for an overwhelming proportion of employment as well as the lion's share of industrial and export output.

The way the Park regime handled the 1973 Organization of the Petroleum Exporting Countries (OPEC) price spikes illustrates the state's aggressive approach to economic development, and specifically Park's commitment to an expansionary and export-oriented approach. The contrast with Taiwan here is especially instructive. As we described in chapter 4, the KMT pursued a conservative monetary policy to tackle inflation brought on by the OPEC crisis. Basically, the KMT slowed the economy almost to a halt. South Korea, in contrast, adopted a different and much more aggressive strategy. Rather than rein in money supply, as the KMT did, the Park regime pursued an inflationary policy by expanding money supply, including taking in new foreign loans. Park's strategy was to increase export trade, which tripled in value between 1973 and 1977, going from about US$3.3 billion in outbound trade to $10 billion. South Korea exported its way out of the crisis. While the Taiwanese economy slowed its growth to just 1 percent in 1974 in an effort to buffer the OPEC price spikes, the South Korean economy grew 8.5 percent in 1974 and 14 percent in 1973 during the height of the OPEC crisis.[14]

From an economic growth perspective, the 1970s were simply extraordinary for South Korea. By every measure, the economy developed at a breakneck pace, growing on average 9.6 percent annually between 1970 and 1979. Per capita income increased from around US$240 to just under $1,600 over the same period, nearly a sevenfold increase in one decade. South Korea's manufacturing sectors became more self-sufficient and less dependent on imported industrial inputs. Its export-oriented strategy paid off, as the total value of exports grew nearly seventeenfold, from about US$880 million in 1970 to $14.7 billion in 1979.

South Korea's economic development, set against a backdrop of authoritarian rule, generated a more politically demanding society, with heightened expectations and increasing frustrations over the lack of political reform. Despite amazing growth rates, opposition to the regime fomented under Park, even more acutely than before.

The size of the middle class increased during the 1970s. Survey results showed that despite benefiting from growth, middle-class South Koreans sought not just economic stability but also gradual political democratization.

Working-class activists felt left behind in South Korea's economic transformation, and labor protests flared up. Workers expected political reform. Park responded by cracking down even harder, inciting more criticism and more opposition, and fueling the conflict between the authoritarian state and society.

The 1970s lifted into political prominence the popular dissident politicians Kim Young-sam and Kim Dae-jung, both of whom called for the end of the authoritarian regime. In the fall of 1979, students at Busan University protested the brutal regime and its stifling Yushin constitution. Thousands of students and activists across the country joined the Busan protesters to criticize the Park regime. They sent a powerful signal to Park that the authoritarian regime had passed its apex of power. There was a glimmer of hope that a democracy-through-strength scenario lay on the horizon.[15]

A shocking turn, however, altered the course of events in South Korea. On October 26, 1979, Korean CIA operatives assassinated Park. The details surrounding his murder remain unclear to this day. Many believe a power struggle between the Korean CIA and Park's inner circle led to his demise. Speculation also suggests that some leaders among the ruling elite felt the regime ought to scale back its repression and that the regime was going too far, in opposition to Park, who unrelentingly pushed for an even stronger crackdown on the opposition. Irrespective of why Park was assassinated, his sudden death left a huge political vacuum, permitting an upsurge of anti-authoritarian activism in South Korean society.

Doubling Down on Dictatorship

In the wake of Park's assassination, the window for democratic reform was pried open again. South Korean civil society demanded the end of authoritarianism. Activists wanted political reform. It appeared that some leaders within Park's regime were looking to soften the regime's repressive tactics. An interim government was formed immediately after his assassination, and it set out to open up politically and undo the dictatorial practices of the previous regime. Optimism was in the air.

In early 1980, during the period known as the "Seoul Spring," opposition activists mobilized in the streets to push for political reform. The interim government rolled back several emergency measures that Park had imposed under the Yushin constitution. Many jailed activists, notably reform-minded professors and students, were released by the interim government. Political dissidents, including opposition leaders Kim Young-sam and Kim Dae-jung, had their civil rights restored.

The interim government also looked to promulgate a new constitution: specifically, one that meaningfully democratized the political system by strengthening the authority of the National Assembly and judiciary, creating fairer electoral rules so that opposition parties stood a chance, as well as curtailing the executive powers of the president. In short, the Seoul Spring was a time of hope for South Korea's activists and a moment of democratic experimentation.

Amid this buzz of democratic hopefulness, however, General Chun Doo-hwan was orchestrating a political power grab behind the scenes. A former Park ally, Chun mobilized the military's support after Park's assassination. He also took control of the Korean CIA. In retrospect, it was clear that it was only a matter of time before the interim government would fall. It indeed came to an abrupt end in the spring of 1980, just months after Park was killed, when Chun formed the Democratic Justice Party (DJP) and promptly took over the civilian administration of the South Korean government.

The Chun regime immediately crushed any momentum toward democracy. According to political scientist John Kie-Chiang Oh, Chun's was "the most nakedly authoritarian regime on the whole in contemporary Korea," even more brutal than Park's. Chun declared martial law in 1980.[16] Opposition leaders Kim Young-sam and Kim Dae-jung were sidelined once again. The National Assembly was suspended, and the Chun regime shut down university campuses, which were hotbeds for opposition activism. The regime decreed new laws that undermined the freedom of the press. The passage of highly restrictive labor laws by the Chun government further curtailed workers' rights.

Student protesters took to the streets, demanding Chun revoke martial law and return to the path of political reform imagined months earlier during the Seoul Spring. The largest protests took place in Kwangju, the capital city of South Cholla Province. South Cholla is far from Seoul, and as the birthplace of popular dissident leader Kim Dae-jung, the province was ripe for opposition activism. Around 100,000 protesters confronted the regime in the Kwangju uprising. The Chun government responded by deploying nearly 20,000 troops to the city and, in late May 1980, ordered them to fire on the demonstrators. Over 500 people died during the "Kwangju massacre," though estimates are as high as 2,000.

Like the Park regime, Chun consolidated his political power through the repressive power of the state security apparatus as well as the rigged elections for the National Assembly. In the 1981 legislative election, electoral gerrymandering guaranteed his DJP a majority of seats in the legislature, even though the DJP polled just over one-third of the vote. Not satisfied with the result, however, Chun altered the National Assembly Election Law to increase malapportionment even more to favor the ruling party. Consequently, four years later, in 1985, the DJP again won a majority of National Assembly seats, even though it polled far short of majority electoral support with just 35 percent of the vote. The opposition New Korea Democratic Party (NKDP) actually lost seats in the assembly, despite growing its share of the popular vote to 29 percent.

The 1985 National Assembly elections were a critical focusing event. They highlighted the regime's blatant abuse of power and the diminishing appetite among South Koreans for autocratic rule, regardless of the economic development promised by the ruling regime. Excessive gerrymandering laid bare Chun's willingness to bend the institutional rules to benefit the DJP regime. Meanwhile, the extraordinary showing of the NKDP reflected the increasing popularity of the prodemocracy, anti-DJP opposition. In the election, the NKDP expanded its base of electoral support, including workers, students, the middle class, and the church. Democratic activists were not going anywhere anytime soon, and if anything, anti-authoritarian opposition galvanized broader-based electoral support.[17] The confrontation between the opposition and the Chun regime was coming to a head. Chun began to feel the pressure.

After the 1985 National Assembly election, Chun signaled he might consider liberalizing the political system, initiating yet another experiment in political reform. The Chun regime released political prisoners, notably popular opposition leaders Kim Young-sam and Kim Dae-jung. Chun also promised to consider introducing direct presidential elections. Between 1986 and 1987, the ruling regime and the opposition attempted to negotiate constitutional reform, which was viewed as a potential concession.[18]

After months of discussion, however, the two sides failed to come to an agreement. This was in part because the ruling party and opposition were too far apart to come to a compromise. The internally fragmented opposition was also unable to form a consensus within its own camp. A brewing conflict between the "two Kims" and their supporters fractured opposition solidarity. Sensing the rift, Chun cut off the negotiations in April 1987, ending the brief liberalizing experiment. A day later, the regime ordered a sweeping crackdown and rounded up 4,000 democracy activists. The 1985 thaw quickly ended and the Chun regime slid back to its authoritarian ways.

The opposition was, predictably, outraged. Over the next several months, democratic protests intensified. The government doubled down on authoritarianism by suppressing the social movements. Increasingly violent, South Korea's political scene was described by the *New York Times* as a "war zone."[19]

Further enflaming the opposition, on June 10, 1987, Chun announced General Roh Tae-woo to be his successor as president and leader of the DJP. Roh was Chun's military comrade and had carried out several of Chun's campaigns to crush opposition activists during his reign, including the Kwangju massacre. Roh was Chun's crony and owed his political ascension to South Korea's authoritarian system. Chun's 1987 succession plan did not portend democratic reform, nor did it inspire confidence among antiregime activists that democracy was on the horizon. Instead, Roh's appointment rubbed salt in the wounds of opposition activists.

After Chun's announcement, an estimated 250,000 prodemocracy activists poured into the streets all over South Korea. On June 19, Chun ordered troops to be on standby to crush the protests. The moment was extremely tense. As John Kie-Chiang Oh writes, "South Korea was on a precipice, facing an unprecedentedly bloody massacre of the people by its military."[20]

Choosing Democracy

In January 1987, six months before the summer protests, the Chun regime detained and tortured a Seoul National University student, Park Chong-chol. Park later died and became a martyr for South Korea's democratic activities. His death further catalyzed the prodemocracy *minjung* coalition of social movements, sparking a new wave of antiregime mobilization. The conflict between state and society peaked when hundreds of thousands of antiregime protesters participated in the Great Peace March of the People in late June 1987.

The regime was again at a crossroads: it could choose to suppress the opposition, or it could politically liberalize and set South Korea on a course toward democracy. This was not the first time a South Korean dictator faced this decision, though in the past—from Rhee to Park and to Chun—the ruling regime always chose to double down on authoritarianism in the end.

On June 29, one week after Chun ordered troops to prepare to put down the opposition, Roh unexpectedly issued a Declaration of Democratization and Reforms. He put forth a democratic blueprint for political reform, including constitutional commitments to human rights, freedom of the press, the release of political prisoners and dissidents, new legal mechanisms to combat corruption, and the devolution of power to local authorities. The reform blue-print proposed to create new laws that curbed the power of the president and to institutionalize checks and balances on the executive branch, including giving the authority to impeach the president to the elected National Assembly. Roh also announced direct presidential elections to be held in December 1987, followed by National Assembly elections in March of the following year. The incumbent regime lifted restrictions on opposition candidates, and popular leaders Kim Young-sam and Kim Dae-jung were allowed to contest the elections. Roh's reform pledge promised a more level political playing field, an essential condition for meaningful democratic transition.[21]

Roh's June 1987 decision to concede democracy was abrupt and unexpected. Democratic openings and experiments had previously emerged in South Korea, as we recounted earlier in this chapter. Opposition politicians had mobilized before. The ruling party had fared poorly at the polls before. This was also not the first time the regime had confronted popular protest. The Kwangju uprising was as intense as the protests of 1987. Yet in 1979, the Chun regime brutally crushed the opposition movement.

Why, then, did Roh concede democracy when he did? In our theory of democracy through strength, incumbent authoritarian regimes are more likely to consider a strategy of democratic concession when they confront clear and strong signals that their grip on power vis-à-vis the opposition is waning and in incipient decline. As we lay out in the introduction to this book, authoritarian regimes can receive four kinds of signals: geopolitical, electoral, contentious, and economic. When regimes receive these signals, they become more likely to concede democracy, especially when the political costs of suppression are prohibitively high (ominous signals) and the incumbent party is reassured it can remain competitive (reassuring signals) in democracy.

Scanning the political-economic landscape when he did in the summer of 1987, Roh would have seen both clear and strong signals that the authoritarian regime was in decline, and that the ruling party was well past its apex of power. Importantly, however, foreboding economic signals were not among them. As in Taiwan, the South Korean economy remained vital and strong throughout the mid-1980s. Industrial development continued to drive economic growth, and chaebol firms were successful competitors in the global economy.

The US government signaled that the authoritarian regime had passed its apex of power when it exerted public political pressure on the regime to democratize. The American government had applied behind-the-scenes pressure before, from the postwar Rhee government of the 1950s until the summer of

1987. The United States quietly excoriated Chun and his crackdown during the Kwangju uprising. However, the United States never publicly called out South Korea's authoritarian government. Prodemocracy activists in South Korea in fact criticized the US government for its seeming indifference to, and at times even outward support for, authoritarianism in South Korea. Activists were especially critical of the United States when President Ronald Reagan invited Chun as the first official guest of his White House administration, and when the United States remained conspicuously silent as the Park and Chun dictatorships sidelined opposition leaders Kim Young-sam and Kim Dae-jung.[22]

The US tactic of privately criticizing while publicly supporting South Korea's authoritarian regime changed in 1987. As the Cold War was coming to an end, the US government became less tolerant of its authoritarian allies. Soon after Chun ordered troops to be at the ready in the summer of 1987, the US government strongly cautioned Chun against this move. A mission led by Assistant Secretary of State for Asia Gaston Sigur "sternly warned" Chun "against the use of the Korean military for political purposes."[23] Earlier that year, Sigur had admonished Chun's authoritarian tactics, encouraging Chun and his allies to "civilianize their politics."[24] In June 1987 Reagan sent Chun a personal letter "imploring him not to use military force in dealing with the unrest."[25]

That the American government turned to overt and explicit criticism of the regime in 1987 for the first time sent a powerful signal to Seoul. The US government, South Korea's most important diplomatic, military, and economic patron, was losing patience with the regime's repressive tactics.

South Korea's dictators were not impervious to the regional diffusion of political reform either. For instance, the events in Taiwan around the same time were noted in South Korea. Taiwan's president Chiang Ching-kuo's decision to concede political reforms starting in 1986 and the lifting of martial law the following year surely influenced Roh's calculations of the political cost of continued authoritarian suppression. Chiang's decision to concede democratic reform had also portended political gains for the incumbent regime in South Korea if it similarly relaxed the political system while it remained relatively strong. Taiwan's example showed how conceding democracy did not have to sound the death knell of the incumbent regime, and that in fact conceding democracy through strength could solidify a ruling party's grip on power.

Internal contentious signals mattered greatly as well. By 1987, the size and scale of the opposition movement overwhelmed the incumbent authoritarian regime. Given South Korea's pattern of democratic development in fits and starts, popular protest against the regime was nothing new. Successive authoritarian governments in South Korea had confronted waves of intense opposition before. The mobilization that occurred in the spring and summer of 1987, however, was of an unprecedented magnitude, signaling to Roh that opposition to the authoritarian regime had reached an unprecedented level of intensity and would be unwavering.

Unlike in Taiwan, where *tangwai* activists were mainly opposition politicians and dissident elite intellectuals, in South Korea, the minjung movement that arose during the mid-1980s mobilized hundreds of thousands of antiregime activists across social classes and political-economic cleavages. The scale and size of the minjung coalition, massive in terms of numbers, were troubling enough for the regime. The breadth of the movement, encompassing and galvanizing so many different activists around a common enemy, telegraphed an ominous signal to the authoritarian regime.[26]

Geopolitical pressure and the emergence of unprecedented contentious politics provided very powerful signals to Chun and Roh that support for authoritarian rule, internally and externally, had waned. However, as in Taiwan, the clearest signal to the regime that it had passed its apex of power was electoral. The ruling party failed to increase its share of the popular vote between the 1981 and 1985 legislative elections, winning just over one-third of the vote in both. Meanwhile, the main opposition party dramatically grew its vote share by 8 percent over the two elections, with the NKDP winning 29 percent of the popular vote in 1985.

In both contests, the incumbent DJP managed to secure a majority of National Assembly seats, but this was due to gerrymandering. Obvious to everyone, including the ruling party, the main reason the DJP maintained its majority in the assembly was that it blatantly cheated and manipulated electoral rules. Compared with the KMT in Taiwan, the DJP's electoral performance was considerably less impressive. Whereas the KMT continued to poll majorities in the popular vote right up to the eve of democratic transition in Taiwan, South Korea's DJP was eking out narrow pluralities at best.

Democratic transition in South Korea was not prompted by economic troubles. Rather, sustained bottom-up grassroots mobilization, electoral decline, and geopolitical pressures signaled to Roh that the ruling regime's once unassailable grip on political power was waning. By the summer of 1987, South Korea's authoritarian system was well into the bittersweet spot, and much further along than the KMT in Taiwan. On one hand, the Chun regime had inherited considerable antecedent strengths. The DJP continued to dominate the legislature even as its popular vote share was shrinking. The regime was in full control of the security apparatus and the South Korean economy was strong. Yet on the other hand, signals that the authoritarian regime was in incipient decline—that it had passed its apex of power—were also clear and increasingly ominous. It was obvious to Roh and Chun that "time was running out for the old form of authoritarian politics."[27]

Clear and strong signals to the regime that its grip on power had weakened presented a democratic experiment scenario to incoming president Roh. Ironically, it was Chun, Roh's predecessor and one of South Korea's most brutal dictators, who advised Roh to concede reform and hasten a democratic transition. According to Chun's recording secretary, he explained that, "in view of the mounting demand for a direct presidential election, accepting such a demand would be the most popular move" for the regime. He further speculated, "This single act should enable Roh to win over the two Kims [opposition leaders Kim Young-sam and Kim Dae-jung]. Thus," he claims, "I told Roh to accept the direct election system."[28] Despite Chun's encouragement, Roh was predictably anxious about conceding democracy, since democratic reform could lead to the defeat and removal of the DJP regime altogether. He worried as well about retribution for those associated with the Chun regime, including himself.

To reiterate: conceding democracy is always a risk, a high-stakes gamble for an incumbent regime. From Chun's point of view, however, the marginal returns of incumbency were decreasing for the authoritarian regime in its existing form. It was in the best interest of the ruling party for the regime to initiate democratic transition, rather than have the regime weaken even further and need to resort once again to massive violent repression. In terms of Chun's own self-interest, democratic concession would also pave a way for him and his cronies to be amnestied for their authoritarian crimes. Chun understood that Roh had to be the one to lead democratic reform, however. Chun could not pull it off. He had no legitimacy as a democratic reformer, given his association with the Kwangju massacre and his repeated silencing of democratic reformers.

Conceding direct presidential elections would make Roh a "hero," Chun reasoned. Encouraging Roh to confidently pursue democratic concession, Chun went so far as to "guarantee his victory." He pointed to the incumbent regime's antecedent strengths, and specifically the party's development record, and how they gave Roh a significant advantage over the opposition. Roh eventually came around to the concession strategy, in part because the ominous

signals of the regime's incipient decline had become so clear, but also owing
to the confidence that the regime retained enough political power to survive
a democratic concession, and potentially even thrive as a democratic ruling
party in the spirit of Japan's LDP or Taiwan's KMT.

The June 29 declaration was a dramatic announcement, a choreographed
public performance by outgoing president Chun with his successor, Roh.
Upon making the declaration, Roh promptly revealed he would bring an eight-
point reform proposal to then-president Chun for his approval. To add more
dramatic flair to the political theater, Roh also announced he would rescind
his presidential candidacy if Chun did not accept the reform proposals. By
doing so, Roh tied South Korea's democratic fate to both his bold declaration
and Chun's willingness to support democratic concession. He portrayed them
both as democratic reformers. In what observers described as an "elaborate
hoax," Chun publicly approved Roh's eight-point proposal on July 1, even
though he was aware of it in advance and even had a hand in drafting it.[29]

Conceding with (Some) Confidence

As we state in our theory, authoritarian regimes are more likely to consider a
democratic concession strategy when they have accumulated antecedent
strengths but after they have passed their apex of power. Regimes are most
likely to concede democracy when they receive clear and ominous signals that
they are in incipient decline and their authoritarian hold on power is waning.
Autocrats need to be reassured, however, that conceding democracy will not
necessarily lead to their demise or political obsolescence. Rather, democratic
concession from a position of strength is a strategic option that likely ensures
the incumbent regime's survival and even potentially its revival as full-blown
rulers in democracy. While conceding democracy is a risky move, the incumbent regime's antecedent strengths provide decision makers the confidence
that embracing rather than rejecting democratic reform can lead to a stable
transition process in which the incumbent party has a great fighting chance to
thrive in democracy.

Amid clear and powerful signals that the authoritarian regime was in incipient decline, Roh still had many reasons to be confident about its stock of political power. The fact the economy was very strong helped the incumbent
ruling party make the case to voters that continuity was in their best interest.
The regime made the case stronger by highlighting the opposition's lack of
experience in managing and growing the economy. In the ten years between

1981 and 1990, South Korea's economy grew at over 9.5 percent per year. Between 1986 and 1988 specifically, the period when Roh initiated democratic reform, the economic growth rate was nearly 13 percent annually. In other words, conceding democracy in 1987 meant the regime transitioned in very "good times." The developmental state's record appealed to middle-class voters, and Roh's promise of political reform neutralized the regime cleavage that had activated middle-class opposition. By conceding democracy, the incumbent regime had a good chance of expanding its core support base.

The specific electoral rules of the game were critical in affirming Roh's decision to move ahead with democratic reforms. Similar to the situation in Japan and Taiwan, the electoral rules for the National Assembly favored the incumbent party, which bolstered the DJP's (and Roh's) victory confidence. Electoral reforms implemented just before the 1988 legislative elections went a long way to even the playing field for all parties but still gave built-in advantages to the incumbent ruling party.

For example, because the DJP attracted voters from across the entire country, the incumbent party had an advantage in winning single-member districts where a plurality (rather than majority) of electoral support won the seat. The smaller, regionally based opposition parties, on the other hand, were at a disadvantage. Both opposition party leaders, Kim Young-sam and Kim Dae-jung, drew their electoral support from their regional home bases. Kim Dae-jung was immensely popular in South Cholla Province, while Kim Young-sam historically drew disproportionate electoral support in his home province of Kyungsang. Both opposition parties were expected to secure wins in their respective regions but would likely fail to outpunch the DJP and Roh on a national scale.

The electoral districts were also drawn up to overrepresent the countryside, where the DJP was historically dominant. Again, this is not unlike the situations faced by the LDP in Japan and the KMT in Taiwan. In the 1988 National Assembly election, district apportionment gave the incumbent ruling party a sizable seat bonus in rural areas. The DJP further shored up its rural electoral support when it announced the government's plan to extend medical insurance benefits to farmers and rural self-employed workers in 1988, in time to coincide with the first National Assembly election.

The proportional representation (PR) rules in the legislative electoral system further benefited the incumbent DJP by giving the largest party a disproportionate share of PR seats. These rules all but guaranteed the ruling party a sizable take of the seats in the National Assembly. Thus while the 1988 National Assembly elections were free and the electoral rules of the game leveled the playing field considerably, they were hardly completely fair. Like the KMT in Taiwan, the incumbent DJP built safeguards into the electoral system to ensure the former authoritarian party decisive advantages in democratic competition.

Where the incumbent regime was less confident about its democratic concession strategy, however, was in its gamble that Kim Young-sam and Kim Dae-jung would split electoral support among opposition voters.[30] Splitting the opposition was the securest route for Roh to win the 1987 presidential election and for his party to succeed in the 1988 legislative contest. If the two Kims somehow unified their disparate political bases, Roh and the DJP faced a strong likelihood they would be defeated at the polls. Chun and Roh assessed the situation in the summer of 1987 and determined the two Kims would not be able to unify their divided constituencies in time for the founding democratic elections.

Their assessment was correct, as it turned out. Kim Young-sam and Kim Dae-jung, despite being allies in the campaign for democracy, had a long history of conflict and enmity between them. They were democratic champions but also fiercely competitive in winning the leadership of South Korea's prodemocracy movement. At times under the Park and Chun dictatorships, the two Kims joined forces, especially during the 1970s and 1980s when authoritarian suppression was most intense. However, the alliances were born out of political convenience, without a clear foundation for a lasting coalition once democratization no longer required a unified opposition struggle.[31]

Prior to the 1987 presidential election, Kim Young-sam and Kim Dae-jung flirted with the idea of running on the same ticket in opposition to the incumbent regime. They recognized that the best way to defeat the incumbent regime was to form an alliance. The two Kims went so far as to form the Reunification Democratic Party in 1987 to contest the presidential and legislative elections. However, the alliance was short-lived. In October 1987, just a few months before the founding presidential election, Kim Dae-jung broke away to form the Peace Democratic Party. As Chun and Roh predicted—and probably prayed—the opposition split.

Leading the process of democratic transition, as Roh did in 1987, not only gave the incumbent regime the levers and power to shape the reform process to its advantage; it allowed the regime to portray itself as the party of reform and as a reformed political party. Recall that in Taiwan, Chiang Ching-kuo portrayed himself and the KMT as credible political reformers by initiating democratic transition. Conservative politicians in Japan pursued a similar strategy, drawing on their prewar democratic ideals and actively crafting the postwar constitution with American occupation leaders. Roh similarly benefited politically by preemptively conceding democratic transition, neutralizing the opposition's key political cleavage.

In the wake of the June 29 declaration, Roh anointed himself the champion of democratization, despite his initial hesitation to embark on political reform. He promptly set out to win back the support of the US government, South Korea's most important geopolitical patron and international economic partner. In September 1987, in a much-celebrated trip to the United States, Roh assured President Reagan that South Korea was on an irreversible path to democracy. He even assured the president a peaceful transfer of power in the event that either Roh or the DJP was defeated in the coming elections. Roh was prepared—or at least he claimed to be—not only to concede democracy but also to concede defeat.

In sum, though not nearly as confident as the KMT was with its democratic prospects in Taiwan, Roh initiated democratic transition in South Korea with a fair degree of confidence that he and the incumbent party could at least survive the transition, and that there was even a possible scenario in which the DJP could thrive and retain power without interruption. A growing economy, a favorable electoral system for the incumbent party, the strong likelihood the opposition would fragment, and the credibility that comes with initiating democratic reform were all sources of confidence that conceding democracy was a risk worth taking.

The gamble paid off handsomely for Roh and the DJP. Roh won the 1987 presidential election with a plurality of support, winning 36 percent of the popular vote. Kim Young-sam came in second with 28 percent, and Kim Dae-jung trailed behind with 27 percent of the national vote. As Roh and Chun anticipated, the two Kims ended up splitting the opposition vote along their regional bases of popular support. Their combined vote share would have resulted in a clear majority for the opposition, reinforcing the notion that had the two Kims unified their bases of support, Roh would have been defeated in the presidential election.

The National Assembly elections told a similar story. The DJP won 34 percent of the popular vote, but because of the skewed allocation rules for the proportional representation seats, the incumbent party ended up controlling 125 seats in the 299-member legislature, or about 42 percent of the total seats. Kim Dae-jung's Peace Democratic Party won 71 seats (or 24 percent of the legislature), and Kim Young-sam's Reunification Democratic Party controlled 59 seats

(20 percent). A fourth and new party, the New Democratic Republican Party, won 35 seats. Though the incumbent ruling party's share of legislative seats was short of a majority, the DJP remained the largest party in the National Assembly. In other words, though the former authoritarian ruling party took a hit in the 1988 democratic elections, it "did not surrender" political power.[32]

Becoming a Normal Democracy

Roh observed in early 1988, "There is a strong wind of change blowing over the country." Echoing Chiang in Taiwan, who similarly noted how "the times have changed," Roh proclaimed, "We will have an era of mature democracy" in South Korea.[33] Roh and Chiang share many parallels with respect to their roles in ushering in democracy. Their decisions to concede democracy were the result of longer processes of developmental transformation in South Korea and Taiwan. Roh and Chiang were not committed democrats themselves, but democracy served their interests and those of their ruling parties well.

Decades of economic development under authoritarian rule eventually set the stage for conservative-led democratic transition. The state-led model of growth transformed their societies, creating citizens who demanded political reform. By the mid-1980s, the two developmental statist regimes recognized that despite having relied on economic performance legitimacy to sustain their authoritarian rule, the regimes had passed their apex of power and entered the bittersweet spot. If there was ever a good time for the authoritarian party to concede democracy, from the point of view of the incumbent regime, this was the time.

Though the South Korean and Taiwanese experiences share many similarities, they were not identical. As we argue in the preceding chapter, Taiwan is the exemplary case of democracy through strength. When the KMT initiated democratic reform, it was in a much stronger position than the DJP was in South Korea. In Taiwan, opposition activists mobilized against the KMT, but not nearly to the extent, in terms of both size and scale, that we saw in South Korea during the 1980s. The KMT's electoral support was declining in the 1980s, but also not as steeply as the DJP experienced in South Korea. In other words, the incumbent regime in South Korea was strong when Chun and Roh conspired to concede democracy in 1987, though not nearly as strong as the KMT was in Taiwan when Chiang initiated democratic reform there.

In our theory of democracy through strength, we are attentive to such differences, noting that incumbent authoritarian regimes array across a spectrum of strength. As we show in the previous chapter, during the mid-1980s, the KMT had *just passed* its apex of power and *just entered* into the bittersweet spot, whereas the DJP was already much further along in its decline into the bittersweet spot. The difference between the KMT and the DJP and their respective strengths was most clear in the two incumbent parties' electoral performance in the run-up to democratic transition. Whereas the DJP's electoral popularity dwindled to the point where it was routinely polling no more than one-third of the vote, the KMT continued to win the majority of votes in electoral contests right up to the moment of democratic concession.

Yet unlike authoritarian regimes that had held on for too long, South Korea's incumbent ruling party had not hurtled through the bittersweet spot entirely. Just as the DJP's situation in South Korea in 1987 was not the same as the KMT's in Taiwan, it was also not analogous to the collapse of the Marcos regime in the Philippines. Rather, the DJP remained powerful enough to survive a democratic transition, even though its prospects in democracy were more uncertain compared with the KMT. Whereas the KMT went from being a very strong authoritarian party to becoming an equally dominant democratic party—going from strength to strength—the DJP transitioned from a relatively strong but weakening authoritarian ruling party into a precarious but still ruling democratic political party.

As expected, South Korea's democracy disembarked onto shakier footing than Taiwan's. The incumbent DJP was in a vulnerable position after the founding presidential and legislative elections. It continued to be the governing party, though its share of electoral support was not decisive and its control of National Assembly seats fell short of a majority. Still, by retaining governmental power, the DJP had the opportunity to become a *normal* democratic party. Likewise, Roh could become a normal democratically elected president.

The DJP and Roh accepted that they needed to win support to govern and could no longer rely on repression to stay in power. Like the KMT in Taiwan and the LDP before it in Japan, the incumbent regime in South Korea moderated its political and economic positions to broaden its electoral appeal and to distance it from its authoritarian past. With respect to the economy, the government continued to focus on growth and development. Economic growth was key to winning back middle-class supporters who earlier defected to the prodemocracy opposition. The DJP started to find its footing as a "catch-all" party as well and, like the LDP and KMT, deliberately expanded its electoral base by promoting a development program of economic "growth with equity." The DJP government extended medical insurance schemes to rural and urban self-employed workers in 1988 and 1989, universalizing access to health care. With bottom-up pressure from unions, it reformed South Korea's labor laws and legislated new policies to grow the small and medium-sized enterprise sector.[34]

Politically, the DJP did not become a democratic spoiler, despite the incumbent governing party's shaky start as a democratically elected government. The DJP did not roll back democratic reform, as we might expect when a former authoritarian party is on its heels, but rather continued to deepen and normalize democratic practices and institutions in South Korea. It made good on Roh's pledge to institutionalize democratic rules of the game and to make constitutional changes. The government opened up political space for civil society and protest. The military was brought under civilian control. The media was left alone. Dissidents were free to mobilize, and opposition parties were free to contest elections.

Most important, the DJP—like the LDP in Japan and the KMT in Taiwan—consolidated its power after 1987 through democratic means as opposed to reverting to authoritarian tactics. Rather than lick its wounds and flirt with democratic recession after its disappointing showing in South Korea's founding elections, the DJP reformed itself as a dominant democratic party. Specifically, it consolidated its political power as a democratic party when it merged with two opposition parties, including Kim Young-sam's Reunification Democratic Party, to form the Democratic Liberal Party (DLP) in 1990. The newly formed party controlled a supermajority of National Assembly seats. While the formation of the DLP consolidated political power into a dominant party, it did not sabotage democracy.

Modeled after the LDP and KMT, the DLP was an ideologically pragmatic and moderate catch-all party. The alliance with Kim Young-sam, one of South Korea's staunchest democratic leaders since the 1970s, gave the DLP democratic credibility among voters. Despite opposition leader Kim Dae-jung's criticism of the DLP, which he initially saw as an assault on democracy, the three-party merger in 1990 hastened the consolidation of the opposition. After the formation of the DLP, Kim Dae-jung mobilized the Democratic Party alliance in 1991, solidifying and stabilizing the civilian two-party system that has more or less endured, despite continual changes to the names of the parties, in South Korea's democracy ever since. When the DLP's Kim Young-sam won the presidency in 1992, South Korea had democratically elected its first civilian president ever in the country's postwar history.[35] What began as yet another reversible democratic experiment has ultimately, to this day several decades later, proved irreversible.

6

China to 1989

TOO WEAK TO CONCEDE

IN THE EARLY HOURS of June 4, 1989, the People's Liberation Army (PLA) fired on student protesters who had assembled that spring in Beijing's Tiananmen Square. After several months of peaceful protest, hunger strikes, pleas to meet with Chinese Communist Party (CCP) leaders, and demands for political reform, the authoritarian regime responded violently, ending China's democracy movement. Scholars estimate that hundreds, perhaps thousands, of students and their allies were killed during the crackdown. Thousands were injured, and several thousands more arrested. Many dissidents fled the country, escaping the regime and abandoning their efforts to build a democratic China from within. Despite the wave of democratic transitions occurring around the world at the time—especially in the communist world—the CCP chose to resist democracy.

The protests and crackdown of 1989 were neither the beginning nor the end of Chinese society's democratic struggle. The Tiananmen Square tragedy suppressed a democratic impulse that had long permeated China's intellectual and activist circles. At the end of the Qing dynasty in the early twentieth century, decades before China was ruled by the CCP, Chinese thinkers already dreamed of a modern and unified nation, and with that, the promise of economic and political development. The New Culture movement, an intellectual and literary movement that emerged in the 1910s, celebrated the liberal arts and rational pragmatism. It appropriated science and democracy as its symbolic totems. In the May Fourth movement of 1919, Chinese intellectuals envisioned a more self-reliant, more powerful, and more democratic China.

The Beijing Democracy Wall movement of 1978 resowed the seeds of democratic activism in communist China, only to be swiftly swept up by the

CCP. Nationwide student protests erupted yet again in late 1986, calling for political reform after China started on its course of economic modernization under Deng Xiaoping. Those too were put down by the CCP regime.

Ever since 1978, when China first opened its doors to international trade and implemented liberalizing economic reforms, the country has been on a path to becoming the modern economic giant that Chinese nationalists long imagined. Yet paradoxically, China's unprecedented economic transformation has been presided over by a ruling party that remains steadfastly antidemocratic. Though the idea of democracy was neither new nor alien among Chinese thinkers and activists, the brutal violence of the June 4 crackdown nonetheless was decisive, delivering the final blow to democratic prospects in China for decades to come. As historian Jonathan Spence laments in the final pages of *The Search for Modern China*, the CCP "that had swept to power forty years before by challenging all the existing social, political and economic norms now seemed to have no purpose but to ensure that it faced no such challenges itself."[1] It was clear in 1989 the CCP had no interest in leading democratic transformation.

Beyond the tragic spectacle of the June 4 crackdown, the events of 1989 also left an indelible imprint on how China watchers think about democratic prospects in the Middle Kingdom. Specifically, the events of 1989 and the regime's resistance to democracy instilled a widespread expectation that democracy in China would come about only when the ruling party was weak; simply put, *democracy can only emerge from the ashes of the regime's total collapse.*

Given the images of democratization that were swirling across the globe in the late 1980s and early 1990s, this "collapsism" perspective made perfect sense. Communist regimes crumbled in the Soviet Union and Eastern Europe because of regime weakness. If Chinese communism survived while other communist regimes died, it could only be because the CCP was stronger than its fallen communist counterparts.[2] Bolstered by the nationalist legitimacy from its successful homegrown revolution and the seeds of performance legitimacy from a decade of promising economic reforms—strengths the Soviet bloc plainly lacked—China was indeed less prone to collapse than many other communist regimes, as Tiananmen Square painfully proved.[3]

Yet as the previous chapters on Japan, Taiwan, and South Korea have shown, authoritarian strength does not make democratization impossible, or necessarily even undesirable for authoritarian incumbents. Strong regimes may not *collapse*, but they can *concede*. Democracy is possible when an authoritarian regime is strong or weak. In our theory, democratization is more likely to stabilize a country when an authoritarian regime is strong, not weak, and when it possesses the organizational strength and has generated the performance legitimacy among its citizens and prospective voters to engineer a democratic transition in which it remains a prominent political party.

Comparing China with its developmental statist neighbors thus offers a very different lesson from comparing it with its distant Soviet and Soviet-backed cousins. Comparative perspective matters in the conclusions we draw. From our perspective, the CCP avoided democratic transition in the summer of 1989 not only because it was *too strong to collapse* but also because it was *too weak to concede* democracy through strength. It lacked the confidence that it could concede democracy and thrive, as seen in our previous three chapters on Japan, Taiwan, and South Korea. Notwithstanding the regime's willingness to use violence in 1989 to suppress the protesters, revealing the blunt and brutal tools of authoritarianism, the CCP had not yet generated the popular legitimacy or accumulated the antecedent strengths to concede political reform with confidence. In the language of our theory, the party lacked the victory confidence and stability confidence in 1989 that it could politically survive democracy and that China would maintain the stability required to continue its rapid economic transformation.

This chapter recounts China's political and economic development from the communist revolution through the late 1980s. The account ends in 1989 to emphasize the regime's relative lack of antecedent strength and confidence at the time to embrace democratic concession, unlike its three East Asian neighbors just discussed. Our thesis is that democracy through strength was not yet historically available to the CCP as a viable option as of 1989; but today, as we contend in chapter 9, after decades of successful membership in developmental Asia, China could democratize with confidence in a fashion similar to that of its democratic predecessors in Japan, Taiwan, and South Korea.

By ending the account in 1989, this chapter properly historicizes China's developmental takeoff and the role of the CCP in leading that development. Due to China's remarkable transformation since then and its rise to superpower status, it can be difficult to contextualize historically its relative underdevelopment and the weakness of the party in 1989, over three decades ago. One might be tempted, understandably, to overestimate China's strength and the strength of the ruling party in 1989 because of their strength today.

The fact is, however, that while gross domestic product per capita in China today is over US$10,000, in 1989 it was only about $300. The economy in 1989 was still largely a peasant economy and not the global industrial powerhouse that it is today. The current regime appears formidable, politically and economically, whereas during the 1980s, the CCP had only just emerged from the chaos and destruction of the Cultural Revolution a decade before. Mao Zedong's reign and then his death in the late 1970s continued to divide the ruling party, and as we show in this chapter, the CCP was far from a unified actor during the Tiananmen Square protests in 1989. In other words, the regime was certainly gathering strength during the 1980s, but it had not accumulated enough strength to concede democracy with confidence.

This warrants a novel interpretation of China's political development and democratization prospects since Tiananmen, which we undertake in chapter 9 on developmental socialism. China watchers hoping for democratization have long wondered, and repeatedly asked, *When will the CCP become so weak that it totally collapses?* According to the logic implicit in this question, the stronger the CCP gets, the less likely democratization will come to China. But if democracy in developmental Asia arises through strength more often than weakness, the relevant question becomes, *When will the CCP become strong enough that it can confidently concede democracy?* In other words, thirty years of developmental success might make democratization in China a nearer prospect rather than an increasingly distant one.

As the remainder of this chapter shows, when compared with the developmental statist regimes explored in chapters 4 and 5, both of which confronted democratization pressures in the 1980s alongside China, the CCP was by far the weakest among them. The Kuomintang (KMT), we contend, was in the strongest position when Taiwan began to democratize during the late 1980s. The Democratic Justice Party (DJP) in South Korea was less strong politically and confronted a considerably larger opposition, though the incumbent ruling party possessed enough accumulated strengths that it reasonably bet democracy would give the party a new lease on life. Taiwan and South Korea conceded democratic reform, we argue, precisely because the incumbent regimes were strong enough, and comparatively stronger than the CCP. Ironically, though not inexplicably according to our theory of democracy through strength, *the weakest authoritarian regime among them was the one that resisted democracy.* The remainder of this chapter explains why.

Mao and Socialist Development

Mao was a patriotic revolutionary. He led the CCP in wars on two fronts: an internal war against Chiang Kai-shek's nationalist KMT and an anti-imperialist war with Japan. Against the odds, Mao's peasant army was the victor in both wars. He mobilized China's vast peasantry with a promise and vision of a unified and strong China, one that would no longer be victim to foreign aggression or to internal efforts to divide the country through civil war. On October 1, 1949, having beaten down the retreated KMT and after Japan's defeat in World War II, Mao proclaimed the founding of the People's Republic of China (PRC).

Lacking an economic bureaucracy and any experience in actual governing, the CCP did not have a comprehensive plan for China's development.[4] Early on, Mao and the ruling party sought—and won—political legitimacy through the party's nationalist credentials and Maoist ideology. Mao's communist vision comprised three core principles. First, China's modernization would come about through socialist development. China would initially perfect an agrarian form of Marxism-Leninism, followed by state-led and state-owned industrial development. China's was to be a planned socialist economy through and through.

Second, China's rise would be a self-reliant one. Playing off a deeply entrenched victimization narrative—citing foreign and imperialist occupations from the British to the Japanese, or the "hundred years of humiliation"—Mao argued that China must look inward to develop itself. The CCP appealed to Leninist antiforeign, anti-imperialist nationalism. Mao's China saw no need to trade with the rest of the world. It did not require foreign technology, shutting its doors to global capital, investment, and influence. China's suspicions of foreign countries ran so deep that in the wake of the June 4 crackdown, nearly a half century later, a key belief among CCP leaders was that the 1989 prodemocracy student movement was the result of foreign meddling, instigated by foreign powers bent on undermining the communist regime. The CCP always insisted that foreign interests are committed to undermining China's rise.

The third and most critical principle of Mao's socialist vision was that China's development would harness the energy of the masses through ideological appeals. By mobilizing the masses—and here Mao had in mind China's peasantry—China's economy would develop through collective hard work and ideological purity and by drawing on a deep reservoir of nationalist and revolutionary spirit among all Chinese citizens. Mao traded on his revolutionary legitimacy, rather than performance legitimacy. The CCP, after all, was a revolutionary party that had defeated its bourgeois enemies, the KMT, in the Chinese civil war, and had won the war against imperialist Japan. Mobilizing the masses through ideological fidelity rather than economic results was critical to Mao's grip on political power. He understood politics to be a battle between his ideological allies and class enemies.

Mao launched the PRC's first five-year development plan in 1952. Recalled as the "mini leap forward," the plan was intended to lay the foundation of a socialist, planned economy. Land reform was carried out early on. Landowners were persecuted, and many executed, because they were deemed class enemies. The first five-year plan reformed the agricultural sector and agrarian life more generally. Farming households were organized into mutual aid societies and then into agricultural cooperatives. Land and farming activities were collectivized during the mid-1950s, destroying the vestiges of land ownership and the independent peasant household. Peasant loyalty was transferred to the collective and the local party secretary, and ultimately to Mao.

The first five-year plan proved to be the high tide of socialism in China. Energized by the PRC's recent founding and Mao's charismatic leadership, the mini leap forward was a successful experiment in early socialist development. From an economic development point of view, agricultural productivity increased, even though the gains were relatively modest and largely the result of hard work and effort, rather than more efficient means of production. Peasants remained poor, but less than before. Politically, China's early socialist experience was successful in energizing and mobilizing the peasantry's support of Mao and the CCP regime. It won the regime legitimacy.[5]

Buoyed by the initial success of the first five-year plan, Mao launched the Hundred Flowers Movement in 1956, in which he invited intellectuals, thinkers, and party officials to assess and even criticize Maoist ideology and the regime's socialist program. "Let a hundred flowers bloom and a hundred schools of thought contend," Mao asserted. Confident at the time—and as it turned out, overconfident—Mao expected praise and affirmation, and initially criticism from intellectuals was tepid. However, as the movement gained momentum and critics became emboldened, more and more contentious voices emerged, questioning Mao's mass mobilization approach to development. Critics pointed out how, in the first five-year plan, short-term productivity gains through hard work were inefficient and unsustainable. They highlighted the imperative of political and party reform, and how the emerging cult of personality around Mao was good for neither the CCP nor the country.

Surprised by the groundswell of criticism, Mao lashed out against his detractors and cracked down. Labeling critics as class enemies and bourgeois counterrevolutionaries, he unleashed the Anti-Rightist Campaign in June 1957, picking off those whose views clashed with Mao and Maoist ideology. By the end of the campaign, a few years later in 1959, several million dissidents had been "reeducated" in the countryside, sent to villages to learn from the virtuous peasants. Hundreds of thousands more of Mao's critics were investigated and dealt with by the regime's security apparatus, imprisoned or disappeared.

The initial years of the PRC revealed some key characteristics of the early CCP and of Mao's political instincts. Politically, power was uncontested and firmly in Mao's personal grip rather than institutionalized in the party. As China's charismatic dictator, he was a strong leader, while the ruling party was organizationally and institutionally weak. Economically, modernization and development adhered to Maoist thought and an unwavering commitment to socialist principles rather than economic pragmatism and market institutions. Ideological purity within the party and, importantly, ideological fidelity among the masses were central to political power. Unlike other developmental regimes explored in this book, Mao's political reign did not depend on economic performance and development as the source of popular legitimacy for the regime. Rather, bottom-up, mass mobilization generated political legitimacy.

Mao's fixation on ideological fidelity influenced the early evolution of the ruling party-state. Notably, Mao eschewed the bureaucratization and professionalization of the CCP. He viewed a developmental bureaucracy as bourgeois excess. He was deeply suspicious of so-called experts. For Mao, to be "red" was far more important than being an "expert." Not surprisingly in such a highly personalist regime, he was paranoid about those who might undermine his political authority inside the CCP. He punished those he feared to be ideological detractors, and he unceasingly worried about potential traitors within the party more generally, and within his own inner circle specifically.[6]

Mao's political instincts shaped the next phase of China's early development. In 1958 the CCP launched a highly ambitious economic development plan, the Great Leap Forward. Building on the achievements of the first plan, the mini leap forward, the Great Leap accelerated and deepened the rural collectivization campaign by transforming producer cooperatives into full-blown communes. Households in the communes lived and worked together, sharing in the provision and production of everything from farming to schooling to other social services. Land, animals for husbandry, and farming equipment belonged to the communes, not to households.

The ruling party imposed price controls and enforced production quotas more strictly, erasing any material incentives for increased productivity. Peasants labored to earn points instead of wages, and they worked to meet state production targets. Critics of the commune system characterized peasants as "subordinates" of the state plan, the commune, and the party secretary. Mao, on the other hand, believed the communal work brigades tapped into the energy of the masses and would accelerate China's socialist modernization.[7]

He was tragically wrong. China experienced the worst famine in human history in the two years after the start of the Great Leap Forward. From an economic and human development point of view, the Great Leap campaign was an unmitigated disaster. Poor crop yields created massive food shortages, leading to widespread starvation. Scholarly estimates suggest that up to 45 million people died between 1958 and 1962 during the Great Leap Forward. Meanwhile, zealous commune leaders overreported agricultural output, even when villagers were starving, in part for fear of failing to meet the state plan and in part to demonstrate their loyalty to Mao and the regime. The Great Leap Forward exemplified the irrationality of ideological rigidity at the expense of pragmatic developmental policy.[8] Mao's China was not a part of developmental Asia.

Mao's missteps were not limited to the domestic front, but extended to foreign affairs. Starting in the late 1950s, Mao criticized China's main geopolitical ally, the Soviet Union, and its leader, Premier Nikita Khrushchev. Mao took umbrage at Khrushchev's denunciation of Stalinism. Contrary to the view of other CCP leaders, he criticized the USSR's foreign policy to engage Europe's Western bloc, which Mao viewed as offensive, revisionist, and as socialism gone astray. His reckless barbs aimed at the USSR, which were not reflective of CCP policy, brought to a boil already simmering tensions between the two powers over their geopolitical strategies for internationalizing communism in the developing world. In 1960 the Soviet Union ceased the flow of economic aid and technical assistance to China, cementing the Sino-Soviet split. The withdrawal of Soviet aid exacerbated China's economic problems at home that had been brought on by the disastrous Great Leap Forward. Geopolitically, the PRC also lost its main communist ally and Cold War patron, leaving China isolated.

Maoism's Demise

By the late 1950s and into the early 1960s, Mao found himself increasingly sidelined inside the party and government leadership. Senior CCP leaders distanced themselves from the Great Leap Forward program and from the Great Helmsman himself. Opponents within the CCP saw Mao as a demagogue and a political liability. Many party leaders resented his growing cult of personality and the personalization of politics, both of which undermined the ruling party's organizational integrity and its political strength. Some within the CCP tried to shift the political spotlight away from Mao. During the 1959 National People's Congress, for instance, the CCP's second-highest-ranking official, Liu Shaoqi, replaced Mao as president of the PRC. The factional lines were drawn.

Mao was down, but certainly not out. Grasping at what personal power he had, he relentlessly and ruthlessly punished his opponents, and at the 1962 party plenum, he launched the Socialist Education Campaign to revitalize socialist ideology. In the wake of the disastrous Great Leap Forward, Mao feared the CCP was becoming overly bureaucratized, dominated by technocratic planners rather than ideological purists. The Socialist Education Campaign was intended to reignite from the bottom up the revolutionary fervor that had energized the masses during the early to mid-1950s. Through socialist education, Mao again emphasized the importance of being "red," by which he meant ideologically pure, over being an "expert," which he saw to be bourgeois and counterrevolutionary. Confronting opposition among his comrades in the party, Mao allied with the military and specifically factional leaders within the PLA leadership who were loyal to him.

By the early 1960s, Mao had set the stage for what would become the Cultural Revolution.[9] In totalitarian fashion, he turned to the masses to carry out the Cultural Revolution beginning in 1966. He used his revolutionary cult of personality to mobilize university students, appealing to their idealism and ideological zeal. The student movement organized into Red Guard brigades, representing millions of young devoted followers of Mao and Maoist thought. Mao instructed the Red Guards to "smash" the "four olds": old culture, old ideas, old habits, and old customs, all of which he considered vestiges of bourgeois tradition, the antithesis to socialist modernity. The Cultural Revolution was carried out from below by the Red Guards, though the puppet master pulling the strings at the top was Mao himself.

The Red Guards wreaked violent havoc on Chinese society. They destroyed temples, demolished buildings, toppled monuments, and torched books. They broke into and razed the homes of people deemed not red enough, and branded them counterrevolutionaries. Red Guards marched to their schools and universities, calling out and even physically beating their teachers and professors, accusing them of teaching traditional and bourgeois lessons. Mao encouraged them to attack local party officials who were not demonstrating their fealty to Mao and ideologically correct Maoist thought. Some Red Guards reported their own family members to the authorities.

China scholar Lucian Pye describes how the chaos of the Cultural Revolution caused by the Red Guards "brought China to the brink of anarchy." He goes on to say that "the assaults on authority were matched by attacks on everyone who in the slightest way deviated from the Guards' view of correct behavior."[10] Violence and chaos were endemic. No official record of the number of deaths resulting from the Cultural Revolution is available; however, based on archival research, scholars estimate that several hundreds of thousands of people died, with the death toll likely as high as in the millions.

While the Cultural Revolution instigated by Mao did tremendous damage to Chinese society and the economy, so too did Mao with respect to the CCP. As the Cultural Revolution intensified on the streets, factional battles within the party leadership heated up. Because his prestige and standing inside the CCP was diminishing, Mao turned to the Cultural Revolution to mobilize his factional power base in the ruling party and attack his enemies. Elite politics became street politics.

With the PLA on his side, Mao went after his two main adversaries in the CCP: Liu Shaoqi and Deng Xiaoping. Liu was stripped of his government post in 1966, along with his deputy chairmanship of the CCP. Mao's PLA ally, Marshal Lin Biao, replaced Liu in the party's second-highest-ranking post. Liu was also purged from the party and vilified, and he died a few years later in 1968, disgraced. Mao also targeted Deng, even though he was at one time Mao's close ally and carried out the 1957 Anti-Rightist Campaign. Mao purged Deng from the party and sent him to the countryside for ideological reeducation, where he stayed until the mid-1970s.

The Cultural Revolution officially ended in late 1968, though the turmoil and rot inside the ruling party continued to fester in Chinese society until Mao's death in 1976 and the arrest of his Cultural Revolution co-conspirators, the Gang of Four. Referred to as the "ten lost years," the Cultural Revolution, and Mao's dictatorship more generally, left China and the CCP in shambles. The party possessed little organizational strength, despite having been in power for nearly three decades. Personalist politics, rather than formal institutions, determined political outcomes. Factional splits and personal enmities shaped internal party politics rather than meaningful policy differences. Political power was vested in individuals as opposed to institutional rules.

The CCP lacked developmental legitimacy as well. Rather than generating performance legitimacy through economic development, such as in other developmental Asian economies, the ruling party under Mao banked on ideological legitimacy and its revolutionary credibility instead. Citizens came to distrust the regime and blamed the CCP for the destruction brought about by the Cultural Revolution and for the developmental disasters of the late 1950s and 1960s. The economy at the end of Mao's reign, internationally isolated and inefficient, virtually stalled. Per capita income in China had barely increased from US$90 in 1960 to just over $150 in 1978, after nearly two decades of socialist development. Meanwhile, its "bourgeois" Asian neighbors had raced ahead.

China's Economic Takeoff

Interim CCP leader Hua Guofeng rehabilitated Deng Xiaoping soon after Mao's death. Deng quickly mobilized his allies within the party around a reformist vision for China's development. He proposed a "second revolution," a fundamental break from Mao and a new path for the ruling party.[11] He politically outmaneuvered Hua and coalesced a powerful reform faction among CCP elders, cementing his status as China's "paramount leader" by 1978.

It was clear to Deng the ruling party needed to undo many of the programs and policies established during the Mao era. More fundamentally, China had to abandon Mao's rigid ideological commitment to socialist development and transform the CCP's modernization program to prioritize social and economic development. Socialist principles continued to guide China's development—after all, the CCP ruled the country—but economic pragmatism instead of ideological purity would drive the ruling party's reform agenda. Ideological appeals and mass mobilization won the CCP power in 1949, Deng reasoned, but socialist idealism and ideological rigidity would not keep the party in power unless citizens benefited from development.

Deng's regime set out to achieve three goals. First, the CCP prioritized economic development. By the late 1970s, reformers in the party were alarmed that many of China's neighbors, including Japan, Taiwan, and South Korea, were outpacing China in terms of economic growth. Deng acknowledged that the Great Leap Forward and Cultural Revolution had set the country back decades. China had fallen behind. Deng adopted a pragmatic approach to economic growth. Critically, he was receptive to more liberal, market-conforming economic policies. Reflecting his pragmatic approach, Deng famously remarked that "no matter if it is a white cat or a black cat; as long as it can catch mice, it is a good cat." He envisioned a new role for the ruling party. Rather than being the arbiter of ideological correctness, as the CCP was under Mao, Deng envisioned the ruling party and state apparatus becoming more technocratic and professionalized, staffed with experts and economic planners.

Deng's second goal was to rebuild the party apparatus. Chinese citizens were unsurprisingly cynical about the ruling CCP after the Cultural Revolution. After nearly thirty years in power, the ruling party had brought more destruction than development. Meanwhile, factional splits and political infighting in the party had done considerable damage to the CCP's ability to govern. Deng set out to get the party's organizational house in order. He crafted a powerful reformist coalition by elevating reform-minded officials such as Zhao Ziyang, Hu Yaobang, and Chen Yun to senior posts in the government and the party. He sidelined Mao loyalists, what remained of them. Deng also institutionalized a more decentralized, collectivist style of political decision-making, in an effort to eradicate the cult of personality that dominated party politics under Mao.[12]

Third, China's new leaders prioritized stabilizing Chinese society. Stability is critical to authoritarian regimes' ability to govern. For the CCP, the imperative of creating stability was paramount for China's modernization, especially given the tumult of the revolutionary civil war prior to 1949 and the developmental disasters that ensued. One way to achieve stability under authoritarianism is to rule with an iron fist, and the CCP retained its repressive capacities, notably through the party's control over the military and the state's internal security apparatus.

However, Deng also recognized the importance of economic performance legitimacy as a source of political power for the regime and a critical component of political and economic stability within society. Consequently, the post-1978 communist regime in China put performance legitimacy—and specifically economic performance legitimacy—at the center of its development plan. Similar to other authoritarian regimes in developmental Asia explored throughout this book, Deng looked to stabilize Chinese society and the regime itself by delivering economic development. He brought China into developmental Asia's fold.

The Four Modernizations campaign was the centerpiece of Deng's reform vision. It prioritized modernizing the agricultural sector, its industries, China's capabilities in science and technology, and its national defense and security. Importantly, the four modernization goals were interlinked: agricultural and industrial development depended on China's adoption of modern technologies, which in turn strengthened the country's capabilities in national defense. To accelerate its modernization in all these areas, China cautiously began opening its doors to the international economy and integrating market-conforming economic policies. The Four Modernizations campaign was in many ways a direct rebuke to Mao-era policies.

Under Deng, the CCP adopted a more market-regarding approach to economic growth. While the state continued to develop plans and targets, the government also introduced market incentives and mechanisms into the economy. The CCP did not jettison socialist planning entirely, but rather permitted market mechanisms to operate *alongside* the state sector. Over time, however, the government increasingly retreated from the economy's commanding heights.

Deng also adopted a more open-door international economic policy. He reversed Mao's inward-looking stance and introduced China's economy to international trade, investment, and capital flows, as well as the adoption of new and foreign technologies. Though the regime remained suspicious of international capital and foreign influence, it realized China could not rapidly develop if it remained closed to the rest of the world.

Deng launched his ambitious reform plan at the CCP plenum in December 1978. The first phase emphasized agricultural reform and abolished the commune system. Though land was still technically owned by the state, control over land was essentially given back to individual households to manage. The "rural responsibility system" meant households, rather than the collective or commune, were responsible for their agricultural production. The government continued to mandate production targets, though procurement prices rose after 1978. The rural responsibility system permitted farmers to sell their surplus (over production or procurement targets) on the open market, which incentivized crop diversification and investment in efficient farming technologies. In 1983, just five years after the reform era began, nearly every peasant household had signed on to the rural responsibility system. Productivity increased, as did peasant incomes, during the early years of reform.

The CCP reformed the industrial sectors in much the same way during the early 1980s. The government permitted a parallel market-based system alongside the state-determined plan. Company managers assumed more responsibilities over production and pricing. As in the rural responsibility system, surpluses could be sold at unregulated market prices, creating competition among firms. The lure of profits and revenues "beyond the plan" incentivized firms to invest in efficient productive capabilities and adopt innovative technologies to gain competitive advantage.

The introduction of market mechanisms unleashed a flurry of entrepreneurial activity, which led to the creation of new companies. Though the state-owned enterprise sector continued to dominate China's industrial landscape, industrial productivity among nonstate firms grew rapidly. Between 1979 and 1990, the non-state-owned enterprise sector grew its share of overall industrial output from 21.5 percent to 44 percent. Town and village enterprises in rural areas more than doubled their industrial output, from under 9 percent to 20.5 percent during the same period. By 1984, goods and services sold by non-state firms accounted for around half of retail consumption in China.

The most radical departure from Mao's vision of socialist development in Deng's reform plan was reversing China's closed-door policy. Deng's reforms opened up China to the international economy in an effort to transform its inward-looking growth model into an export-oriented industrialization one.[13] Similar to other East Asian developmental states in their earliest stage of industrialization, China created special economic zones in key cities along the coast to attract foreign direct investment (FDI) and develop an export base for Chinese firms. The zones increased the inflow of FDI from virtually zero in 1978 to nearly US$1.5 billion by 1984. The flow of FDI led to the creation of joint ventures in strategic industries. It also brought opportunities for companies and factories operating in China to sell their products in global markets.

Not surprisingly, international trade increased rapidly after 1978, growing from approximately US$20 billion to over $100 billion in 1988. Chinese exports, specifically, grew five times, from just US$10 billion to nearly $53 billion over that decade. Step by step, China was belatedly "joining" developmental Asia by opening its doors to international trade and investment.[14]

Yet it is important to stress that Deng's 1978 reforms were not tantamount to the marketization of the entire Chinese economy. The government's production and procurement plan remained China's economic core. The CCP did not completely relinquish its controls over pricing, nor did it give up its regulatory power to enforce production quotas. Rather, Deng's reforms introduced market mechanisms alongside the planned economy.

The state did not shrink. For instance, the state-owned enterprise sector continued to be massive. Government banks similarly retained a very strong hand in controlling and directing the flow of credit and domestic investment. Labor mobility as well as the ability of firms to hire and fire continued to be constrained by state regulations. The government did introduce incentives such as market pricing, but only for surplus production. In these respects, economic reform during the late 1970s was an effort by Chinese reformers to gradually *grow out of the plan* but not replace the socialist planned economy. The relentlessly and unabashedly capitalist developmental states of Northeast Asia remained a world apart.

Nevertheless, Deng's reforms were a radical departure from the Maoist era of socialist development as well. Productivity and consumption rose under Deng.

Poverty levels, especially in the countryside, dropped dramatically, as peasant household incomes grew early on in the reform era. Inflation was under control and prices remained stable. More and more workers from the countryside found employment in firms and factories popping up in cities and villages. China also maintained a positive balance of trade. The economy grew at nearly 10 percent per year from 1978 on, in line with Asia's other dynamic developmental states. In short, the early economic returns on Deng's reform plan were encouraging.

Accelerating Reform

Ruling party leaders shared a broad consensus that China needed to grow out of the planned economy. China's economic reform trajectory was on dual tracks, with the socialist plan representing one track alongside a second, complementary, market-oriented track. The 1978 reforms, they agreed, were an encouraging first step, though there was disagreement among them regarding the next phase of reform. The debate was about how, on the one hand, to maintain a socialist economy in which the state continued to play a critical role while, on the other hand, implementing market-regarding reforms. The disagreement among CCP leaders during the mid-1980s was not about the direction in which the economy was heading but rather about the speed and scope of reform.[15]

Cautious reformers in the CCP, such as party elder Chen Yun, proposed short-term austerity measures to rein in creeping inflation starting in the mid-1980s.[16] He sought to reimpose a more direct planning role for the government as well. For Chen's faction, the socialist track needed to continue to grow, not shrink, in proportion to the market. The state-planned sector, including state-owned enterprises, must continue to be dominant over the nonstate sector. Go-slow reformers worried that unfettered marketization and internationalization would destabilize China's economy.

On the other side of the debate, Premier Zhao Ziyang and CCP secretary-general Hu Yaobang pushed to accelerate the pace and expand the scope of liberalizing economic reform. They proposed injecting more, not fewer, market mechanisms into the economy. Whereas Chen and his allies in the party argued in favor of growing the state-planned socialist track, reformers like Zhao and Hu looked to freeze the size of the planned economy while accelerating the development of the market track. Over time, the marketized segments of the economy would dwarf the planned economy.

Zhao's vision won out. In October 1984 the ruling party introduced the second phase of the reform program, doubling down on Zhao's aggressive reform agenda. While state-owned firms were required to meet production targets, they were able to respond to market prices for surplus beyond the plan. Managers gained more authority in how they ran their companies as a result. Party interference declined, as the role of the party secretary diminished inside companies. State enterprises got into the market boom, diversifying and intensifying their production capabilities to meet government targets in addition to generating market revenues outside the plan. The government opened the door to experiments in alternative property and enterprise ownership schemes, including the introduction of cooperative, leasing, and stock ownership systems. This would have been unthinkable during the Mao era.

The CCP tinkered with how the government executed the planned part of the economy to simulate market conditions for state-owned firms. Rather than agreeing to annual production plans, the state gradually implemented a contracting system for industrial producers. Under this scheme, instead of production quotas, firms signed long-term multiyear contracts with the state. While firm managers took on the risk to meet their contractual obligations, they also gained the autonomy to strategically manage the company. The contracting scheme intensified competition among firms, which in turn incentivized enterprises to increase their production capabilities and productive efficiency.

Labor reform accompanied market reform. Before, wages were controlled and the government constrained labor mobility. After 1984, however, worker contracts, wages, and bonuses were increasingly tied to firm revenue and profitability. This change enabled enterprise managers to make rational market decisions when it came to wage-setting and worker contracts. A more competitive and less rigid labor market benefited firms, as they were less constrained in how they managed workers.

From the point of view of workers, however, labor reform presented a double-edged sword. On one hand, contracts replaced guaranteed employment for industrial labor, presenting more uncertainty to wage earners. On the other hand, because contracts and wages were determined by enterprise revenue and profitability, workers were incentivized to increase their productivity with the expectation of higher incomes.

Whither China's Fifth Modernization

In an effort to consolidate the ruling party's authority, one of Deng's key priorities after the tumultuous years under Mao, the CCP figured out how to generate popular legitimacy by delivering economic performance. China's economy grew at an average annual rate of 11.5 percent between 1983 and 1988, even faster than the initial reform period that began in 1978. During the 1980s, industrial development drove economic growth. While the farming sector stagnated somewhat, industrial growth skyrocketed. Industrial output grew from 8 percent annual growth during the first reform period between 1978 and 1983 to nearly 18 percent annually in the five years from 1983 to 1988. Even though China was still very far from rich, many Chinese people were becoming richer. They acknowledged Deng's leadership and the CCP's role in guiding China's remarkable development.

We know from the rest of developmental Asia that social and economic development leads to new expectations among citizens and new demands of the state. Development, as we have argued in this book, creates *more demanding citizens*. Development, paradoxically, breeds its own discontents. China was no different. That sweeping economic reforms were not accompanied by equally transformative political reforms meant there was no political pressure-release valve for citizens to voice their grievances and no arena for those grievances to be addressed. From the start of the reform period, critical voices occasionally emerged and openly challenged the legitimacy of the ruling party.

In 1978, political activist Wei Jingsheng advocated for a "fifth modernization" and mobilized the Democracy Wall movement, demanding democratic reform. Activists wanted to participate in political life. The protest movement had popular appeal because it recognized the people's suffering under Mao and their frustration with the Cultural Revolution and the destruction left in its wake. The Democracy Wall movement also appealed to protesters because of the promise of holding the ruling party accountable into the future, to ensure the tragedies of the 1950s and 1960s did not happen again.

The CCP regime crushed the movement that same year, not surprisingly. Political protests regularly broke out throughout the early part of the 1980s, though the regime easily dealt with political flare-ups. Protests tended to be local and far away from Beijing, the seat of political power. Having just emerged from the chaos of the Mao regime, the party was too unpopular, politically weak, organizationally broken, and politically illegitimate to concede political reform. Indeed, to concede at the time may have spelled the party's imminent demise, as would soon transpire across so much of the communist world.

Building Pressure, Weakening Regime

The antiregime protests that erupted a few years later in 1986 in Beijing, how-ever, sparked a deeper anxiety inside the party. That December, students took to the streets again to protest the authoritarian regime. Fang Lizhi, a university professor in Beijing and himself a member of the CCP, led the movement. He called out party leaders for their unethical behavior and corruption. He pointed to China's lack of democracy as the ruling party's failure and unful-filled promise to modernize the nation.

Fang criticized the regime's so-called representative institutions as authori-tarian window dressing, from the rubber-stamp National People's Congress at the very top to fixed village elections at the bottom. He questioned the extent to which the party had reformed itself, and whether the rule of law and formal institutions inside the party had effectively replaced the personalist politics of the Mao era. In many respects, Fang and his followers were calling out the party in a very public way.

Though the ruling party confronted protest movements regularly, the 1986 student protests were especially distressing for the regime for a variety of rea-sons, not least because they attracted national attention. The government at-tempted to muzzle the media but with little success. The students gained more and more allies in society, fomenting frustration with the regime. By 1986, political reform was no longer an abstract wish—something the intellectual classes debated among themselves—but rather a real reform agenda sought by many. By the end of December that year, antiregime protest movements mobilized in cities all across China, culminating on December 20, when 30,000 students, along with tens of thousands of other local protesters, marched in Shanghai to demand political reform.

The 1986 protests reflected deep legitimacy challenges facing the re-gime.[17] Despite extraordinary economic growth during the early part of the decade, the economy was beginning to show worrying signs of structural problems. The introduction of market reforms, and specifically market com-petition, contributed to economic uncertainty as company bankruptcies increased along with unemployment and worker incomes declined. Wage growth in the industrial sector was stagnant after 1986. At the same time, the increased flow throughout the economy of new industrial capital and credit—which grew over 25 percent per year after 1984—drove up consumer inflation rates. Inflation in 1985 was near 12 percent, a severe increase from just over 2 percent inflation in the preceding years. Consumer prices for food increased by 23 percent, making it difficult for industrial workers to make ends meet.

After several years of focusing on industrial development, growth in the agricultural economy, which at the time still employed the vast majority of workers in China, had slowed considerably by the mid-1980s. Agricultural productivity flattened, as neglect of the sector in terms of investment and the integration of new technologies contributed to deteriorating infrastructure in the countryside. Poor planning led to a decline in irrigated arable land. To make matters worse, government procurement guarantees shrunk as multiyear production contracts replaced annual quotas. State prices for agricultural products decreased as well, as the government was stuck in a fiscal bind. In some reported instances, the government gave peasants IOUs in lieu of cash payment. Consequently, rural incomes did not grow from 1985 to 1988, exacerbating the effects of inflation. China's developmental boom was leaving peasants behind.

Despite its efforts to grow out of the plan, the Chinese economy began to experience the pains of economic reform during the mid-1980s. The accelerated reforms implemented in 1984 introduced new market mechanisms, but without undoing or reforming the state plan. As a result, the CCP's liberalizing reforms of the mid-1980s were a patchwork of compromises and, at times, contradictory policies. For example, the economy was awash in credit, which was a shot in the arm that got industrialization going, but also drove up inflation. In another example, the imposition of price controls without the government's fiscal capacity to align prices and incomes adversely affected already poorer farmers and workers at state-owned firms.

Because it was designed to placate both the more liberal and more cautious voices in the party, the reform program failed to address many deeper structural challenges of marketization and implement the so-called hard reforms. The reforms of the mid-1980s kicked the can of hard reform further down the road. It was not just a lack of political will to take on the hard economic reforms but also the lack of administrative capacity in the state that stymied reform. Implementing difficult reforms required a strong state to guide the process. Still reeling from decades of manipulation and abuse by Mao and his anti-bureaucratic champions, however, the state lacked the capacity to follow through.

The state was still weak. Marketization reforms required the decentralization of power away from the central state apparatus. Provincial governments and local administrations gained more authority and consequently developed their own subnational strategies for economic growth. Provincial authorities, instead of the central state, leveraged their regulatory powers, for example, to set procurement targets and prices, channel industrial investment, seed new industries and sectors, develop joint ventures with foreign investors, and importantly, collect taxes and other revenues for provincial, not central, coffers. Provincial and local developmental states were supplanting the national developmental state. As a result, the central state's share of fiscal revenue fell dramatically after 1978, going from the equivalent of 35 percent of gross national product to 20 percent a decade later.

The central government came to rely on borrowing from local and provincial authorities, leading to increasingly dire deficit situations for the central state. It was not until the mid-1990s that the national government reformed the tax system. Until then, however, the state was markedly weak, without the administrative or fiscal capacity to direct China's reform process through the difficult bumps it experienced during the mid-1980s.[18] Unlike in Japan, Taiwan, and South Korea, there was no prospect of a strong developmental bureaucracy in China to stabilize and weather the storms of more difficult political and economic reforms.

To make matters worse, spiking inflation and stagnant incomes exacerbated socioeconomic inequality. Contrary to the regime's commitment to a socialist economy, the benefits of growth during the 1980s failed to reach the majority of the people. Economic problems undermined social solidarity. Popular consumer campaigns such as the "Eight Bigs" (ownership of a color television, a refrigerator, a motorcycle, and other conspicuous consumer goods) emphasized social disparities during the Deng years, in stark contrast to the shared austerity of Maoist socialism. Corruption among party officials and entrepreneurs was getting out of hand, specifically in the coastal cities and special economic zones, where business wheeling and dealing was especially pronounced. Reporting on increasingly rampant corruption amplified the divisions between the haves and have-nots and further undermined the party's fragile legitimacy.[19]

In other words, China's remarkable economic growth was not able to mask the troubling trends in the economy and society and the difficult reforms that needed to be undertaken. Aggregate economic growth alone was unable to subdue and placate the rising tidal wave of antiregime protesters. The regime's developmental pact—the insistence on political acquiescence amid the promise of economic development—started to unravel by the mid-1980s, only a few years after it had begun. Intellectuals, students, workers, and ordinary Chinese directed their frustrations toward the CCP. Political pressure on the regime was building, and without any pressure-release valve in the political system, the situation looked likely to explode.

The momentum of the December protests carried over into January 1987 and showed no signs of slowing. The regime had had enough and decided to end the uprising. The hard-line faction galvanized around a harsh authoritarian response and quashed the student movement. The university dismissed Professor Fang Lizhi from his post, and the party purged him from its ranks. The CCP authorities cleared the students out of Tiananmen Square and elsewhere around the country.

Cracking down on the protesters on the streets was not enough. Members of the party would have to pay as well. That month, party secretary-general Hu Yaobang was forced to resign his position and his leadership of the CCP. His reputation as a liberal reformer set him up as the scapegoat for the regime's hard-liners. Hu's public demotion also sent a clear signal to prodemocracy activists that the CCP was not going to tolerate demands for political reform. The CCP subsequently named Zhao Ziyang party chief. Zhao's past associations with Hu, however, made him a marked man, and it would only be a matter of time before the hard-line faction in the party turned against him too.

The following year, 1988, was a very difficult one for China's economy. All of the challenges that had emerged a few years earlier came to a head. Grain production continued to fall due to weather and poor harvests. People were going hungry. Peasant incomes declined as state prices for staples decreased. Labor unrest was on the rise, as workers confronted the threat of unemployment and wage cuts across China's industrial sectors. Inequality continued to go up as well, and Chinese society became increasingly stratified across regions, between the cities and the countryside, and between workers and the rising new professional and middle classes. Inflation rates soared to over 20 percent that year, which, combined with declining wages and rural household incomes, made life miserable for most. That summer, consumers desperately hoarded staple goods, driving up inflationary pressures on the cost of essentials. Internationally, China's exports sagged, which led to trade deficits. The inflow of FDI fell short of targets as well that year.

Perhaps most explosive for the regime was when a report came out that revealed that 150,000 party members had been investigated and punished for corruption in 1987, and that 25,000 of them had been pardoned. If the social, economic, and political challenges that year were the proximate cause of what came in 1989—the tinderbox that sparked the Tiananmen protests—then public revelations of the party's rampant corruption were the match that set it off.

The Tiananmen Massacre

Student protesters mobilized in early 1989 to demand political reform. The movement galvanized when former CCP leader Hu Yaobang died on April 15. Democratic activists lionized Hu as a liberal reformer—a progressive image that, ironically, the party reinforced when it scapegoated him for the 1987 student uprising—and his death mobilized student protesters all over China. The party had indirectly created a democratic martyr. Students assembled in Tiananmen Square to mourn Hu's death and demand the regime initiate political reform.[20]

Throughout the spring of 1989, students peacefully protested in the square. They asked to confer with senior party leaders, though the regime largely ignored their requests. The few times student leaders met with CCP officials, they and their demands were summarily dismissed. In May, the students went on a hunger strike, generating more sympathy and support across the country. Secretary-General Zhao Ziyang went to the square to bring a sympathetic message to the students. He implored them to end their protest and go home. Zhao's comrades in the CCP saw his overtures as a betrayal of the party and its increasingly hard-line stance on political reform. Though he was one of the party's leaders who had boldly set China on its developmental path, the CCP purged him and placed him under house arrest at the end of May.

Hu's and Zhao's demise revealed not only the brutal swiftness of the CCP but also how the ruling party lacked the formal institutions to manage and reconcile internal political conflict. Despite Deng's goal to consolidate the ruling party in the wake of the Cultural Revolution, the CCP continued to rule and govern largely through informal mechanisms. Uncertainty, as opposed to routinized formal practices, informed how party officials maneuvered and mobilized support within the CCP. Efforts by Deng to institutionalize a more collectivist, consensus-building style of decision-making fell apart when the party experienced crises. Notably, though it had been in power for nearly forty years, the CCP lacked a formal process for leadership succession. By the 1980s, Deng himself did not have any formal leadership posts in the party or government, even though he exercised a tremendous amount of political power in his informal role as paramount leader.

The CCP's lack of organizational resilience was consequential, as the party became deeply divided in the 1989 crisis. The lines between the liberal reformist and hard-line factions began to harden in 1987, when the party politically scapegoated Hu. By the spring of 1989, internal party divisions were so pronounced and irreconcilable that when the CCP confronted a mounting political challenge, it reverted to its old ways of managing internal conflict by purging and expelling its own. It was unable to stay unified, and instead aired its rifts publicly by openly sacrificing popular leaders who had fallen out of favor. Records from internal party meetings after the Tiananmen crackdown show that CCP leaders blamed disunity within the party leadership for the 1989 "rebellion," and that the deep divisions inside the party reflected the CCP's weakness. Even the CCP itself conceded it was not a cohesive party.[21]

By mid-May, an estimated one million protesters had assembled in and around Tiananmen Square. The movement spread across the entire country, mobilizing students, workers, and ordinary Chinese citizens who supported the students. Demonstrators openly and brazenly demanded Deng resign and step down as China's leader. Within the CCP, hard-liners led by Premier Li Peng rallied to decisively and violently end the Tiananmen protests. The distance between the two factions was so great and irreconcilable that the "contradiction" and conflict among them were an "all-or-nothing" contest.[22] Compromise, by this point, was out of the question. The hard-liners won the internal party struggle when Deng endorsed Li's plan to crack down. The regime declared martial law on May 20 and PLA troops soon surrounded the square.

Despite the military's show of potentially lethal force, the troops could not initially disperse the protesters. Over the next week or so, chaos and disorder poured into Beijing's streets, portending more instability for the regime, something the CCP desperately feared. By early June, the pressure from the standoff between the PLA troops and the protesters was untenable. Foreign officials watching the scene unfold in Beijing worried the CCP regime had few remaining options. The ruling party arrived at the same conclusion. Tragically, on late June 3 and into the morning of June 4, the CCP ordered PLA soldiers to enter the square and to fire on the student protesters, bringing to a tragic head what history would come to know as the Tiananmen Massacre.

Resisting Democracy

The CCP regime did not collapse during the summer of 1989, nor did it succumb to the Tiananmen protesters' demands and lead China in a transition to democracy. One interpretation of the events of 1989 is that the ruling party's resistance to democracy was a function of the regime's resilience and strength. Put another way, despite the CCP being on its heels politically, it was *not weak enough* to be overthrown by the prodemocracy protesters, nor was the ruling regime either so unpopular it collapsed under the weight of its illegitimacy or so divided as to crumble through waves of internal defections.

The assertion that the CCP was not weak enough to transition to democracy informs the dominant view or conventional wisdom surrounding democratic prospects in China: that democratic reform will come about when the regime is so weak that it cannot survive. Democracy, in this scenario, emerges from the ashes of a collapsed CCP regime. The collapse-cum-democracy perspective has remained the dominant view among China watchers in China and the rest of the world ever since.

Following this logic, some argue that because the CCP regime did not crumble in the summer of 1989, and shows even fewer signs of weakening and collapsing as the country becomes richer, more developed, and more powerful, expecting democracy to come to China is a fool's game. The regime is even less likely to collapse today because it is stronger. Apologists for the authoritarian regime contend that China and the CCP need not democratize, as the resilient "China model" provides an alternative, and some might argue superior, route to modernity. Democracy, they insist, is not a defining feature of a country's political modernization.[23] Meanwhile, democratic hopefuls hunt for cracks in the ruling party's authority and signs the regime is about to collapse.[24] Either way, *China will democratize only when the ruling party is weak.*

In our theory, which draws lessons for China from East Asia rather than Eastern Europe, *China is more likely to democratize when—and in part because—the ruling party is strong.* Obviously, China's authoritarian regime did not collapse in June 1989, nor did the Tiananmen protesters overthrow the government. But collapse is not the only way that democracy comes about; authoritarian concessions are also possible. And we contend that as of 1989, the CCP was *not strong enough to concede democracy with confidence,* and this helps to explain why the regime chose to eschew a democratic path then.

The party, while strong enough to violently put down the Tiananmen protesters in 1989, was organizationally weak, having failed to institutionalize mechanisms to mediate party politics and mitigate internal conflict. Furthermore, the bureaucratic state lacked the fiscal and administrative capacity to implement difficult social, economic, and administrative reforms. The CCP lacked the antecedent strengths and thus the confidence to concede democracy. It did not look like the developmental authoritarian regimes in Taiwan, South Korea, and Japan, which chose to concede democracy through strength.

The CCP was unpopular at the time, lacking the victory confidence that incentivizes strong regimes to concede political reform. The fact that the events of the spring and summer of 1989 occurred so soon after China and the ruling party emerged from the destruction of the Cultural Revolution and the disastrous consequences of the Great Leap Forward meant the CCP regime was in the early stages of building its credibility and political legitimacy. The CCP in 1989 did not yet have a strong "usable past," a developmental record of achievement it could lean on to stably guide China's development; if anything, the recentness of the Mao years saddled the party with an "unusable past." The CCP understandably feared chaos and disruption, and lacked the stability confidence that the country and the party could manage its tumultuous political crisis without ready recourse to a full battery of repressive controls.

Compared with the KMT and other dominant catch-all parties in developmental East Asia, the CCP lacked organizational capacity and political appeal.[25] Though the Taiwanese and South Korean DJP regimes confronted popular pressures from below, especially in South Korea, in neither scenario was the opposition as destabilizing as the successive waves of protest that erupted in China throughout the 1980s. It is worth remembering that in postwar Japan and in Taiwan and South Korea during the late 1980s, democratic transition occurred in periods of economic growth and stability, rather than crisis. The latter half of the 1980s was anything but stable in China.

Our theory of democracy through strength expects that stronger ruling parties are most likely to concede democracy and promote a stable transition when they are only slightly past the apex of their power. The KMT in Taiwan was the strongest of the affirming cases examined in this book so far, while South Korea's DJP was the weakest. But in both cases, along with conservative politicians in Japan, the incumbent regimes were nonetheless *strong enough* that they conceded democracy with confidence. China's CCP in 1989, however, was weakest among them.

Looking ahead, we can also conclude that the CCP in 1989 was not yet anywhere near what would become its apex of power in the reform era. The party was not a waning political power either, an authoritarian regime that had hurtled through what we call the bittersweet spot. Rather, the CCP in 1989 *was a party on the rise*, and one that needed to put more distance between its developmental record and the destruction of the decade before, accumulate more organizational and institutional strength, continue to lead China's development and create a more compelling usable past, and put the ruling party in a position where democracy through strength was even a plausible option. As the CCP would become much stronger after 1989, we might think of the tragic Tiananmen epilogue not as the end of the road for China's democratization struggles, but as a prologue to China's next stage of political and economic development.

7

Developmental Militarism

REVERSIBLE EXITS

THE CASES IN the developmental statist cluster introduced in chapters 3–5 were unusual in their historical authoritarian strengths, which enabled them to initiate and carry out comparatively smooth democratization pathways. The fact, however, is that few authoritarian regimes have ever built such impressive strengths, in terms of either their institutions or their economic track records, even in developmental Asia. This was the central lesson of chapter 6, where the Chinese Communist Party lacked the "usable past" necessary to countenance democratic concessions during the Tiananmen Square protests of 1989. As we now move into our developmental militarist cluster—Indonesia, Thailand, and Myanmar—we encounter additional cases with intermediate rather than highly impressive institutional strengths and "usable pasts."

And yet, despite these relative authoritarian weaknesses, Southeast Asia's three historically militarized regimes have all pursued democracy through strength, at one time or another, in a manner resembling what we have already seen in Japan, Taiwan, and South Korea. In Thailand in the 1980s, Indonesia in the late 1990s, and Myanmar in the early 2010s, military regimes substantially reduced repression, opened up political space, and allowed competitive elections as a way of sharing power with civilian politicians. This process tended to unfold at moments when militaries were relatively confident that political stability could be maintained or improved by increasing electoral competition, not snuffing it out.

Whether this reversible experiment actually culminated in democratic transformation and the long-term survival of the incumbent regime mostly hinged on whether the military's stability confidence was fulfilled. This primarily depended, in turn, on varied legacies of institutional development under militarized rule. Indonesia has enjoyed more democratic success than either Myanmar or Thailand since the turn of the millennium because of the inherited strength of party and state institutions built up under Suharto's authoritarian New Order during the previous millennium. Myanmar and Thailand, on the other hand, have chronically lacked strong and popular parties representing old elites sympathetic to military interests and have been more persistently beset by regional insurgencies threatening national stability. They thus experienced rockier, more incomplete, and ultimately more reversible exits from militarized rule than Indonesia.

From one perspective, our three developmental militarist cases are simply weaker versions of what we encountered in our three cases in the developmental statist cluster. Yet the purpose and payoff of our clustered analysis lie in illuminating how cases in different clusters are also *different types* of political economies and authoritarian regimes. The developmental militarist cases are qualitatively different from the developmental statist cases in at least four important ways. This necessitates a different kind of narrative from the ones offered in our most paradigmatic democracy-through-strength cases.

First, in this chapter, our analysis centers more on stability confidence than victory confidence. Unlike ruling parties, ruling militaries do not need to win elections to protect their elite privileges and prerogatives. Even when they are not highly confident that the introduction of democratic elections will deliver victory to the most pro-military parties, military leaders can nonetheless support democratization if they are confident that stability will not be compromised in the political transition. Stability includes continued economic development, uninterrupted corruption opportunities, guaranteed immunity from prosecution for past human rights abuses, manageable conflict with the military's opponents, and relative peace with historically rebellious regions. In all three of the militarist cases, preemptive democratic experiments at least initially rested more on the military's confidence in these areas than on their expectations of positive results in national democratic elections. Victory confidence still matters, but stability confidence is paramount when it comes to the world of developmental militarism.[1]

Second, more than in any other cluster, this stability confidence centered on the manageability of regional and separatist insurgencies on the territorial periphery. In all three militarist cases, armed and organized threats to the political center either were absent (as in Thailand) or had been defeated (in Indonesia and Myanmar) during initial processes of authoritarian consolidation.

The same cannot be said for threats to territorial integrity, smoldering in the national periphery. Recall that a major reason for stability confidence in Japan, Taiwan, and South Korea was that the communist threat was primarily external rather than internal. Although the internal threat was not absent in Indonesia, Thailand, and Myanmar, it became manageable in all three cases over the course of the Cold War. The waning communist threat was a major source of stability confidence across the militarist cluster. Separatist threats generally loomed much larger and have posed a consistent threat to democratic consolidation that has been absent in the developmental statist cluster.

Third, democratization through strength has also led to qualitatively different outcomes in the militarist cluster from those in the statist cluster. Whereas democratization saw civilian leaders moving from strength to strength in Japan, Taiwan, and even in semi-militarized South Korea, democratic experiments ushered in an era of what we call civilian-military cohabitation in Indonesia, Myanmar, and Thailand. By democratizing at moments of relative strength, military leaders could play a leading role in designing the rules of the democratic game, including the preservation of substantial military prerogatives alongside newly democratically elected civilian leaderships.[2]

We refer to these arrangements as cohabitation because democratization meant neither the veneer of demilitarization nor an overseer role for the military; instead, it meant more of a peer relationship between civilian and military leaders as relative equals, with each side enjoying its own sizable political bailiwicks. The fact that military leaders could remain standing alongside democratically elected civilians in appointed parliamentary seats, at least during the early days of democratic experiments in all three cases, contributed to the stability confidence so fundamental to democracy through strength. As we saw in chapter 3, the era of Taisho democracy during the 1920s in Japan resembled such cohabitation, demonstrating how such democratic cohabitation arrangements are ultimately tenuous and, as we saw in Japan in the 1930s, reversible.

Fourth, democratization meant substantially different outcomes for the political economies of the militarist cluster. Although corruption was and remains a problem in all three developmental statist cases, it is not the core dynamic that makes their economies function. Japan, Taiwan, and South Korea were all resource-poor countries where techno-nationalism and highly efficient manufacturing paved their parallel "pathways from the periphery."[3] By contrast, Indonesia, Myanmar, and Thailand are all resource-rich countries, highly dependent on foreign direct investment (FDI) to move from low-income toward middle-income status in recent decades.

The upshot has been rampant corruption opportunities for military officers, both when they have been in power and when they have stood alongside democratic civilian leaders in cohabitation arrangements. Therefore, the expected continuity of opportunities for grand corruption has underpinned preemptive democratic experiments in the militarist cluster. Militaries in this developmental Asian cluster have thus done what Barrington Moore, echoing Karl Marx and Friedrich Engels, once argued the bourgeoisie must ultimately do to protect its fortunes—trade the right to rule for the right to make money.[4]

The Three Cases to Come

Our case studies begin with Indonesia. Similar to the South Korean case explored in chapter 5, Indonesia's authoritarian regime was neither a purely party-dominated nor military-dominated autocracy. Suharto's New Order dictatorship (1966–98) was born in one of the most violent counterrevolutionary outbursts of the Cold War era, with hundreds of thousands of suspected communists perishing at the hands of the Suharto-led military and its conservative (largely but not exclusively Islamist) allies.[5] Opening the country up to Western and Japanese investment, Suharto ushered Indonesia into developmental Asia and oversaw three decades of spectacular economic growth as well as impressive poverty reduction and substantial urbanization. No feature of Indonesia's political economy under Suharto was more striking than its grand corruption, however.

Politically speaking, Suharto installed a tightly managed electoral authoritarian regime. A new authoritarian party, Golkar, was built with military and bureaucratic backing to "success" multiparty authoritarian elections every five years. When the corruption-ridden Indonesian economy was devastated in 1997–98 by the Asian financial crisis, Suharto exited power as a profoundly weakened leader. But it would only be in the following year that his successor, B. J. Habibie, would dismantle the New Order's many authoritarian controls and move Indonesia swiftly to free and fair democratic elections in 1999. The relative smoothness of this democratization process and the cohesive support for it among party and military elites as it progressed can only be understood against the backdrop of authoritarian and conservative strengths—and thus confidence—accumulated over more than three decades of Suharto's rule.

This was neither the first time nor the last time that a developmental militarist regime in Southeast Asia would concede democracy through strength. After devoting the bulk of this chapter to detailing the Indonesian trajectory from development to democracy, we turn to the militarist cases that preceded (Thailand) and followed in Indonesia's footsteps (Myanmar).

From the late 1970s through the late 1980s, Thailand's long-dominant authoritarian elite—its monarchy, military, and bureaucracy—gradually moved the kingdom to civilian rule under fully democratic conditions. This followed a tumultuous democratic experiment from 1973 to 1976, during which the collapse of a corrupt military triumvirate led to three years of intense ideological polarization, culminating in a brutal crackdown on leftist elements in the nation's capital of Bangkok.[6] As in South Korea in the early 1960s, democracy through weakness in Thailand in the mid-1970s proved destabilizing and was quickly, brutally reversed.

What followed was not a return to full-blown authoritarian rule, however, but a gradual process of democratization through strength in which the military and its technocratic allies introduced elections and devised a new constitution and electoral system. The new rules of the game ensured that party politicians could not concentrate enough power to reign supreme over the military and, especially, the monarchy of King Bhumipol. This gradually democratizing system survived a military coup and power grab in 1991–92 and remained steady until the Asian financial crisis of 1997–98 devastated the Thai economy. In response to the crash, democratic politicians wrote a new constitution that concentrated more power in the prime minister and encouraged a consolidation of the perennially fragmented party system.[7]

Despite undeniable twists and turns, one could argue that from approximately 1980 to 2006, Thailand boasted Southeast Asia's most stable democracy. This broadly confirmed the confidence of its originators that democratization would help preserve conservative and stable outcomes. However, the meteoric electoral ascendancy of populist tycoon Thaksin Shinawatra in the early 2000s would prove the electoral Achilles' heel of the country's ruling oligarchy.

Thaksin's rise occurred against the backdrop of Thailand's lack of a powerful conservative party, even of the intermediate caliber of Indonesia's Golkar. The fact that Thai democracy has careened and collapsed over the past fifteen years is inexplicable without understanding how victory confidence in Thailand has been hindered by conservatives' continued dependence on the monarchy rather than a cohesive conservative political party.[8] One must also appreciate how Thaksin's Thai Rak Thai party was perceived as a threat to Thailand's entrenched power structure, shaking stability confidence as well.

Few would have imagined before 2011 that Myanmar, formerly called Burma, would follow Indonesia's and Thailand's footsteps on the trajectory from developmental militarism to democracy through strength.[9] Yet Myanmar's fragile, incomplete, violence-ridden, and ultimately reversed democratic experiment from 2011 to 2021 was actually decades in the making. After the socialist and isolationist military-led regime of Ne Win teetered on the brink of collapse during the popular uprising of 1988 and saw its party allies suffer a landslide defeat at the hands of Aung San Suu Kyi's National League for Democracy (NLD) in 1990, it cracked down hard and became one of the post–Cold War world's most notorious rogue dictatorships. While the world condemned and sanctioned the brutal regime, remarkably, it began charting a long and fraught path toward democracy through strength, despite the military's atrocious developmental track record and its fateful delay in constructing a conservative party vehicle to compete on its electoral behalf.

Myanmar's dictatorship prized stability confidence, as we would expect in a military regime. Once it managed over the course of the 1990s and 2000s to snuff out popular unrest, resolve internal military factionalism, forge peace agreements with many of the deeply divided nation's ethnic armed organizations, and most importantly impose its preferred constitution, which protected military privileges, the military regime enjoyed sufficient stability confidence to open up the political process in 2011, seemingly overnight.

Although the military's favored party was decimated in the NLD landslide electoral victory in 2015, the military itself retained the powers and privileges it valued most, even after peacefully accepting the results of what can only be described as a fully democratic electoral shellacking. The result from 2015 to 2020 was not merely a mildly liberalized but unreformed military regime, but rather a bona fide system of cohabitation in which a freely constituted civilian and democratic regime jockeyed for primacy with the military-led side of the state.

On February 1, 2021, Myanmar's reversible democratic experiment was tragically reversed. The NLD's second landslide electoral win in November 2020 clearly heightened military fears that its prerogatives could not easily withstand an NLD so strongly legitimated and emboldened. This prompted military commander Min Aung Hlaing to pull the plug on civilian-military cohabitation, likely to secure his own personal political interests as much as the military's political interests. One cannot understand either how Myanmar's democratization experiment began in 2011 or ended in 2021 without appreciating how much more confidence in democratic processes the ruling military possessed at reform's beginning than at its end.

Indonesia

Indonesia is one of the most surprising democracies in the world today. On virtually every global indicator, Indonesia looks more likely to be authoritarian than democratic. The country is on the poorer side of middle-income status; the population is overwhelmingly Muslim, as well as ethnically diverse; the territory is recurrently threatened with disintegration by armed regional insurgencies; and the region where Indonesia lies, Southeast Asia, is hardly a neighborhood in which democracies diffuse and spread. None of these features augur well for Indonesia's democratic prospects.

Lacking the conventional "democratic prerequisites," Indonesia's democratization is seemingly best explained as a case of democracy through weakness. This interpretation is hardly without merit. The authoritarian regime of former general Suharto had become highly personalized and irredeemably corrupt by the 1990s. The Indonesian economy was absolutely devastated by the Asian financial crisis in 1997–98.[10] Urban protests erupted, and the military was split over whether to defend the aging president. By the time student protests overwhelmed and occupied the nation's parliament in Jakarta, and a series of top regime supporters began calling for the president's immediate resignation in a cascade of elite defections, the Suharto regime had simply run its course.[11]

Suharto resigned on live television on May 21, 1998, to the cheers and relief of millions, handing power to his vice president, B. J. Habibie. One year later, free and fair democratic elections were held in Indonesia for the first time in forty-four years. The incumbent Golkar party finished a distant second in the parliamentary polls. After Habibie's "accountability speech" was rejected in the special parliamentary session in November 1999, a pairing of perhaps the two most prominent Suharto critics—liberal religious cleric Abdurrahman Wahid and nationalist icon Megawati Sukarnoputri—were selected as president and vice president. Indonesia's miraculous democratic transition was completed, though its democratic consolidation remained anything but assured.

More than twenty years later, however, Indonesia remains a democracy, having experienced its fifth peaceful national election in 2019. After shooting dramatically upward with the transition of the late 1990s and staying basically steady in the first decade of the 2000s, Indonesia's democracy indicators have softened only slightly, albeit very worrisomely, throughout the 2010s.

The preceding narrative portrays Indonesia as a consummate case of democracy through weakness, which, as we readily concede, is not an entirely inaccurate account. But it is an incomplete account, and in certain respects it is fundamentally misleading. It is incomplete in the sense that Indonesia's incumbent authoritarian elites beyond Suharto enjoyed considerable and lasting political strengths at the time of transition in the late 1990s, despite the depth of the sudden economic shock. It is misleading in that Suharto's fall and his removal from office in 1998, which most assuredly occurred at his weakest political moment, did not constitute Indonesia's democratization. A dictatorship can often remain standing (or get restored quickly) after a particular dictator falls.[12] Yet in Indonesia, a weakened dictatorship was replaced in relatively short order by a surprisingly strong democracy. This was only possible because incumbent authoritarian elites retained substantial antecedent strengths that Suharto himself had lost.

For all its glaring differences from the developmental statist cases of Japan, Taiwan, and South Korea, Indonesia's experience with democratization displayed certain key parallels. It was, we argue, another case of democracy through strength. As in Japan, the devastation of a *country* coincided with relative political advances by its leading civilian *conservatives*, including those who could fare well in free and fair elections.

Similar to the Kuomintang (KMT) in Taiwan, the authoritarian Golkar party possessed an impressive party infrastructure and a credible decades-long developmental track record. This gave some measure of confidence that it could fare reasonably well in fully democratic elections, especially in rural and remote areas. The parallels with South Korea are even stronger. In Indonesia, as in South Korea, massive urban cross-class protests were a major stimulant to democratic change, the military played a role rivaling that of the ruling party in overseeing the transition process, and democratic elections ultimately served to divide and temper the strongest opponents of military rule, whereas worsening authoritarian repression had increasingly unified and emboldened them.

The upshot was that Indonesia's incumbent authoritarian elite remained standing throughout the country's democratization process. So much so, in fact, that the military practically stood in a status of cohabitation with elected civilian leaders for the first several years of the transition, particularly by enjoying appointed seats in parliament from 1999 to 2004.[13] But that has not meant that the eventual outcome has been less than democratic. Rather, it has meant that democratization proved surprisingly stable and durable, despite all the reasons Indonesia seemed such a poor candidate for democracy either to emerge or to endure. As elsewhere, Indonesian democratization through strength was a reversible experiment, and what matters most is that—unlike in Thailand or Myanmar, for reasons our theory should help illuminate—it is still yet to be reversed after more than two decades.

There is a fascinating analogy here between democratization in Indonesia and Japan. As we saw in chapter 3, Japanese democratization unfolded at a time when the country was at its weakest. Yet civilian conservative politicians and bureaucrats were arguably at their strongest, given American support, the decimated military in the wake of the war, and a weak Left. Similarly, in Indonesia, the nation's economy was a basket case, but its conservative elites had enough political strength to be looking ahead with some confidence about their political futures. There is also a parallel with South Korea in that the Indonesian military, driven more by stability confidence than victory confidence, was a leading player in realizing Indonesia's transition to democracy through strength. The same will be true, in fact even more true, in the purer military regimes of Myanmar and Thailand discussed later in this chapter.

Authoritarian Economic Development

Economic factors might immediately point one to a "weakness" rather than "strength" interpretation of Indonesian democratization. Among all the countries that have democratized since the global "Third Wave" of democratization began in the 1970s, none has done so amid more dramatically worsening economic conditions than Indonesia.[14] Unlike in Taiwan and South Korea, democratic transition did not occur in Indonesia during "good times." The drop in economic growth rates from the start of the Asian financial crisis in 1997 until its bottom in 1999 was truly precipitous. This plunge in real economic output was paralleled in the financial sector, where Indonesia's currency (the rupiah, or Rp) plummeted from over Rp 2,000 per US dollar to under Rp 13,000 per US dollar in a matter of weeks. The private banking sector collapsed under the weight of its dollar-denominated debts.

To the extent that democratizing during economic crisis produces rockier outcomes than democratizing in good economic times, the conditions surrounding Indonesia's democratic transition could hardly have been less auspicious. To be sure, its democratization was the polar opposite of "non-crisis transitions" in Taiwan, South Korea, and Thailand (explored later in this chapter), if viewed from a strictly short-term economic perspective.[15]

Yet a longer view is essential to appreciate Indonesia's considerable economic strengths as well as its weaknesses at the moment when democratization commenced. Indonesia's fall was so dramatic and devastating in large measure because its rise had been so stratospheric and sustained. Suharto's authoritarian rule from 1966 to 1998 may have famously been an era of colossal corruption, but it was also unmistakably an extended period of rapid and steady growth, accompanied by remarkable reductions in extreme poverty and the emergence of a sizable urban middle class—very different in degree, but not in kind, from what earlier unfolded across the developmental statist cluster. Simply put, the Suharto regime brought Indonesia into developmental Asia and achieved tremendous economic success.

When Suharto seized power in the counterrevolutionary bloodbath against the Indonesian Communist Party (PKI) and its suspected sympathizers in 1965–66, the country was an economic pauper. Hyperinflation and hunger ran rampant from the late 1950s through the mid-1960s, as Indonesia's founding father and president, Sukarno, mismanaged the economy terribly during the country's years of "Guided Democracy" (1959–65). The economy was overwhelmingly agricultural yet far from self-sufficient in rice, the nation's staple crop.

By virtue of massive influxes of foreign aid, oil revenue, and economic reforms designed to generate investment both foreign and domestic, the Indonesian economy had made a dramatic turnaround by the mid-1970s. Far from catering to urban dwellers at the expense of the countryside, Indonesia's economic policy makers made both rice self-sufficiency and family planning their highest priorities, easing the rural misery that had helped galvanize the PKI's rise to become one of the largest communist parties in the world.[16]

Economic growth spiked considerably in the 1980s, especially after the US-Japan Plaza Accord strengthened the yen and directed a flood of Japanese FDI into Indonesia and its low-wage industrializing neighbors. Through rapid industrial development as well as dramatically stepped-up extraction of valuable and exportable natural resources, Indonesia's gross domestic product (GDP) per capita surpassed US$2,000 by the late 1990s. Urban areas were increasingly filled with educated middle-class citizens who resented the Suharto regime's astonishing corruption, rankled under its smothering blanket of authoritarian controls, and fully expected the regime to keep stepping up its delivery of developmental benefits. As we see throughout developmental Asia, economic modernization did not automatically incubate "democratic values" in Indonesia, but it certainly cultivated a more politically demanding citizenry.[17]

Authoritarian Institutional Development

Sometimes authoritarian regimes build institutions that a democracy can inherit and turn to purposes of democratic stability, even if that was by no means the original intent of those institutions' creators. As in the developmental statist cluster, the key institutional foundations of the regime's authoritarian controls—Indonesia's ruling party and state apparatus—could be repurposed toward stabilizing democratic ends after Suharto was pushed from office in 1998. Yet stable democratization remained extraordinarily unlikely until Indonesia's strongest institution of all, the military, gained the stability confidence necessary to countenance the uncertainties of a democratic transformation.

Institutional development under Suharto's authoritarian regime was especially impressive in two domains, both of which ultimately paid surprising and unintended dividends for democratic stability. The first was state capacity, so vital for stability confidence; and the second was party strength, so crucial to victory confidence. As with incumbent ruling parties in developmental Asia's other cases of democracy through strength, the fact that Golkar competed in multiparty elections for over twenty-five years, as skewed and unfair as those exercises were, provided Indonesia's authoritarian elites with electoral experience that could be carried over into a post-authoritarian era.

Authoritarian institutional strength always begins with the state, and in Indonesia as in most of the postcolonial world, the contemporary state apparatus has identifiable origins in the colonial period. The Dutch colonial state had been renowned for its governing effectiveness, albeit mostly for repressive and extractive purposes. This institutional inheritance, however, was squandered during Indonesia's first two decades of independence.[18] Once the authoritative executor of commands across the vast archipelago, Indonesia's postcolonial bureaucracy found itself starved of resources and bereft of operational autonomy during the hypermobilized years of nationalist revolution, parliamentary democracy, and Sukarno's Guided Democracy. As a charismatic populist, Sukarno profoundly mistrusted political parties, but he respected bureaucrats even less. By the time he was toppled in the confusion of conspiracy, communism, and a coup d'état that ripped the country apart in 1965–66, the Indonesian state was in no position to govern. There was scarcely a functioning private economy to govern in any event.

The tide turned dramatically with Suharto's takeover. In the transition's first phase, anticommunist elements in the Indonesian military, led by Suharto and allied closely with Islamic civil society, unleashed a horrific bloodbath against the communist PKI and its suspected sympathizers. Hundreds of thousands died. It was on this mountain of corpses that Suharto's New Order would be built. Yet with the truly enormous and epically tragic exceptions of the PKI and, after the mid-1970s, the restive ex-Portuguese-ruled province of East Timor, the Suharto regime governed not so much through brutal and violent repression as through smothering coercion and sweeping co-optation. The anticommunist mass killings were not the exception that proved the rule; they were the exception that established New Order rule.[19]

The centrality of anticommunism in the construction of the Suharto regime's identity and its political institutions had profound consequences for the regime's accumulation of strengths. On the one hand, it gave Suharto and his elite allies an appealing justification and ample leverage for rebuilding the state under deeply authoritarian auspices, as a bulwark against reemergent communism. It is impossible to understand the strength of the New Order regime without understanding the forcefulness of the communist challenge that directly preceded and inspired it. Yet the regime's utter annihilation of organized communism meant that its stability confidence could be more readily restored as the Cold War drew to a close.[20] As we have seen in the cases of Japan, South Korea, and Taiwan, democratization through strength was facilitated by the weakness of the internal communist challenge; the same was equally true, and probably of even more pivotal importance, in the case of Indonesia.

It was only through the wholesale reconstruction and revamping of the Indonesian state after Suharto took power that the New Order regime became as stable—even, for long stretches, boringly stable—as it was. While the military was the political heart of the New Order, it was by no means the regime's organizational entirety.

Suharto invested massive new resources in the developmental bureaucracy, at first thanks to the revenue floods of Western foreign aid and the oil boom in the 1970s, and later by virtue of the soaring revenues made possible by restored economic growth and inward floods of FDI.[21] Military officers were routinely given a variety of leading positions in government ministries, but this was more to ensure the political loyalty of the bureaucracy than to install military (i.e. nonexpert) governance. Bureaucrats were entrusted and empowered to govern, in areas ranging from family planning to rice self-sufficiency to the management of price volatility in vital basic commodities. Considering that bureaucrats overwhelmingly supported the New Order as a bulwark against communism and as a welcome legitimation of their technocratic impulses, Suharto did not have to worry that they needed military oversight to do his regime's bidding.

The state-building process that unfolded during the three decades of the New Order resulted in a highly impressive track record of economic growth and a remarkable run of relative political stability. To be sure, both growth and stability were fueled by colossal corruption that ultimately helped bring the Suharto regime down in the 1997–98 Asian financial crisis. Furthermore, regime stability was occasionally interrupted by ominous signals of growing organized opposition to authoritarian rule. Yet the fact remains that a state apparatus quite capable of governing stably was one of the Suharto regime's most important by-products.

The second critical domain for institutional development under Suharto's New Order was in political parties. Since the regime had such widespread support across the political spectrum, it did not fear a return to highly controlled electoral and party politics within the first decade of its founding. Although the Suharto regime was military led, it commanded highly organized civilian support. Moreover, the ratio of civilian to military power grew significantly over time, as Suharto cultivated civilian allies to help him personalize power vis-à-vis his most powerful rivals in the military.[22] Party development and electoral politics provided these supportive civilians with routes to status and largesse, even under the suffocating coercive blanket of New Order rule.

As with the incumbent authoritarian parties in Taiwan and South Korea, party development also allowed civilian politicians to develop the political skills and clienteles necessary for success in democratic elections when they eventually came. Most significantly, Suharto quickly supported the building of a regime-supporting political party called Golkar after seizing power. The party's name reveals both its origins and its governing purpose. Short for *golongan karya* (functional groups), Golkar was a political vehicle constructed from the wide variety of conservative political organizations that arose to counter the radical leftist mass mobilization of Sukarno and the PKI during the early to mid-1960s.[23]

In formal terms, Golkar was not a political party but an umbrella organization—symbolically, a hovering banyan tree—under which these conservative political organizations could shelter and coalesce. This made it easier for Suharto to mandate that all Indonesian civil servants become Golkar members, since the organization was a bureaucratic superministry as well as a partisan vehicle. Golkar would compete in national elections every five years against the two "semi-opposition" parties that the regime permitted to form, the Islamic PPP (United Development Party) and the nationalist PDI (Indonesian Democratic Party), and predictably crushed them.[24] In essence, the state apparatus itself assumed the electoral role of a political party, without surrendering any of the powers or resources it held by virtue of being Indonesia's ultimate sovereign authority.

By both hook and crook, Golkar commanded overwhelming electoral support from the New Order's founding election in 1971 until its final election in 1997. Its primary functions were to secure the support of civil servants throughout the Indonesian archipelago and to deliver reliable landslides in unfair and unfree elections. And deliver Golkar did, in large measure through the intimidating shadow of coercion, but also because the political and economic successes of the Suharto regime made acquiescence a relatively bearable choice for most Indonesians most of the time. As growth rates soared and poverty rates declined, Golkar secured 63 percent of the popular vote in the regime's inaugural elections of 1971 and gained supermajority vote shares throughout Suharto's reign: 62 percent in 1977, 64 percent in 1982, 73 percent in 1987, 68 percent in 1992, and 74 percent in 1997. Not once did Golkar poll less than 62 percent of the popular vote.

Golkar's reliable, rhythmic electoral landslides reflected its impressive, fully nationalized party organization and political infrastructure, especially on the many "Outer Islands" beyond Java. Concerned that the restoration of electoral politics in the 1970s could return Indonesia to the kind of mass mobilization that culminated in the anticommunist genocide of the mid-1960s, the Suharto regime imposed a "floating mass" policy to stifle opposition. This meant that only Golkar could have branches at the local level, while the two state-sanctioned semiopposition parties could not. It also meant that radical civil society was utterly uprooted in the countryside. Simply put, Golkar enjoyed expansive national reach, an advantage denied to its competitors.

Decades of rapid economic growth allowed avalanches of patronage to flow from Jakarta to the provinces. Golkar politicians developed reputations in many locales as reliable providers of basic public goods. Hence, while elections were a democratic farce in Suharto's Indonesia, the ruling party was a significant source of authoritarian institutional reach and might. Golkar was inextricably intertwined with the state apparatus, which had regained much of its impressive colonial-era functionality after the New Order's rise. The

restored prestige of the bureaucracy and the concomitant devastation of organized radical elements in society lent an important degree of stability confidence to Golkar leaders, even amid the tumult of the Asian financial crisis
and in the wake of Suharto's popular overthrow.

Shocking Signals

Democratization through strength is a product of signals received by the incumbent authoritarian regime, not just its accumulated strengths. In Indonesia's case, those signals were unmistakably momentous, taking the form of
severe shocks. A personalized regime that seemed uneventfully stable in the
first half of 1997 was overturned in dramatic fashion by the first half of 1998.

Of the four common types of shock that can signal a strong regime's entry
into the bittersweet spot where a democracy-through-strength scenario is
most likely to arise, Indonesia suffered two massive ones: economic and contentious. Soon after Golkar romped to its best-ever result in Suharto's 1997
electoral swan song, the devastation of the Indonesian economy and subsequent urban protests clearly signaled that epochal changes were afoot. By far
the hardest-hit economy in the Asian financial crisis, Indonesia saw its currency free-fall from 2,250 per US dollar to approximately 17,000 per US dollar
in a matter of months.

The eruption of student-led protests did not focus strictly on economic
concerns, moreover, as the key legitimacy claim of Suharto to be the nation's
"father of development" was obliterated by a crisis that only worsened as his
political responses became ever less consistent and coherent.[25] Once a consummate "protection pact" that enjoyed widespread elite support for its success at bridling political instability, the Suharto regime crumbled in the face
of cross-class protests that condemned the president for bringing the Indonesian nation to the brink of collapse with his corruption and brutality.[26]

To be sure, the economic and contentious signals of the Asian financial
crisis were not entirely unprecedented for the Suharto regime. When volatility
in oil prices shook the economy and sparked a massive student-led protest
movement in 1978, the regime teetered then as well, but it ultimately survived
and reasserted its dominance through the party, state, and military institutions
discussed earlier.[27]

The regime also persistently struggled to control Indonesia's robust Islamic
civil society, fronted by the world's two largest Muslim associations, the
Nahdlatul Ulama and Muhammadiyah, as well as its effervescent nationalist

community, eternally inspired by the revolutionary example of Sukarno, Indonesia's first president.[28] It was no accident that the three most important opposition figures of the late New Order were precisely the leaders of these three groupings: Abdurrahman Wahid (Nahdlatul Ulama), Amien Rais (Muhammadiyah), and Sukarno's daughter Megawati Sukarnoputri (who led the semiopposition PDI party). As in South Korea during the Seoul Spring of 1987, the unity or division among these opposition leaders weighed heavily in considerations of victory confidence when the incumbent regime confronted the choice whether to democratize through strength after Suharto's forced exit in May 1998.

Indonesia's nationalist civil society conveyed the strongest and clearest signals of incipient regime decline. In June 1996, more than a year before the financial crisis shattered the Suharto regime's stability, the regime faced its biggest challenge in urban unrest since the upsurge of 1978. After Megawati ascended to the leadership of the semiopposition PDI and began using it as much more of an oppositional vehicle to the regime, Suharto engineered her removal. Outrage exploded among Megawati's red-clad followers, who refused to vacate Jakarta's PDI headquarters when their leader was toppled. The riots and crackdown that followed sent a clear signal that the Suharto regime was past its prime. Backroom skulduggery over who would succeed Suharto after the 76-year-old president's inevitable departure from power became the talk of the town in Indonesia's elite political circles.

Overall, however, signals of regime decline were neither loud nor clear before the Asian financial crisis hit. The predominant expectation was that Suharto would eventually hand power to a chosen successor who would keep the authoritarian machinery of the New Order state running smoothly. Suharto's shifting desire to give the vice-presidency to military leaders versus civilian allies fueled speculation as to his intentions. His grooming of his eldest daughter for political leadership raised the worrisome specter of a dynastic succession. But nobody appeared to be in a position to stand in Suharto's way, whatever he was to decide.

Still, it is vital to distinguish the regime's stability from its predictability. At the time the financial crisis hit, Suharto had grown increasingly unpredictable and had made no viable plans for his succession. Economic downturn quickly turned into political panic. The return of democracy thus brought at least the prospect of renewed predictability to the rhythms of regime politics and economic policy. As in South Korea, ongoing protests never threatened to topple the post-Suharto leadership in violent fashion, but they did raise the undesirable possibility of continued instability if democracy did not replace authoritarianism.

Conceding with Caution

For all the instability and uncertainty that accompanied Suharto's removal from office in May 1998, the hastening of free and fair national elections that immediately followed it promised to help restore stability rather than further undermine it. This was especially true because no radical leftist parties were credible contestants for elected office: a lasting legacy of how Suharto's New Order regime had managed and, at times, massacred its leftist rivals.

Furthermore, competitive elections promised to divide the New Order's three most popular opponents into different party vehicles, whereas Suharto's authoritarian abuses of power had brought them together as a unified, and thus far more formidable, opposition bloc. The introduction of democratic competition promised to divide the opposition in Indonesia, as it did in South Korea when its democratic champions Kim Young-sam and Kim Dae-jung failed to unify, thus splitting the presidential vote and allowing the ruling conservatives to remain in uninterrupted power.

Indonesia began its democratization process in May 1998, when Suharto was forced to step down after more than thirty years in power by massive student-led protests. Yet as we stressed earlier in this chapter, a dictator's fall is not tantamount to democratization. Democratization does not merely lie in the toppling of a hated autocrat, but rather requires the introduction of difficult political reforms to make free and fair elections possible. Ending a dictatorship does not equal establishing a democracy. Even when the masses initiate a democratization process through contentious street actions, politicians must install democratic rules of the game through field-leveling reforms.

These political reforms were introduced by Suharto's civilian vice president and presidential successor, B. J. Habibie. With Suharto's ouster, Habibie ascended not only to the presidency but to de facto leadership of the incumbent authoritarian ruling party, Golkar. Although Golkar had always shared the stage with the military under Suharto, the vicissitudes of Suharto's fall left Indonesia with a Golkar-dominated civilian government. It also left Golkar with a leader lacking significant popularity and without any basis of legitimacy for his unexpected presidency. Much like Roh Tae-woo in South Korea, Habibie rose to the presidency as the handpicked successor of an outgoing military autocrat, seemingly auguring authoritarian continuity rather than a sudden democratic rupture.

Golkar was thus in a far stronger position than Habibie himself; the party was strong while the president was weak. Unlike the many pure military regimes and single-party regimes with no recent electoral experience that transitioned to democracy after the Cold War, Indonesia became a democracy in 1999 with a firmly established electoral system already in place. Party competition had been tightly governed under the New Order, but it had not been completely absent. Moderate and conservative politicians, and specifically those who were affiliated with Golkar, knew that elections were something they could continue to win, at impressive levels if not at the landslide levels of the authoritarian era.

The crisis that felled Suharto in 1998 left Golkar weakened but by no means destroyed. In fact, it was the only political party with an established presence at the local level across the entire Indonesian archipelago. For all the uncertainty that surrounded Indonesia's democratic transition in 1998 and 1999, deeply established electoral procedures were more a source of stability than of instability for the incumbent party. The stoutness of the Golkar-led party system that had been built under the Suharto regime was critical to the surprising democratic stability that followed it.

None of this is to say that Indonesia's ruling party was equivalent in its antecedent resources to Taiwan's KMT. Golkar was substantially weaker. Yet Golkar was sufficiently strong and robust to provide considerable victory confidence to Suharto's successors. As new president Habibie considered how best to hold on to the crown that had been so unexpectedly and precariously perched on his head, Golkar's territorial advantage over any other party was a crucial strategic consideration. Habibie could thus call, within days of assuming office, for expedited national elections in 1999 (moved up from 2002) and dramatically liberalize Indonesia's restrictive laws on political parties and the media with relative confidence about Golkar's prospects, especially in non-Javanese provinces. He possessed ample information to project that the ruling party would coast to victory across much of Indonesia's vast periphery, even as its reputation in most of Java was deeply damaged in the wake of Suharto's downfall. As a native of Sulawesi, Habibie himself had grounds for confidence that such results would strengthen his fellow non-Javanese politicians within the Java-dominated Golkar hierarchy. This democratization strategy also went hand in hand with Habibie's aggressive pursuit of decentralization, which promised to place more authority and resources where Golkar's advantages and hopes of continued incumbency were strongest. Habibie was mustering up whatever powers he and the incumbent party possessed to democratize through strength.

Habibie's ascension to the presidency left him in a perilous position, for sure, but not an impossible one. Suharto's resignation had lowered the crest of the swelling protests but had not calmed the contentious waters entirely. Habibie also confronted opposition to his leadership within Golkar itself, where his many rivals saw him as a weak Suharto surrogate undeserving of presidential power.

Under the circumstances, therefore, a new infusion of democratic legitimacy seemed to offer Habibie the most promising strategy for taming urban protests and solidifying his position as president. He could portray himself as a democratic reformer and compete for support on those grounds, as we saw conservative elites do with great success in postwar Japan, South Korea, and Taiwan. This was an especially compelling strategy to Habibie and Golkar because Indonesia's main superpower benefactor, the United States, was sure to keep essential economic aid flowing to help Indonesia recover from its ongoing financial cataclysm if democratic elections were in the offing.

Hence Habibie's quick announcement of expedited democratic elections not only reflected a strategic response to the whirlwind of economic, contentious, and geopolitical signals that he was receiving; it also represented his best hope for remaining in office. Recognizing his tenuous position at the helm of Indonesia's most powerful party, Habibie resigned as Golkar's executive chairman in July 1998 but helped install an uncharismatic apparatchik, Akbar Tandjung, as the party's new head. Habibie thus put himself in a position to ride Golkar's electoral coattails to a full term as president, as the newly elected parliament would select the next president at a special session in October 1999.

The antecedent strength of his Golkar party was thus central to Habibie's strategy to concede electoral democracy (rather than responding to ongoing protests by bringing Suharto and his family to justice, for instance). It also explains why Golkar elders acquiesced to Habibie's democratization strategy with no open pushback. "The holding of a general election under new electoral laws was central to Habibie's efforts to acquire legitimacy and met with no opposition" in the Golkar-dominated parliament, Harold Crouch concludes. This was partly because Golkar was in almost as serious need of a new brand of legitimacy as Habibie himself. "It was obvious that Golkar would suffer a substantial loss of support, but the party still hoped to remain among the major political forces."[29] More cynically, expedited democratic elections represented an expedited opportunity for Golkar elites to reckon with Habibie's fraught party leadership, replacing him with a less disliked alternative sooner rather than later.

Golkar's mix of active support for and quiet acquiescence to expedited democratic elections reflected its considerable, if steeply declining, victory confidence. "The Golkar-dominated government was making the best it could of a bad situation to salvage at least some of its influence and power," Crouch argues. "Although the new election laws were basically damaging to its electoral prospects, it was still able to gain small but significant concessions in its own interest while it appreciated that its long-established nationwide political machinery would allow it, at least in the short term, to retain a strong position in decentralized regional government."[30]

New elections promised to channel political competition into the electoral arena, where Golkar's built-up resource advantages were substantial. These accumulated strengths elevated Golkar not only over Indonesia's fledgling opposition parties but also importantly over the military, which could play no direct role in elections and whose long-standing relationship with the ruling party was legally severed soon after Suharto's downfall. These advantages were backstopped by an electoral system that overrepresented non-Javanese provinces, where Golkar was strongest. Thus, while Habibie himself conceded democracy from a weak personal position, the fact that Golkar publicly supported his call for early elections suggests that it rightly perceived the party's enduring strengths in Indonesia's newly born democracy.

Nevertheless, by failing to concede democracy before the calamitous economic downturn and contentious upsurge of 1997–98, Golkar narrowly but fatefully missed its most golden moment to concede and thrive. The party conceded democracy in the bittersweet spot, though it had fallen further (and far faster) from its apex of power than the more powerful and strongest regimes, notably Taiwan's KMT, that we examined in the developmental statist cluster.

This helps explain why the emergent Indonesian Democratic Party of Struggle (PDI-P), led by nationalist icon Megawati Sukarnoputri, placed first in the June 1999 parliamentary polls, gaining an edge of 33 percent to 20 percent over second-place Golkar in popular votes. Malapportionment narrowed this parliamentary seat advantage of 33 percent to 26 percent, however. In addition, the military's appointed seats allowed the ancien régime's two powerhouse institutions—Golkar and the military—to combine for nearly 34 percent of the parliamentary seats, slightly surpassing the PDI-P. As expected, Golkar gained the largest vote share in half of Indonesia's twenty-six provinces, affirming its lasting territorial reach.

The 1999 election results were a colossal decline from Golkar's golden days of authoritarian hegemony, when stage-managed quinquennial elections consistently delivered the official party over 60 percent of the national vote. Yet with its continued control over subnational offices and its command over political networks in Jakarta, Golkar maintained its political centrality under democracy while shedding its authoritarianism. Not only did Golkar avoid obsolescence under democracy; it avoided even going into opposition.

Cohabitation and Coalitions

The stabilization of Indonesian democracy in the wake of the June 1999 elections and October 1999 transfer of power was a story of party, state, and military institutions. The role of the military loomed especially large at the outset of the transition, because state failure loomed especially large as a potential outcome during Indonesia's tumultuous transformation. The provinces of East Timor, Aceh, and West Papua all presented credible separatist claims. Ethnic and religious violence erupted in various parts of the archipelago, most notably in the eastern Indonesian districts of Ambon, Maluku, and Poso. Riots against Indonesia's ethnic Chinese minority hit as close to home as Jakarta itself. Islamist terrorism also delivered repeated blows, most infamously in Bali.

Leading country experts quite seriously asked whether the republic could endure without the military holding it all together by force. Less than a decade removed from the collapse and disintegration of the Soviet Union and Yugoslavia, the notion that power holders in Jakarta might fail to keep the country intact and minimally governable was hardly far-fetched.

The inheritance of a relatively strong state proved up to these challenges, however. Remarkably in hindsight, and even in real time, East Timor was permitted to exit Indonesia by popular referendum, though pro-integration militias long backed by the Indonesian military inflicted a horrible price on East Timor's people for so choosing. Not only was it surprising that East Timor was allowed to secede; equally remarkable was the lack of separatist sentiment in other parts of the archipelago that, like East Timor, had sizable Christian majorities. Even as Christian communities feared eradication in the deadly religious conflicts that erupted in demographically divided districts like Ambon and Maluku, no wider push for Christian separation and self-determination gathered steam.

Steeled by over three decades of military rule, the Indonesian military and security services were quickly and efficiently deployed to conflict zones across the archipelago, and they restored peace in surprisingly short order. A national policy of decentralization also allowed provinces to split, making local ethnoreligious conflicts more tractable. Islamist terrorism was also effectively snuffed out by the state's highly professionalized intelligence services. In sum, Indonesia's young democracy avoided state failure because the inherited state apparatus was capable enough to prevent the republic from violently unraveling.

Importantly, while the Indonesian military was strong enough to help keep the country together, it did not use this strength to reassume direct control of the political system and roll back Indonesia's democratic experiment. Herein lay perhaps the biggest surprise of Indonesian democratization. During the years preceding Suharto's fall, the overwhelming consensus among Indonesia watchers was that his New Order would be followed by some variety of collective military rule. Yet this did not come to pass. A key reason was that Suharto increasingly personalized, factionalized, and to some extent Islamicized the military during his final years in power. This left the Indonesian military in Suharto's final days as the country's most powerful actor, but not a highly cohesive one, rife with factional splits.

Of particular importance was the intense factional rivalry between Suharto's son-in-law, Prabowo Subianto, who commanded the military's strategic units in and around Jakarta, and the national head of the military, Wiranto. Prabowo proved ready and willing to unleash violence as a way of justifying martial law and his own assumption of dictatorial powers, much as his father-in-law had done in 1965. Wiranto and other professional soldiers, meanwhile, saw Prabowo as an opportunist who was a scourge on the military rather than a savior of national stability. It was more important to Wiranto and his ilk to restrain Prabowo and restore military unity during crisis times than it was either to keep Suharto in power or to salvage the military's leading governance role.

Herein lies a vital lesson from all three developmental militarist cases, contrasting sharply with the expectations of a democracy-through-weakness scenario. In canonical transitions theory, military leaders negotiate an exit from power, and thus initiate a democratic transition, when they are too divided among themselves to keep ruling in stable fashion.[31] However, in Indonesia, and as we will also see shortly in Thailand and Myanmar, the worsening of military rivalries presented occasions not to democratize but to settle those rivalries through purges. *Only after military unity was restored* and *only from a position of renewed cohesion and strength would the military support democratization*, rather than conceding democracy as a last resort from a severely weakened and fragmented position.

This is not to say the military simply stepped aside in Indonesia. For the first five years of Indonesian democracy, the military retained a sizable proportion of appointed parliamentary seats, and prominent military officers played a major role in electoral politics. Indeed, Indonesia's first directly elected president, Susilo Bambang Yudhoyono (SBY; 2004–14), was one of the top military officials of the late Suharto era. Yet the military surrendered its parliamentary seats with little fuss in the constitutional revisions that followed democratization, in plenty of time for the 2004 national elections.

The best explanation for why the military conceded such constitutional revisions lies in the institutional inheritance of Indonesia's party-state. Electoral support in 1999 and 2004 did not flow to former radical opponents of the New Order or to proponents of root-and-branch military reform; it flowed instead to conservative and moderate parties and politicians with deep experience in Indonesia's military-led political system.

Once again, the continued leading role played by Golkar was critically important. The former ruling party remained one of Indonesia's top electoral performers in 1999 and beyond. It also consistently secured leading roles for itself in governing coalitions and cabinets. Although a wide variety of new parties have emerged during Indonesia's twenty-plus years of democracy, most of them have derived their leadership from former leading figures of Golkar. To the considerable extent the military could continue to rely on moderate politicians with familiar New Order roots, there was simply no reason for military men to dominate the civilian arena. The continued relevance of Golkar provided potential democratic spoilers, especially the military, with the stability confidence necessary to support Indonesia's democratic transformation.[32]

Stability confidence was fulfilled in the economy as well as the political system. By the early 2000s, Indonesia had returned to its familiar trajectory of strong growth driven by foreign direct investment, natural resource exploitation, and light manufacturing exports. Golkar remained the most identifiably probusiness major party in Indonesia, which was critical in stabilizing the economy after the financial crisis of the late 1990s. Credited with presiding over decades of economic growth, Golkar still appealed to many voters for its "usable past," even though its programmatic differences with other leading parties were minimal.

Golkar was not removed from power after its second-place finish in the June 1999 elections or even after Habibie's "accountability speech" was rejected at the October 1999 special session of parliament, at which point the president resigned. Having already been formally led by Akbar Tandjung rather than Habibie for more than a year, Golkar did not miss a beat. In fact, it played the kingmaker role by denying the presidency to Megawati and delivering it to a much weaker figure in Abdurrahman Wahid, whose National Awakening Party (PKB) controlled only 11 percent of parliamentary seats. This gave Golkar the leverage necessary to dominate Indonesia's first democratic cabinet, securing seven portfolios for the former ruling party to the PDI-P's five. Golkar then took the lead in impeaching President Wahid after he expelled Golkar and PDI-P figures from his cabinet, and landed five cabinet posts under President Megawati from 2001 to 2004. Golkar's uninterrupted leadership roles in democratic Indonesia rested not on any exceptional mass popularity but on its unrivaled elite networks and alliances accumulated during its long authoritarian reign.

The party may only be moderately effective at electioneering, but it is extremely skilled at postelectoral bargaining. By taking the lead in crafting a system of "party cartelization" and "promiscuous powersharing," Golkar ensured itself unbroken representation in the presidential cabinet after democratization.[33] It also ensured that politics would not take on a polarized ancien régime–versus–opposition cast. Much as in South Korea, democratization through strength in Indonesia divided the multiple opposition parties—some nationalist, some Islamist—that had once unified in their shared struggle to topple Suharto's authoritarian New Order. But whereas dictatorship had temporarily unified Golkar's opponents during Suharto's final days, democracy divided them once again. It would also channel them into Golkar-guided power-sharing schemes.

Starting with the decisive democratic reforms introduced by President Habibie in 1998 and 1999, Golkar remained steadfastly committed to the process of regime transition. Its central role in devising a battery of constitutional reforms between 1999 and 2002 showed that the party had no intention of either being left behind during the democratic era or moving backward to the authoritarian era.[34] Coming in a strong second in the founding democratic elections confirmed the former ruling party's confidence about its future prospects in democracy.

Golkar's electoral fortunes improved in the 2004 elections. This time the party placed first in the parliamentary polls. Golkar veteran Jusuf Kalla gained the vice presidency under the presidency of retired general SBY, then captured the leadership of Golkar. Though SBY fronted a new party called the Democrat Party (PD), the new president rushed to ally with Golkar in a manner that made the PD look like Golkar's junior partner.

Once again, Golkar gained more cabinet seats than any other party, including the president's. It was only after the 2009 elections, in which Golkar placed second behind the PD, that newly reelected president SBY asserted himself vis-à-vis Golkar by choosing a non-Golkar running mate and granting his PD six cabinet seats to Golkar's three. Even so, more than a decade after President Habibie first conceded democracy during a tumultuous time for the former ruling party, Golkar remained firmly and uninterruptedly ensconced in the executive branch. Meanwhile, recognizing that party politics was in safely moderate hands, Indonesia's military gave up its appointed seats in parliament by 2004 with nary a whimper, mitigating a potential threat to Indonesia's democratic prospects.

Golkar's electoral viability was not a merely transitional phenomenon. While far short of the electoral performance exhibited by the authoritarian successor party in Taiwan, Golkar remained popular enough to hold its own in the electoral arena, and then practically to dominate Indonesian party politics at the vital coalition-building stage. From 2004 to 2009, just as in the period from 1999 to 2004, Golkar held more cabinet seats than any other party, including the PD, the party of the newly and directly elected president, SBY. In addition, it consistently and predictably captured the largest number of executive positions at the subnational level during this period, given that President Habibie's original embrace of democratic reforms was largely prompted by his recognition that Golkar enjoyed a massive infrastructural grassroots advantage across Indonesia's sprawling archipelago. Hence, for a full decade after Indonesia's democratic transition, Golkar remained its most powerful political party.

The bottom line is that due to its ability to maintain electoral viability and orchestrate various power-sharing arrangements in a multiparty system, *Golkar has never had to go into opposition during the entire democratic period, after choosing to democratize from strength.* Furthermore, it achieved this uninterrupted executive access despite generating weaker electoral returns than either the KMT in Taiwan or the Democratic Justice Party (DJP) in South Korea. In other words, Golkar may have conceded democracy as well as its unchallenged dominance of Indonesia's party system, but it has still never been forced to concede outright defeat; a feat that neither the KMT nor the DJP (nor even Japan's LDP) can claim. Indonesia's former authoritarian party has continued to thrive, moving from authoritarian strength to democratic strength.

What Golkar learned since democratization began in Indonesia was not so much how to lose power outright as how to win leading positions of power even as voters increasingly shifted toward alternative parties at the ballot box.[35] It has been Golkar's mastery of backdoor negotiating, and not any growing skill at public electioneering, that best explains its successful adaptation to the rough-and-tumble nature of democratic competition.

Indonesia's democratic transition exemplified the staying power of hold-over elites whose roots were from the Suharto era. When Golkar's electoral performance slipped, President SBY's PD picked up much of the slack, winning the parliamentary elections outright in 2009. The specter of an ex-Suharto ally prevailing through a new party vehicle inspired imitations. Two additional retired generals and a wealthy businessman, all of whom had been top contenders for the Golkar chairmanship in 2004, formed three additional parties that gained back the vote share Golkar had lost. Whereas Golkar alone won 22.4 percent of the national vote in 1999, in 2014 the vote share for all five parties led by Golkar-based and military-rooted elites (including Suharto's former son-in-law, Prabowo) more than doubled, to 48.7 percent of all votes in national parliamentary elections.

Golkar has lost its unrivaled dominance since conceding democracy over twenty years ago, though Indonesia's party system has remained dominated by parties with deep roots in the New Order era, and more proximate roots in the post-democratization version of Golkar itself. The military gave up its seats in the national parliament as of 2004 but remained politically untouchable in most other respects. To the degree that new social forces found entry into national politics, it has not shifted Indonesian politics in any radical new directions, either politically or economically. It is these relative weaknesses in democratic quality that best explain why Indonesian democracy showed growing signs of stagnation by the 2010s.[36]

The upshot of the Indonesian case is a democratic transformation that has been rockier and less robust than in Taiwan or South Korea but of greater stability and predictability than the nascent democracies that arose from "purer" military regimes in Thailand and Myanmar. Indonesia shows that neither the developmental state nor the ruling party needs to be extraordinarily strong for a democracy-through-strength scenario to be viable over the long term. In contrast, the cases of Thailand and Myanmar show in the remainder of this chapter how democracy through strength can unfold more shakily and reversibly, and ultimately unsuccessfully, in cases with even less antecedent authoritarian strength.

Thailand

Two decades before Indonesia's ruling party and military began conceding democracy through strength, Thailand's ruling monarchy and military attempted and accomplished something quite similar. In Thailand's case, however, the democratic experiment was far more gradual, and it unfolded under boom conditions rather than bust conditions. These propitious economic conditions help explain why, despite Thailand's lack of a formidable ruling party like Indonesia's Golkar, it was nonetheless able to become, arguably, Southeast Asia's strongest democracy for a full quarter century, from the early 1980s until the mid-2000s.[37]

Stability confidence was always comparatively higher in Thailand than in Indonesia, even if victory confidence for the incumbent authoritarian party was stronger in Indonesia. Since stability confidence counts for more than victory confidence in the developmental militarist cluster, it should be no surprise that Thailand's authoritarian leaders conceded democracy long before those in Indonesia. It was also no surprise, however, that the inability of conservative, military-friendly civilians to win democratic elections led the Thai military to reverse its democratization experiment in the mid-2000s, while the predictability and moderation of the Indonesian party system helped the military there stay out of parliament, if not entirely in its barracks.

It needs to be pointed out that Thailand's political regimes have long been notoriously unstable. One of the most famous facts about the kingdom is that it has experienced an astonishing 19 coups, 12 of them since 1932, when constitutional constraints were first imposed on the absolute monarchy. This has meant a regime arrhythmia of coups and constitutions, with 20 constitutions and charters introduced since 1932. The overall pattern of instability is unmistakable both over the long haul and more recently.

Of the Thai regime's many chutes and ladders, several are of particular significance at the outset. From 1973 to 1976, Thailand experienced a classic case of democracy through weakness: a brief interregnum marked by instability and ended by a brutal coup. Instead of reinforcing closed military rule, however, the new regime led by General Prem Tinsulanond commenced a gradual process of conceding democracy and ceding power to freely elected civilians over the course of the 1980s. After a brief reversal to military rule in 1991–92, Thailand's upward democratization trajectory continued until its illiberal turn under strongman Prime Minister Thaksin Shinawatra starting in 2001, and the first coup against Thaksin and his allies in 2006.[38]

In the discussion to follow, we treat the long stretch from 1978 to 2006 as Thailand's incremental—and several times interrupted—experimentation with democracy through strength. Only when the rise of populist electoral juggernaut Thaksin shattered both the victory confidence and, more importantly, the stability confidence of the Thai military and monarchy in the early 2000s did Thailand's democracy through strength trajectory become blocked by authoritarian retrenchment. Even so, the Thai military regime's current effort to restore cohabitation with civilian politicians, although very much on its own terms, bears some important resemblances to the events of the 1980s. The fate of the Thai military's latest, exceedingly guarded liberalization experiment will hinge once again on their own stability confidence, as well as that of their allies—especially in the monarchy.

Authoritarian Economic Development

More than any other case in this book (except perhaps Hong Kong), stability confidence in Thailand has been a product of remarkable capitalist development rather than robust civilian political organizations. Thailand's growth trajectory and baseline level of development surpassed those of either Indonesia or Myanmar. With wealth levels lying as close to Malaysia (from the much richer developmental Britannia cluster) as to Indonesia, Thailand has long been one of the central players in developmental Asia's stratospheric economic rise.

To a degree unusual in developmental Asia, Thailand's rapid growth was a tale of free-market orientation more than state interventionism. The Thai economy was forced open in the 1850s by British pressure, which integrated the kingdom into world trade flows as a leading exporter of rice. Like Meiji Japan, Thailand was ruled in the late nineteenth and early twentieth centuries by "modernizing kings" (Mongkut, 1851–68 and Chulalongkorn, 1868–1910), who worked closely with bureaucratic allies to keep formal colonialism at bay.

Instead of a highly activist and interventionist Japan-style developmental state, however, Thailand developed a professionalized financial bureaucracy that kept the kingdom out of debt as a way of preserving national independence.[39]

This resulted in a state apparatus that was expert and prudent enough to balance the budget and preside over export-led capitalist economic growth, but not to steer the Thai economy decisively away from its basic comparative advantages in abundant natural resources and affordable labor, as we saw in the developmental statist cluster.[40]

Thailand's resource-dependent and relatively laissez-faire developmental model meant that tremendous growth was accompanied by endemic corruption and ever-worsening inequality. Even still, owing to Thailand's growth trajectory, poverty reduction was significant, which laid the critical foundations for stability confidence as pressures to democratize began to increase in the 1970s. From a staggering level of 88.3 percent in 1962, the incidence of poverty in Thailand shrank to 48.6 percent by 1975, 27.2 percent by 1990, and just 9.8 percent by 2002.[41] Consistent economic improvement surely helps explain why Thailand experienced relatively mild class-based mobilization, in comparative perspective, for most of its modern history.[42]

Authoritarian Institutional Development

Thailand's strong developmental track record compensated in important ways for its weak civilian institutions. One of very few countries in the developing world to avoid formal colonization entirely, Thailand germinated neither strong conservative nor strong communist parties, which often arise through mass struggles for national independence.

Instead, the military and monarchy played outsize political roles in Thailand. From the military coup that ended the absolutist monarchy in 1932 until the rise to power of Field General Sarit Thanarat in 1957, the monarchy played the minor partner in this alliance. However, Sarit saw the young king Bhumipol as an indispensable ally in his push to build a stronger Thai state and a richer industrial economy during his fourteen-year rule (1957–71). The moral authority and political clout of the Thai monarchy skyrocketed during this period, making the king a pivotal player in all questions of authoritarianism and democratization to follow.[43]

Wherever ruling monarchs are strong, conservative parties tend to be weak.[44] The most important conservative party in Thailand, the Democrat Party, made its appearance in 1946 as the country began routinizing competitive elections in the aftermath of its quasi-fascist interlude immediately before and during World War II. Yet the Democrats were never able to consolidate conservative political forces under its party banner. Rather than consistently throwing its considerable weight behind the conservative Democrats, as the Indonesian military did behind Golkar, the Thai military generally sought to keep the party system fragmented and weak so that no single party challenged the ruling military-monarchical alliance. Stability confidence in Thailand rested on the relative weakness of organized forces that might challenge the ruling conservative oligarchy rather than on the stoutness of conservative political organizations, such as parties, to defeat all comers.[45]

While Thai parties suffered from fragmentation, the Thai military had been hamstrung by internal factionalism. The roots of Thailand's lack of military cohesion can be found in the fierce ideological and personal conflicts between the two leading figures in the 1932 coup against the monarchy, Pridi Phano-myong and Plaek Phibunsongkhram. The military's internal divisiveness was never fully resolved during the Cold War, as the mildness of the internal communist threat (unlike in Indonesia) and the manageability of separatist sentiment (unlike in Myanmar) gave Thai elites little impetus to band together and organize politically.[46]

Ultimately, military fragmentation paved the way for Thailand's democracy-through-weakness episode from 1973 to 1976. As popular protests challenged the rampant corruption under the ruling military triumvirate that replaced Sarit after his premature death from cirrhosis, the king threw his moral support behind those demanding the triumvirate's removal and a decisive move toward democratic elections.

As so often occurs when democracy arises through authoritarian weakness and collapse, the period between 1973 and 1976 was marked by instability and polarization. Coinciding with communist North Vietnam's march to victory over South Vietnam, the rise of progressive popular forces during Thailand's unstable democratic interlude blared the alarm bells. When leftist students tried to mobilize mass support in the conservative and quiescent countryside, the Thai military-monarchy alliance struck back with ferocity. After paramilitary "Village Scout" forces massacred leftist students at Bangkok's Thammasat University in August 1976, the military returned fully to power.[47] Democracy through weakness ended abruptly and violently.

Yet a return to full authoritarianism was no panacea for political stability either. Once the threat of radical students was neutralized, the Thai military began a gradual process of gathering the strengths necessary to democratize in a far more stable fashion than what had occurred in 1973.

Signals and Concessions

The dominant political figure throughout Thailand's slow-moving democratization-through-strength era was Prem Tinsulanond, a military commander with impeccable ties to the crown. By early 1980, Prem had simultaneously assumed the roles of commander in chief of the Royal Thai Army, minister of defense, and prime minister. By the time he left office in 1988, handing over the post to democratically elected Chatichai Choonhavan of the Chart Thai Party, Prem had presided over a decade of rapid economic growth and piecemeal democratic reforms. Far from exiting the scene, however, he assumed the presidency of the king's Privy Council for the long remainder of his life, from 1988 to 2019. It was from this lofty yet secretive position that Prem became the center, alongside King Bhumipol himself, of Thailand's "network monarchy," until his death at the age of 98.[48]

The system Prem assembled over the course of the 1980s was dubbed, jokingly and not entirely unfairly, "Premocracy." The jibe captured the fundamental point that military elites retained substantial powers and the monarchy enjoyed overwhelming influence, even as free and fair elections put civilian politicians formally in charge of the political regime. Yet the shift to a civilian-led regime nonetheless constituted a major democratic transformation. Furthermore, the shift occurred when times were good, stability confidence was rising, and military leaders could dictate the terms of transition without needing to negotiate their exit with a democratic opposition. Having briefly democratized through weakness in the early 1970s, Thailand democratized through strength, incrementally but more sustainably, over the course of the 1980s.

A declining communist threat was one of the most important factors in the Thai military's rising stability confidence. Geopolitically speaking, Vietnam's bloody unification under communist rule in 1975 led not to the encroachment of heightened leftist pressure into Thailand but to the dramatic and violent splintering of the communist bloc itself. Communist Vietnam invaded communist Cambodia while communist China invaded communist Vietnam, and Southeast Asia became a hothouse for Sino-Soviet rivalry rather than shared expansionist purpose. Thailand's homegrown communist insurgency, never one of Southeast Asia's most threatening, quickly disintegrated after Prem offered communists a blanket amnesty in 1980.

Prem had serious housecleaning to do within Thailand's chronically factionalized military. Although he was solidly backed by the king and he began moving Thailand in a decisively liberalizing direction when he became prime minister, this by no means represented a reform consensus among military officers. Through the Young Turks coup of April 1981 and a series of assassination attempts on Prem's life, hard-line elements in the military tried to reverse Thailand's gathering democratization trend.

Not only did these revanchist efforts fail; they backfired. Far from pushing Prem and the king in a more conservative direction, these violent outbursts discredited proponents of direct military rule and exposed the dangers that excessive military involvement in everyday politics posed to national stability.

The upshot was a military apparatus that was both relatively unified and far more supportive of decisive democratic reforms. In a clear reversal of the predicted democracy-through-weakness trajectory of military-led democratization, a divided military did not prompt democratization in Thailand. Only once those divisions were dealt with and military unity restored could military-led democratization proceed through strength. Moreover, Thailand's democratic transformation consisted of preemptive unilateral concessions and not the bilateral negotiations between regime soft-liners and opposition moderates expected in the canonical literature on democratic transitions.[49]

In moving Thailand toward democracy, the military and monarchy needed to ensure that elections would not deliver political power to any organized force, such as an opposition political party, that was both eager and able to surpass their combined power and influence. Luckily for the military and monarchy alike, no such organized oppositional force even existed. Unlike in Indonesia and, as we will see shortly, Myanmar, where the descendants of mass nationalist movements posed a direct electoral challenge to the military's dominance, Thailand in the 1980s exhibited only the weakest articulation of the masses and lower classes in political parties or organizations of any kind. If democratic elections were to deliver political power to civilian politicians, they would surely be overwhelmingly elite, pro-business candidates who had already found great success and felt comfortably acclimated to life under military-monarchical influence and a freewheeling capitalist economy.[50]

Democratic elections also offered military elites new avenues to power in their own right. Even more than in Indonesia, military leaders in Thailand became party leaders as democratization unfolded. Most notably, but far from uniquely in the Thai case, retired general Chatichai Choonhavan, the son of a former army commander in chief, formed the Chart Thai Party, which won a plurality of votes in the 1988 national elections. Chatichai's prime ministership from 1988 to 1991 was notorious for spreading power and resources, often in highly corrupt fashion, across the full range of elite political actors in Thailand. Foreshadowing what would occur a decade later in Indonesia and a quarter century later in Myanmar, civilians in Thailand won considerable power through free and fair national elections but without the military losing its power in the process. Cohabitation, not the military's total political displacement, was the rule in Thailand as in all of the cases in the developmental militarist cluster.

What makes this shared pattern of regime change qualify not as superficial liberalization but as substantial democratization is the fact that it was accompanied by dramatically improved protections for political rights and freedoms. There was no imperative for Thai ruling elites to restrict the electoral arena in an "electoral authoritarian" fashion, since no parties emerged to challenge the developmental status quo, never mind winning popular majorities. Nor did Thailand face any intense identity or ethnic conflicts in the country's major population centers pressing the military to maintain an illiberal democracy to keep restive minorities in check. Insurgency in the Muslim-majority South would only flare up later during the early 2000s, with predictably devastating consequences for Thailand's reversible democratic experiment.

Coda: Reversals and Replays

With stability confidence in hand and with no worries that elections could usher powerful critics into national office, Thailand's reformist elites were willing and able to level the electoral playing field, open up the press, and remove restrictions on civil society over the course of the 1980s with considerable confidence. Democracy through strength had come to Thailand. It lasted for a good while, though not forever.

The preceding discussion made clear that Thai democracy arose in the 1980s during economically good times and on the military's own terms. It was a case of democracy through strength, not weakness. Yet with Thai civilian political organizations being as unimposing as they were, this strength fell well short of what we have seen in the developmental statist cluster of Japan, Taiwan, and South Korea, or even Indonesia. The fact that Thailand's democratization experiment ultimately proved especially reversible makes sense given our explanatory framework, particularly the role that strong conservative parties play in making authoritarian-led democratization work.[51]

Importantly, the rhythms of regime reversal in Thailand were a product of shifting—and especially waning—elite confidence. The first interruption of

Thai democratization came in 1991, when the extreme corruption of the Chatichai government and his "buffet cabinet" gave the military a perfect pretext to return to power.

Yet the pretext had a short shelf life. With the Cold War over and communism eliminated as a meaningful threat, democracy in boom-era Thailand caused little elite anxiety. When coup leader Suchinda Kraprayoon tried to renege on his promise to return power to civilians in May 1992, massive urban protests and the king's timely intervention ensured that Premocracy was quickly put back on track.

The Asian financial crisis of 1997–98 ironically deepened Thai democracy rather than undermining it. Instead of discrediting democracy, the crisis signaled that Thailand had too little of it. After forcing oligarchic prime minister Chaovalit Yongchaiyudh from office, the 1997 constitution strengthened political parties and parliament while also legally enshrining a more complete battery of liberal rights for citizens. Prompted by the financial crisis, the reform constitution promised a civilian government that was less fragmented and more responsive to popular desires. This undid the status quo biases in the electoral system introduced under Premocracy in the 1980s.[52]

Paradoxically, improving Thai democracy after 1997 ultimately endangered it. Taking advantage of new electoral rules that encouraged a more consolidated party system, Thailand's richest man, media tycoon Thaksin Shinawatra, bankrolled a new party juggernaut, Thai Rak Thai (Thais Love Thais), to win an outright majority of parliamentary seats for the first time in Thai history in 2001.

This represented a new challenge to Thailand's shaky democracy. The Thai military and monarchy had never confronted such concentrated civilian power before, and they did not respond well. Prompted by worsening security conditions in the Muslim-majority South and growing middle-class protests over Thaksin's brazen corruption, the military once again toppled Thai democracy through a coup in 2006.[53] Thailand's old military-monarchical alliance no longer had confidence in democracy, and military-led authoritarianism returned.

For the past fifteen years, Thai ruling elites have essentially been trying to bring back the 1980s. Experiments since the 2006 coup with returning substantial power to conservative politicians through highly skewed general elections (in 2007, 2011, 2014, and 2019) were interrupted by yet another coup in 2014 and repeated disqualifications of parties deemed destabilizing (2007, 2008, 2019, and 2020). Unless and until the Thai military and monarchy develop the victory confidence to believe that their political party allies can defeat progressive and pro-Thaksin parties in fully democratic elections, as well as the stability confidence that their interests will be protected no matter who wins democratic elections, developmental militarism will continue to mean regime militarization in Thailand.

Myanmar

Of developmental Asia's six cases of democracy through strength, Myanmar began its democratic experiment in 2011 with the least strength. Predictably, it progressed the least in establishing democracy during its decade of democratic experimentation from 2011 to 2021. And although the full authoritarian reversal that tragically occurred in February 2021 with a military coup was far from inevitable, our theory does shed light on why Myanmar started a democratic experiment when it did in the early 2010s, and also why it was always the most likely case in developmental Asia for a decisive and deadly reversal of democratization to take place.

As we have seen in Indonesia and Thailand, cases of "developmental militarism" all conceded democratic reforms from positions of considerable strength and confidence, though considerably less authoritarian strength than in the developmental statist cases of Japan, Taiwan, and South Korea. Myanmar manifestly lacked even the intermediate levels of party strength of Golkar in Indonesia or Thailand's bureaucratic strength when democratic reforms commenced there in 2011, much to the world's surprise, under the leadership of General Thein Sein. Myanmar's military regime was also saddled with a developmental track record that fell far short of its developmental militarist neighbors, never mind Asia's developmental statist cases. For so many reasons, Myanmar is our hardest case to make for democracy through strength.

Yet even in Myanmar, we insist, the dramatic democratization trend over the course of the 2010s is more accurately seen as having arisen in a moment of authoritarian strength and military regime confidence than of weakness. The democratizing reforms that began in 2011, which peaked with free and fair national elections in 2015 and continued to make incremental progress until the democratic plug was pulled in 2021, were not initiated at a moment when the military regime faced *shrinking choices*. Democratizing reforms in Myanmar only bore even the modest, bitter, and fleeting democratic fruit they did because the military regime perceived *shrinking risks* from pursuing them due to its growing stability confidence.[54]

In some ways the hardest argument for us to make is not that Myanmar's military pursued democracy through *strength* but that it pursued democracy *at all*. We are not claiming that its democratic transition was ever completed, much less consolidated. Yet the comparability and similarities of the Myanmar trajectory to the Indonesia and Thailand trajectories just described are striking. Intriguingly, if one compares the Varieties of Democracy (V-Dem) liberal democracy scores across the developmental militarist cluster, Myanmar had almost precisely the same score in 2019 (0.25) that Indonesia had in 1999 (0.27) and Thailand had in 1989 (0.26).

In other words, the reversible experiment of democracy through strength was very much still in process in Myanmar when its second free and fair national elections were held in 2020. It could have proceeded quickly and successfully like Indonesia's did in the 2000s, or gradually and successfully like Thailand's in the 1990s. Yet it would be reversed entirely, much as we saw occur in Thailand in the 2000s and 2010s, but much more quickly, brutally, and emphatically than in the Thai case.[55]

It was the rising stability confidence of Myanmar's military that made the democracy-through-strength experiment of the past decade possible in the first place. There was every reason to believe that if the civilian government led from 2015 to 2020 by national icon Aung San Suu Kyi and the NLD could refrain from dominating politics too thoroughly and defer to military prerogatives in handling regional separatist insurgencies as well as maintaining its corrupt position at the heart of the nation's booming economy, Myanmar's military-led democratization of the 2010s could well have stayed on its steady if shaky track into the 2020s. There is no single observable cause of democracy's failure besides the February 2021 coup itself. Yet the military's antecedent weakness and deteriorating confidence that its interests could be met in cohabitation with the civilian NLD were enormous contributors to this unfortunate, still unfolding outcome.

Authoritarian Economic Development

Myanmar is the polar opposite of Thailand in one key respect: the relative importance of capitalist economic development in generating the authoritarian strength needed to pursue democracy through strength. In Thailand, economic development under military rule was absolutely pivotal to the regime's democratic prospects; in Myanmar, economic development under military rule would be more fairly described as pitiful. No authoritarian regime in developmental Asia had a weaker economic track record than Myanmar's military regime when it commenced democratic reforms in 2011.[56]

From the time the military seized power in 1962 amid a growing welter of separatist threats until the massive "8/8/88" protests and crackdown in 1988, economic development in Burma was defined by "the Burmese Way to Socialism." This was nothing more than a Burmese way to stagnation. The autarkic and paranoiac Ne Win regime remained entirely outside the economic dynamism occurring across developmental Asia, including in neighboring Thailand. With a developmental model resembling that of North Korea much more than that of South Korea, Burma clearly remained a "nonmember" of developmental Asia so long as the Burmese Socialist Political Party (BSPP) ostensibly presided.

If authoritarian regimes always democratized through weakness and via collapse, 1988 should have sounded the death knell for authoritarianism in Burma. The economy was completely collapsing and civil society was erupting in protest, as was the situation in so much of the socialist world in the late 1980s. Revolutionary pressure from below was palpable. Burma's military responded by abolishing the BSPP and reasserting its own dominance in the civil-military equation.

In so doing, it looked throughout the 1990s as if Myanmar—as Burma's military renamed the country in 1990—was doubling down on what one might justifiably call a "better North Korea than South Korea" political-economic model. While China and Vietnam started forging a new "developmental socialist" cluster in Asia through decisive capitalist reforms (see chapter 9), Burma's military stood aside and licked its wounds. Under the military regime, the country deservedly became one of the world's most contemptible pariah states.

Yet even during the dark days of the 1990s, the military regime's rhetoric was beginning to shift. Changing the country's name from Burma to Myanmar represented an act of national self-assertion that signaled preparation for a nationalist economic drive, throwing autarkic socialist economic ideologies by the wayside. After cracking down on the 1988 democracy protests and refusing to accept the results of the 1990 elections, which Aung San Suu Kyi's NLD won in a landslide, Myanmar's military declared its commitment to a long-term path to a new constitution and a restoration of civilian rule. Having resisted democratization through weakness during both the popular uprising of 1988 and its landslide electoral defeat in 1990, the military professed its intention to democratize through strength over the longer term, but entirely on its own terms.

Politically speaking, this seemed like nothing but hot air throughout the 1990s and 2000s. The military regime had no credibility when it came to pronouncements about political reform. No signs of political liberalization or loosening were evident for two decades. Economically speaking, however, the 2000s began to look starkly different. Over a decade after China and Vietnam became latecomer members of developmental Asia as founding members of the developmental socialist cluster, Myanmar was doing the same by belatedly joining the developmental militarist cluster.

As of 1991, Myanmar's GDP was under US$200 per capita, where it had been mired since the military seized power in 1962 nearly four decades before. By 2001, however, this had nearly doubled to $377 per capita, and by 2011, the year that military leader Thein Sein shocked the world by announcing preemptive democratic reforms, it inched above $1,000 per capita (a threshold Thailand and Indonesia had both surpassed way back in the 1970s). As in Thailand in the 1980s, Myanmar's reversible democratic experiment of the 2010s unmistakably unfolded as economic tides were rising rather than falling—albeit from a comparatively unimpressive starting point.

Authoritarian Institutional Development

Authoritarian rule in Myanmar has always been military rule. This meant regime weakness in one sense, but strength in another. It was a source of weakness because the military neither built nor permitted the development of any civilian political organizations that could help govern the population and bolster its rule.[57] Most notably, successive military regimes intentionally frustrated the development of a workable state and an authoritative political party. The military relied on pure force to stay in power to a far greater extent than military-led regimes in either Indonesia or Thailand.

Yet pure military rule resulted in a strong form of authoritarianism in Myanmar in that the ruling military was remarkably cohesive.[58] We have seen how factionalism chronically weakened Thailand's military-led regime and how personalism did the same to Suharto's regime during the 1990s. Critically, Myanmar's authoritarianism was weakened by neither of these forms of fragmentation. The military may have ruled alone, as a single organization, but it also ruled forcefully, with a singular sense of purpose. Simply put, the strength of military rule rested in the fact that it was so *solidary*, while its weakness derived from the fact that it was so *solitary*.

This cohesion and shared purpose had its roots in the birth of Burma's military itself and the onset of military rule. Like Indonesia's military, Burma's was built by occupying Japanese forces during World War II and developed a strong nationalist esprit de corps from resisting the postwar reestablishment of European colonization. Even more vitally, Burma's military was soldered into a cohesive force by endemic separatist rebellions that rocked the new nation between independence in 1948 and the onset of military rule in 1962. The military never fractured throughout its reign from 1962 to 2011, even as it repeatedly used overwhelming force against antiregime protesters, most famously and dramatically in 1988 and 2007, in ways that usually expose and exacerbate fault lines within the military.[59]

When the ruling regime did experience its most serious instance of military factionalism, sparked by the political rise of General Khin Nyunt in the early 2000s, it did not have the democratizing effects anticipated by canonical transitions theory. As in Thailand in the wake of its Young Turks coup in the early 1980s and in Indonesia during the late 1990s with the elimination of Prabowo Subianto as a contender for power, military factionalism in Myanmar in the early 2000s was dealt with *by purging the prime source of friction along with his allies rather than succumbing to a democratic exit.* As in Thailand and Indonesia, only once the military successfully reestablished internal cohesion when it sidelined the Khin Nyunt faction did it begin its process of democratic concessions. Instead of divided militaries democratizing from weakness, as widely expected, military regimes in developmental Asia have first overcome their divisions, then democratized through strength.

Part of this process in Myanmar included belatedly launching a military-backed political party. In 2010, on the eve of democratizing reforms, the regime founded the United Solidarity and Development Party (USDP) in anticipation that competitive elections would soon be restored. This new party vehicle had virtually no chance of holding its own in free and fair elections against the wildly popular NLD behind Aung San Suu Kyi, the daughter of Burma's great nationalist hero, student, and military leader, Aung San, as well as the charismatic champion of Burma's democracy movement for nearly a quarter century in her own right.

Yet the formation of the USDP provided the military at least some hope that, in alliance with appointed military members of parliament and smaller parties representing ethnic minorities, the USDP might help limit the NLD's power after it inevitably prevailed in elections once they were restored. Even if the USDP could not win elections, it could lessen NLD dominance, and thus help maintain ultimate military supremacy, albeit in cohabitation with an NLD-led civilian government instituted by fully free and fair elections.

Conceding to Cohabitate

The Myanmar military's decision to end outright military rule was in one sense shockingly sudden, and in another sense almost imperceptibly incremental. It was sudden in the sense that Thein Sein announced a wide array of dramatic liberalizing reforms at a moment when nobody was expecting it, since the regime was not in any imminent trouble whatsoever. Reforms began when active domestic opposition was in abeyance, rather than during a moment of upheaval such as the so-called 8/8/88 uprising or Saffron Revolution of 2007.

Ironically, as a regime that had been almost perpetually on crisis and even literal war footing for fifty years, Myanmar's military conceded a democratic opening in a moment when the economy was improving and politics was stabilizing. Like Thailand's in the 1980s, Myanmar's military miraculously managed to generate a "noncrisis" democratic transition. As Morten Pedersen rightly puts it, Myanmar's military embarked on reform when "it was in a stronger position than ever before."[60] And as Min Zin and Brian Joseph similarly summarize, "Despite retaining a firm hold on power and facing no urgent domestic or international threats, the military began to shift course."[61]

And yet, as sudden as the military regime's pronouncements seemed at the time, Myanmar's democratization through strength was an incremental story as well, and one that continued to unfold gradually over the course of the 2010s. After watching the NLD romp to victory in the 1990 elections, the military tossed the results in the waste bin but also promised to restore democratic elections once Myanmar promulgated a new constitution.

It took almost twenty years, but in 2008, the military's self-made constitution was railroaded into existence via referendum. This was of course the furthest cry imaginable from the participatory, negotiated constitution-making processes that have ended authoritarian rule in so many parts of the world. Nevertheless, Myanmar's military unilaterally imposed a new constitution on the country that promised to deliver the kind of "disciplined democracy" they had been promising to bestow, albeit with absolutely no credibility behind their commitment, for two long decades.

At the same time, the military was gradually solidifying ceasefire agreements with virtually every regionalist rebel army it confronted.[62] Since the raison d'être of military rule had always been to keep the country from breaking apart, these peace deals were the most important element in the military's stability confidence by the early 2010s. Stability confidence was also enhanced by the military's dramatic decision to move the national capital in 2005 from Yangon (Rangoon) to the new, distant, sleepy inland metropolis of Naypyidaw, where neither student radicals nor activist monks could possibly use massive protest to bring government to a halt.

Victory confidence was another matter entirely, however. Fearful of another 1990-style NLD landslide, the military delayed the first national elections until 2015. This gave the Thein Sein regime a bit of breathing room to build up the newly formed USDP, to generate support for minority ethnic parties in areas where the Burman-dominated NLD might not be expected to fare as well, and to continue improving its track record of economic development and, with it, its paltry performance legitimacy. Indeed, the fact that dramatic liberalization reforms after 2011 allowed the lifting of almost all international sanctions prompted a new influx of FDI into Myanmar and the promise of further accelerated economic development. The former hermit military regime was both civilianizing its power structure and positioning itself in developmental Asia with growing confidence.

Yet if the military ever hoped the USDP could prevent the NLD's long march to eventual electoral victory, it could harbor no such wishful illusions after the by-elections of 2012. Testing the waters, the military regime allowed several dozen free and fair by-elections to gauge the NLD's continuing strength. The NLD won 43 of the 44 seats it contested. This made it a foregone conclusion that the 2015 national elections would be another NLD wipeout.

By tweaking electoral laws to ensure that Aung San Suu Kyi could not become president, however, due to her being the widow of a British national, the military kept its chief rival at least partly in check. More importantly, by ensuring that every state ministry dealing with issues of national security and defense stayed by constitutional dictate in military rather than civilian hands, the military tried to guarantee that its rightful lack of victory confidence would not spill over to shatter what mattered far more if democratization were to proceed as planned: its stability confidence.

Coda: Losing the Confidence Game

Even when Myanmar's democratization story seemed to be proceeding largely apace in the mid-2010s, it had a deeply dark underside. In response to a deadly attack against its personnel by the Arakan Rohingya Salvation Army in 2016,

Myanmar's military unleashed a horrific campaign of ethnic cleansing and genocide against the Bengali-speaking Muslim minority, known as the Rohingya, in northern Rakhine State. In a country where Buddhist nationalism reigns over civilians as much as the military, the Rohingya found themselves utterly friendless. Aung San Suu Kyi infamously defended the military and its murderous campaign against the Rohingya before the International Court of Justice at The Hague in late 2019, spoiling even further her tattered credentials in the international community as an icon for human rights.

Against the backdrop of the narrative and theory just outlined, the connivance of democratically elected politicians like Aung San Suu Kyi with the military in Myanmar should appear as predictable as it is reprehensible. The military's halfhearted commitment to the democratization process always depended first and foremost on its stability confidence, which depended primarily, in turn, on its free hand to deal with regional and separatist insurgencies in whatever way it deemed fit. If civilian leaders had tried to get in the way of the military's war-making prerogatives in the immediate aftermath of winning the NLD landslide in 2015, they would not have been allowed to cohabit in power with military leaders long enough to compete for power again in the elections of 2020.

Having dedicated the better part of her adult life to freeing her own (ethnically Burman, religiously Buddhist) people from the half-century-long scourge of military rule, Aung San Suu Kyi was not about to abandon her democratization mission on behalf of Myanmar's marginalized Muslim minority. Nor was her stance a problem within the NLD or among Myanmar's majority-Buddhist population. Unsuccessful as she may have become as an international human rights heroine, Aung San Suu Kyi was seeking sustained success as a national politician in an incredibly difficult, delicate democratization context.[63]

As its second democratic national election in November 2020 loomed, Myanmar seemed to face at least two chronic risks to its continued democratic emergence. The first, as noted, was that the military's stability confidence would become increasingly threatened by regional unrest as civilians tried to restrain the military from handling its enemies in its own preferred manner. It was not so much the sheer severity of internal conflicts as the ability of civilian and military elites to stay in accord over how these threats to stability should be managed that loomed over Myanmar's fragile democratic experiment like a sword of Damocles.

Of course, whether any regime that helped preside over the kind of inhuman maltreatment the Rohingya have suffered should be considered to be traveling a path toward democracy is another question entirely. It is unfair to place the Rohingya disaster on the doorstep of democracy itself, however. Myanmar's military has a long and notorious record of abusive conduct both on the country's periphery and in its major population centers, a track record that events since the February 2021 coup are only underscoring. There is no reason to believe the Rohingya would have fared any better if Myanmar had not been experimenting with democracy at the time the conflict tragically escalated.

A second chronic threat to Myanmar's democratic experiment, which lies outside the boundaries of our theory, could be seen in the electoral dominance of the NLD itself. As the past decade of global democratic backsliding makes abundantly clear, freely and popularly elected governments are all too capable of using their democratic mandates to undermine their opponents and critics in illiberal ways. The completion of Myanmar's reversible experiment with democracy through strength was always uncertain, and not only because it depended on whether its military stayed confident of its strength. It also always hinged on whether the NLD would remain committed to democracy and resist the temptation to hold on to and exercise political power in autocratic ways.

As it turns out, we will probably never know. Despite the fact that Myanmar's democratic experiment had just given the country its freest and most prosperous decade in its entire history, and did so according to the military's own meticulously constructed road map, Myanmar's military leadership nevertheless decided to torpedo civilian-military cohabitation and restore full military rule in its February 2021 coup. One could hear echoes from Thailand in its power grab. Like Thaksin Shinawatra, Aung San Suu Kyi had proved unbeatable at the polls. Like Thailand's military, Myanmar's military had historically failed to build the credible party vehicle and legitimating developmental track record necessary to compete at the polls with an electoral juggernaut. A coup was the only bullet it had left in the chamber.

In the final analysis, the reversal of preemptive democratic experiments via coup d'état in both Thailand and Myanmar suggests a caveat to our theory of victory confidence and stability confidence. We have argued throughout this book that in the developmental militarist cluster, stability confidence should matter more than victory confidence, because militaries (unlike ruling parties) can retain their prerogatives no matter who wins elections. And yet, in both Thailand and Myanmar, crushing electoral victories by iconic rivals provided the occasion for military coups. We would submit that it was not the electoral results themselves, however, but the military's lack of confidence that it could maintain its political primacy against such rising civilian rivals that doomed each country's democratic experiment. Perhaps for the Thai and Myanmar militaries, if not for the Indonesian military, nothing counts as stability confidence except its confidence in its own political dominance.

Conclusion

The developmental militarist cluster of Indonesia, Thailand, and Myanmar is both far economically poorer and far democratically poorer than the developmental statist cluster of Japan, Taiwan, and South Korea. Modernization theory would correctly predict this correspondence of relative economic and political underdevelopment. Yet it would not predict the next twist in our story: the refusal by far richer authoritarian regimes in the developmental Britannia cluster of Singapore, Malaysia, and Hong Kong to concede democracy through strength in ways seen in the preceding chapters.

Before our story shifts to developmental Asia's cases of "democracy avoidance," however, we should emphasize the striking and surprising similarities across the six diverse cases of democratization just detailed. From the wealthy developmental states of Japan, Taiwan, and South Korea to the military-led developing economies of Indonesia, Thailand, and Myanmar, authoritarian regimes have proved both willing and able to pursue decisive and preemptive democratic reforms when they expected to thrive—or at least minimally survive, in the weakest cases—in their aftermath. Dictators across the globe self-servingly equate democratization with political collapse and instability. Developmental Asia's six cases of democracy through strength show that the end of authoritarianism need not mean a loss, or even a decline, in political order.

8

Developmental Britannia

EMBITTERED AUTHORITARIANISM

DEVELOPMENTAL ASIA is not Sinocentric. Before Japan created the region, before America reshaped it, and long before any specter existed of China dominating it, the greatest power along the rim of the Pacific was Great Britain. From the Opium Wars of the mid-nineteenth century until World War II in the mid-twentieth century, the Union Jack flew higher in Asia than any rival banner. What China calls its century of humiliation was Britain's century of hegemony.

This chapter charts the economic and political trajectories of those polities where East Asian developmentalism was preceded by British imperialism: Singapore, Malaysia, and Hong Kong. The results have been surprising. On a global level, British colonial legacies are generally associated with stronger democratic prospects after independence. Even in Asia itself, India's surprising democracy has long been traced, at least in part, to the relatively virtuous legal and electoral legacies of its years under the British Raj. The sheer size of India means observers tend to associate British rule in Asia with democracy, much as the awesome girth of China can mistakenly make Asia seem altogether authoritarian.[1] Yet to India's east, the collision of British rule and Asian developmentalism—the forces that forged the developmental Britannia cluster—has not produced *democratic advantages*. As we now explore, and attempt at least partly to explain, it has led to *democracy avoidance*.

Riches without Reforms

Developmental riches are one thing; democratic reforms are quite another. The preceding chapters have shown that democratic reforms can proceed through a similar overarching logic—the logic of democracy through strength—from economies as rich as Japan and Taiwan to developing economies like Indonesia and Myanmar. Though the course of democratization either remains rocky or has been reversed entirely in the developmental militarist cases, in all six cases the incumbent authoritarian regimes chose to experiment with democracy when they were confident a transition could be relatively stable. In the developmental statist cases, these experiments came with the justified expectation of staying in power without interruption.

This chapter shows that even extraordinary levels of capitalist economic development do not necessarily lead strong authoritarian regimes to attempt democratic reforms, however. Unlike in our statist and militarist clusters, in developmental Britannia—Singapore, Malaysia, and Hong Kong—the general pattern has been democracy avoidance, not democracy through strength. Yet the costs and risks of instability resulting from democracy avoidance have grown as surely as levels of economic development. All three authoritarian regimes have clearly passed their apex of power, missing their opportunity to democratize in the most stabilizing manner possible. Once an authoritarian regime enters this "bittersweet spot," we contend, continuing to avoid democratic reform as decline worsens propels the incumbent regime into an age of *embittered authoritarianism*. Once a regime has passed its apex of power, it can experience a surprisingly steep decline from strength to weakness.

The disastrous costs of delay for political stability, and for the authoritarian incumbents themselves, are most obvious in Malaysia and Hong Kong. In Malaysia, the dominant authoritarian coalition's failure to begin pursuing democratic reforms from their apex of strength in the mid- to late 1990s culminated in their outright loss in the 2018 national elections. The years since have seen Malaysia devolve from one of Asia's most predictable polities to one of its most unpredictable. Somewhat analogously, in Hong Kong, the failure of pro-Beijing politicians to begin addressing popular demands for democratic reform since the handover from British rule in 1997 have hastened the city's downward spiral from enviable stability to near ungovernability.

Singapore's authoritarian order remains in much stronger shape. The ruling People's Action Party (PAP) in many ways resembles Taiwan's Kuomintang (KMT) at the time of its transition. However, Singapore's near future is liable to look more and more like Malaysia's and Hong Kong's recent past and present, rather than Taiwan's, if it chooses to continue avoiding democratic reforms. Despite its avowed exceptionalism, Singapore can never fully escape or expunge the distinctive features of the developmental cluster that it inherited from a century and a half of direct British rule.

What are the core features of the developmental Britannia cluster? And what are their central lessons for democratic reforms and democracy avoidance?

The most striking feature is the cluster's *sustained authoritarianism after decades of rapid capitalist development*. With the possible exceptions of Japan and Germany in the late nineteenth century, and with the looming potential exception of China in the decades to come (see chapter 9), nowhere else in the world has ever witnessed anything similar. Recall that the developmental statist cluster all democratized upon reaching "developed country" status; the developmental Britannia cluster, on the other hand, did not. Sustaining authoritarianism for decades at extraordinarily high levels of capitalist development presents a challenge for authoritarian regimes in the Britannia cluster that their counterparts in the statist cluster (Japan, Taiwan, and South Korea) strategically chose not to encounter.

As we have argued throughout this book, sustained economic development does not necessarily inculcate democratic citizens; but it does nurture more demanding citizens. An impressive economic track record might generate performance legitimacy for an authoritarian regime at lower levels of economic development and for a considerable time. Over time, however, national wealth breeds societal ingratitude. Only by providing more and more developmental public goods can authoritarian regimes hope even to stay in place in terms of public support.

Societal demands have manifested in many ways in developmental Britannia. More than in any other cluster, societal intolerance of political corruption and abuses of power is especially intense. This, we contend, is a consequence of colonial inheritance and the accumulation of extreme wealth. Strong legal institutions constructed under British rule instilled an expectation of legality among citizens in the Britannia cluster that has no parallel elsewhere in developmental Asia, where bureaucracies and militaries tend to fill the yawning legal void produced by weak courts.

These strong legal institutions are double-edged. On the one hand, effective legal institutions have given authoritarian regimes in Singapore, Malaysia, and Hong Kong a powerful tool for establishing social control. On the other hand, they have also raised expectations of legality to the point that society practically takes them for granted. If there is any value that bourgeois development seems to foster, it is a deep distaste for and self-interested aversion toward corruption. Expectations of party-state incorruptibility in Singapore, a sacrosanct "rule of law" in Hong Kong, and an active professional governance role for the judicial system in Malaysia are essential and distinctive features of how these authoritarian regimes have long operated. These high expectations present profound constraints under which these authoritarian regimes must labor.

Something similar can be said about electoral institutions, another way in which developmental Britannia is distinctive as a cluster. Largely as a product of British rule, nowhere in developmental Asia are competitive multiparty elections more a part of the political DNA than in developmental Britannia. Electoral and legal institutions are as fundamental to the manner in which citizens in Singapore, Malaysia, and Hong Kong are governed as the kind of bureaucratic and military institutions that perpetuated state dominance in the statist and militarist clusters, respectively.

What these distinctive electoral and legal features amount to is this: authoritarian regimes in developmental Britannia have become increasingly hemmed in as they have each confronted an increasingly demanding citizenry. Unlike in the developmental socialist cluster to be discussed in chapter 9 (most notably China), authoritarian rulers in Singapore, Malaysia, and Hong Kong are not able to rejuvenate their legitimacy by gradually building a professional judiciary, introducing competitive multiparty elections, or providing expanded and improved basic public goods like education, health care, and housing. They are not viable options in the reform toolkit that other authoritarian developmental regimes might deploy, *because these reforms were already implemented long ago in developmental Britannia.* They represent a historical artifact of their British colonial heritage, and their fruits for good governance have long been the expected privilege of being a Singaporean, Malaysian, or Hong Konger.

As authoritarian regimes in developmental Britannia struggle to keep their citizens quiescent and to maintain their own political power, their options are either to provide better and better economic and governance outcomes or to become more democratic. As we argue in this chapter, failing to accomplish either has paved the path to electoral defeat in Malaysia and a revolutionary upsurge in Hong Kong. Singaporean authoritarianism must now operate in the distant yet looming shadow of both.

The Three Cases to Come

Despite being in the same developmental cluster and sharing a common political heritage, all three cases in developmental Britannia have a history and dynamic all their own. They also lie in different spots on the spectrum of authoritarian strength, which we have argued throughout this book portends the kind of democratic transition they could expect if they muster the courage to attempt it. Singapore is the obvious leader, and for purposes of clarity that is where our analysis to follow will begin.[2]

To understand Singapore, one should recall the discussion of Taiwan and the role of the KMT in Taiwan's development and eventual democratic transition (chapter 4). Much as the KMT and its developmental state factored into Taiwan's democratic transition through strength in the 1980s and 1990s, Singapore's PAP also has the electoral might and developmental track record to ensure that it would thrive under fully democratic conditions, should it ever choose to introduce them. Indeed, Singapore has found outright repression so unnecessary in recent decades, and has so faithfully followed the Westminster system of competitive multiparty elections for over half a century, that the ruling PAP could level the playing field with the deeply divided Singaporean opposition and continue to dominate, making barely a ripple in the process.

Yet Singapore still stubbornly resists taking the Taiwanese path. We offer an explanation for why in this chapter. For all its comparable strength with the KMT, the PAP has received very different signals regarding its incipient decline and has thus adopted the very different strategy of democracy avoidance rather than democracy through strength. For all its claims of geopolitical vulnerability, Singapore is nowhere near as dependent on the United States as Taiwan was during the Cold War. Contentious politics in Singapore has been comparatively mild, and there has not emerged a sustained opposition such as the *tangwai* movement in Taiwan. Most importantly, electoral signals of PAP decline, which we argue present the clearest signals of a ruling party's staying power, remain relatively mild and muddy.

Singapore thus represents our first example of what we refer to as *the tragedy of dominant-party politics*. In Singapore—as in Hong Kong, Malaysia, and Cambodia—dominant authoritarian parties failed to democratize from their positions of lofty (though still quite variable) strength and waited too long to deliver democracy in the most stabilizing manner possible, thereby entering the ranks of "embittered authoritarian" regimes. Simply put, they missed their window of opportunity in the bittersweet spot to transition from a position of incumbent authoritarian strength to eventual democratic strength. The consequences of democracy avoidance can be tragic indeed, especially for the societies they govern.

Malaysia is the clearest example of this trajectory. It provides a cautionary tale for would-be political reformers who ultimately choose to avoid preemptive democratic reforms. As of the mid-1990s, the country's ruling United Malays National Organization (UMNO) party and Barisan Nasional (BN; National Front) coalition were at an apex of power so rarefied as to rival Singapore's PAP and Taiwan's KMT. Yet with no signals of incipient decline, there was no pressure for democratic reform. This all changed in 1997–98, however, when the dual hammer blow of the Asian financial crisis and the dramatic emergence of the democratic *reformasi* movement delivered economic and contentious signals indicating that the golden age of stable authoritarian hegemony was at an end.

If Prime Minister Mahathir Mohamad had simply fulfilled his existing promise at the height of the economic crisis to transfer power to his hand-picked heir apparent, Deputy Prime Minister Anwar Ibrahim, Malaysia would almost certainly have commenced a path to democracy through strength. Anwar was poised to play a parallel historical role in Malaysia to the one B. J. Habibie was just beginning to play in Indonesia's democratic transformation. However, the deeply authoritarian Malaysian prime minister strategized otherwise, and tragically rallied UMNO and the BN behind democracy avoidance instead.

Mahathir's repressive turn did not salvage UMNO-BN strength; to the contrary, it subverted it. Economic development had expanded the Malaysian middle class to the point where an increasingly authoritarian and more deeply corrupt and abusive ruling party could no longer reliably generate majority electoral support, even under Malaysia's highly skewed and unfair electoral system, backed by a battery of authoritarian controls over media and expression. Ironically, UMNO-BN's steady decline eventually led Mahathir himself to join the opposition coalition as its prime ministerial candidate, helping deliver defeat to UMNO-BN in 2018 for the first time in its history.

Rather than conceding democracy without conceding defeat, like Taiwan's KMT, *UMNO-BN conceded defeat without conceding democracy*. Whether a democracy will eventually arise from this period of political upheaval remains uncertain. What is vital for our purposes here is that 2018 marked a power transition from weakness rather than strength because Malaysia missed its bittersweet spot entirely. Therefore, whatever democracy might emerge from Malaysia's transition will likely be far less functional and stable than the democracies in the developmental statist cluster. It would also be less functional and much less stable than Malaysian democracy would have been if UMNO-BN had democratized through strength rather than losing power through weakness.

Hong Kong has experienced regime decline as insuperably and gradually over the past two decades as Malaysia. During the same period when Malaysia was struggling to adjust to life after the Asian financial crisis, Hong Kong had to cope with the massive fallout of its 1997 transition from British to Chinese control. To be sure, the fact that Hong Kong exists under Chinese sovereignty has meant that any decision to democratize through strength is out of local hands; in this sense it is an awkward fit for our comparative and theoretical analysis. Yet the case contains powerful lessons about the prospects of democracy through strength in this cluster of cases. Since Britain departed so recently, in 1997, Hong Kong remains by historical inheritance the most British place in developmental Britannia. Its political and economic institutions have proved, predictably from the perspective of our clustered analysis, to be a terrible fit with Chinese sovereignty. Hong Kong's rule of law and liberal, competitive electoral environment have strained mightily in Beijing's developmental socialist shadow.

As in Singapore and Malaysia, the regime response in Hong Kong—as implemented by its pro-Beijing local political establishment—has been democracy avoidance rather than democracy through strength. In political terms, Hong Kong's electoral arena and liberal rights protections have diminished substantially over the past two decades, frustrating the territory's burgeoning democratic energies. Moreover, against the backdrop of Hong Kong's financial flair, the local government's unwillingness to extend a more robust social safety net has left Hong Kong's working and middle classes in an increasingly perilous position, struggling to secure affordable housing and suffering the squeeze of the city's stratospheric inequality.

This combination of political and economic strains culminated, not surprisingly, in a series of massive popular uprisings beginning in 2014, as well as the shocking electoral defeat of Hong Kong's pro-Beijing conservatives in local elections in 2019. The local pro-Beijing regime has become immensely unpopular in recent years. In other words, Hong Kong's leaders missed their best chance to democratize when they were still at their strongest. They now have few options besides fuller democratization, as improbable as that may now be under Chinese sovereignty, or continued repression, as they struggle to make one of the world's richest cities governable and stable once again. No longer in a position of strength, the Hong Kong administration has moved toward illiberal regime closure and increasingly forceful repression. At least for now, Beijing and its local Hong Kong allies have slammed the window shut.

Singapore

We begin with Singapore because of its relative simplicity and clarity with respect to its authoritarian strength. With the possible exceptions of the KMT in Taiwan and the Liberal Democratic Party (LDP) in Japan, no political party in developmental Asia has generated as much performance legitimacy and political dominance as Singapore's PAP. The ruling party has long been regarded as the architect and master of one of the world's most capable, effective, and controlling authoritarian Leviathans. Armed with impressive party-state infrastructure, PAP leaders have presided over Singapore's incredible rise, during which it has become one of the richest countries in the world. Although the PAP puts its power and popularity to an electoral test every five years, it is never a fully free and fair contest. Spectacular wealth and party strength have led not to democratic concessions in Singapore, but rather consistent democracy avoidance.[3]

Singapore thus stands as a clear testament to one of this book's central tenets: democracy *through* strength does not mean democracy *because* of strength. Nothing can force strong authoritarian regimes to democratize. Democracy through strength is ultimately a strategic decision made by an incumbent authoritarian regime. As we have shown in the earlier chapters of this book, it takes clear and sometimes ominous signals of incipient decline to make a democracy-through-strength scenario increasingly likely, and shifting strategies of regime legitimation are necessary to bring it to fruition. The remainder of this section details Singapore's authoritarian strength, offering an explanation for why signals have not pushed the PAP to rethink its strategy and to democratize preemptively like similarly strong regimes in fellow high-income economies such as Taiwan and South Korea.

Authoritarian Economic Development

Singapore is one of the richest and most strictly governed countries on earth. The island's rise to riches, now nearing US$60,000 per capita, began long before independence. British rule leveraged Singapore's commercial entrepôt potential as well as the absence of local dynastic or feudal obstacles to economic transformation to make it one of Britannia's richest colonies even before World War II.

The immediate postwar period witnessed even more pronounced economic gains. British rulers and their local elite allies built stronger and more fiscally extractive state institutions in a counterrevolutionary response to the upsurge of labor and racial unrest following Japan's wartime occupation.[4] By the time Singapore gained self-rule in 1959, gross domestic product (GDP) per capita was already over US$3,500, a middle-income threshold that South Korea would not reach until 1978, Thailand would not reach until 1995, and China would not reach until 2008.

Singapore's spectacular postwar record of economic development was a product of the city-state's integration into the international economy, its export orientation, and its eager openness to inward foreign investment. As postwar Asia became developmental Asia, Singapore was never going to stand to the side or go it alone. Even before Japan became the engine of Asian developmentalism during the 1970s and 1980s, Singapore was already a haven for investment from European and American firms, a bustling trading hub for natural resources and processed goods, and a major exporter of manufactured products to the world's industrialized countries.

Unlike the developmental statist economies of Japan, South Korea, and Taiwan, Singapore relied more on the importation and adoption of foreign technology than indigenous technological development in its path to high-income status.[5] Very much like the cases in the developmental statist cluster, however, Singapore has managed to generate rapid and sustained economic growth without access to substantial natural resource wealth.[6] This economic strategy was buttressed by the British colonial emphasis on the development of legal institutions that, under authoritarian conditions as under colonial conditions, assert state rule more than they constrain it. This helped Singapore become not only one of the world's richest economies but also one of the world's least corrupt countries.

The PAP government's efforts in poverty reduction have been impressive, and welfare provision has been universalistic in scope albeit far from generous in scale. Adequately funded and professionally managed public education, health, and housing have long been the birthrights of every Singaporean citizen. Although increased immigration of high-income expatriates has recently worsened inequality from above, and growing inflows of low-income workers have exacerbated pressure on public services from below, the fact remains that Singapore is a highly developed economy and a highly urbanized middle-class society.

And yet the regime has never embraced substantive democratization. There is no version of modernization theory that can make sense of Singapore's endurance as an authoritarian regime governing a society with a per capita income reaching US$60,000.

As we have seen in other parts of developmental Asia, economic development generates performance legitimacy and improves an authoritarian regime's stability confidence when it substantially reduces poverty and expands the middle class. Successful and balanced economic development also improves the regime's victory confidence when the ruling party can trade on an imposing developmental record.

The PAP is a consummate example of both kinds of regime confidence. These feats would not have been possible, however, without the same levels of institutional strength and capacity that undergirded economic miracles in the developmental statist cluster. The regime's strength was a product not only of its record of developmental success but also its formidable institutional strengths. By the 1950s, Singapore's colonial state was already one of Asia's strongest and most capable. By the 1960s, the ruling PAP emerged to become one of Asia's strongest governing political parties as well.

The party-state's initial path to dominance was anything but smooth, however. Hard as it is to believe now, Singapore was one of the most contentious and mobilized cities in Asia in the aftermath of World War II. Specifically, labor unions and the socialist movement were radical and ascendant. A combination of selective repression by the government and broad electoral incorporation gradually transformed organized labor from a force for the opposition into an active and cooperative player in Singapore's decolonization state-building project. The PAP began its life as a consummate nationalist united front, positioning itself to be a dominant and left-leaning party after self-rule was granted in 1959.

Like many nationalist united fronts, the PAP was deeply fragmented internally. The party's socialist and predominantly Chinese-speaking left wing coexisted uneasily with its procapitalist, British-friendly, and mostly English-speaking center.

This coexistence constituted an invincible if incoherent electoral juggernaut. Reflecting its emerging catch-all appeal, the PAP won 43 of 51 parliamentary seats in 1959, unified by one overarching goal—namely, the handover of sovereignty from the British. By 1961, two years after self-rule was won, the ruling party officially split, with the left wing, led by David Marshall, forming the new Socialist Front (Barisan Socialis) and the now more cohesively centrist PAP fronted by Lee Kuan Yew. Consequently, the PAP's majority in parliamentary seats dwindled to just a 26–25 advantage after 1961.

By 1963, the political situation had become even more complicated and contentious. Fearful that Singapore was unviable as a small city-state, PAP centrists and British colonialists pushed for the island's merger with the expanded Federation of Malaysia. This heightened political polarization across both ideological and ethnic lines. At the time, Malaysia was governed by a fervently antisocialist, Malay-led coalition, while Singapore was led by a Chinese-dominated party that still paid lip service to socialist principles and expressed a bitter distaste for the ethnic favoritism that governed politics in the rest of Malaysia. In the 1963 parliamentary elections that accompanied the Malaysian merger, the PAP managed to ward off challengers from both socialist and Malaysia-wide contenders, winning 37 of 51 seats.

The subsequent period from 1963 to 1965 proved the Malaysia experiment to be a nonstarter. The PAP's vision of a "Malaysian Malaysia" in which non-Malays enjoyed fully equal political status to indigenous Malays was fundamentally anathema to the ruling UMNO-dominated Alliance coalition. Ethnic tensions became unbearable, and intermittently violent. In August 1965, Singapore and Malaysia officially split. Singapore would henceforth be governed by a resolutely procapitalist ruling party that had no compunction about using authoritarian measures to ensure political stability and rapid economic growth.

What emerged was one of Asia's strongest authoritarian developmental states. Shorn of its leftist and Chinese-educated wings, the PAP forged an ironclad alliance with a meritocratic, capable, and professional bureaucracy that shared the ruling party's commitment to open international markets and tight social control. Foreign investment soon poured in and industrialization accelerated. Meanwhile, in an effort to ensconce the PAP in power, the ruling party-state pumped its ample tax revenues into expansive social services, most famously the public-housing program that encompassed over 90 percent of Singaporeans by the late 1970s. Even as inequality gradually increased, absolute poverty, a vivid recent memory, became a thing of Singapore's past.

Weak Signals, Old Strategies

The PAP accumulated tremendous strengths over the course of the postindependence period in Singapore, making it a prime candidate for a democracy-through-strength scenario to unfold. However, such a scenario is most likely prompted when the incumbent regime receives clear and strong signals that it has passed its apex of power and that the democratic choice presents the most reassuring path forward for the regime. This is where the PAP's path diverged from that of Taiwan's KMT and other developmental democracies.

Whereas the Democratic Justice Party (DJP) regime in South Korea received strong signals of its decline and the KMT clear signals of its waning electoral popularity, the PAP has received only very weak and inconsistent signals of incipient decline over the past two decades. Nothing transpiring in Singapore's economic, electoral, geopolitical, or contentious arenas has clearly and ominously signaled there is anything remotely urgent about pursuing preemptive democratic reforms as a way of mitigating rising pressures. And yet the PAP regime is clearly past its prime, and the costs it must pay simply to maintain its levels of electoral support are inexorably rising.

The PAP's long-term electoral record is every electoral authoritarian regime's dream. In the 1960s and 1970s, the PAP was effectively a single-party regime because opposition first boycotted, then woefully underparticipated in the electoral exercise. When the opposition finally committed itself to entering the electoral fray during the 1980s, it was deeply divided. Although dozens of opposition parties have come and gone, they have typically presented the PAP with challenges from the left. For instance, the current opposition mantle is shared by the Workers' Party and Singapore Democratic Party.

One of the key reasons for the PAP's assured electoral success is Singapore's Westminster-style electoral rules, common across the developmental Britannia cluster, which ensure a massive seat bonus whereby the winning party's seat share typically far outstrips its vote share. Not that the PAP has needed any such malapportionment help: the ruling party has never polled less than 60 percent of the popular vote, and only in 2020 did its share of parliamentary seats ever slip below 90 percent (and then only to 89.9 percent).

Paradoxically, however, the certainty of PAP electoral landslides has not been reflected in entirely consistent voter support. Valleys tend to be followed by peaks, and peaks by valleys. In 1991, 2011, and 2020, the PAP's vote share sank close to 60 percent. These worrisome results from a PAP perspective, however, were punctuated by massive rebounds, with vote hauls of 75 percent in 2001, 66 percent in 2006, and 70 percent in 2015. The PAP has thus shown a capacity to continually revitalize its popular support, mitigating any sense the party is in an inevitable or even incipient decline. Still, the party's towering apex—the long period from 1968 to 2006 when it never won a smaller seat share than 95 percent—was clearly a bygone era by the mid-2010s.[7]

Singapore's PAP is thus firmly ensconced in the bittersweet spot, where democratization would surely be accompanied by continued PAP electoral dominance, and indeed even solve certain governance and stability challenges in the process. Put another way, the incumbent ruling party's resounding accumulated strengths would help keep it in power and help keep Singapore politically stable should the PAP choose to democratize through strength.[8]

The ruling party has found itself on slightly shakier ground in the past decade or so. Surveys conducted by the nonpartisan Institute of Policy Studies after each recent election show both the limits and softness of PAP support.[9] Of particular importance were worrying signals in the institute's 2015 survey, when the PAP had just secured a historic landslide win in the aftermath of two major events: Singapore's fiftieth national day (known as SG50) and the passing of the city-state's revered founding leader, Lee Kuan Yew. If early signals of trouble can be uncovered at one of the PAP's brightest recent moments—a momentary apex within a longer bittersweet spot, we might say—the case that the PAP is in incipient decline would be that much stronger, even before the party's all-time-low seat share in the subsequent 2020 campaign.

Without question, the PAP has succeeded mightily in focusing citizens' minds on questions of development and performance when they vote every five years. The developmental party-state has produced developmental voters. When offered eighteen options for governance priorities, the most commonly chosen answer among Singaporeans was the "need for efficient government," deemed either very important or important by 98.5 percent of respondents. On this dimension, the PAP continues to be a winning proposition.

Yet efficient government, the PAP's calling card, was far from all that Singaporean voters were demanding. Over 90 percent of respondents in the 2015 survey listed concerns that were emphasized not by the PAP but by opposition parties, including "government help for the needy," "fairness of government policy," and "cost of living." The last concern was especially troubling for the PAP because of growing anger among Singaporeans over rising prices in what is already one of the world's most expensive cities. Voters identified "cost of living" to be the top priority. The fact that, even during one of the PAP's brightest recent moments in the sun, more voters identified an opposition talking point than the PAP's preferred themes—law and order, efficient governance, economic growth, and national security—was a clear sign of PAP vulnerability to growing opposition strength. Even worse for the PAP, cost of living was not something its old development model was well equipped to manage, as economic growth and inequality continue to rise in tandem. It remains the PAP's biggest political problem, for which its existing economic model offers no clear solution.

Worrisomely for the regime, approximately one-third of Singapore's voters will not vote for an unreformed PAP under any circumstances. In the 2015 survey, 35.1 percent of respondents identified their top priority to be "government transparency and accountability." Since this reflects the PAP's Achilles' heel, it is hard to imagine the PAP winning these voters back without fundamentally reforming its political approach to give these voters what they want. The solid and sizable base for Singapore's opposition means that every election is actually in the hands of swing voters and not the ruling party. In 2015, remarkably, 46.2 percent of voters did not make up their minds on whether to support the PAP or opposition until after nomination day. Seventy percent of those late-breaking voters went to the PAP in 2015, but in future elections such decisive advantages among weakly affiliated voters cannot be taken for granted.

The PAP's loosening grip on political dominance has been the result not only of changing voter preferences and priorities but also of party politics, within both the ruling and opposition camps. Between 2015 and 2020, the biggest changes in the Singaporean political landscape were increasing faction-alism within the PAP, on the one hand, and increasing coordination among its opponents, on the other.[10] As Lee Kuan Yew's son, Lee Hsien Loong, prepares to exit the stage after nearly two decades as prime minister, there is no consen-sus on who comes next, and even the Lee family itself has become openly di-vided over their patriarch's legacy. Succession problems are common in nondemocratic regimes, and expose an institutional weakness in authoritarian ruling parties. Meanwhile, Singapore's opposition parties showed greater ca-pacity to coordinate in the recent 2020 elections and enjoyed unprecedented trust from voters as responsible full players in national politics. Postelection surveys indicate that rising "party credibility" among the PAP's rivals, more than any other factor, drove the substantial swing toward the opposition.[11]

In a city-state where levels of everyday protest are vanishingly low, geopo-litical pressure for democratic reform is weak, and the economy churns along by virtue of a propitious location as much as prudent policy, it is highly un-likely that any type of ominous signals besides electoral ones will budge the PAP from its current path of democracy avoidance. This path is not simply the status quo, however, but a gradual and unceasing shift into the kind of welfarist authoritarianism the PAP has long eschewed in theory, if not in practice.[12] As the ruling party confronts an increasingly cooperative and responsible opposi-tion, the PAP is reputationally hindered more than it is operationally bolstered by its lingering authoritarian controls. For a regime with such an impressive record of developmental success, its authoritarian character is its main repu-tational demerit.

To see how wealthy authoritarian regimes shed their repressive character without losing power or sacrificing economic development, the PAP would do well to consider the developmental statist cluster of Japan, Taiwan, and South Korea: three exemplary tales of democracy through strength. On the flipside, to see what happens when a well-off authoritarian regime relies too much on coercion instead of concessions after receiving clear signals of incipient decline, the PAP should take a closer look at some cautionary tales: the recent descent into "embittered authoritarianism" and political destabilization in the other members of developmental Britannia. We begin with an extensive discussion of Malaysia, then turn our attentions more briefly to Hong Kong.

Malaysia

The parallels between Malaysia and Singapore used to be striking. As of the mid-1990s, the neighboring rivals, once briefly joined in the same Malaysian federation from 1963 to 1965, were the world's two clearest-cut examples of authoritarian regimes that were smashing success stories of capitalist catch-up development. In 1995, the year we consider to be the apex of Malaysia's long-ruling party (UMNO) and coalition (BN), it would have been hard to say which regime was more dominant, politically secure, and unchallenged. In that year's election, the BN won 65.2 percent of the national vote—an even higher vote share than the PAP received in Singapore's 1984, 1988, 1992, and 1997 elections—and because of the electoral system's built-in seat bonus, a whopping 84.4 percent of parliamentary seats.[13]

In what follows, we explore how the invincible UMNO-BN regime of 1995 devolved into a defeated and vanquished electoral-authoritarian regime by 2018, a mere two decades later. Malaysia's authoritarian rulers did not concede democracy when they were strong, so they wound up having to concede power, vanquished, when they were weak. Malaysia's was an example of a strong authoritarian regime that experienced *the tragedy of dominant-party politics*, a cautionary tale in which an incumbent regime that was strong enough to concede with strength chose to avoid democratic reform, producing its own peril. Once the incumbent regime's position substantially worsens, as it did in Malaysia, it becomes too late to concede democracy without conceding defeat. Malaysia's BN reached this weakened status by the 2013 national election, when it first lost the popular vote. It continued hurtling through the "bittersweet spot" until the opposition defeated it outright in 2018, removing the ruling UMNO party and its partners from power for the first time since independence in 1957.

Authoritarian Economic Development

As in Singapore, a remarkably stable electoral-authoritarian regime in Malaysia rested on a foundation of spectacular economic growth and the regime's ability to translate developmental success into performance legitimacy. Malaysia has maintained its consistent "hybrid regime" status throughout its postindependence history, even while achieving impressive economic transformation.[14]

Malaysia's economy was highly globalized throughout the colonial era, similar to the other cases in the Britannia cluster. As a world-leading exporter of tin and rubber, British Malaya was a relatively wealthy colony even before World War II. As in Singapore, the immediate postwar period in Malaysia was marked by substantial mass mobilization in both communist and communalist guises, prompting the construction of a much stronger and more extractive and coercive state apparatus. The economy remained deeply dependent on British capital investment in natural-resource industries after independence was maintained through a convivial handover between chummy elites in 1957. Malaysia was not especially poor at the time, but it was initially more of a revenue-generating neocolonial resource-dependent economy than a developmental state. The oil boom of the 1970s made Malaysia a good bit richer, thanks to its status as a petroleum exporter, but only reinforced the resource dependency of its national economy.

This economic model underwent two dramatic shifts, culminating in Malaysia truly "joining" developmental Asia in the early 1980s. First, ethnic riots in 1969 led the ruling UMNO party to build a wider ruling coalition (the aforementioned BN) and impose a battery of new authoritarian controls.[15] In economic terms, UMNO forced through the New Economic Policy (NEP) in 1971, which sought to transfer wealth from the minority Chinese population to the majority, indigenous Malay community. The core idea was that a less ethnicized distribution of economic inequality would make a repeat of the 1969 riots less likely.[16] There would only be enough "pie" to be redistributed, however, if capitalist development continued and even accelerated. Hence by the early 1970s, the ruling UMNO-BN regime was politically committed to rapid economic growth, substantial redistribution through aggressive state intervention, and continued integration into global commodity markets.[17]

A decade later, this economic strategy would launch Malaysia into developmental Asia. Rising to power in 1981, Prime Minister Mahathir Mohamad immediately exhorted his countrymen to "look East."[18] British investments in the plantation sector were nationalized. Protective tariffs were jacked up in many heavy industries, notably in the automobile sector, to prompt a seismic shift from agricultural and petroleum dependency to import-substitution industrialization.

As in South Korea, Taiwan, and Singapore, however, this did not mean any retreat from global economic integration. To the contrary, the goal was to attract waves of new foreign direct investment (FDI) in manufacturing so that local firms could work with multinational corporations to turn Malaysia from a still relatively resource-dependent economy in the world's semiperiphery into a leading producer and exporter of high-tech manufactured goods.

This economic transformation was primarily driven, as elsewhere in developmental Asia, by Japanese investment and American consumer markets. By the mid-1980s, upward pressure on the Japanese yen prompted a deluge of outward manufacturing investment across East and Southeast Asia. Malaysia was a leading beneficiary.[19] While Japan faced increased trade protectionism in the United States, the same was not true of its Asian neighbors where Japanese multinationals were among the leading exporters. Malaysia positioned itself in the 1980s and 1990s as a key node in developmental Asia, exporting profitable advanced manufactured goods across the Pacific with a huge assist from Japanese technology and investment.

To be sure, this developmental model faced substantial problems and pitfalls. Fostering a new class of Malay tycoons through state intervention unsurprisingly yielded a new class of Malay rentiers, not entrepreneurs. Corruption and inefficiency abounded in emerging heavy industries. For example, the national car project, Proton, was predicated on outdated Japanese technology and never generated the desired export income. Spectacular new infrastructure—including the Petronas Towers, the world's tallest building when its construction was completed in 1996—transformed the Malaysian landscape. However, this all came at the cost of ballooning dollar-denominated corporate debt, backed implicitly by the authoritarian regime that had largely brought these Malay-led national champions into existence. The costs of foreign-debt-led economic transformation became painfully clear when the Asian financial crisis crashed on Malaysia's shores in 1997.

Before discussing the momentous effects of the crisis on Malaysia's authoritarian regime and political economy, it is essential to appreciate how successfully Malaysia managed to insert itself into the booming regional economy of developmental Asia over the course of the 1980s and 1990s. By no means did

Malaysia become a technological leader or innovator in the mold of a Japan, South Korea, Taiwan, or even Singapore. But investment-friendly policies allowed Malaysia to become a leading exporter of finished manufactured goods thanks to the massive amounts of high-tech investment pouring in from other parts of Asia. Combined with continuing natural-resource exports, this structural shift into export-oriented manufacturing had transformed Malaysia from a low-income neocolony by the time the Asian financial crisis hit into an upper-middle-income, fast-growth miracle. It was also an extraordinarily strong, stable, and institutionalized authoritarian regime.

The rapid growth and sweeping structural transformation of the Malaysian economy during the 1980s and 1990s could not have been accomplished without robust political organizations. The powerful party-state apparatus, like Singapore's PAP-led party-state, had its roots in the conservative elite response that bridled communist and communalist unrest during the decolonization period. Paradoxically, the exigencies of responding to the social disorder and instability of the 1940s, 1950s, and 1960s left Malaysia with the political organizations necessary to cement an extraordinarily stable authoritarian system by the early 1970s.

To start, Malaysian political elites of all ethnic backgrounds were folded into the UMNO-led party coalition at the dawn of independence. Indeed, the general elections of 1955, which paved the way for Britain's departure in 1957, delivered approximately 80 percent of the national vote and 98 percent of the parliamentary seats to UMNO and its party allies. Intriguingly, conservative coalescence in the waning days of British rule paralleled an analogous and virtually simultaneous process in Japan under postwar American occupation. In both cases, departing imperial powers helped crush the extreme Left and facilitate collaboration among the conservative local elites positioned to rule in the occupiers' stead. Both Malaysia and Japan thus passed through a period of electoral authoritarianism under external occupation en route to independence, at which point full-blown independent democracies were supposed to emerge.

Electoral competition quickly resuscitated democratic roots in postwar Japan, but it could not grow deep democratic roots in independent Malaysia. By the beginning of the 1970s, Malaysia returned emphatically to electoral-authoritarian status, while Japan never did. Informed by our theory, the reason for these divergent paths was simple: *Malaysia's ruling elite lost its victory confidence and stability confidence, while Japan's did not.* Malaysia's 1969 elections saw ethnically based opposition parties denying the UMNO-led coalition its two-thirds majority of national parliamentary seats for the first time. This was a huge shock to the ruling coalition, which won over 70 percent of all parliamentary seats in the 1959 elections and over 85 percent in 1964. Since control over constitutional amendments required a two-thirds parliamentary supermajority, the 1969 electoral results directly threatened Malay ethnic supremacy.

The ethnic riots that followed the shocking electoral setback ensured that the UMNO-led coalition suddenly lacked not only victory confidence but stability confidence as well. We argued in chapter 3 that Japan never backslid into electoral authoritarianism during the Cold War era, unlike so many of its pro-American Asian neighbors, because the LDP's victory confidence and stability confidence were never badly shaken. In fact, we showed that after 1947, with America's reverse-course policy, conservative confidence grew. In Malaysia two decades later, the opposite occurred.

In terms of institution building and the accumulation of authoritarian strength, however, the UMNO-BN government did not become less institutionalized as it became more authoritarian after the early 1970s. Nor did the ruling coalition become less institutionalized as it became more personalized under the authoritarian rule of Mahathir after the early 1980s. Party and state institutions remained strong, in the sense of both reliably organizing diverse elites behind a common purpose and predictably delivering massive electoral landslides to the ruling coalition.[20]

In the first four elections that UMNO-BN contested as a full-blown authoritarian regime, in 1974, 1978, 1982, and 1986, a highly unified ruling coalition won approximately 85 percent of all parliamentary seats every time. The connection between elite cohesion and electoral strength was undeniable. It was only after UMNO suffered a temporary factional split in 1987 that the BN took any real electoral hit, sinking to a 70 percent seat share in 1990.

Although it never meaningfully threatened authoritarian domination, UMNO's factional split from 1987 to 1995 is still quite informative. The combination of an economic downturn and Mahathir's increasingly personalistic grip on power led two leading UMNO rivals to form an alternative Malay-led party. The UMNO clone, called Semangat '46 (Spirit of '46, named for the year of UMNO's founding), dented UMNO-BN's dominance in the 1990 election, seemingly signaling the "incipient decline" we see portending democratic reforms.

Yet the devil is in the details. Democratization theory expects factional splits, like the one UMNO experienced in 1987, to make democratic reforms more likely. However, that only holds for democracy through *weakness*, not strength. When relatively strong and cohesive authoritarian regimes suffer factional splits, their immediate driving imperative is to repair the split, including through severe repression if necessary. Indeed, the so-called Operasi Lalang (Weeding Operation) in 1987 saw Mahathir imprison over one hundred critics under Malaysia's draconian Internal Security Act. In the preceding chapter, we saw how factional splits in military regimes like Myanmar and Thailand led to purges and repression rather than authoritarian retreats in the developmental militarist cluster. Malaysia in the late 1980s and early to mid-1990s illustrates that the same logic can apply to party-dominated authoritarian regimes as well.

By 1995, with UMNO's brief factional split behind it, the BN rebounded and enjoyed its best electoral result ever, regaining its typical seat share at around 85 percent and an unprecedented vote share surpassing 65 percent. After its crushing 1995 electoral win, UMNO-BN was at its apex. Semangat '46 dissolved and its members returned to the UMNO fold. The economy was roaring. The ruling party's supremacy, both over the military and over its opponents in generating electoral support, was unchallenged. The state was a strong, cohesive, and successfully extractive state by any reasonable measure. And UMNO-BN's developmental track record was one of the envies of the developing world. Lacking any clear signals of incipient decline, there was no pressure on Malaysia's authoritarian regime to leverage its strength by democratizing through strength.[21]

Triple Shock

Between 1997 and 1999, Malaysia's long-ruling UMNO-BN government received three powerful signals of its incipient decline. In late 1997, the Asian financial crisis brought Malaysia's economy to its knees and its debt-driven development model into disrepute. In late 1998, the first massive democratization protests in the nation's history erupted, in the form of the *reformasi* movement. Then, in late 1999, the UMNO-BN government took a substantial electoral hit, losing almost 10 percent of both its 1995 vote share, declining from 65.2 percent to 56.5 percent, and its seat share, from 84.4 percent to 76.7 percent.

In just two years, the incumbent regime in Malaysia had received three of our theory's four types of ominous signals in rapid succession: economic, contentious, and electoral. However, they occurred in a succession that made preemptive democratic reforms less likely rather than more likely. As our theory reiterates: democracy through strength commences when incumbent powerholders choose it as their best strategy to maintain their power.

The essence of being a strong authoritarian regime that is in the bittersweet spot, as opposed to a weak regime in the throes of its death spiral, is that no signals or pressures can be strong enough to *force* democratic change. Doubling down on repression is always an option for regimes that still lie close to their apex of power.

And this was the option Prime Minister Mahathir chose. The 1997–99 crisis swiftly hurtled Malaysia's UMNO-BN regime past its apex and into its bittersweet spot, but Mahathir's repressive strategies to confront the regime's crisis only ensured that it would keep accelerating downward into embittered authoritarianism, rather than seizing the opportunity to pursue transformative reforms and gain UMNO-BN a new lease on life as a dominant democratic party and coalition.

Before detailing the three signals as they unfolded in sequence, we should foreshadow why the sequence mattered. Importantly, the 1997 economic crisis did not lead to any political crisis for over a year. Disagreement at the top of the party between Mahathir and his popular deputy Anwar Ibrahim on how to respond to the crisis, in terms of both economic reform and democratic reform, prompted Anwar's unceremonious sacking rather than elite accommodation between the two leaders. It was *only after the ruling party split* that the contentious and electoral signals of incipient decline hit UMNO-BN in late 1998 and 1999. Just as in 1987, a split within UMNO resulted in a structural weakening of the regime that made a unified reform strategy to respond to crisis more difficult and unlikely.

Consider a simple sequential counterfactual to demonstrate our point: if the economic signals had been immediately followed by other ominous signals, Mahathir would have been under enormous pressure to salvage UMNO-BN's slipping position by handing the reins of power to Anwar, who, as his popular deputy among Malaysian voters, was poised to lead Malaysia on a new trajectory of democracy through strength. As it turned out, however, by the time protests erupted on a massive scale over a year later, Anwar had already been purged and UMNO had already split; indeed, his purge was the shocking event that sparked the protests themselves.

Hence, *the open party split preceded and in many ways contributed to the strong and clearest ominous signals* of regime decline. Unlike in Taiwan and South Korea, the rising popular protests that made democratic reforms an urgent consideration were confronted by a freshly fragmented authoritarian regime. While alternative theories predicated on regime weakness would contend the party split should have made democratization more likely in Malaysia during the late 1990s, in our theory, elite splits make democratic reform too threatening and thus too risky to undertake for the regime, and thus less likely unless and until the elite split can be repaired.

Economic Signals

There can be no question that the economic shock constituted an ominous signal to the UMNO-BN regime. After leveling Thailand's economy in August 1997, the Asian financial crisis spread, with Malaysia one of its next unwitting victims. The crisis was such a shock because Malaysia did not have enormous public debt, which had been the primary driver of various financial crashes during the Cold War era. Rather, it was a highly leveraged private sector, and especially the fact that those massive private-sector debts were denominated almost entirely in dollars, that led international investor confidence in the Malaysian economy to crater. Capital fled, the stock market and currency crashed, and the government had to ratchet up interest rates to stop the bleeding, threatening an avalanche of corporate bankruptcies as a direct result.[22]

Malaysia's prime minister and heir apparent split over how best to respond to the economic crisis. Enjoying impeccable reformist credentials abroad, Anwar urged Malaysia to take decisive steps to restore international investor confidence. This meant taking some harsh medicine, including cutting public spending, postponing major infrastructure projects, and letting at least some well-connected businesses fail. Prime Minister Mahathir, on the other hand, was deeply resistant. Unconvinced the crash signaled anything structurally deficient in Malaysia's highly successful growth model, Mahathir struggled even to pay lip service to the need for fundamental reforms. Whatever conciliatory reform concessions he could muster were drowned out by his paranoid polemics blaming Jewish currency speculators for trying to bring a rising Muslim power to its knees.

Throughout the first year of the economic crisis, Mahathir and Anwar coexisted in a tense equilibrium. Economic policy largely followed Anwar's lead, by sheer necessity. Restoring investor confidence was essential to any lasting recovery, even if that meant major short-term pain. Mahathir essentially disavowed his government's own policies, stubbornly insisting that nothing had been wrong with Malaysia's development model until dark outside forces attacked it. The tensions showed signs of bursting into open conflict in June 1998, when an Anwar proxy publicly criticized corruption at the highest levels of UMNO at the party's annual meetings, in an obvious shot across the bow at Mahathir and his personal network.

Mahathir ultimately resolved the tension by force. At the end of August 1998, he struck a double blow against Anwar and his reformist approach to the economic crisis. First, in the most heterodox response to the crisis in developmental Asia, Malaysia imposed capital controls and fixed the value of the national currency, preventing further capital flight and currency speculation. The next day, Mahathir sacked Anwar from all his positions and had him purged from UMNO on charges of corruption and sexual misconduct. Hence, by the beginning of September 1998, it was clear that Malaysia's strong authoritarian regime had chosen to respond to ominous economic signals by becoming more illiberal both economically and politically, rather than seizing the window of opportunity to liberalize both the political system and economic model while UMNO-BN was still dominant and even effectively unchallenged.

Contentious Signals

The sacking of Anwar did not end Malaysia's political crisis, but rather marked its beginning. Notwithstanding the obvious political tensions within the ruling coalition, the country and its people had remained entirely peaceful and quiescent throughout the first year of the economic shock, despite all the economic pain. That was how thoroughly dominant UMNO-BN was at the time. Removing and slandering the country's most popular politician changed all that, however. Within hours of Anwar's ignominious purge, the first mass-based democratization movement in Malaysian history erupted in the capital city of Kuala Lumpur.

The upsurge in street protest was unprecedented in modern Malaysian history. The core demand of the new *reformasi* movement was justice for Anwar. Given his long-standing reputation as an advocate of democratic reforms, and considering the brazenly authoritarian manner in which he was purged, the movement quickly became defined by its demand that Mahathir step down and a more democratic dispensation be installed. Only a few short months after massive street protests and booming cries for reform ushered in a dictator's removal and a ruling party's democratic reinvention in Indonesia, something similar had suddenly become thinkable in Malaysia.[23]

Although UMNO had split and become weakened with Anwar's sacking, it was not too late for the incumbent regime to experiment with democracy through strength. Even after his dismissal, Anwar continued to insist that he wished to return to UMNO and take Mahathir's place.

The path to an Indonesian scenario was actually quite straightforward. If enough support could be mustered within UMNO to replace Mahathir with Anwar as party leader, Anwar could have followed in the footsteps of B. J. Habibie, Roh Tae-woo, and Chiang Ching-kuo by initiating democratic reform. The size of street demonstrations, spreading from Kuala Lumpur to the far corners of the country, made it clear that a yearning existed for democratic change. There was simply no question that an Anwar-led UMNO-BN would have romped to victory in the elections that had to be called by 2000, especially considering how little political damage the ruling coalition had been taking as punishment for the financial crisis.

Electoral Signals

However, a democracy-through-strength scenario did not come to pass, because it was not the scenario Mahathir chose. Anwar was arrested and then beaten in prison. Mahathir unleashed the state's highly capable coercive organizations to bring the *reformasi* street protests to heel. The regime's response to Malaysia's first-ever democratization movement was not reform but repression.

Ironically, though not unexpectedly, Mahathir's decision to imprison Anwar and repress his followers tore UMNO apart for good. Neither the economic crisis nor the Mahathir-Anwar factional dispute had divided UMNO beyond repair, but the purge and crackdown did. Within weeks of Anwar's imprisonment, new opposition parties and coalitions emerged, drawing from within the ranks of UMNO itself, to challenge UMNO-BN hegemony.

The most important of these new parties was Keadilan (Justice). For as long as Anwar was in prison—and he stayed in prison from 1999 to 2004—the Keadilan party was led by his wife, Wan Azizah Wan Ismail. Crucially, the party was multiethnic in character and committed to democratic transition. This made it a far greater threat to the ruling UMNO-BN than the predominantly ethnic Chinese (Democratic Action Party, DAP) and ethnic Malay (Partai Islam Se-Malaysia, PAS) opposition parties, which lacked cross-ethnic appeal and centered on advancing the cause of their own ethnoreligious communities more than overturning authoritarianism. Once Keadilan joined the

DAP and the PAS in a new opposition coalition, it meant that UMNO-BN faced its stiffest challenge since independence.

It responded to the growing electoral challenge with repression. Not content with jailing Anwar alone, the Mahathir regime disqualified six additional Keadilan candidates before the national elections in November 1999. Fueled by Malay outrage over Anwar's flagrant mistreatment at Mahathir's behest, the elections saw UMNO lose 17 parliamentary seats, declining from 89 to 72. As a whole, the UMNO-BN coalition lost almost 9 percent of its vote share from its 1995 peak, shrinking from 65.4 percent to 56.5 percent, and delivered 14 total seats to the opposition, slipping from 162 to 148 out of 193.

In other words, the 1999 election clearly signaled that UMNO under Mahathir was losing major ground, and that the opposition coalition symbolically led by Anwar from prison had made major gains. To be sure, the ruling coalition still controlled over 75 percent of parliamentary seats, and in that respect it was not on the verge of losing power. But like many of the other regimes explored in this book, including the very powerful KMT during the 1980s, the Malaysian ruling coalition was clearly experiencing incipient decline.

More to the point, the 1999 election was a straightforward referendum on Mahathir's repressive leadership, and it showed Malaysian voters', especially ethnic Malay voters', willingness to abandon UMNO in unprecedented numbers. When combined with the ominous signals delivered by the economic crisis of 1997 and the massive democratization movement of 1998 and 1999, UMNO's electoral setback in 1999 put the potential benefits to UMNO of a preemptive democratic strategy in plain sight.

Superficial Reforms and Embittered Authoritarianism

Despite dragging UMNO to new electoral depths, Mahathir held fast to power for four more years, while Anwar languished in prison. If Mahathir had taken the signals of the 1999 elections seriously, resigned from office, and handed the reins either to Anwar or to another UMNO politician brave enough to implement decisive democratic reforms, the UMNO-BN coalition could have likely stopped the political bleeding. According to our theory, it could have set itself up for a long run as a dominant though democratic party along the lines of Japan's LDP and Taiwan's KMT.

Instead, Mahathir clung to power long enough to ensure there would be no decisive and explicit break from the past. The years immediately following 1998 would be Malaysia's first years of embittered authoritarianism, not democratization through strength, as in neighboring Indonesia. By the time Mahathir resigned his office in frustration at the age of 78 in 2003, his twenty-two years of purge-happy rule left UMNO devoid of major political talent in its upper echelons. Power was not passed to a decisive reformer or visionary, but to a bland and uninspiring technocrat and yes-man, Abdullah Badawi.[24]

It is a testament to how much damage Mahathir's repression did to UMNO's popularity that under Badawi, after Mahathir had left the scene, the party roared back to electoral strength in 2004. UMNO-BN was heavily aided by its ongoing strangulation of Keadilan (renamed the People's Justice Party in 2003) as well as its steeply gerrymandered and malapportioned electoral system. However, UMNO's bounce back, once released from Mahathir's iron grip, was substantial nonetheless. Partying like it was 1995 (and not 1999), UMNO-BN gained 50 additional seats, 37 of them by UMNO alone. Meanwhile, the opposition coalition, fragmented and battered, practically collapsed.

Unfortunately for UMNO, it learned all the wrong lessons from its 2004 recovery, while Malaysia's opposition learned all the right lessons from its 2004 collapse. Leading UMNO politicians failed to recognize that 2004 was a honeymoon election for Badawi, giving him a whopping mandate to make Malaysia more open and less stifling than during its Mahathir era. They behaved instead as if UMNO-BN was once again invincible and in no need of meaningful reform.

Badawi proved not to be a liberalizing leader but a feckless one. He did not block the courts from releasing Anwar from prison early for medical reasons, but neither did he confront or discipline leading UMNO politicians who began delving into ugly Malay supremacy to burnish their own images with the party rank and file. At best, Badawi could be described as the authoritarian good cop who followed Mahathir, the consummate authoritarian bad cop. Badawi did not renew UMNO and lead it down a democratic path when the party had regained some strength. Like Mahathir before him, he missed another, albeit fleeting, window of opportunity. A second shot at seizing the bittersweet spot had been squandered.

Meanwhile, Malaysia's highly diverse and divided political opposition put its many differences aside and unified behind a prodemocratic, antiauthoritarian agenda. As we have seen in Indonesia and South Korea, authoritarianism can be a powerfully unifying rallying point for opposition groups who otherwise have little in common. If Malaysia had democratized after 1998, UMNO-BN's opposition would surely have remained fragmented and incapable of unseating the ruling coalition, opening the door to continued incumbent dominance. Instead, Badawi neither repressed his opponents to eliminate them like Mahathir nor reformed the party to electorally defeat his opponents like Roh Tae-woo did in South Korea.

These repeated missteps on the part of the weakening regime set the stage for the historic elections of March 2008. With Anwar out of prison, opposition rallies swept the nation like in no election before, even though Anwar was disqualified from contesting. The results of the 2008 elections were shocking to anyone with 2004 in their rear-view mirror, but not to those who saw the deeper signals that were so clear in the 1999 elections. Even with the entire electoral system skewed in its favor, UMNO-BN lost 12.5 percent of its vote share (from 63.9 percent to 51.4 percent) and with that 58 parliamentary seats, its advantage slipping from 198–21 to 140–82 vis-à-vis the opposition. The ruling coalition held on to its narrow voting majority, but it had lost its critical two-thirds supermajority in seats.

Again, UMNO-BN learned the wrong lessons. UMNO blamed Badawi for the coalition's poor results and forced him to resign. UMNO replaced him with a less accommodating figure in Najib Abdul Razak. A dynastic scion in Malaysia's elite, rather than a talented and popular politician in his own right, Najib was no answer for what ailed UMNO by this time. Rather than moving the regime in either a decisively reformist or repressive direction, he floundered by pursuing an incoherent mixture of both, relying on stepped-up patronage to the Malay majority and good old-fashioned authoritarian malapportionment to hang on to power by his fingernails.

At the heart of Najib's strategy was eliminating Anwar through a second round of sodomy and corruption charges. Incompetently handled, the legal attack failed to reimprison Anwar before the pivotal 2013 elections that were on the horizon. Najib made bold reformist promises like abolishing the Internal Security Act, but these came to naught and rang hollow among voters. Meanwhile, the Anwar-led opposition was emboldened by its 2008 gains and formally consolidated into a new multiethnic coalition, the Pakatan Rakyat (People's Coalition).

Predictably, 2013 saw UMNO-BN continue to hemorrhage voters. This time it lost the popular vote outright, 50.9 percent to 47.4 percent. All manner of electoral malapportionment meant that UMNO-BN only lost seven seats, however, which resulted in its majority shrinking to 133–89.

Rather than taking responsibility for the setback and trying to incorporate the democratic agenda that was clearly gaining the opposition Pakatan Rakyat so much support, Najib made the colossal error of blaming his losses on a

"Chinese tsunami." Any hope that UMNO-BN could ride non-Malay support to a big victory in 2018, as it did in 1999, quickly went up in smoke. Furthermore, any hope that Najib might aim for more openness in order to win big again as the ruling coalition did in 2004 evaporated when Anwar was reimprisoned in 2015.

After 2013, nothing besides repression could possibly save a ruling coalition that refused to reform. The coup de grace came when Najib became embroiled in a monstrous corruption scandal, the 1MDB affair, in which the prime minister appeared to have siphoned US$700 million into his personal accounts from a state-run development company. Smelling blood, and reviling Najib for sidelining his son from UMNO leadership positions, Mahathir came back into politics, but this time as the opposition Pakatan Rakyat's prime ministerial candidate, with Anwar still languishing in prison. As the 2018 elections approached, UMNO-BN's biggest problem was not that Mahathir was such a formidable opponent but that Najib was such a terrible and discredited leader.

May 2018 would finally see the embittered UMNO-BN authoritarian regime put out of its misery. Despite all the unevenness and unfairness of another authoritarian election, and despite the opposition's most popular politician being imprisoned and unable to campaign and lead it, UMNO-BN was decisively routed. Even with the opposition Pakatan Rakyat splintering on the eve of the election, opposition parties seized 113 of 192 seats, gaining 45 new seats. UMNO-BN lost an astonishing 54 seats, with several going to smaller parties. The coalition that for decades never came close to losing its *two*-thirds seat majority found itself winning only *one*-third of the votes, 33.8 percent. After two painful decades of decline under embittered authoritarianism, Malaysia's UMNO-BN had not conceded democracy without conceding defeat, as we saw in other cases in developmental Asia like Taiwan, Japan, South Korea, and Indonesia. Rather, it conceded an embarrassing defeat without ever conceding democracy.

Coda: Authoritarian Weakness, Democratic Uncertainty

Ever since UMNO-BN lost power in the elections of May 2018, Malaysian politics has been in flux. Saddled with a prime minister, Mahathir, whose commitment to democratic reform was entirely superficial and opportunistic, the new ruling Pakatan Harapan (Coalition for Hope) could never gain its footing in governing Malaysia or planting stable democratic roots. Mahathir promised to hand power to Anwar after an unspecified transitional period, but this promise lacked credibility on its face. Formed as a negative coalition against Najib, the Pakatan Harapan had no common purpose as a ruling coalition.

Today, Malaysian politics no longer pits an authoritarian ruling coalition against a democratic opposition coalition, as it primarily did from 1998 to 2018. It now sees a new Malay-only coalition led by UMNO, the Perikatan Nasional (National Alliance), facing off against a pluralistic Pakatan Harapan coalition led by Anwar's People's Justice Party. The tectonic shift is most evident in Malaysia's leading Islamist party, PAS, switching sides from the Anwar-led Pakatan Harapan to the UMNO-led Perikatan Nasional. Political competition in Malaysia is now defined by a relatively liberal, cosmopolitan, and urban-dominated coalition on the one hand, and a more religious, conservative, and rural-dominated coalition on the other.[25]

Malaysia's democratic hopes are by no means permanently dashed, however. The same actors in civil society and opposition parties who spent the past two-plus decades pressing for democratic reform continue to fight their uphill battle. Which way Malaysia will tip in the coming years is beyond the capacity of this book's theoretical framework to tackle. What we can say with confidence is that UMNO's failure to reform during its bittersweet spot has led to unprecedented fragmentation and flux in Malaysian national politics. Neither democracy nor stability has been well served by UMNO's failure to reform when conditions were ripe to concede from strength. Malaysia is thus a cautionary tale that other strong authoritarian regimes should heed.

Hong Kong

There is one enormous difference between Hong Kong and every other case considered in this book: it is not self-governing. Although Taiwan also lacks formal sovereignty and international recognition as an independent nation-state, its own leaders determine the island's course. Hong Kong is in a very different position. Despite its status as a "special administrative region" negotiated in Hong Kong's handover from British rule to Chinese suzerainty in 1997, the territory has never enjoyed more than a very fragile autonomy from Beijing. Nobody in Hong Kong has the authority to decisively shape its political direction.

Hong Kong's exceptionalism in some ways makes it incomparable and ineligible for inclusion in this book's analytical framework. But considering Hong Kong's analytical importance as an economic cornerstone of developmental Britannia (and of developmental Asia as a world-historical phenomenon), as well as its real-world importance as its democratization struggle unfolds, it should not be excluded. There is no gainsaying the fact that incumbent politicians in Hong Kong lack the free hand and political agency required to pursue democracy through strength, even if that was the path they might sincerely and strategically prefer. Any decision of that magnitude needs to come from Beijing. But it is also true that Hong Kong exhibits all of the moving parts of our theory. Without unrealistically assuming that democratic reforms are a matter of local incumbent choice in Hong Kong, as elsewhere in developmental Asia, we can still assess whether and how it became a candidate for democracy through strength in ways that parallel the other cases explored in this book.

In the pages that follow, we clarify the parallels between Hong Kong and our other two cases in developmental Britannia. Like Singapore, Hong Kong became spectacularly wealthy under authoritarian rule, allowing multiparty elections and developing strong legal institutions, but never giving opposition a legitimate chance to win political power. Like Malaysia's, Hong Kong's failure to pursue decisive democratic reforms when local elites were still in a strong position has led to destabilization and embittered authoritarianism. Nowhere are the costs of democracy avoidance more painfully and abundantly evident.

Authoritarian Economic Development

Hong Kong's experience of development without democracy is a tale almost two centuries in the making. In the mid-nineteenth century, the Opium Wars allowed the United Kingdom to seize Hong Kong from China and convert it into a free port after 1842. In 1898 Britain claimed territories adjacent to Hong Kong on the Chinese mainland under a one-hundred-year lease. It was this agreement that would eventually put Hong Kong on a gradual glide path from British to Chinese rule with a handover date of 1997.

In economic terms, Hong Kong is a vivid example of how much wealth could be accumulated under British colonial rule, wherever the British had a free hand to install their own preferred arrangements instead of ruling indirectly through local feudal potentates. It was the linkage between freewheeling British capitalism and the pulsating energies of the postwar Asia-Pacific economy, however, that made Hong Kong spectacularly rich. Hong Kong's economy began skyrocketing in the 1970s, as developmental Asia's Japan-led boom began driving more and more of the region's economic dynamism.

Once sparked, the fire of economic growth in Hong Kong was unrelenting. From an impressive upper-middle-income base of approximately US$5,000 GDP per capita as of 1980, the past four decades have seen Hong Kong's per capita wealth multiply by a factor of ten, now approximating $50,000. About half of that increase occurred before the 1997 handover and the other half occurred after, underscoring how Hong Kong's economic development model was and remains robust enough to deliver spectacular aggregate results under both British and Chinese control.

Much like Singapore's, Hong Kong's economy boomed by blending lucrative property development, liberal rules on inward manufacturing investment, and its location as a crucial export entrepôt. This is no panacea, however, for the extreme inequality that afflicted and continues to afflict Hong Kong society. As elsewhere in developmental Asia, rapid and sustained growth has also nonetheless contributed to the elimination of absolute poverty, even if not complemented by extensive social welfare or economic redistribution.

Authoritarian Institutional Development

Capitalist economic development cannot reach the lofty heights seen in Hong Kong without strong political institutions in place. In this regard, nothing has been more important than Hong Kong's legal system, a hallmark of the developmental Britannia cluster. It is quite simply a legal system built for unleashing and supporting capitalism. The British colonial state was constructed to remove all fetters from those who could accumulate capital, and to place fetters on those who would challenge the wealthy oligarchy through demands for representation or redistribution.

For most of Hong Kong's long history as a British colony, it was governed by a conservative alliance of bureaucrats and judges. The Legislative Council was not directly elected and lacked democratic legitimacy. Police could be counted on to repress labor and leftist unrest whenever it erupted, and it erupted often. It was only after the Sino-British Joint Declaration of 1984 promised to fulfill Hong Kong's long-scheduled handover to China in 1997 that politics began to shift in a more liberal direction in Hong Kong, and when democratic aspirations became more strident.

The declaration included a clause indicating that the Legislative Council would eventually be a fully popularly elected body, though this was aspirational. Beijing was obviously reticent about substantial democratic reforms before the handover, and British authorities—an oligarchic alliance of bureaucrats and barristers—wanted to avoid conflict with the Chinese regime. Instead, so-called functional bodies were permitted to elect a handful of representatives to the Legislative Council starting in the mid- to late 1980s, while the general population remained very much uninvolved.

This smooth trajectory toward a friendly transition from one form of colonial authoritarianism to another was interrupted by events on the Chinese mainland. After the Tiananmen Square massacre of 1989 (see chapter 6), Hong Kong's largely liberal and, it must be mentioned, overwhelmingly Cantonese population became anxious about whether the rule of law, so central to Hong Kong's governance, could persist under Chinese Communist Party (CCP) rule. For all its lack of popular inclusion in political decision-making, British Hong Kong was a place where liberal freedoms were at least broadly and generally respected. The fear that Beijing might roll back freedoms of association, speech, and the press led many in Hong Kong's nascent political class to demand a larger role for locally and popularly elected representatives as a check on the CCP's looming authority.

This simmering controversy came to a head under the governorship of Chris Patten from 1992 to 1997. From a comparative perspective, it is worthwhile recalling how democratic self-rule emerged from imperial domination in Japan, Malaysia, and Singapore in the 1950s. As the Americans and British slowly retreated from these imperial entanglements, they essentially pursued an experimental period of electoral authoritarianism, slowly and carefully expanding the role of competitive elections while continuing to keep a strong repressive grip on the communist Left. All three cases saw a peaceful and friendly handover of power from colonial governors to conservative elected politicians.

Patten surely would have loved to accomplish precisely the same feat in Hong Kong. Simply put, he would have loved for Hong Kong to democratize through strength. Confident that freer and fairer elections would not lead to leftist victories or any other sort of destabilization, he unilaterally opened half of the Legislative Council to be decided by universal suffrage. This is the main reason why the early 1990s are the only moment in Hong Kong's history when a stepwise improvement in democratic quality gets registered in global data sets. Nearly half a century of regime immobility and authoritarian stasis was broken by the slight democratic improvements under Patten's brief rule.

Patten was rightly confident that elections would not be destabilizing to Hong Kong for the exact same reason leaders in the developmental statist cluster (Japan, Taiwan, and South Korea) reached the same conclusion.

Decades of rapid development had produced a developmental electorate. As an early experiment in controlled political opening, Hong Kong's first and final elections with full suffrage under British rule proceeded without a hitch. Conservative politicians thrived, as we would expect, though they were not yet organized into any popular or well-rooted ruling party. This failure either to foster the party organization of Hong Kong's conservatives or to submit them to regular tests of electoral popularity put them in a much weaker position than their counterparts in Malaysia or Singapore when the Union Jack was lowered for the final time in 1997.

Signals and Sclerosis under Chinese Rule

In the 1984 treaty that ratified Hong Kong's transfer from British to Chinese authority, China committed to rule Hong Kong under the principle of "One Country, Two Systems" for fifty years, from 1997 to 2047. This entailed a very different dynamic to controversies over democratic reform in Hong Kong from that in either Malaysia or Singapore. In those latter two countries, the big question has been whether and when dominant authoritarian parties might choose to liberalize the system. In Hong Kong, however, the political atmosphere has been dominated by fears that China will retract the liberal freedoms Hong Kongers have long enjoyed, rather than by hopes that local incumbents will open up a more competitive and level political playing field.

The peculiarity and distinctiveness of Hong Kong's authoritarianism in this regard needs to be underscored. It is not simply that Hong Kong's ultimate fate is decided in Beijing. It is that whereas most electoral authoritarian regimes combine highly competitive multiparty elections with full suffrage, on the one hand, with unfair restrictions on the partisan opposition and civil society, on the other, Hong Kong is closer to the reverse. British rule did more to enshrine liberal rights protections than full formal electoral inclusion.[26]

Post-handover politics in Hong Kong has mostly been about gradual retreats from rights protections previously granted, and not gradual advances in elections. Like its counterparts in developmental Britannia, Hong Kong has traveled the path of embittered authoritarianism, not democratization through strength. Worse yet for Hong Kong, the regime has not stalled or avoided democracy but instead deepened authoritarian rule by chipping away at what rights had been installed by the British colonial regime.

Notably, Hong Kong's electoral saga of the past twenty-five years has not been over election results but the electoral system itself.[27] At stake have been two basic issues: whether suffrage will be universal, and whether all candidates need to be vetted by Beijing-backed nominating committees. On both of these fronts, the pro-Beijing and prodemocracy camps remain miles apart. As of the early 2020s, Hong Kong's electoral system is no more democratic than it was in the late 1990s. While electoral inclusion stalled at a low level, rights protections have been receding from a high level. The central controversy has long been Beijing's insistence that Hong Kong either pass a new security law itself or have one passed for it. As with elections, compromise between pro-Beijing and prodemocracy forces has proved impossible.

This reform sclerosis has been consistently met with signals of public dissatisfaction with the pro-Beijing regime. These signals have been both contentious and electoral, and they have been getting louder and clearer, not fainter and fuzzier. The first major contentious signal came in 2003, when hundreds of thousands of Hong Kongers took to the streets to oppose the new Beijing-backed security law.[28] As in many instances before, Hong Kong's local government backed down in the face of massive protests. The typical result in these confrontations is not a victory for reformers, however, but rather stalemate between the two sides. Calculating that time is ultimately on their side, pro-Beijing leaders have thus tended to rescind objectionable laws in the face of massive public outrage, reserving unchecked authority to reintroduce more restrictive laws at a later, calmer time.

But times have not gotten calmer. Instead, the credibility of the local regime and its "One Country, Two Systems" pact have plummeted. Hong Kong's contentious atmosphere reached a fever pitch in late 2014, when the government's ongoing failure to introduce full suffrage was inflamed by video evidence of police abuse against democratic protesters. The Umbrella Movement paralyzed Hong Kong for almost three months.[29] Protests eventually simmered down, but through exhaustion rather than political concessions. Underlying tensions were not resolved or even assuaged.[30] It was only a matter of time before a successor to Umbrella would erupt.

The tinder was relit in 2019. The proximate cause was a new extradition law that allowed the Hong Kong authorities to send criminal suspects to the mainland for trial. Although the law was explicitly tailored to target criminal behavior rather than critical political speech, Hong Kong's pro-Beijing puppet government had no credibility to commit to such limits on the law's applicability. Understandably and unsurprisingly, Hong Kong's democratic opposition saw any Hong Kong law as the handiwork of the CCP regime in Beijing. At a moment when the shocking human rights abuses of Xi Jinping's government in Xinjiang gained global attention, Hong Kong's smoldering citizenry was poised to explode.

The protests and riots of 2019 would make the Umbrella Movement look like a tea party. The standard move by Hong Kong's government to suspend the bill at the first sign of major protests only galvanized protesters to demand the bill's complete withdrawal. Police crackdowns produced stronger demands rather than quiescence. For the first time in Hong Kong's contentious two decades of Chinese rule, the city descended into a downward spiral of police violence and public rioting. Stability confidence was good and shattered. Any faint hope for even a democratic experiment with stability confidence was eliminated.

Local elections in 2019 destroyed pro-Beijing politicians' victory confidence in turn. For twenty years, conservative forces fared reasonably well in competitive elections, even though parliament's lack of authority in Hong Kong gave voters every reason to register protest votes rather than votes to keep economic development on track. The main pro-Beijing party, the Democratic Alliance for the Betterment and Progress of Hong Kong (DAB), saw its fortunes plummet in an election with a historic turnout. As voter turnout skyrocketed from 47 percent to 71 percent in 2019, the DAB saw its 119–43 seat advantage over its main rival, the Democratic Party, dramatically reversed into a 91–21 seat deficit. In the aggregate, pro-Beijing parties saw their 331–124 seat edge over the prodemocracy camp converted into a 388–89 defeat in terms of legislative seats.[31]

Unlike in Malaysia, losing seats in Hong Kong does not mean losing power. In the irony of all ironies, the United Kingdom might be the birthplace of parliamentary sovereignty, dating back to the Glorious Revolution of 1688, but it failed completely to transfer the same fruit to its final major colony even as it hoped to plant some democratic seeds to counter China's inevitable authoritarian reach. Sovereignty in Hong Kong has always rested entirely in the hands of a local chief executive and the external powers who effectively appoint it. At one time, that meant the British imperial office in Whitehall, and now it means CCP headquarters in Beijing.

Hong Kong offers another cautionary tale from developmental Britannia. It demonstrates that even the most spectacular record of economic development is no permanent substitute for political legitimacy. By the 1980s, Hong Kong's developmental successes had groomed a developmental and demanding citizenry. This, we have argued, was one of the key impetuses for democratization through strength in cases like Japan, Taiwan, and South Korea. Unfortunately, Hong Kong has never been governed for the benefit of its general population. It has always operated to benefit external sovereigns and their wealthy local allies. It has never been a democracy, even if it looked to be on that path as recently as the 1990s. Enriched but not enfranchised, Hong Kong's people have revolted against the eternal denial of their popular sovereignty, leaving no clear pathway back to political governability.

Our theory provides no obvious guidance on how an embittered authoritarian regime can regain lost footing. As in Malaysia, Hong Kong's ruling conservatives no longer have the option of both introducing fully democratic elections and winning them freely and fairly. By this point, conceding democracy would almost surely mean conceding defeat. The main reason this is unlikely to happen is not that the status quo is stabilizing. It is that both the CCP and its Hong Kong allies prioritize their own continuing power and incumbency over the economic welfare and political rights of Hong Kong's citizens.

Conclusion

No cluster in developmental Asia defies the expectations of modernization theory more emphatically than developmental Britannia. Where capitalist development was most impressive, such as in the developmental statist cluster (Japan, Taiwan, and South Korea), stable democracy has been the result. Where capitalist development has been most delayed, in the developmental socialist cluster (China, Vietnam, and Cambodia), authoritarianism remains unbent and unbroken. The fact that cases in the developmental militarist cluster (Indonesia, Thailand, and Myanmar) have all experimented with democratic reforms is better explained by political factors—especially the propensity for military rulers to seek smooth exits—than by economic factors. Yet even there, the wobbliness and reversibility of democratic experiments are surely related to the region's relative poverty vis-à-vis the developmental statist cluster, most starkly.

Unlike these other three Asian clusters, developmental Britannia flies straight in modernization theory's face. Developmental successes have rivaled those of the developmental statist cluster, yet democratic reforms have not followed in development's long train. Something about British colonialism gave its authoritarian inheritors a stubborn belief that they could maintain and sustain economic development and stability without needing to submit themselves to free and fair tests of their popularity and legitimacy. In Singapore, that confidence in never-ending authoritarian stability in a wealthy society remains strong. The lessons of embittered authoritarianism, as seen in Malaysia and Hong Kong, suggest that confidence may ultimately be misplaced.

9

Developmental Socialism

DOMINANCE AND DEMOCRACY AVOIDANCE

NOT SO LONG AGO, the natural way to divide Asia was into capitalist Asia and socialist Asia. Nowhere in the world was the Cold War more divisive or more determinative of a region's development. Two waves of violent communist revolutions—in China and North Korea in the late 1940s, and Vietnam and Cambodia in the mid-1970s—drove a long and deep ideological wedge through Northeast and Southeast Asia alike. In the three clusters discussed thus far—developmental statism, Britannia, and militarism—defeating communism lay at the heart of the dominant political and economic institutions that rulers built. But in China, North Korea, Vietnam, and Cambodia, ruling parties sought not to construct stronger developmental defenses against revolutionary socialism but to build revolutionary socialism itself.[1]

Communism is obviously anathema to developmental capitalism. It would only be with the jettisoning of autarkic economic planning that socialist Asia could "join" developmental Asia and stop opposing it tooth and nail. As detailed in chapter 6, China led the way. While that chapter explored pre-1989 China as a singular socialist *case*, this chapter situates contemporary China in the developmental socialist *cluster* that has emerged since the 1990s. It will show that China continues leading the way, economically soaring above its developmental socialist neighbors. The ruling Chinese Communist Party (CCP) has not loosened its grip on power, however, even as it softened its governing touch in the decades immediately following the totalitarian Maoist era.

China's reform era began in the late 1970s. Yet by the end of the 1980s, the CCP's violent crackdown on democratic student protesters in Tiananmen Square had made it abundantly clear that reform only meant developmental and capitalist economics, not democratic and electoral politics. China's was not a dual transition, as in much of Eastern Europe. As we argue in chapter 6, China in 1989 was *too strong to collapse* like the Soviet Union, but also *too weak to concede* democracy like Taiwan and South Korea. Unlike its socialist brethren in the Soviet Union and Eastern Europe, China's CCP steadfastly avoided democratizing through weakness.[2] And unlike its neighboring Asian cases in the developmental statist cluster, the CCP lacked the strength and confidence to experiment with democracy.

Vietnam started making a parallel developmental shift about a decade after China, in the late 1980s. With the collapse of the Soviet Union, their superpower patron, Vietnam decisively parted company with North Korea, where the Kim family dynasty consistently rejected political and economic reforms alike. As the ruling Communist Party of Vietnam (VCP) reformed and opened up Vietnam's impoverished and inward-looking economy, it needed to decide whether to follow an electoral and democratic path to postcommunist political modernity (as in much of Eastern Europe) or to salvage the political model of single-party socialism by moving decisively away from the development model of economic socialism (as in China). Vietnam chose the latter path, and the ruling VCP accomplished a very similar feat to that of China's CCP: maintaining single-party domination while advancing rapid national economic development.

Cambodia's road to development has been much rockier. As of the early 1990s, the genocidal communist Khmer Rouge were still fighting an insurgency against the socialist Cambodian People's Party (CPP) regime that Vietnam installed in Phnom Penh through invasion in the late 1970s. United Nations (UN) intervention brought the Khmer Rouge out of the jungle and forced the CPP to accept relatively free and fair multiparty elections to qualify for massive multilateral aid. For over twenty-five years, Cambodian politics has been a story of the Hun Sen–led CPP trying to develop the national economy and destroy, not simply defeat, its opposition. For all its important differences from China and Vietnam, Cambodia has similarly traveled a path from autarkic socialism to high-growth nationalist economic developmentalism under single-party rule throughout the post–Cold War era. Cambodia's authoritarian trajectory has not meaningfully diverged from China's and Vietnam's, despite multiparty elections.

By the 2010s, all three developmental socialist cases had become viable candidates to pursue democracy through strength, with China the strongest candidate of all. Yet as in the developmental Britannia cluster, none have done so. What is it about developmental socialism that makes it more democracy avoidant than the cases in the developmental statist (Japan, Taiwan, and South Korea) and developmental militarist (Indonesia, Thailand, and Myanmar) clusters?

The socialist cluster's lower overall development is a necessary part of the story, but not the entire story. If the developmental militarist cluster was not too underdeveloped to experiment with democratic reforms, neither is the developmental socialist cluster. Indeed, if any country in the socialist cluster is on a path to becoming a high-income dictatorship, it is certainly China. As it continues to get rich at an unprecedented speed, China nonetheless seems increasingly inclined to avoid democracy like Singapore. It seems disinclined to choose democracy through strength, as its rivals Japan and Taiwan did once their regimes accumulated sufficient confidence that democratic transition would neither spell their own demise nor destabilize their developmental trajectories.

China's rivalry with democratic Japan and Taiwan matters. One of the main reasons for China's persistent democracy avoidance, we argue, is geopolitical. The end of the Cold War dramatically improved China's relations with South Korea, but not with Japan or Taiwan. Historical grievances against Japan, an intense desire to unify Taiwan with China, and enduring perceptions that Japan, Taiwan, and South Korea are all weak puppets of the United States continue to shape China's view of democracy. Moreover, as Sino-US relations worsen in the current era of Xi Jinping and of growing bipartisan consensus in Washington that China is a threat to the current international order, the prospects that geopolitics might support democratic reform in China, as they did with its neighbors in the developmental statist cluster, have become even more remote.

Geopolitics plays out differently in Vietnam and Cambodia. As Cambodia tries to cast aside the multiparty system foisted on it by UN intervention, the Hun Sen regime has cast its geopolitical lot almost entirely with China. There is thus *regime diffusion and emulation* within the developmental socialist cluster that mirrors what we saw earlier in the developmental statist cluster. But whereas Japan's successful democratization through strength helped inspire confidence in similar reforms in Taiwan and South Korea, China's successful single-party democracy avoidance has emboldened Cambodia (like Vietnam before it) to emulate China's authoritarian example.

Vietnam's geopolitical story is shifting in a very different direction. Hanoi increasingly looks at Beijing with the same sort of resentment and trepidation that Beijing looks at Tokyo and Washington.[3] As China's strength rises, Vietnam has grown closer to the United States. If Vietnam comes to believe that American support is both essential for its survival and contingent on deepening political reforms, geopolitical signals will make democracy through strength more likely. The growing geopolitical rivalry between the United States and China is reshaping the developmental socialist cluster as we speak, with a mix of favorable and unfavorable implications for democratic prospects in the region.

With so many differences among them, does it even make sense to consider China, Vietnam, and Cambodia a single developmental cluster? We believe it does, for several key reasons. Most obviously, all three cases have attempted transitions from socialism to capitalism, and the linkage between development models and modes of democratization—the path from development to democracy—is at the heart of our comparative analysis. Most importantly for our explanatory purposes, which center on victory confidence and stability confidence, China, Vietnam, and Cambodia share *violent revolutionary histories*. In all three cases, ruling socialist regimes can credibly claim to have brought relative peace and order to a formerly war-torn society. Enduring specters of historical conflict not only give these socialist parties a rough sort of Hobbesian legitimacy; they also make stability confidence especially hard to come by, and democratic reforms especially risky to countenance.

Socialist ideology also matters in another fashion potentially detrimental to stability confidence. In the developmental statist and Britannia clusters, citizens experienced rising living standards through capitalist development. Income and wealth inequality was a by-product of state-led capitalist growth. In contrast, in the developmental socialist cluster, decades of anticapitalist socialization and socialist ideology have legitimated the rejection of growth-enhancing but inequality-deepening policies. Democratic transition could therefore strengthen leftist populism in the developmental socialist cluster, and more significantly so than in any other cluster in developmental Asia, with deleterious consequences for continued economic development.

Turning from stability confidence to victory confidence, the fact that authoritarian China and Vietnam lack competitive multiparty elections puts them in an entirely different category from the other developmental clusters. Of greatest importance, China and Vietnam are *immune to clear electoral signals of incipient decline*. Such signals helped prompt democratic concessions in Taiwan and South Korea, and could still do so in Singapore. Single-party dictatorship, such as we see in China and Vietnam, is not necessarily more *deeply* authoritarian than multiparty authoritarianism, but it is *differently* authoritarian in this critical sense. Having failed to respond to clear electoral signals of incipient decline in the 2010s with democratic reforms, Cambodia rejoined the ranks of single-party dictatorships and is now devoid of clear electoral signals of its strength, similar to the regimes in China and Vietnam.[4]

Finally, successful nationalist revolutions led by communist parties in China and Vietnam (though far less so in Cambodia) provide a popular and legitimating narrative for permanent single-party rule, which can serve as an effective substitute for electoral democratization, especially if economic development continues apace. Although it is certainly self-serving for these regimes to continue democracy avoidance, it is not entirely insincere to claim that socialist single-party rule can be responsive to popular wishes in ways that competitive multiparty democracies often fail to provide. The more that multiparty democracies stumble at meeting contemporary governance challenges, the louder this alternative narrative will surely grow, most notably in contemporary China, to which we now turn.

A Strong China

As of 1989, the CCP was simply too weak to democratize through strength. Tiananmen Square was a story not only of *resilience to collapse* but also of *refusal to concede*. The CCP lacked the antecedent strength and regime confidence necessary to go down the path of Japan, Taiwan, and South Korea. This was the main lesson of chapter 6, in which we argued that China in 1989 was only just beginning its transition from socialism, distancing itself from the disasters of the Mao era, and belatedly entering the ranks of developmental Asia.

Three decades hence, China is recognized in this chapter in its rightful place as the uncontested leader of Asia's developmental socialist cluster. Rich beyond anyone's earlier prognostications, China and the CCP regime that leads it are powerful enough to consider transitioning from a position of strength. However, even after gathering tremendous regime strength, China remains highly unlikely to do so, due largely to features shared with the other countries in the developmental socialist cluster.

Like Vietnam and Cambodia, China remains a developmental latecomer with enormous lingering problems of relative poverty and inequality, problems that are especially pronounced given the regime's socialist heritage. It also has a history of devastating internal conflicts that makes stability confidence especially prized by the regime and by China's people, but a confidence that is also especially hard to come by. Lacking any history of multiparty elections, the CCP also lacks the clear evidentiary grounding for victory confidence that characterized dominant parties in the developmental statist and developmental Britannia clusters. Perhaps most significantly, China's geopolitical positioning as America's greatest superpower rival practically rules democratization out on nationalist grounds. Even if democracy through strength would prompt the greatest leap forward to democratic freedom for the Chinese people, China's leadership—especially under Xi Jinping—seems adamantly opposed to pursuing it.

Strengthening the Economy

In the immediate aftermath of the 1989 Tiananmen crackdown, the CCP embarked on a path of economic retrenchment, austerity, and the reinforcement of state control. Economic liberalization, China's leaders reasoned, had prompted demands for political liberalization. The entire system thus needed to be reined back in if China was to avoid another disaster.[5]

Spearheaded by Premier Li Peng, the regime quickly recentralized control of the economy, putting emphasis on the state-planned, socialist development model favored by the Li faction. The years preceding the Tiananmen protests, according to Li's view, were evidence of the liberalizing economy run amok. The CCP, after 1989, prioritized rebalancing the economy, even if it meant slowing down growth. The state reduced inflation by reintroducing price controls. The government rejuvenated the state-owned enterprise (SOE) sector through protectionist policies and an increasing flow of credit to state firms.

Though the retrenchment reforms were effective in bringing down inflation, they "overshot" their intended effect with immediate and severe consequences for China's economic growth. Notably, productivity quickly declined, as well as consumption. Recall that over the decade from 1979 to 1988, China's annual economic growth rate hovered around 10 percent; in 1989 and 1990, it plummeted to just 4 percent.

Soon after, the government shifted gears again, swinging back toward a liberal economic reform agenda. Deng Xiaoping embarked on his famed Southern Tour in 1992, visiting key southern provinces and cities that had quickly become the dynamic engines of China's early industrial development. Deng signaled that China had to continue, even accelerate, its reform path, embracing market incentives, foreign investment, and international trade. Jiang

Zemin, who became president in 1993, took his cues from Deng and introduced the concept of the socialist market economy. By explicitly adopting the "market" model and moniker, Jiang's pronouncement was a critical turning point in the CCP's evolving economic development strategy.[6]

The objective of the post-1992 transition to a socialist *market* economy was to "grow out of the plan." Undoing the 1989 retrenchment measures, the state reintroduced market pricing for goods and services. The government extended price liberalization further in key strategic consumption sectors, including in energy and food markets. The Jiang administration implemented a raft of enterprise reforms, increasing labor mobility and wage flexibility, which accelerated the growth of private businesses. The state encouraged more capital mobility to finance private-sector enterprises. The Shanghai Stock Exchange, currently among the world's largest bourses, was reestablished in 1990 after it had been shut down in 1949 when the People's Republic of China (PRC) was founded.

The CCP also created space for the burgeoning private sector by reforming the SOE sector. This did not happen quickly though, as SOE reform was (and continues to be) relatively laggardly due to the potentially massive labor disruptions arising from the privatization and scaling back of SOEs. Herein lies just one of many ways that China's socialist legacy matters, and one of the factors that differentiates China from its developmental Asian neighbors without a socialist past.

To jump-start the SOE reform process, Jiang announced the "hold big, release small" campaign in 1997. State planners and managers were encouraged to "let go" of underperforming SOEs while maintaining control over large ones, specifically those in strategic industries. Reforming the SOE sector gradually, along with the rapid growth of the private enterprise sector, altered China's industrial landscape. By the late 1990s, the SOE sector accounted for only 28 percent of total industrial output. Meanwhile, private-sector companies accounted for the vast majority of China's industrial output as well as exports.[7]

To get its fiscal house in order, the CCP implemented important tax reforms in 1994, introducing several new levies to generate revenues for the central state. Most significantly, the reforms centralized fiscal flows to the central government. Previously, the vast majority (upwards of 80 percent) of fiscal revenue stayed in provincial coffers, constraining the central government's ability to allocate resources for national defense, infrastructure investment, and other strategic initiatives like national economic development. Before

1994, the central government was forced to run chronic budget deficits, at times even needing to borrow from local and provincial governments in exchange for IOUs.[8]

The 1994 fiscal reform drastically increased the size of the central budget and the state's capacity to make strategic investments in the economy. Between 1995 and 2012, central tax revenues more than doubled. Though local and provincial governments took a hit in their share of the fiscal pie, they gained more autonomy to develop their local economies. Less dependent on fiscal largesse, regional governments embraced market opportunities to attract foreign investment, develop profitable firms, shutter nonperforming ones, and grow their export earnings. Simply put, the fiscal reform accelerated China's market reforms while also strengthening the most important of all authoritarian institutions: the central state.

The CCP regime liberalized its rules and regulations governing incoming foreign direct investment (FDI). Between 1979 and 1999, China's accumulated inward FDI grew to over US$300 billion and increased to around $1 trillion a decade later. By the mid-1990s, just a few years after Deng's Southern Tour, foreign-invested firms accounted for one-fifth of industrial output and 40 percent of total exports.

Foreign manufacturing firms were drawn to China because of its abundant labor supply and massive consumer market. They were also attracted to the special economic zones and their preferential tax arrangements, especially in China's export-friendly coastal provinces. In preparation for its 2001 entry into the World Trade Organization (WTO), China committed to reduce import tariffs across most sectors and sought more FDI to fuel its export industries. The government unified and then devalued the Chinese currency to facilitate trade and specifically to increase Chinese exports. As part of Jiang's "going global" strategy, China permanently reversed its trade deficit starting in the mid-1990s.[9]

Hu Jintao succeeded Jiang Zemin as China's president in 2003, appointing Wen Jiabao as premier. In most respects, the Hu-Wen administration (2003–13) continued the high-growth, globally oriented trajectory that Jiang initiated a decade before. Rapid economic growth bolstered the ruling regime's performance legitimacy. China was becoming richer, and this generated support for the CCP dictatorship.

The Hu administration recognized, however, that the fruits of China's development were not benefiting most people, and that many, especially those inland and in the countryside, were being left behind. If the regime expected to politically trade on its economic performance, aggregate growth alone was not going to be sufficient to sustain its legitimacy. The "quality of growth," as Hu put it, needed more attention.

During the early 2000s, China's rural economy was suffering. Rural town-and-village enterprises that initially benefited from the post-1978 reforms were being squeezed by private-sector competition. By the mid-1990s, rural enterprises, which had been critical for absorbing rural labor surpluses and providing wage-based employment earlier on in the reform period, were basically obsolete. Fearful that imbalanced growth might incite political opposition to the regime, the CCP focused on rural development, encouraging more industrial growth in China's interior provinces and providing tax relief for rural households.

By the 2000s, the economic gulf had widened severely between interior western provinces and those on the coast. Soon after taking power in 2003, the Hu government doubled down on the "western development" initiative, introduced during the late 1990s to reduce regional economic inequalities.[10] Many in the CCP leadership worried the emergence of "two Chinas"—the rich coastal cities and impoverished inland provinces—would foment dissatisfaction and potentially diminish political support for the ruling regime and its development strategy. The Hu-Wen government allocated disproportionately more resources to western provinces for infrastructure development to promote trade and commerce, industrial investment into strategic growth sectors, and tax breaks to attract foreign investment and create preferential export zones.

The Hu government also prioritized social policy reform, specifically the gradual expansion of state-financed social insurance programs. Despite decades of economic growth and the state's commitment to socialist development, China's government-run welfare programs actually excluded many of the rural and urban poor. Lower-income families did not enjoy a social safety net, meaning they paid for social services on their own. Prior to the mid-2000s, for example, out-of-pocket spending on health care exceeded government funding.[11]

The Hu regime reversed this by increasing the state's share of the national health care bill. In 2006 public financing for health care was higher than out-of-pocket payments for the first time since the early 1990s. In 2009 the government implemented a new and far-reaching health insurance scheme, covering not just rural and urban workers but also unemployed residents and nonworking dependents. Largely publicly financed, the universal insurance program expanded coverage to 95 percent of the population, ensuring access to health care and medicine for nearly all citizens, irrespective of their employment situation. These social policy reforms were very popular among Chinese citizens, generating more support for the CCP regime.

In sum, the CCP's economic development record is nothing less than staggering. By 2010, China surpassed Japan as the world's second-largest economy. Per capita income skyrocketed from the early 1990s onward, lifting China into the upper tier of the world's middle-income countries and pulling hundreds of millions out of extreme poverty, an unprecedented human development achievement. If current president Xi Jinping can make good on his lavish promises, extreme poverty in China will be eliminated completely through a mix of exorbitant public spending and continued economic growth.

China has also become the world's largest trading economy in terms of overall trade volume and exports. China has aggressively diversified its markets in the global North as well as in emerging economies in Southeast Asia, Central Asia, and Africa. At one time criticized for their lack of global brand appeal, Chinese corporations are now competing in consumer markets once dominated by American, Japanese, and European brands. In 2001 only 11 Chinese firms were listed in the world's Fortune 500; by 2020, Chinese firms accounted for 124 of the 500 largest firms in the world, eclipsing the United States (with 121 companies) and more than doubling Japan (with 53 companies).[12]

Chinese companies are not only huge; they are climbing the global value chain. Benefiting from years of public- and private-sector investment into universities, research labs, scientific and technological research, development, and commercialization, Chinese firms are challenging established global leaders in cutting-edge technologies.

China's economic presence on the world stage has grown in other ways. In recent years, China has led the way in forming ambitious transnational investment consortia, such as the Belt and Road Initiative and the Asian Infrastructure Investment Bank. Chinese firms have also become among the world's largest sources of outbound direct investment, fueling economic development in other rising economies in the global South.

Accumulating Regime Strengths

China's extraordinary economic development has generated tremendous performance legitimacy for the regime. However, while economic growth is an important source of an authoritarian regime's political support, it is not the only one. Moreover, as we have seen in other parts of developmental Asia, economic growth heightens societal demands for better government performance, even as it enhances regime legitimacy. Since the 1989 Tiananmen massacre, the ruling party in China has been on a clear trajectory of *accumulating strengths*, including but not limited to economic performance legitimacy.

A weakened regime in the shadow of June 4, 1989, the CCP quickly rebuilt the party apparatus. Importantly, it institutionalized an internal leadership succession process, a mix of informal norms about factional balancing and formal mechanisms for meritocratic promotion up the party ranks. Predictable leadership succession, a key feature of authoritarian party strength and durability, ensured more stability inside the party and dampened the factional divisions that earlier weakened the CCP under both Mao Zedong and Deng Xiaoping. As far as leadership successions went, the transition from Jiang Zemin to Hu Jintao in 2003 was politically uneventful, as was the next leadership transition to Xi Jinping.

The CCP also actively rebuilt and reshaped its membership base. Given the party's efforts to grow the economy and pursue a pragmatic rather than an ideological path to development, former "class enemies" such as private-sector entrepreneurs were integrated into the party ranks. In rapidly modernizing China, capitalist entrepreneurs were an important base of support if succored, and a potential source of political opposition to the ruling party if smothered. That said, despite Deng's ideological pragmatism, the party's socialist heritage made it difficult to embrace private entrepreneurs. Co-opting entrepreneurs into the CCP was slow.

This process of co-optation gathered steam in the early 2000s. In 2002, outgoing president Jiang offered a new mass slogan at the National People's Congress (NPC): the "three represents." The ruling party, he stated, must represent China's efforts to develop the highest forms of productivity, to perfect China's socialist culture, and to represent the interests of the Chinese people. The evolving party, therefore, committed itself to representing the interests of entrepreneurs as well, which signaled an open door to private entrepreneurs to become party members.

They did in droves soon after. Estimates suggest that nearly half of China's private entrepreneurs are CCP members. Whether because the CCP successfully co-opted these "red capitalists" or they already shared similar views to the ruling party's, China's emerging entrepreneurial class did not demand political reforms, as many CCP leaders initially feared (and some external observers initially predicted). Instead, entrepreneurs were generally supportive

of the ruling party and the political status quo, and they were viewed as partners rather than adversaries of the CCP. Simply put, entrepreneurs strengthened the ruling party's governing coalition.[13]

After Tiananmen, the CCP created new channels for bottom-up input, generating new modes of popular participation and new sources of political legitimacy among citizens. The Chinese People's Political Consultative Conference
(CPPCC) is celebrated by the regime as an institutional mechanism through
which citizens can voice their opinions on all matters of politics and policy,
from domestic policy to foreign affairs. The CPPCC is composed mainly of
party members, though it also includes functional organizations representing
different sectors of society, such as the youth league, businesses, trade associations, labor organizations, and other CCP-affiliated political organizations.
Accountable to the NPC, the CPPCC has positioned itself as the national
sounding board for societal input, including political grievances. It is intended
to provide the pressure-release valve that was so tragically missing in the run-
up to the June 1989 crisis.

Efforts to create what Chinese officials have called "consultative authoritarianism" reach down to the local level. For instance, the CCP implemented
village election reforms during the late 1990s to make rural elections more
transparent and less corrupt. Though these elections remain far from competitive, electoral reform resulted in increased citizen participation in local politics
and governance. Similarly, the proliferation of urban neighborhood associations starting in the 1980s was intended to generate more societal input into
local urban affairs. To improve local governance and government responsiveness, the CCP regime has also encouraged local-level experiments in consultative practices to create more avenues for citizen input into policy matters.[14]

Before the recent crackdown under Xi, the regime actually welcomed the
growth of civil society, and specifically the formation of so-called nongovern-
mental organizations (NGOs). Chinese NGOs have to be registered with the
authorities; hence, they are referred to as "government organized NGOs," or
GONGOs. Currently in China there are over 500,000 registered GONGOs,
with estimates of potentially millions more unregistered civil society groups
operating in China.

The NGO sector is not necessarily antagonistic to the regime, as we tend
to expect in other societies. The government actively collaborates with civil
society groups, especially those involved in social service delivery and other
nonpolitical causes. From the point of view of the authoritarian regime, so
long as civil society actors—including those that are unregistered—refrain

from explicitly political activities, the government has been willing to nurture their development.[15]

The CCP during the 1990s and 2000s became increasingly, though still selectively, tolerant of political dissent and protest. The internet began to provide a critical forum for citizen feedback, including grievances with the government. Recently the regime has suppressed "netizen" activism, though the internet continues to be a site, albeit carefully monitored, for politically subversive activity. In terms of popular mobilization and protest, literally hundreds of small protests began to occur daily in China. Almost all of these protest "incidents" have been small in scale, involving only a few individuals. Protests have also tended to be about local concerns, from whistleblowers of corrupt local officials to NIMBY (not in my backyard) grievances. For the CCP, political dissent became an important though carefully managed source of feedback for the regime, provided that localized political dissent is contained and does not spread or mobilize larger protest movements.[16]

What this all adds up to is the fact the CCP today, unlike in 1989, is a very strong, popular, and highly adaptive ruling party. It has accumulated strengths upon strengths since the reform era began over four decades ago. After 1989, the ruling party successfully reorganized internally and consolidated its power. It generated popular legitimacy among citizens and political support at the helm of China's extraordinary economic, social, and political transformation. And most importantly, it adapted and evolved and, at least for several decades, conveyed a softer, more tolerant, and more open regime. The CCP today is not the CCP as it was under Mao, nor the ruling party in 1978 at the start of the reform era, nor even in 1989 when the regime chose to crack down and violently put an end to the Tiananmen Square protests.[17] In other words, if the CCP was *gathering strength* during the 1980s, as we argue in chapter 6, we can unequivocally say the CCP today is a party that *possesses extraordinary strengths* and is strong enough to consider conceding democracy through strength.

Ominous Signals?

Compared with the ominous but still reassuring signals that ushered in preemptive democratic concessions in cases as far ranging as South Korea, Indonesia, and even Myanmar, indicators of incipient decline in China remain unalarming and unclear to the CCP. At the same time, after four decades of accumulating political and economic strengths, the CCP's ability to continue accumulating such strength may be waning. There are signs the ruling party may have reached, or is imminently approaching, its apex of power.[18]

The pace of China's economic development has slowed, going from an average of 10 percent annual growth to the current "new normal" of around 6 percent beginning in the mid-2010s, and slowing even further amid the coronavirus pandemic that began in 2020. This slowing trend is not a surprise. Economists contend that President Xi, upon taking power in 2013, inherited an economy in need of major structural reform. Difficult reforms were required if the Chinese economy was to continue growing at the same rate as before. Productivity declined in the Chinese economy beginning in the early 2000s. Emerging economies in Southeast Asia and other parts of the developing world started to undercut China's competitive advantage in abundant and cheap manufacturing labor. Chinese firms began moving their factories offshore, seeking cheaper labor markets elsewhere, just as foreign firms looked to China and fueled the country's rapid industrial development during the 1980s.

While domestic consumption has been on the rise in recent years, a large portion of China's gross domestic product (GDP) growth can still be attributed to investment. China's investment-led growth strategy, however, is potentially reaching its limits. President Xi's current efforts to increase rural incomes and reduce inequality serve in part to address the investment-consumption imbalance by increasing household spending in China. Skeptics fear these efforts may be too late, however, as local economies are wrestling with their addictions to investment-driven growth. Rebalancing may mean ultimately slowing down the economy, which could prove politically perilous for the regime.

China's economy is also increasingly saddled with huge debt burdens. Recent concerns about Evergrande and other highly leveraged real estate development consortia threaten to destabilize China's financial markets. The SOE sector, which has been a target of difficult reforms since the 1990s, continues to drain government investment resources as well. The sector remains awash in nonperforming loans, reflecting the inability or unwillingness of the state to let go of nonproductive, zombie firms. In addition, local governments are carrying unsustainable debt loads, as they meet their economic growth targets through debt-financed investment. Household and consumer debt is also on the rise at the micro-level, as housing prices and the cost of living more generally continue to skyrocket in China's cities.[19] Growing indebtedness is throwing China's economic fundamentals out of whack.

Rising levels of inequality pose a serious political and economic challenge to the CCP regime, especially given the party's commitment to a socialist ideology. China's Gini coefficient increased from under 0.3 at the start of the reform era in the early 1980s to nearly 0.5 in the 2000s. Unofficial estimates have it much worse, suggesting China's Gini coefficient could be nearer to 0.6, which would rank it among the most unequal societies in the world.

Growing levels of inequality are due in part to stagnancy in rural wages during recent years and the overall decline in economic opportunities and productivity in the countryside. Rising prices have exacerbated income inequality in the cities. Growing inequality is not experienced in terms of income inequality alone, however. Wealth disparities are becoming especially pronounced in China, as access to housing and education is increasingly constrained. Intergenerational wealth transfers have widened China's wealth gap. Such egregious levels of disparity cut to the core of the CCP's socialist ideology and identity.

Balancing economic growth with other politically relevant concerns poses difficult challenges for the current regime. Chinese citizens have turned their attentions to—and expressed their dissatisfaction with—their quality of life. Just as the Hu-Wen administration presciently focused on the "quality of growth" rather than just aggregate growth, Chinese people have become increasingly attentive to postmaterialist concerns. Consumer safety, for example, has become a lightning rod for citizen dissent and popular mobilization. So-called NIMBY issues and grievances, such as land grabs by the state and the costs of rapid urbanization and displacement, are also coming to the political fore. Environmental concerns regarding air pollution and access to clean water have put the government on the defensive.[20] The CCP is increasingly confronted with myriad political and economic challenges.

How the regime chooses to respond to emerging protest and contentious politics illuminates whether it perceives such challenges as benign or as existential threats.[21] It looks increasingly as though the CCP perceives them as the latter. Though it has portrayed itself to be a more tolerant and consultative regime, the ruling party continues to invest significant resources into its internal security apparatus, developing sophisticated suppression tactics to root out politically sensitive dissenters. That the CCP regime routinely deploys costly technologies for internet monitoring, press and social media censorship, CCTV surveillance, misinformation campaigns, the threat of imprisonment, and even violent repression suggests the ruling party assesses emerging contentious politics as threats to the stability of the regime. For all the CCP's strengths accumulated through China's incredible development, its repressive turn under the current Xi regime does not imply stability confidence, but rather the opposite.

In addition to economic and domestic political challenges, the geopolitical situation for China has become increasingly fraught. More and more countries are critical of China and its human rights record, its territorial claims in the region, and its expanding economic clout internationally. As China becomes more powerful on the world stage, its neighbors are becoming more skittish and anxious about China's bullying, and other major powers are becoming more deeply suspicious of China's rise.

This represents a big change from the 1990s, when China first integrated itself more fully into the international economy and established important footholds in global governance institutions such as the WTO, the World Bank, and Asia's many regional organizations. Communist China was not an ally to the rest of the world, but it was also not its enemy or challenger. Today, however, it is increasingly perceived as, and behaves as though it is, a geopolitical rival of the United States and its allies. Global criticisms of Chinese policies— from the regime's treatment of Muslim Uighurs in Xinjiang, to security concerns about Chinese firms, to accusations of unfair trade policies—are contributing to increasingly unfriendly and competitive pressures on China from the rest of the world.

The future political, economic, and diplomatic consequences of the current rivalry with the United States are ambiguous. It is not clear, for instance, whether Chinese leaders themselves view geopolitical headwinds to be a worrying signal and as pressures that could harm the regime and its political legitimacy at home. It is clear, however, that prolonged trade wars, diplomatic spats with formerly friendly countries, border skirmishes that repeatedly flare up, and a growing chorus of international condemnation of China's domestic and international actions will make it more and more difficult for China to continue modernizing in as smooth a fashion as it has over the past four decades.

Having developed a truly extraordinary track record of economic development, the CCP regime seems to be nearing a critical inflection point. It could either take the path of political reform toward a more liberal future or double down on Xi's authoritarian turn. Our theory of democracy through strength can help inform this analysis.

As we have shown throughout this book, strong regimes are most likely to choose to concede democracy when they have passed their apex of power.

Moreover, the closer the authoritarian ruling party is to that apex, the more likely the transition will be stable and the incumbent ruling party holds on to power. Simply put, the stronger the regime, the better for the incumbent if it chooses democracy.

The signals the CCP regime has received over the past decade or so, from economic to geopolitical, do not necessarily mean the ruling party is in incipient decline. At the present moment, the CCP enjoys widespread political support, and the performance legitimacy it generated over the past forty years provides the ruling party with considerable political and economic strength—for now.

Given that the CCP in China is a *candidate case* for democracy through strength, we do not know—as we cannot know for certain what the future holds—whether in fact the regime has passed its apex of power and is in the bittersweet spot. As we saw with the cases in the developmental Britannia cluster, waiting to find out with certainty, however, can pose real and possibly existential threats to the incumbent regime.

A recurring theme throughout this book is that development begets its own discontents. Past success, by virtue of people's rising expectations of future success, generates pockets of dissent that can quickly become full-blown opposition. Bruce Dickson describes this conundrum as the Tocquevillian paradox, or the "revolution of rising expectations," that he contends is at the core of the "dictator's dilemma." In the case of China, Dickson speculates that "even if the Party does not face organized opposition at present, it may be undone by the revolution of rising expectations."[22] Though the challenges the CCP currently confronts may not be ominous in their immediacy, they nonetheless signal social, economic, political, and geopolitical challenges that may not be resolvable by the regime in its current form.

Just as China's current economic growth model has reached its limits and needs to be substantially reformed, the performance legitimacy formula the regime has relied on to date to maintain its political dominance might also soon expire. The CCP's decisions to increase its suppressive and repressive capacities in recent years, and the hardening of its authoritarian grip on power under President Xi, suggest the incumbent party senses that the best way to confront these looming obstacles is by moving China further away from, rather than closer to, the stable, strong-state democratization pathway of its closest Northeast Asian neighbors.

Despite the stability and victory confidence the CCP *should* possess given its accumulated strengths over the past four decades, it seems the regime is choosing to eschew the democracy-through-strength option. As we saw in chapter 8 in the cases of Malaysia and Hong Kong, and as we explore later in this chapter in the case of Cambodia, eschewing this path comes with big risks of its own.

China's Democratic Prospects

In our theory of democracy through strength, we highlight the paradox of incumbent party strength. When "a ruling party enjoys substantial incumbent capacity, this not only increases its ability to sustain authoritarian rule, but can lessen its imperative to do so."[23] Put another way, when an incumbent party is strong enough to maintain its authoritarian grip on political power for the time being, it is also strong enough to concede democracy without conceding defeat, thus increasing the likelihood it might choose the democratic path.

In our view, the CCP is clearly strong enough to choose either path; it is in a spot that is far less bitter than sweet. China's ruling party can credibly claim to have orchestrated and overseen China's extraordinary development. The party today, unlike in 1989, has a compelling "usable past" that it can exploit to generate electoral support for the party to lead China into its next phase of social, economic, and political modernization. The CCP's track record is not limited to economics, either. Governance reforms to increase the regime's consultative capacity reflect the party's growing responsiveness to citizen demands and input. The CCP's embrace of capitalist entrepreneurs reflects its ability to adapt to China's developmental evolution. Chinese citizens broadly support the regime, recognizing the party's past role and historical record.[24]

Simply put, the party's economic and political developmental track record would be its greatest ticket to stability and victory in a democratic future. In this respect, China keeps looking more and more like its developmental statist neighbors, and less and less like the former Soviet bloc that collapsed three decades ago. In China's mix of developmental socialism, the regime's commitment to economic growth and developmentalism has kept increasing, while the weight of socialism has lightened.

The CCP ought to be confident that if it democratizes on its own terms and timing, China will remain stable. If the CCP were to lead the transition process, much as the Kuomintang (KMT) did in Taiwan, the incumbent regime would most assuredly put in place the institutional safeguards and constitutional provisions to ensure a stable transition process.[25] Contrary to fears that democracy would bring chaos and instability, one could expect a more level, democratic playing field in China to bring about the political pressure-release valve needed to defuse some of the political tensions inside China, including more peacefully and sustainably managing relations along China's restive periphery. Indeed, one of the core lessons learned from the developmental statist cluster is that democratic transition can likely foster more, not less, political stability in China.

The ruling party in China is popular. Not only do Chinese citizens support the governing regime, as expressed in almost every opinion survey; most people support the CCP specifically, which should give the incumbent party ample victory confidence. Of course, citizens criticize the party and the regime, and would likely criticize it more and more openly in a democracy. Critics of the CCP, for instance, would form an opposition to the CCP in a multiparty democracy. Yet there is, at present, no viable alternative to the incumbent CCP. If China were to democratize, there is no conceivable challenger that could unseat it as the ruling party in the near term. Moreover, as we saw in the developmental statist cluster, opponents of an authoritarian regime can come to electorally support an authoritarian successor party after it democratizes the political system. In other words, the CCP should have as much confidence that conceding democracy would not spell its defeat as the incumbent ruling parties did in Japan, South Korea, and Taiwan, if not more.

There are many inside China who argue that democratic transition would derail China's development. Critics point would-be democratic reformers to the Soviet example and the cautionary tale of glasnost and perestroika. In China, the lesson learned from the Soviet example is that democratic transition brings about political instability and economic chaos. It also spelled the political demise of the Communist Party of the Soviet Union (CPSU). Nothing good came from democratization, according to this critical narrative.

That is the wrong lesson to take from the Soviet example. Democratic failure in the former Soviet Union and the death of the CPSU were due to the incumbent ruling party's *collapsing* rather than *conceding*. The CPSU began conceding mere half measures of liberalizing reform at a time when the regime was already delegitimated and unpopular, such that when a democratic opening emerged, the incumbent ruling party was swiftly kicked out. If the Chinese regime takes anything from the Soviet example, it should be that waiting too long after a ruling authoritarian party passes its apex of power makes democratic transition less stable and less advantageous for the incumbent. As we showed in the Britannia cluster, when a regime avoids democracy for too long, surpassing its "best-before" date, it increases the risk of hurtling through the bittersweet spot altogether, resulting in either what we call embittered authoritarianism (Hong Kong and, increasingly, Singapore) or even the authoritarian regime's outright defeat (as in Malaysia).

Obstacles to Chinese Democracy

Despite a compelling case for the CCP regime to concede democracy through strength, the prospects of democratic transition remain unlikely in China, even remote. The political trajectory the current regime is on does not bode well for democracy in China. Some speculated that Xi Jinping's early efforts to consolidate his own personal power within the party were intended to lay the groundwork for a possible democratic concession scenario. The CCP's tightening authoritarian grip on power and the deployment of more repressive tactics in recent years, however, suggest that those hopes were misplaced, and that Xi and the CCP are not preparing for a more liberal political system.[26] Xi's move to remove term limits on the presidency in 2018 affirms the CCP's current trajectory away from democratization.

Speculation about Xi's intentions aside, however, there are structural reasons why a democracy-through-strength scenario is highly improbable in China. First, potentially ominous signals that the CCP regime is in incipient decline or has passed its apex of power remain too unclear in China. As we contend in our theory, the clearest signals of a ruling party's hold on power, be it on the rise or diminishing, are electoral. Recall that in our exemplary case of democracy through strength, Taiwan, elections provided feedback loops for the KMT regime to gauge its popularity among voters. The KMT's hold on power was never in doubt, especially as martial law prohibited opposition parties from forming, though the ruling party had to reckon with its dwindling electoral support during the 1970s and 1980s. Elections clearly signaled to the incumbent ruling party its strength was on the decline.[27]

In China, electoral signals are at best unreliable and at worst nonexistent. Village and township elections provide little clarity because corruption, graft, thuggery, and voter intimidation distort reliable information to the CCP about its popularity and support. In the absence of clear signals, the ruling party may be less confident about its democratic prospects, a problem evident in all authoritarian regimes lacking multiparty elections.

Second, the CCP has proved very adept at deflecting political blame away from the central leadership. Amid the rise in contentious politics after 1989, the party effectively localized dissent. In addition to deploying the security apparatus to suppress any potential uprisings, the ruling party in Beijing has diverted political blame to local cadres. Despite Xi's anticorruption campaign, which has uncovered the extensive rot inside the party and among government officials, most citizens continue to trust and support the central regime, while lacking trust in local officials.[28]

Third, the CCP is highly resistant to any geopolitical pressures to democratize. As we recount in this book, countries in the developmental statist cluster confronted varying degrees of pressure from the United States to concede democracy. China, however, has never been an ally of the United States, and hence it is impervious to the transnational linkage effects that directly and indirectly promote democratization.[29] Indeed, it increasingly sees itself as a rival to the world's wealthy democracies. Other states, including most importantly the United States, increasingly view China as a rival as well. The democratic "pull effect" that encouraged the developmental statist cluster to concede democracy is absent in contemporary China. If anything, the geopolitical competition between China and the United States has created a repellent or "push effect," widening the gap between democratic prospects and socialist authoritarian resilience.

Finally, the prospects of democracy are not very appealing to the CCP. Democratic backsliding worldwide has become increasingly prevalent in recent years, as elected leaders turn to populist appeals and polarizing politics to win political power. Democracies increasingly appear unstable because they *are* unstable in many parts of the world, including among younger, more recently transitioned democracies where the global "democratic recession" is most pressing.[30] Furthermore, many in China believe the CCP regime is already democratic, pointing to the government's efforts to create more consultative mechanisms, the implementation of the rule of law, and public support for the regime. The CCP is not a liberal or even electoral democracy, but it claims to be differently democratic in ways that accommodate some political participation and responsiveness.[31]

The assertion that liberal democracy is a Western construct and hence ill suited for Chinese society has unsurprisingly gained traction among Chinese leaders and citizens, as well as foreign cheerleaders for the CCP. According to Dickson's recent survey data, most Chinese believe China is "already democratic" and that transition to liberal electoral democracy is both unnecessary and undesirable.[32] Jie Chen contends that China's middle class is not in favor of democracy but is supportive of the CCP regime.[33] China's leaders are even championing an alternative "China Model," as Daniel Bell puts it, which is potentially more attractive to China than democracy.[34] Neither the incentives to democratize nor democracy's appeal is sufficient to compel the CCP to choose democracy, even if the regime is in the ideal position to concede democracy through strength, and to continue to thrive in a new Chinese democracy.

Vietnam

Like China, Vietnam did not democratize through weakness when the Cold War ended. There would be no communist collapse. Instead, over the past three decades, Vietnam has joined the ranks of developmental Asia as a member of the region's developmental socialist cluster. It has achieved this through an impressive battery of market-oriented and externally oriented economic reforms, not unlike what we saw in China. Socialist legacies and practices surely persist, again as in China, in the continued prominence of state enterprises in the national economy and in the vanguard single-party role played by the Vietnamese Communist Party (VCP). Socialist legacies notwithstanding, in broader comparative and historical terms, the economic transformation of Vietnam since the end of the Cold War has been nothing short of astonishing.

In most respects, the following analysis will paint Vietnam as a slightly weaker version of the developmental socialist case we explored in China, and thus a weaker candidate for democracy through strength. The VCP regime is strong enough to democratize through strength, while confronting only faint and fuzzy signals that democratic reforms are necessary and only weak pressures to do so. However, Vietnam is meaningfully different from China, and not just measurably weaker than China, in at least two key ways.

The first key difference lies in Vietnam's political institutions: a difference more pronounced as China has become increasingly personalized under Xi Jinping. Most simply put, Vietnam has a surprisingly *centrifugal* power structure for an enduring single-party socialist regime. Provinces have real authority; parliament makes real decisions, after holding real televised debates; the VCP's critics have real opportunities to make their voices heard both online and in street protests; and real political power is shared among VCP leaders who fully expect to be replaced in a regularized, predictable manner.

All of this was not so terribly different from China prior to 2013, between the Deng and Xi regimes. Perhaps the most important change during the Xi era has been China's return to a more *centripetal* power structure, with Xi as the unchallenged personal center. China's provinces, parliamentary institutions, protesters, and potential successors to the party's leadership all have less room to maneuver under Xi than before. In all these domains there is substantially greater latitude in Vietnam than in China. Whether this means Vietnam's authoritarian institutions are now becoming "stronger" or "weaker" than China's is debatable. What is undebatable, however, is that the two socialist neighbors' authoritarian institutions are becoming ever more different from one another.

What is also undebatable is a second key difference: Vietnam's position in the world of geopolitics. Whereas China's deepening geopolitical rivalry with the United States makes democratization there less likely, the fact that Vietnam sees China as a greater threat and rival than the United States makes democratization there *more* likely. When considering which type of signals are most likely to shift Vietnam's regime trajectory in the years to come, geopolitical signals seem to be the most significant. However, since geopolitical signals are neither the clearest nor strongest signals to a declining regime in our theory, immediate prospects for Vietnam to democratize through strength remain quite low.

Economic Strengths

During the Cold War, Vietnam allied itself closely with the Soviet Union, unlike China, which went its own way after the Sino-Soviet split of 1959. This had profound implications for Vietnam's political economy, including its mode of exit from state socialism and entry into developmental socialism. Whereas China blended socialism with autarkic technonationalism during the Mao years, Vietnam was highly aid dependent after expelling the French from its north in 1954 and repelling the Americans from its south by 1975.

Somewhat paradoxically, this deep external dependency under Cold War socialism made it easier for Vietnam to internationalize and open its economy to the capitalist world as the Cold War ended. Its initial "joining" of developmental Asia in the late 1980s may have come a bit later than China's; but once it started, it was less hesitant. Socialist Vietnam also adjusted more comfortably than China to the rules of regional economic engagement in developmental Asia, even while attaining much lower levels of aggregate development than its behemoth neighbor to the north.

Vietnam's socialist economy also differed from China's because its socialist revolution was different. The most significant deviation from the Chinese experience was simply the depth and scope of social transformation in the Vietnamese revolution. Although Vietnam fought a social revolution as surely as China did, the ruling VCP triumphed through a united-front strategy that required considerable compromise with noncommunist forces.[35] It was thus more hindered than the CCP in its ability to revolutionize property relations, eliminate markets from the mainstream of economic life, and demand ideological fidelity as Mao did when he proclaimed the PRC. This was especially true in the South, where VCP rule was more belated and tenuous. Market relations began largely prevailing in the Vietnamese countryside as early as 1979. But whereas China's rural marketization of the late 1970s represented a major shift in direction after Mao's death and Deng's political rise, in Vietnam this signified the VCP's failure to transform and socialize the rural sector in the first place.[36]

The VCP's hard push for socialism in the 1970s might not have effectively transformed Vietnam's political economy, but it certainly badly disrupted it. Echoing the horrors of the Great Leap Forward in China, Vietnam's agricultural system buckled under the pressures of forced collectivization, producing virtual famine conditions in city and countryside alike by the late 1970s.[37] To make matters considerably worse, Vietnam found itself at war both with Cambodia, which the VCP invaded to topple the genocidal Khmer Rouge in 1978, and with China, which subsequently invaded Vietnam in retaliation for overthrowing the Khmer Rouge, which was the CCP's ally. There was no prospect whatsoever for Vietnam's fledgling socialist economy to gain solid footing and make substantial strides forward under such hostile conditions, both from within and from without.

Socialism thus proved a shallower affair in Vietnam than in China before both countries embraced "market socialism." This embrace was more of a survival mechanism than an ideological shift in the Vietnamese case. Although the VCP's 1979 plenum "acknowledged the useful role of the private sector, and granted greater autonomy to local governments," Tuong Vu argues, "Party leaders considered these measures a temporary retreat but not permanent policies because they apparently contradicted the Marxist vision of socialism."[38]

Yet the retreat would soon prove permanent. Geopolitical shifts were happening all around Vietnam. With Mikhail Gorbachev's rise to power in the Soviet Union, the client would mimic the patron. In the USSR, perestroika was the economic watchword as of 1986, and by the end of that year, the VCP formally announced its own strategy of doi moi (renovation). The battery of liberalizing and internationalizing economic reforms entailed in doi moi amounted to Vietnam's "joining" developmental Asia in one fell swoop.[39] The death of VCP leader Le Duan in 1986 after he had led the party for over twenty-five years also contributed to the momentum for decisive, radical economic reforms under the new leadership of Nguyen Van Linh, a southerner with the impeccable revolutionary credentials necessary for legitimating the VCP's decisive new departures from socialist orthodoxy.

Doi moi never meant democratization, just as China's Four Modernizations never meant political reform. To draw a Soviet analogy, doi moi was heavy on the perestroika and light on the glasnost. Although Nguyen Van Linh has at times been called "Vietnam's Gorbachev," it is more accurate to call him Vietnam's Deng Xiaoping. Brief flirtations with political liberalization in 1988, and specifically greater freedom of the press to help the VCP get a handle on corruption, were swiftly reversed as communist regimes toppled in Eastern Europe and China's CCP found itself on its heels in 1989.[40] Like China's ruling communist party, Vietnam's VCP steadfastly avoided democratizing through weakness.

Fortunately for Vietnam and the VCP, dramatic reforms aimed at internationalizing the economy came at an especially propitious moment, just as the 1985 Plaza Accord was unleashing a flood of Japanese investment into Southeast Asia. Without a scientific or industrial base that could even rival post-Mao China's, Vietnam nonetheless possessed a relatively widely educated population, as one would expect given its recent socialist past. The results were remarkable from a global perspective, albeit par for the course where developmental Asia is concerned. Annual GDP growth rates for Vietnam shot above 5 percent by 1988 and have not fallen below that impressive annual clip in the subsequent three decades, even during the Asian financial crisis of the late 1990s and global recession of the late 2000s.

Very much in the spirit of developmental Asia, pursuing rapid development and elevating Vietnam's place in the regional pecking order became "the dominant concern of Vietnam's political leadership" by 2000, as "the momentum toward extensive regional and global engagement became irresistible."[41] Growth peaked at nearly 10 percent per year during the mid-1990s, in the wake of America's lifting of sanctions against Vietnam in 1994, and has typically averaged in the 6–7 percent range over the past several decades. According to World Bank figures, in 2020 the Vietnamese economy was over forty times larger than it was in 1990.

The point is not that Vietnam is now rich, or even comfortably middle income. Since Vietnam joined developmental Asia from an especially parlous economic state, even three decades of consistent rapid growth have not been enough to overcome the destructive legacies of brutal wars and socialist economic mismanagement. For our explanatory purposes, the critical point is that the VCP has an extraordinarily strong economic record, above and beyond the revolutionary legitimacy it enjoys from ridding the Vietnamese nation of French and American occupation.

Institutional Strengths

Vietnam's economy could not have been successfully "renovated" under doi moi unless its governing institutions were substantially reformed. Institutional reform did not mean democratization or even multiparty competition under continuing authoritarian controls, and certainly not the development of the rule of law. It did, however, mean rebuilding the party-state in significant ways. While Vietnam's economic transformation was comparatively less momentous than China's during the 1990s, its ruling institutions have arguably surpassed China's in how dramatically they have been transformed since their Cold War communist heyday.

Party reform began with a thorough housecleaning in personnel from top to bottom. By 1988, 80 percent of the VCP's 400 party district chiefs had been replaced across the country. The VCP also instituted a system of competitive elections for its leadership positions, so that one-third of the Central Committee would be replaced on a regular basis.[42] Ngyuen Van Linh did not come anywhere close to establishing one-man rule, with a coalition of forces arising by the late 1980s to limit, but not to reverse or even stymie, his internal party reforms.[43]

This was part and parcel of what may well be the VCP's most impressive institutional accomplishment of all: the consolidation of collective leadership and regularized succession. Every five years, Vietnam's leadership ranks are reshuffled like clockwork. While China's CCP managed something similar in Deng's planned handover to Jiang (1993–2003) and then Hu and Wen (2003–13), the wheels of predictable power sharing came off completely under Xi in 2016, when he removed term limits on his stint as China's most powerful leader.[44] Although the VCP is certainly riven with factionalism, like the CCP, the party put institutions in place, and has sustained them, to manage that endemic problem.

Power sharing among elites is not only more predictable in Vietnam than in China; it is also more encompassing. Decision-making in Vietnam's ruling party takes place within a central committee that is more than five times larger than the CCP's Politburo in China, permitting a much wider range of interests to be expressed in national policy. Perhaps most significantly, the territorial representativeness of the VCP's Central Committee encourages much higher levels of interprovincial revenue transfers, a critical factor contributing to the lower levels of income inequality in Vietnam than in China.[45] To the extent that relative income equality reinforces a regime's stability confidence, Vietnam's VCP is potentially in a stronger position to concede democratic reforms than China's CCP, and to expect a less rocky transition.

Vietnam also paralleled and, again, arguably surpassed reform-era China in its construction of avenues for public consultation. Vietnam's legislature, the Vietnamese National Assembly (VNA), is politically active and even publicly accountable in ways that China's equivalent, the National People's Congress (NPC), cannot rival. The media is also substantially freer in Vietnam than in China, especially online, providing the VCP more unvarnished public signals of where it is coming up short.[46] Like most if not all socialist systems, the VCP's strong suit is mass organization, with its Fatherland Front of VCP-affiliated social movements providing an enduring direct linkage between ruler and ruled. The VCP has gone so far as to establish local, grassroots institutions for everyday governance that operate under the principle that "people know, people discuss, people act, and people monitor."[47]

Vietnam thus possesses an array of institutional strengths both for managing elite conflict and for sustaining mass connectivity that most authoritarian regimes sorely lack, even including the CCP in China. To be sure, none of these institutions can take the place of regular multiparty elections in precisely gauging popular support, deciphering public demands, and generating victory confidence. Yet the fact remains that Vietnam is less "closed" than its Chinese neighbor to the north, which has important implications for how receptive the VCP is to signals and pressures for deeper political reform.

Absorbing Shocks to the System

In comparative perspective, Vietnam's reform era has been a relatively low-drama affair. Signals of trouble for the regime are few and far between in a system that, while it surely struggles and suffers setbacks, is a hard one to shock. There have been no major urban protests and thus no massive crackdowns; no surprising electoral setbacks; no precipitous economic downturns; and no threats of geopolitical isolation. These are precisely the kinds of signals that tended to trigger preemptive democratic reforms elsewhere in developmental Asia. Especially when compared with the tumultuous and traumatic four decades that preceded doi moi, the past four decades have been as close to smooth political sailing for Vietnam as any in its modern history.

Yet the VCP is not impervious to the signals most likely to spark democratization through strength. Although Vietnam does not permit regular multiparty elections, the relatively freewheeling character of the national parliament, the VNA, gives the VCP election-like signals of the popularity of specific policies and politicians, if not necessarily the regime writ large. At least several independent politicians typically hold seats in the VNA, giving at least a flavor of what a multiparty government might look like, something that is absent in China (but which was critical in predemocratic Taiwan, South Korea, and Indonesia). Enough competitive action and critique take place in the VNA to have spawned a veritable cottage industry in political science on how much accountability and responsiveness there is in its procedures.[48] Like other nondemocratic institutions, a robust authoritarian parliament is double-edged: it helps produce the institutional capacity to avoid democratic transition, but it can also offer ruling politicians valuable experience and increase their confidence that multiparty democracy would not destabilize the system.

Vietnam is also more receptive than China to signals of dissent and disapproval from civil society, especially since China entered the more repressive Xi era. As Benedict Kerkvliet has chronicled from the postwar unification of Vietnam to the present, peasant and worker unrest and noncooperation have long constrained and shaped VCP economic policy making, and anti-VCP dissent regularly percolates up from dissidents and activist intellectuals.[49] From the violent peasant protests in Thai Binh Province in 1997, which led to the dismissal of over a thousand party officials, to the urban strike wave that pressured the VCP to make its proposed social insurance law more generous in 2015, contentious signals have prompted governance reforms in Vietnam, if not yet democratizing reforms.[50]

There are also visible signs of trouble with Vietnam's economic model. Far more than China, Vietnam has become trapped in something of a "partial reform equilibrium," a condition in which the initial beneficiaries of partial reform become obstacles to deeper reforms that would empower a wider range of beneficiaries.[51] The predictable result has been massive endemic corruption, centered on the narrow nexus between SOEs and enterprising state officials.

At least until recently, pressure to resolve these structural problems was far less imposing than the problems themselves. Accountability for corruption during the first three decades of doi moi was virtually absent. The ineffective-ness of anticorruption campaigns was best captured by a local idiom: "bathing without washing the head."[52] The VCP's propensity for holding votes of no confidence in the VNA and creating performative but ultimately toothless watchdog institutions was described by one analyst as nothing more than the "repackaging of bad governance."[53]

Vietnam's current leadership has seen corruption as a more urgent problem, however, and taken more dramatic corrective measures. Emulating but by no means matching Xi's centralization of power and sweeping campaign against elite corruption in China, VCP leader Nguyen Phu Trong has stepped up anti-corruption efforts substantially since beginning his second term as party chief in 2016. Having been selected for an unprecedented third term in 2021, his lasting impact on the VCP could prove substantial. Yet collective leadership still remains entrenched in Vietnam, suggesting that the equilibrium path of high growth, corruption, and party factionalism will be difficult to dismantle and thus most likely to persist. This equilibrium, for all its flaws, has proved extremely resilient and absorptive of the political and economic shocks that elsewhere made more dramatic reforms seem urgent.

Geopolitical Possibilities

Both before and during the ongoing anticorruption campaign, growth in Viet-nam remained steady and steep. The Asian financial crisis of 1997–98 had little effect, and the dip in economic development during the 2008 global recession was mercifully fleeting. The main economic concern in Vietnam is not the rate of growth but the fact that economic growth has become increasingly depen-dent on Vietnam's biggest rival: China. This has prompted the VCP to show great interest in multilateral initiatives toward trade liberalization such as the Trans-Pacific Partnership, initiatives that frequently exclude China.

While deeper trade liberalization would surely hurt many inefficient Viet-namese firms, "Hanoi was willing to expand international engagement with any country—including the United States—that could support Vietnam's economic development and consequently its ability to avoid overdependence on a single or small number of foreign actors."[54] In much the same way that anxiety and resentment over growing Chinese economic domination prompted preemptive democratizing reforms by Myanmar's military in the early 2010s, the fiercely anticolonial VCP could see democratization as a key feature of its survivalist drive to diversify its external dependencies.

It is ultimately in its geopolitical rivalry with China where the clearest prospects for "bittersweet signals" for the VCP have arisen. On one hand, China's growing clout over its immediate neighbors in Southeast Asia is an *ominous* signal for the VCP regime if it persists with its developmental status quo. "Vietnam's near-exclusive security threat comes from the growing economic and military power of its much larger neighbor to the north, China."[55] On the other hand, strengthening diplomatic overtures from the United States and the other three members of the so-called Quad (Australia, India, and Japan) present the kind of *reassuring* signals that portend a warm embrace of Vietnam should it pursue decisive democratizing reforms. Importantly, America's outreach to and warming embrace of Vietnam gathered momentum under recent Democratic and Republican administrations alike in the United States, which suggests American support for Vietnam has a level of bipartisan predictability and reliability often lacking in its other bilateral Asian relationships and multilateral commitments.

A core lesson from developmental Asia's historical democratization experience is that strong authoritarian regimes can transition into democracies at their own behest and on their own timetables. No developmental socialist regime has yet attempted this. But Vietnam combines both the significant strength and strategic interest in allying with the United States and other major democratic powers that makes democratization through strength a plausible, even if still unlikely, scenario. So long as Vietnam's current single-party system remains capable of absorbing potential shocks, however, such preemptive reforms remain less likely for the VCP than they would be beneficial for Vietnam.

Cambodia

Without question, the weakest authoritarian regime in Asia's developmental socialist cluster is Cambodia. As we have seen in Asia's other developmental clusters, authoritarian weakness is anything but good news for democratization. The strongest rulers have enjoyed the opportunity to thrive after preemptive democratization, while the weakest rulers have essentially doubled down on authoritarianism, retreating to their repressive fortresses due to their lack of victory and stability confidence.

The Hun Sen regime had built up enough strength by the mid- to late 2000s for the ruling regime to concede democracy through strength. However, the ruling CPP missed the bittersweet spot for democratic reform, much as

Malaysia's ruling United Malays National Organization–Barisan Nasional (UMNO-BN) did during the same period, as explored in chapter 8. This left Cambodia's regime in a state of what we call *embittered authoritarianism*, unable to thrive in either authoritarianism or democracy. Instead of conceding democracy, Hun Sen clung to power by crushing Cambodia's formidable opposition and stepping up repression of the country's vibrant civil society, both fading remnants of its fleeting stint as a more pluralist political system during the early 1990s interregnum under UN peacekeepers. Geopolitically, this strategy to repress rather than concede has required deepening Cambodia's dependency on China, wedding it more tightly to the developmental and steadfastly authoritarian socialist cluster and alienating it from the world's far more numerous wealthy democracies.

For all its economic successes since joining developmental Asia in the 1990s, Cambodia's ruling CPP has devolved into a one-man, embittered single-party regime, rather than developing stronger political organizations to reap the performance legitimacy generated from its strengthening economy. Having lost the popular vote outright in 2013, the Hun Sen regime no longer had grounds for confidence that preemptive democratization would allow the CPP to play a leading role in Cambodian politics. Like China's during the 1980s, Cambodia's ruling regime after the 2013 election debacle concluded that it was too weak to concede with confidence. Cambodian society—especially its political opposition—has paid a steep price.

Emerging from a Cataclysm

No country had further to climb to join developmental Asia than Cambodia. By the early 1970s, it had been reduced to a carpet-bombed catastrophe of a country. It was ruled by American-backed military man Lon Nol, stampeded by Viet Cong forces along the Ho Chi Minh Trail, and shattered by American bombs and chemical weapons that pursued Viet Cong forces to no avail.

Then things got even worse. The communist Khmer Rouge overthrew the US-backed regime in 1975 and proceeded to inflict a mass genocide on the Cambodian people that lasted four years and led to millions of deaths. The Khmer Rouge was toppled in 1979 by Vietnam's VCP and the national army it commanded. With the Khmer Rouge and its leader, Pol Pot, on the run, the VCP installed a puppet communist regime in Phnom Penh fronted by Heng Samrin, a Khmer Rouge defector.

For the next decade, Cambodia was the grass that elephants stampeded in late Cold War politics. On one side, the Soviets backed Vietnam and its new Cambodian client regime headed by Heng Samrin, while on the other side, China, the Association of Southeast Asian Nations (ASEAN), Cambodia's own exiled monarchy, and even the UN and United States backed the Khmer Rouge as Cambodia's legitimate government, despite its unspeakable crimes, all in a bid to curtail Soviet and Vietnamese influence.

Clearly, the Cold War could not end soon enough for Cambodia's people. When it did, the UN helped broker a peace agreement between the Khmer Rouge and the Vietnamese-backed regime in the Paris Peace Accords of October 1991. Amid the euphoria and global optimism that followed the collapse of communism in the Soviet Union and Eastern Europe, the UN promised billions of dollars in aid to support Cambodia's transition to multiparty democracy under the watchful eyes of the UN's Blue Helmets and foreign civilian advisers.[56]

Unlike China and Vietnam, therefore, Cambodia did not exit the Cold War as a functional single-party communist regime that had been the product of a homegrown social revolution. It was a disaster area. There was not an entrenched socialist economy that needed to be reformed; there was a war zone that needed to build an economy. There was no triumphant revolutionary party that basked in considerable nationalist legitimacy; there was a puppet regime whose main source of legitimacy was that it was not the Khmer Rouge.

After replacing Heng Samrin as leader of Cambodia's Vietnam-installed socialist ruling party, eventually renamed the CPP, Hun Sen became the leader of Cambodia's turbulent transition from a literal Cold War minefield into a modern nation-state with a functioning economy. Considering that Cambodia was still reeling in the Khmer Rouge's ideological aftermath, and keeping in mind that Vietnam itself was no longer striving to build any communist utopia in its own right, it should be no surprise that Hun Sen and the CPP wore their ideological commitment to socialism ever so lightly.

With billions in foreign aid flooding in to grease the wheels of Cambodia's fragile peace process, and with international socialism discredited by the Soviet collapse, the CPP set its sights on winning competitive elections in 1993, and thus regaining the iron grip it had held on power—thanks to Vietnamese support—from 1979 to 1991. The ruling party treated the 1993 elections as an exercise in coercion as well as mobilization. The CPP leveraged its control over the state apparatus to recruit an astonishing two million new members into the party, but also to unleash death squads that killed several hundred opposition campaigners.[57] The CPP's main opponent was a royalist party called Funcinpec, led by the aging king Norodom Sihanouk's son, Prince Norodom Ranariddh. Given the king's close ties to China and active support for the Khmer Rouge against the Vietnamese invaders and their local proxies, the rivalry between the CPP and Funcinpec was fierce from the get-go.

The 1993 elections produced a stalemate. Despite the intimidation its supporters faced, Funcinpec enjoyed just enough physical UN protection to help it eke out a narrow win over the CPP, 45 percent to 38 percent in the popular vote and a 58–51 advantage in legislative seats.

The CPP refused to concede defeat, however. Since the CPP still controlled the state apparatus, and most importantly its coercive organs, its refusal to concede quickly became a fait accompli. In the face of the CPP's recalcitrance, backed by a repressive state, the Funcinpec and CPP forged a power-sharing arrangement, better described as cohabitation than coalition. The UN begrudgingly endorsed both the 1993 elections and the deal that followed them, departing with its mission only partly and tenuously accomplished.

Cohabitation proved too much for Hun Sen's CPP to bear. Much like Myanmar's military in 2021, Cambodia's ruling CPP blew up the democratically agreed-on power-sharing pact by force in July 1997. Funcinpec was expelled from the political executive, dozens of royalist military officers were extrajudicially executed, and Prince Ranariddh fled to France before settling down to exile in Thailand.

With power thus seized, Hun Sen and the CPP began building up their authoritarian strengths against the stiff headwinds of global condemnation for their violent 1997 coup. That Cambodia benefited from its location among so many wealthy and booming developmental neighbors allowed the CPP to orchestrate a minor economic miracle in the decades that followed. Developmental success starting in the late 1990s, combined with ongoing coercion over an increasingly fragmented and weakening opposition, put the ruling CPP in a dominant enough position to concede democracy through strength by the mid-2000s. However, as in Malaysia at almost the same time, it was not to be.

Gathering Economic Strength

Cambodia's post–Cold War economic transformation has been remarkable. With no established command economy or entrenched socialist interests in place to block economic liberalization, the Hun Sen regime made rapid economic development through "resurgent capitalism" its core objective.[58] Even before the civil war and Cold War had ended, the Vietnamese-installed regime had brought a Vietnam-like acceptance for small-scale rural enterprises and independent food production to the countryside. After toppling the Khmer Rouge, the new CPP regime sought to stabilize the situation "simply by indulging Cambodians in their return to prerevolutionary practices."[59] Socialist rhetoric notwithstanding, actual CPP policies have always been characterized by what renowned Cambodia historian David Chandler calls "unrevolutionary caution."[60]

Still, Cambodia had remained utterly dependent on Soviet aid for its survival throughout the 1980s and shifted to similar abject dependence on global development aid in the 1990s. In the wake of destructive civil war, its needs were overwhelming. Even as of 1998, Cambodians had the lowest life expectancy in Asia. Two-thirds of the population remained illiterate, making Cambodia "more comparable to the war-torn states of sub-Saharan Africa than to the economic tigers of Southeast Asia."[61]

As we have seen in other parts of developmental Asia, however, poverty is not an insurmountable obstacle to rapid economic transformation. Even the poorest countries in Asia's hothouse of a developmental neighborhood can boom by opening themselves up to foreign aid and investment, and by removing internal barriers to private enterprise. This was basically all that Cambodia did, and all that it needed to do. From 1998 to 2007, its annual economic growth rate skyrocketed to nearly 10 percent, which ranked it among the fastest-growing economies worldwide. Growth rates consistently continued to range around 7 percent in the decade that followed. In 2019 Cambodia's growth rate was "the fastest among ASEAN states."[62]

In the context of strongman rule and endemic corruption, Cambodia's developmental miracle has by no means benefited all. Inequality is increasing, environmental degradation is rampant, and labor repression is commonplace. Cambodia's economy today remains highly dependent on foreign aid and investment as well as on natural resources.[63] Nevertheless, while acknowledging that Cambodia clearly belongs at the bottom end of the economic spectrum of strength in the developmental socialist cluster—the cluster itself being one of the two poorest in developmental Asia, alongside developmental militarism—it is clear that the former war-torn basket case has legitimately if belatedly joined the ranks of developmental Asia. "A country that had no paper currency 35 years ago now has a flourishing retail banking sector, while investment funds raise capital for further entrepreneurial ventures," Sebastian

Strangio notes. "The economy is slowly starting to diversify away from low-skilled garment production into more sophisticated forms of industry, such as vehicle manufacturing, electronics, and sporting equipment."[64]

Still, in comparative regional perspective, the developmental transformation led by Cambodia's CPP has been moderate in how much it has reached the average Cambodian citizen. And as we now show, this middling developmental transformation has generated only middling levels of performance legitimacy for the regime, which has translated into the CPP's middling electoral performance.

Muscling to Dominance

Though a far cry from either China's CCP or Vietnam's VCP in its organizational strength and historical revolutionary legitimacy, Cambodia's CPP managed to seize authoritarian power in 1997 with nearly two decades of incumbency and experience under its belt. Built by the VCP in its own image, the CPP by the 1990s was "a cohesive organization with political networks stretching far into the countryside." In the true fashion of a socialist party, furthermore, the CPP "continued to control the military, the police, the bureaucracy, and the courts."[65] The question was whether it would continue to put its strengths to the test of multiparty elections, or whether it would install an uncontested single-party regime in the image of its founder, the VCP.

Both the world-historical moment and Cambodia's deep aid dependency counseled the former. It would take a multiparty election to get Cambodia back in the world's good graces. The 1998 election was a far more authoritarian affair than the 1993 vote, as the CPP enjoyed the unbridled power to dominate media coverage and deploy state agencies to intimidate opposition candidates and voters. Nevertheless, the CPP's victory was a relatively narrow one. Having lost to Funcinpec by a margin of 45 percent to 38 percent in 1993, the CPP prevailed with a margin of 41 percent to 32 percent in 1998, with the newly emergent Sam Rainsy Party securing another 14 percent of the vote. Rather like South Korea's incumbent authoritarian party, which ushered in competitive elections during the late 1980s, Cambodia's ruling party in the late 1990s counted on opposition fragmentation to help pave its way to ongoing domination.

Over the following decade, Hun Sen's CPP built on this slim electoral advantage to ascend to a new apex of authoritarian power. Besides its grip over the central state apparatus, the CPP also gathered strength by leveraging its tight control over the countryside. This was witnessed in the local commune elections of 2002, in which the CPP crushed Funcinpec by a margin of 68 percent to 20 percent. Bereft of access to both rural vote banks and state patronage, Funcinpec began to falter and splinter. In the 2003 national elections, it was again on the losing end, but by an even bigger margin, with the CPP winning 47 percent of the vote and almost 60 percent of all parliamentary seats, or 73 out of 123. Funcinpec and the Sam Rainsy Party won approximately 20 percent of the vote each.

It was thus evident by 2003 that the CPP could rely on a combination of coercive state power, rural party infrastructure, opposition fragmentation, and growing performance legitimacy accrued from the booming economy to dominate Cambodia's multiparty elections. In case the 2003 electoral signal of the regime's strength was not clear enough, 2008 produced an even mightier landslide for the CPP. With Funcinpec in tatters and the Sam Rainsy Party victimized by state manipulation and intimidation, the CPP secured 58 percent of the national vote and 73 percent of parliamentary seats.

Hence, like UMNO-BN in Malaysia, the CPP had coercively muscled and competently governed its way to an apex of electoral power by the mid-2000s. "Many voters were genuinely happy with the stability and development brought by CPP rule."[66] But also like UMNO-BN, the CPP would miss this golden opportunity to liberalize the system at its moment of strength, and suffer a swift downturn that would make it all but impossible for the Hun Sen regime to concede democracy with confidence by the mid-2010s.

Ignoring the 2008 electoral signal came back to bite the Hun Sen regime in 2013. The regime's stepped-up harassment and forced exile of Sam Rainsy only heightened his claim to opposition leadership, echoing Malaysia's experience from repressing Anwar Ibrahim around the same time. Human rights activist Kem Sokha joined forces with Rainsy to form the new Cambodian National Rescue Party (CNRP) in 2012. This unified the opposition and made the 2013 campaign a straight fight between Hun Sen's CPP, with its overwhelming and historically rooted strength in the countryside, and the reformist opposition CNRP, which mobilized an urban-led, predominantly youthful anti-CPP coalition.

The results were a shock to Hun Sen and the CPP, but strikingly similar to what transpired in Malaysia just five years earlier. The CPP failed to win a majority of the vote, narrowly edging out the CNRP 49 percent to 44 percent in votes and 55 percent to 45 percent in seats. The result was so close that the CNRP had every reason to believe that it would have won a free and fair vote. For ten months, it boycotted parliament in protest.

The years from 2013 to 2018 were filled with many twists and turns, but the overall regime trajectory was clear: Hun Sen and his CPP would not let itself face another head-to-head challenge with the CNRP on anything remotely resembling a level playing field. Having eschewed the opportunity to transition to democracy when the CPP was strong a few years before, the incumbent regime found itself on its heels, with less confidence and less incentive to concede democracy. The death knell for multiparty competition was sounded in 2017, when the CNRP made inroads where they were least expected during the local commune elections, which the CPP had thoroughly dominated five years before in 2012. Although the CPP still won 70 percent of all local positions, the CNRP fared much better than it had in the past, securing a result that "would have seemed unthinkable in 2012."[67]

A regime clearly past its apex, the CPP struck back rather than concede reform. Within months, the CNRP was forcibly disbanded, with both Rainsy and Sokha subjected to the full weight of the repressive Hun Sen regime. The CPP did not face a single formidable electoral challenger in 2018, as it did in 2013, but rather twenty splintered parties with no mass support. CNRP leadership called for a boycott of the vote. The second-biggest vote-getter in 2018 would be not an opposition party but spoiled ballots, making up 8.5 percent of the total.[68]

For all intents and purposes, Hun Sen's CPP had returned to fully closed, single-party authoritarianism by 2018. It saw signals of electoral decline and responded by baring its iron claws. Looking back, one could reasonably conclude this was the result Hun Sen always wanted. Consistent with Cambodia's position in the developmental socialist cluster, the ruling regime always seemed motivated by an agenda of reestablishing the single-party rule it enjoyed in the 1980s. Reasonably competitive multiparty elections were tolerated as long as global development aid was a matter of economic life and death and continued to flow into the post–civil war economy. But as China came to play an overwhelming and unconditional role in supporting Cambodia's economy, Hun Sen gained the leeway he needed to avoid democratizing through strength in the 2000s, so he could deepen his one-man rule after his weakness had been fully exposed in the 2010s.[69]

Conclusion

The developmental socialist cluster is entirely a cluster of democracy avoidance. Perhaps this is partly because these three cases remain so early in their economic development trajectories. Perhaps modernization theory will look good over the long haul, with China, Vietnam, and Cambodia all *eventually* moving in more democratic directions as they climb the ladder of national wealth.

Yet there are distinctive features of the developmental socialist cluster that make this sanguine, hopeful trajectory less likely than in those cases we have examined in the developmental statist and militarist clusters, even as socialist China surpasses the wealth of the latter and eventually catches up to the wealth of the former. Throughout the cluster, the absence of clear and powerful signals of incipient decline, the ideological legacies of socialist development and revolutions, the historically grounded anxieties over renewed instability, and ever-growing hostilities with the United States (especially for China) make one pathway to political modernity—democracy through strength—especially unlikely to unfold.

In Cambodia, the specter of democratization through collapse continues to hang over the regime as it contemplates the mortality of Hun Sen. It is no longer clear whether the CPP could expect to thrive in any postauthoritarian scenario, as it likely would have had the incumbent regime initiated genuine political reforms when it was at its strongest after 2008.

In China and Vietnam, by contrast, the potential for democratization through strength and by concession remains ever present. Louder and clearer signals of incipient regime decline against a backdrop of general political stability and regime confidence present the best prospect for China's CCP and Vietnam's VCP to follow this well-traveled route. As long as these regimes retain and do not squander their accumulated strengths by avoiding democracy for too long, stable democracy through strength remains a path that can be chosen, and a path, we submit, that is very much worth choosing.

Conclusion

DEMOCRACY'S UNIVERSALITY AND VULNERABILITY

THE QUESTION OF democratic prospects over the long term hinges on the questions of political stability and economic development. Wherever democracy cannot contribute to stability, it cannot be expected to last. Wherever democracy cannot be expected to coexist with economic development, it cannot be expected to be introduced in the first place. Democracy may very well be a *universal* value, in that people everywhere would generally prefer to be governed democratically than autocratically, all else being equal.[1] But nowhere in the world is democracy the *ultimate* value, in the sense that people anywhere can be expected to prioritize democracy over a peaceful and prosperous way of life. Without peace, prosperity, and stability, democracy is fragile, as we have witnessed in recent decades, with more and more of the democratic gains made during the Third Wave in the latter half of the twentieth century giving way to democratic recession in so much of the world.

Just as democratic deterioration can be undiscriminating when it comes to geography—from the most tenuous democratic bargains in the developing world to supposed democratic stalwarts among wealthy societies—democratic possibility is also universal and unbounded. This book has demonstrated that democracy is as much an "Eastern" phenomenon as a "Western" one; it has no cardinal directions. The fact that democracy is a universal value but not the ultimate value holds true regardless of which continent one stands on. Yet as we show in this book, it has primarily spread in parts of "developmental Asia" where authoritarian rulers were confident that democratization would not lead to political destabilization or to their own unceremonious removal from power.

Where those confident expectations were fulfilled, notably in the developmental statist cluster (Japan, Taiwan, and South Korea), democracy has endured and remained stable. In regimes less confident about future stability and victory, however, democracy may have been introduced, but its path to consolidation has been rocky and at times reversible, a pattern exemplified by the developmental militarist cluster (Indonesia, Thailand, and Myanmar). Where democracy has delivered unwelcome surprises to old authoritarian elites, either by threatening them with a total loss of influence and status or by undermining political stability, democratic experiments have generally ended with authoritarian reversals. Weak authoritarian regimes that lack such confidence altogether, we show, have generally avoided democracy, fearful that in democracy's wake their societies might implode or that the introduction of competitive democracy might spell their permanent political obsolescence.

By examining twelve cases in what we call developmental Asia, we have shown how democracy can both inspire universal aspiration and foment universal trepidation. The aspiration comes from democracy's promise to contribute to human freedom and flourishing. The trepidation comes from democracy's intrinsic disruptive potential. By unleashing competitive passions into the public square, it can all too easily deteriorate into gridlock, polarization, and chaos.

Nothing about these dueling aspirations and trepidations is uniquely Western or Eastern, however; nothing about them is either modern or ancient. Democracy's fate in the remainder of the twenty-first century, therefore, hinges on the same factors and forces that have determined its fate in every century until now. Either democracy finds a way to speak to the eternal questions of peace and prosperity, or autocrats will eventually subdue it into silence, and find ample public support for their decisions to do so.

Democracy and Stability

The second decade of the twenty-first century has made it abundantly clear that authoritarianism is as prolific as democracy. Democratic values on their own are no defense against the rise of authoritarianism anywhere, even in the most "consolidated" or "mature" democracies, because authoritarianism can appear to offer a ready-made solution to problems of societal division, political instability, economic decline, and violent conflict. Authoritarianism also stands as a permanent temptation to leaders who are either so enamored with their own visions for a righteous society or so covetous of unchecked power that democracy, by offering full political rights to their enemies, becomes perceived as a hindrance to their nation's progress instead of one of its cornerstones.

Authoritarian antecedents, however, are not necessarily anathema to democratic prospects. Authoritarian success does not close off a democratic future. Specifically, in this book we argue that democracy can arise from authoritarian strength whenever antecedent authoritarian state and party institutions are strong. Accumulated strengths result from a developmental track record that inspires confidence among leaders within the incumbent regime about their popular legitimacy, while generating more demanding citizens within society. When authoritarian regimes receive clear and early signals of their weakening grip on power, they are more likely to experiment with a democratic pathway if they are confident that democratic transition will neither destabilize the country's trajectory for peace and prosperity nor trigger their own political death spiral. Regimes with ample confidence may therefore strategize that a democratic route to winning power can help them maintain their political relevance, or even dominance.

In other words, democracy through strength presents a paradox: an authoritarian regime is more likely to concede democracy when it is strong, yet its prevailing strengths may encourage that regime to maintain its authoritarian rule. Signals of decline, both ominous and reassuring to the regime, are critical in helping it navigate its decision to stay the authoritarian course or initiate democracy through strength. We have seen this play out in a variety of historical contexts, from the relatively smooth and gradual transitions in postwar Japan and Taiwan, to the far rockier and more uncertain transitions in post–Cold War Indonesia and Thailand.

One way to interpret the argument and evidence offered in this book is that democracy should *only* be pursued through strength.[2] We indeed contend that stable democratization is more likely when the incumbent regime is in a relatively strong position. We have also shown that stronger authoritarian regimes in developmental Asia have democratized in a smoother and more stabilizing fashion than the region's weaker authoritarian regimes. Yet this should not imply that weaker authoritarian regimes must remain stubbornly authoritarian for purposes of stability and development. For several reasons, even democratizing *through weakness* can sometimes address the problem of instability and underdevelopment more effectively than remaining authoritarian indefinitely, or even in the short term.

For starters, weak authoritarianism is the worst of all worlds. Freedoms are denied, and so is good governance, because good governance requires strong institutions.[3] To paraphrase James Madison, weak autocracies are neither empowered to govern society nor required to control themselves. From there, literally anything might seem like an improvement.

Yet to be sure, democratization does not necessarily solve the problem of state governance and state strength. Under certain conditions, the dislodging of a weak authoritarian regime can precipitate societal breakdown and even civil war or international conflict.[4] Just because "après moi le déluge" is a perpetual dictatorial assertion does not mean it is always a lie. Indeed, weak autocrats often stay in power precisely by keeping their societies divided and demoralized, incapable of self-governance absent the dictator's mediation and directives. They claim their societies will implode if they are no longer in control. Weak dictators make the status quo a misery while also making any exit from the status quo an even more terrifying prospect.

The critical point is that an authoritarian regime needs strong state institutions to be durably stable. A strong leader can stabilize an authoritarian regime and oversee economic development for a time; but just as no man is an island, neither is any man an institution. Mao Zedong's cult of personality contributed to the Chinese regime's institutional and organizational weakness on the eve of the Tiananmen protests in 1989, making it impossible for the Chinese Communist Party to democratize from strength. Personalist strongman rule undermines regime confidence, from Mao's China to Syngman Rhee's South Korea. An iron fist is but a poor and passing substitute for an iron cage. Hence when looking at weak authoritarian regimes, the urgent question is whether their leaders are striving to build stronger political institutions, even if not democratic institutions.[5] Where they do, autocrats not only improve the lives of their subjects in the short run; they also unwittingly lay the potential groundwork for democratization through strength in the longer run.

This means we should be looking at authoritarian regimes through lenses other than the standard lens of "democracy promotion." Whether an authoritarian regime is durable is not simply a question of how long its subjects must suffer without democracy. It is also a question of how well they live now, and how promising their prospects are to experience a stabilizing democratization outcome over time. Authoritarian regimes that make genuine collective efforts to promote economic development, improve popular welfare, and build more predictable and durable political institutions should be offered the international community's conditional encouragement rather than unrelenting pressure. By laying a stronger foundation for eventual stable democratic transition, gradual authoritarian strengthening is generally a preferable outcome to sudden and total authoritarian collapse.

International advocates for democracy, in other words, should ironically be on the lookout for long-term democratic prospects in *strong* authoritarian regimes rather than cultivating and exploiting sources of authoritarian weakness to encourage a potentially disastrous regime collapse. The implication is not that authoritarian regimes must singly pursue economic development before countenancing democratization, however. As we have argued in this book, it is much easier and far more straightforward to democratize preemptively during relatively stable times than it is to continue to build up stronger political institutions and generate an impressive economic track record under perpetual authoritarian conditions.[6] We insist that both of these approaches can be viable paths from the dismal equilibrium of weak and personalized authoritarianism to improved political stability and economic development.

Why might a weak state be more stable under democratic than authoritarian conditions? Because whereas authoritarian regimes require state strength to be stable beyond the uncertain writ of any individual ruler, democracies can become functionally stable even in the absence of a strong state. The key to stability in transitional democracies is not exclusively the strength of the state, but the crafting of an inclusive *political settlement* binding all leading political actors into the democratic game.[7] Even in the presence of weak state institutions, the predictable rhythms of democracy can emanate from an underlying agreement to transfer power peacefully through competitive elections, and to exercise power judiciously through executive constraints. Democracy works when the winners do not punish the losers, as they accept that they too might eventually suffer the inconvenience of losing.[8] Domestic tranquility and stability need not come from the power of a Hobbesian state that overawes all; they can also arise from all sides' confidence that no such Leviathan will be turned against them by their rivals.

Long-term democratic stability in places such as postwar Japan, Taiwan, South Korea, and even Indonesia was won because both the democratic champions in the opposition and the incumbent authoritarian successor parties eventually became self-interested agents for democratic persistence. Together they regularized democracy, locked into a game in which neither side could destroy the other and both sides potentially benefited. This is the basis of democracy's durability.

It would be naïve to suggest that introducing democracy necessarily and always increases stability; but no more naïve than to believe that remaining authoritarian necessarily provides lasting stability. Authoritarian regimes appear stable until they are not, and upon crumbling, they reveal the scars of authoritarian decay and institutional rot masked by the regime.

Therefore, because democratization through strength delivers the universal value of democracy without undermining the ultimate values of peace and prosperity, every authoritarian regime with the potential to build stronger institutions should be expected to be laying the necessary institutional foundations for a possible democratic future. And if the political conditions are not propitious for an authoritarian regime to build stronger institutions and a wealthier economy, moving decisively to negotiate a lasting political settlement with opposition forces offers a more reliable and durable path to peace and prosperity than the interminable, cynical waiting game of weak dictators: "après moi le déluge."

The Tragedy of Dominant Parties

A central lesson of this book is that democratization need not emerge from the ashes of a collapsed authoritarian regime. In fact, one interpretation of our analysis is that we are better off growing democracy from the soil of strong existing authoritarian regimes, to avoid the difficult scenario of seeding democracy in the detritus of authoritarian collapse. If democracy is going to spread to the many corners of the world where authoritarian rulers still actively avoid it, it will have to be because those authoritarian rulers come to see democracy as compatible with their own self-interest.

Even when teeming crowds numbering in the hundreds of thousands bring down a despised dictator, there are virtually always incumbent political elites behind the scenes who wisely welcome a decisive democratizing change. To be ruled by an autocrat always means accepting the existential political uncertainty of living under a government both electorally irremovable and legally unbound and unrestrained.[9] Democratization means swapping one set of political risks and uncertainties for another.[10] Our point, however, is that democracy is not so risky for either the incumbent regime or society at large when it is pursued from a position of authoritarian strength.[11]

There is another implication that applies to any authoritarian regime, even relatively weak ones, that have chosen a strategy of democracy avoidance for any appreciable length of time. Simply put, time is almost never on the autocrats' side. Nothing is forever, including the life span of the seemingly most stable of autocratic regimes.

Delaying democratic reforms does not make an authoritarian regime grow stronger roots. Over time, public dissatisfaction with authoritarian rule is likely to grow in tandem with the size of the middle class. Ironically, the more economically successful the regime, the faster it creates the conditions for its own growing opposition, an increasingly demanding citizenry that foments a Tocquevillian revolution of rising expectations.

Only the most spectacularly successful authoritarian regimes can provide the middle class with enough economic blandishments to compensate for a denial of democracy over the long haul. Singapore is a case in point. As we have shown in this book, even in rare cases like Singapore and possibly post-1989 China, the ranks of the dissatisfied are likely to grow with every year that authoritarianism remains in place, especially over the long run.

In this book, we have encountered a diverse set of dominant authoritarian parties that failed to pursue democratic reforms when they were still at or near their apex of power, only to see their popularity plummet while they stubbornly remained authoritarian. In Malaysia, the regime missed its bittersweet spot and lost power entirely, at least for a time. The regimes in Hong Kong and Cambodia similarly missed the window of opportunity to concede democratic reform from a position of strength, leaving them with fewer and fewer options to rejuvenate their rule, and ultimately mired in embittered authoritarianism. These regimes provide a lesson and a cautionary tale, *the tragedy of dominant parties*, for Asia's remaining authoritarian ruling parties in China, Singapore, and Vietnam: authoritarian strength is a resource that can be converted into lasting democratic stability, but waiting too long to cash in on that resource by democratizing through strength can lead to that regime's irreversible decline.

Perhaps the ultimate implication of our book for authoritarian regimes around the world is that preemptive reform provides excellent insurance against the almost certain destruction that follows sudden and total regime collapse: an outcome, we contend, that even the most fervent democracy promoters should never promote. Even the most successful authoritarian regimes should recognize that building institutional strengths and expanding the economic pie can never serve as a permanent substitute for democratization, but that doing so now can lay the firmest foundations for democratization to succeed in the future.

The smoothest path to democracy may be different for strong and weak authoritarian regimes. The strong can make new democratic concessions on their own timing and their own terms, while the weak ones must typically forge new political settlements with their opponents through unpleasant and unfamiliar processes of inclusive negotiation. With both paths, however, the process of transformation will almost surely be smoother the sooner it begins.

NOTES

Chapter 1

1. Although the Asian continent spreads all the way from Oceania through Russia to the Middle East, by "Asia" we refer strictly to the southwesterly sweep of nonlandlocked countries from Japan to the eastern edge of the Indian subcontinent.

2. Of our twelve cases, Hong Kong and Taiwan stand apart for not being internationally recognized as "countries" or "nations." But Taiwan is self-governing enough, and Hong Kong is informatively comparable enough to the other two cases in what we shall call the "developmental Britannia" cluster (Singapore and Malaysia), to warrant their inclusion.

3. The most common way to explore patterns of democratization widely across both Northeast and Southeast Asia has been through edited volumes. Worthy examples include Morley (1993); Laothamatas (1997); Sachsenroder and Frings (1998); Johannen and Gomez (2001); Alagappa (2004); Diamond, Plattner, and Chu (2013); Hicken and Kuhonta (2015); and Croissant and Hellman (2020).

4. We explore the more general global pattern of "authoritarian-led democratization," a broader category of which democracy through strength in Asia is an exemplar, in Riedl et al. (2020). Our argument that democratization can mean a new life rather than the end of the road for authoritarian elites closely parallels that of Albertus and Menaldo (2018, 2014). For compelling cross-national quantitative evidence that authoritarian incumbents very frequently retain power after accepting democratic elections, see M. Miller (2021a, 2021b). Haggard and Kaufman (2016, 348–49) see "institutional transitions" as one recurrent type in which "authoritarian elites could, through incremental changes, abide by commitments they themselves had made, which moved systems in a more open direction." Langston (2017) provides an excellent study of such processes in the case of Mexico.

5. Grzymala-Busse (2002) famously calls this a "usable past" for former authoritarians: in her case, former communists in Eastern Europe.

6. Boix (2003) and Acemoglu and Robinson (2006) argue that extreme economic inequality hinders democratic transitions by posing an extreme threat of economic redistribution to the wealthy. Haggard and Kaufman (2012, 2018) and Slater, Smith, and Nair (2014) find that actual political transitions rarely fit the redistributive model, but this does not mean that perceived redistributive threats are irrelevant when autocrats and their allies ponder the risks of democratization. Ansell and Samuels (2014) challenge the redistributive model at its very roots, offering the argument and considerable evidence that the greatest threat to expropriate the rich comes from an authoritarian state, not the democratically emboldened poor.

7. Tocqueville ([1858] 1955, 180–87) famously argued that reforms could spark rather than snuff out revolutionary pressures. If this is true, we should expect to see most democratic experiments get reversed as society radicalizes. In our reading of de Tocqueville and by our own logic, however, it is not the mere promise of reforms but the failure to fulfill public reform promises that most predictably raises revolutionary pressures.

8. This is consistent with Dahl's (1971) memorable claim that democracy becomes more likely as the costs of repression begin to exceed the costs of toleration. Our analysis seeks to assess how those competing costs—which are really more like competing risks—actually get perceived and assessed as concrete historical processes.

9. Hutchcroft (2000) provides the most compelling analysis of how American colonialism bequeathed a much weaker bureaucratic state in the Philippines than other colonizers did elsewhere in Asia.

10. On war by miscalculation, the classic work is Fearon (1995); on democratization by miscalculation, see Treisman (2020). An equally classic work of international relations that aligns more closely with our logic is Keohane (1984), which argues that dominant nations can respond to relative decline by building *international institutions* that help them preserve much of the hegemonic status quo. Hegemonic ruling parties in developmental Asia have accomplished something quite similar by introducing *democratic institutions*.

11. Authoritarian regimes might also liberalize elections from a position of strength and confidence yet only reform as far as to become what Yonatan Morse evocatively calls a "tolerant hegemony." A prime African example is Tanzania after the Cold War, where "the more open electoral process was not forced liberalization, but a sign of the regime's confidence in its ability to contest the election" (Morse 2019, 22). Historically low levels of physical repression surrounding the electoral process in Singapore and Malaysia can be understood in similar terms.

12. The literature on Northeast Asian developmental states is massive, befitting the topic's colossal world-historical importance. Studies include Johnson (1982); Haggard (1990); Wade (1990); Woo (1991); Evans (1995); Kohli (2004); Doner, Ritchie, and Slater (2005); Vu (2010); J. Wong (2011); and Ang (2016).

13. Our definition of developmental Asia is broader than some common definitions of "developmental states," and narrower than others. Inclusion in developmental Asia requires more than simply having a state that sees its role as promoting economic development (as in broad definitions), but demands less than having a state capable of fostering national technological upgrading and export competitiveness in the world's leading economic sectors (as in the strictest definitions).

14. The existence of victory confidence and stability confidence thus presupposes that a regime also enjoys *immunity confidence*, or the confidence that defeat after democratization would not be accompanied by legal punishment for behaviors under authoritarianism (Nalepa 2010). By our definition, a regime that enjoys immunity confidence but not victory or stability confidence can only democratize through weakness, not strength, because conceding democracy indeed means conceding defeat—just not a crushing defeat that includes entering prison as well as exiting office.

15. We use "incumbent" and "conservative" interchangeably because once authoritarian regimes become incumbents, they take on a conservative sheen at least insofar as they seek to retain their own power. That being said, developmental Asian authoritarian regimes have also

been conservative in the more specific sense that they have been more doggedly committed to pursuing rapid market-oriented growth than to building redistributive welfare states. This ideological conservatism in developmental Asia is a feature not only of ruling parties but of ruling militaries as well. Nor is conservativism in developmental Asia limited to the economic sphere. For an argument that "moral conservatism" underpins accountability claims in Southeast Asia more than "democratic assertiveness," see Rodan and Hughes (2014, 3). For the perspective that the conservatism of Confucianism shapes democratic outcomes in Northeast Asia, see Bell and Li (2013) and Sungmoon Kim (2014). To the extent that Confucian ideologies make democracies more conservative, they should only reinforce the stabilizing effects of strong institutions emphasized in this book. As for whether Confucianism is a barrier to democratization itself, the cases of Japan, South Korea, and Taiwan speak volumes, at a loud volume.

16. See Ziblatt (2017) on how strong conservative parties smoothed more "settled" democratization pathways in Western Europe than the "unsettled" paths followed by countries where conservative parties were weak. Riedl (2014) similarly traces the stability and consolidation of party systems in Africa to legacies of strong, rurally rooted authoritarian parties.

17. Kuhonta's (2011) argument that Malaysia has surpassed Thailand in pursuing equitable development because of its stronger civilian political institutions can be extended to the developmental Britannia and developmental militarist clusters more generally.

18. We first elaborated our causal theory of strengths, signals, and strategies in Slater and Wong (2013).

19. Levitsky and Way (2010).

20. Schedler (2013).

21. This is also not to say that illiberal democracy is a preferable form of government to electoral authoritarianism; arguably, illiberal democracy is far worse. It is simply to insist that considerable democratic content still exists in regimes that abuse power *after winning elections* rather than abusing the advantages of incumbency *to win elections* in the first place.

22. Loxton (2015); Loxton and Mainwaring (2018).

23. Slater (2003) elaborates this logic.

24. Slater and Fenner (2011). Also see Levitsky and Way (2010); Slater (2010b); and Hassan (2020).

25. On the combination of bureaucratic and patrimonial features in China, see Ang (2016); in Thailand, see Doner (2009).

26. See T. Lee (2015) for a stellar analysis of military cohesion and defection in response to popular uprisings in the Philippines, Indonesia, China, and Burma. Greitens (2016) offers a more general theory for why authoritarian regimes' coercive institutions varied in their cohesion in Taiwan, South Korea, and the Philippines.

27. Treisman (2020).

28. As with the literature on developmental states, the literature on how ruling parties help sustain authoritarian rule is vast. Among many others, see Huntington (1968, 1991b); Geddes (1999); Slater (2003, 2010b); Magaloni (2006); Brownlee (2007); B. Smith (2007); Gandhi (2008); Levitsky and Way (2010); and, more recently, Morse (2019) and Meng (2020).

29. These rising development-driven demands do not necessarily include democratization, however, as Bellin (2002), Tsai (2007), and Rosenfeld (2021) have most recently argued and shown. Whether they do depends much on the political economy of state dependence and

market orientation, as our clustered and development-centered approach to democratization will attempt to capture.

30. Gunitsky (2017) provides the definitive account for why geopolitical shocks create democratic and autocratic waves. For a sophisticated analysis of when and why foreign pressure succeeds in pushing reforms in autocratic contexts, contingent upon how it interacts with domestic politics in general and rulers' calculation of their likely fates in particular, see Escriba-Folch and Wright (2015). On the frequent tension between supporting democratization and potentially undermining the economic and security benefits of a foreign alliance, which helps explain the extreme inconsistency in American foreign policy most notably, see McKoy and Miller (2012).

31. The introduction and empirical chapters in Shih (2020) explore the importance of institutional strength, among other factors, in helping authoritarian regimes survive economic shocks.

32. Slater and Wong (2013).

33. Talmadge (2015, 24) captures this logic eloquently in her study of authoritarian regimes' battlefield effectiveness: "Ambiguous signals from the environment are unlikely to provide adequate motivation for such important changes in long-standing practices that protect the regime, while truly unambiguous signals may come in the form of such devastating, regime-rocking battlefield defeats that recovery is impossible in the timeframe the adversary allows." In such cases, nothing needs to be done until there is nothing left to be done.

Chapter 2

1. Efforts to juxtapose the developmental trajectories of Northeast and Southeast Asia with a single theoretical framework are rare. Pempel (2021, 2005) has been a trailblazer in this regard, focusing somewhat more on distinguishing the diverse economies, ranging from developmental to predatory, than the diverse political regimes, ranging from democratic to autocratic, that populate the Pacific Rim.

2. Although the Opium Wars preceded Meiji reforms and projected British-style capitalism into Asia before Japanese-style developmentalism, this did not plant the seeds for developmental Asia because the region is defined by its Japan-like features, while Britain-like features only define one of its four clusters.

3. The term "revolution from above" was coined by Trimberger (1978), who treated Japan as one of her core cases of the concept. On *fukoku kyohei*, see Samuels (1996).

4. Hatch and Yamamura (1996) and Hatch (2010) provide indispensable analyses of how Japan's developmental spread into Asia both began and evolved.

5. On the substantial diversity in developmental outcomes arising out of British colonialism, with cases of highly transformative postcolonial growth like Hong Kong, Malaysia, and Singapore being more the exception than the rule, see Lange (2009).

6. Studies of authoritarian legal development in developmental Britannia include Silverstein (2008) on Singapore, Tam (2013) on Hong Kong, and Moustafa (2018) on Malaysia.

7. Coppedge et. al. (2020). The Varieties of Democracy project does not establish arbitrary thresholds for where authoritarianism ends and democracy begins. But it might be helpful to compare our four developmental Asian clusters to well-known regimes outside Asia to give a

sense of how they shape up in comparative perspective. With its score hovering around 0.8, the developmental statist cluster approximates the robust liberal democracy of the United Kingdom; closer to 0.1, the developmental socialist cluster is in the same ballpark as Vladimir Putin's strongman regime in Russia. The militarist cluster lies close to the wobbly but surviving democracy in Nigeria (around 0.3), while the Britannia cluster is more comparable to the durable hegemonic electoral regime of Yoweri Museveni in Uganda (approximately 0.25).

8. Huntington (1991a, 598) asserted at the Cold War's end that "the halfway house cannot stand," meaning that regimes combining electoral and authoritarian features would either fully democratize or revert to closed authoritarianism. The ubiquity of "hybrid regimes" after the Cold War indicates just how wrong this claim was.

9. Crouch (1995) examines how repression and responsiveness were combined in Malaysia before the Mahathir regime took its repressive turn in the late 1990s and early 2000s. Elstrom (2021) explores mixed strategies of repression and responsiveness to labor in China, again mostly before the CCP's repressive turn under Xi Jinping. While competitive elections and authoritarianism are apparently easy to combine, pace Huntington, the combination of genuine responsiveness with physical repression might be harder to sustain.

10. On these processes in East Asian cases, see Looney (2020). On the politics of land reform in autocracies more globally, see Albertus (2015).

11. Ginsburg and Moustafa (2008).

12. For global quantitative evidence that regional and separatist rebellions are strongly associated with both the rise and endurance of military rule, see Eibl, Hertog, and Slater (2021).

13. On the greater prior emphasis on social and economic rights than civil and political rights in Chinese historical development—reversing the Western European sequence of rights extensions famously posited by Marshall (1950)—see Perry (2008). For the more general point that democracy is always at least somewhat vernacular, understood differently in different societies, see Schaffer (1998).

Chapter 3

1. Dower (1999).

2. Haddad (2012), 7.

3. Gordon (2014).

4. Trimberger (1978).

5. Evans and Rauch (1999) demonstrate how meritocratic recruitment into national bureaucracies reliably predicts economic development in a large sample of developing world economies.

6. Johnson (1982).

7. Quoted in Takenaka (2014), 96–97.

8. See Scalapino and Masumi (1962); Takenaka (2014).

9. Gordon (1991), 50. This conceptualization of Taisho-era imperial democracy bears striking parallels to the uneasy periods of military and civilian cohabitation in Thailand, Indonesia, and Myanmar, discussed in chapter 7.

10. Takayoshi (1966); Takenaka (2014), esp. chap. 6.

11. Gordon (1991), chap. 9.

12. Duus and Okimoto (1979).

13. Gordon (2014), 229.

14. Rinjiro (1983), 354.

15. For a detailed account of the negotiations during the constitutional drafting process in 1946, see Dower (1999), chap. 13.

16. Quoted in Dower (1999), 376.

17. Quoted in Dower (1999), 400.

18. Kohno (1997), 34.

19. Przeworski (1991).

20. Kohno (1997), chap. 3.

21. Johnson (1982); Pempel (1992).

22. Grzymala-Busse (2002).

23. See Scalapino and Masumi (1962); Nakamura (1994); Dower (1999), chap. 17.

24. J. Miller (2019), 61–62.

25. Cha (2016).

26. See Pempel (1990, 1992); Kohno (1997); Krauss and Pekkanen (2010).

27. Johnson (1982).

28. Milly (1999); Kasza (2006). Postwar Japan posted rapid economic growth rates while maintaining a very egalitarian distribution of income, a pattern emulated by its developmental progeny, Taiwan and South Korea.

29. Wong (2004a, 2004b); Peng and Wong (2008). All of the major social policy legislation introduced in postwar Japan—and in the other developmental statist cases—was promulgated by the incumbent conservative ruling parties. For a comparison of welfare-state expansion in East Asia with that in Latin America and Eastern Europe, see Haggard and Kaufman (2008).

Chapter 4

1. Tien (1989), 64.

2. Dickson (1996).

3. Tien (1989), 67–68.

4. Dickson (1997).

5. Johnson (1999), 39. For an excellent historical and historiographical account of the developmental state concept, see Haggard (2018).

6. Amsden (1985); Gold (1986); Haggard (1990); Wade (1990).

7. See Looney (2020).

8. Wade (1990), 272. See also T.-J. Cheng (1990); V. Wang (1995). The KMT pursued an SME-led growth strategy in part to prevent the concentration of economic power in the hands of local Taiwanese industrialists.

9. J. Wong (2020). Taiwan's strategy of adjustment to the OPEC price spikes was the opposite of South Korea's response, which was to accelerate, rather than rein in, economic productivity. The contrast is further explored in chapter 5.

10. Breznitz (2008); J. Wong (2011).

11. Tien (1989), 42.

12. Wong (2004b), 57–61. See also Ku (1997).

13. Winckler (1984); T.-J. Cheng (1989).

14. T.-F. Huang (1996); Rigger (1999).

15. Chu (1992).

16. See Wachman (1994). For an anthropological perspective on Taiwanese identity, see Melissa Brown (2004).

17. Rigger (2001).

18. Tsang (1999), 1.

19. Chao and Myers (1998), 133.

20. Jacobs (2012), 61.

21. Chao and Myers (1998), 93.

22. Quoted in Moody (1992), 92.

23. Rigger (1999), 128.

24. Chu (1992), 104–5.

25. Haggard and Kaufman (1995).

26. Dickson (1997), 213.

27. Jacobs (2012), 63.

28. Quoted in Chao and Myers (1998), 126.

29. Hu (1993); Rigger (1999).

30. Dickson (1997); Mattlin (2011).

31. J. Wong (2004b).

32. Albertus and Menaldo (2014).

33. Slater and Wong (2018).

34. T.-J. Cheng (2008); Wong (2008).

35. Slater and Wong (2018).

Chapter 5

1. Heo and Roehrig (2018), 104.

2. Wagner (1961).

3. See Sunhyuk Kim (2000).

4. For an in-depth account and analysis of the Rhee period, see S.-J. Han (1974). On Rhee's fall from power, see Q.-Y. Kim (1983).

5. E. Kim and Kim (1964).

6. Y. Choi (1978).

7. Oh (1999), 51–52.

8. See B.-K. Kim and Vogel (2011).

9. World Bank (1993).

10. Amsden (1989); Woo (1991).

11. Evans (1995).

12. B.-K. Kim (2011); Moon and Jun (2011).

13. Oh (1999), 59.

14. J. Wong (2020).

15. J.-J. Choi (1993).

16. Oh (1999), 87.

17. Koh (1985); T.-J. Cheng and Kim (1994).

18. Saxer (2002).

19. Quoted in S.-J. Han (1988), 54.

20. Oh (1999), 93.

21. Han (1988).

22. Shorrock (1986).

23. Oh (1999), 93.

24. Fowler (1999), 280.

25. Quoted in Heo and Roehrig (2018), 106.

26. Koo (1993); N. Lee (2007).

27. Cotton (1989), 252.

28. Oh (1999), 94. For a detailed account of Roh's decision-making in the spring and summer of 1987, see Oh (1999), chap. 5.

29. Saxer (2002), 61.

30. On both the difficulty and indispensability of opposition unity in removing autocratic regimes through the ballot box, see Arriola (2013) and Ong (2022).

31. Cotton (1989, 1997); B.-K. Kim (1998).

32. S.-J. Kim (1994), 187.

33. Quoted in S.-C. Lee and Campbell (1994), 42, 45.

34. J. Wong (2004a, 2004b).

35. On South Korean conservatives' process of "learning to lose" under democracy, see B.-K. Kim (2008).

Chapter 6

1. Spence (1990), 747.

2. Nolan (1995).

3. The chapters in Dimitrov (2013) provide excellent treatments of why communism collapsed in some cases but not others, including China and Vietnam.

4. Pye (1991).

5. Friedman, Pickowicz, and Selden (1991).

6. Dikotter (2013).

7. White (1993).

8. MacFarquhar (1983); Dikotter (2010); Yang (2012).

9. For a comprehensive and detailed account of the years leading up to the Cultural Revolution, and specifically Mao's role in instigating the revolution, see Roderick MacFarquhar's three-volume series, *The Origins of the Cultural Revolution* (1974, 1983, 1999), esp. vol. 3.

10. Pye (1991), 302.

11. White (1993), chap. 1.

12. Lieberthal and Oksenberg (1988); Baum (1996).

13. See Zweig (2002).

14. See Y. Huang (2005).

15. For comprehensive accounts of the zigs and zags of the post-1978 economic reform era, see Naughton (1996) and Wedeman (2003).

16. In the Chinese political economy literature, Chen Yun and his CCP allies are often referred to as "conservative" reformers, distinct from more liberal reformers such as Zhao Ziyang. For the purposes of our analysis, however, we refrain from using this term because in this book, "conservative reform" refers to more market-regarding, liberal economic reform.

17. Spence (1990).

18. Naughton (1996), chap. 7.

19. Spence (1990).

20. Unger (1991); Ogden et al. (1992).

21. Nathan (2019). See also National Security Archive (2001).

22. Dittmer (2001), 482.

23. Bell (2015); Tang (2018).

24. Shambaugh (2008). See also Shambaugh's influential *Wall Street Journal* essay "The Coming Chinese Crackup" (2015).

25. Dickson (1997).

Chapter 7

1. For ruling militaries, the politics of stability is very tightly intertwined with the politics of impunity. For an interpretation of Thai political history as one centered on military impunity, in both autocratic and democratic times—an insight that applies equally well in Indonesia and Myanmar—see Haberkorn (2018).

2. The developmental militarist cases thus more closely approximate Albertus and Menaldo's (2014) "gaming democracy" model than the developmental statist cluster, where conservative elites in all three cases proved "game for democracy" (Slater and Wong 2018). Consistent with our theory, Indonesia gamed democracy least (Horowitz 2013), and South Korea gamed democracy most, in their respective clusters.

3. Haggard (1990).

4. Moore (1966).

5. Roosa (2006, 2020).

6. Bowie (1997) provides a chilling anthropological account of the August 1976 killings.

7. Hicken (2006) offers the definitive institutionalist treatment of this dramatic shift.

8. Slater (2013) compares the more severe "democratic careening" in 2000s Thailand than in Taiwan.

9. Sundhaussen (1995) astutely and precociously recognized how Myanmar's generals saw Indonesia as a potential model, albeit before the Suharto regime fell.

10. For a sophisticated argument that the Suharto regime simply could not hold its diverse elite coalition together with any economic policy response to the crisis, see Pepinsky (2009). On the Indonesian fiscal state's incapacity to respond effectively in any event, see Hamilton-Hart (2002).

11. J. Sidel (1998) provides a particularly riveting firsthand account and historical analysis.

12. The contrast between Indonesia after the fall of Suharto and Egypt after the fall of Hosni Mubarak is especially revealing here. See Mietzner (2014) for a comparative account, stressing the need for civilian elites to remain unified to keep a recently ousted military out of politics.

13. Horowitz (2013) offers the definitive theoretical and historical account of how post-1999 constitution-making in Indonesia—"an inside job" among elite insiders, devoid of popular

input—ironically furthered democratic consolidation. Shair-Rosenfield (2019) deftly explores how elites gained knowledge and experience through iterated reform episodes over time.

14. Huntington (1991a, 1991b) coined this famous phrase in reference to the worldwide wave of democratizations between the mid-1970s and early 1990s.

15. Haggard and Kaufman (1995).

16. B. Smith (2007) compellingly argues that Indonesian state-building in the late 1960s and early 1970s *preceded* the global oil boom, leading to more fortuitous results for the economy and more fortifying effects on the authoritarian regime than in cases in which state-led development *followed* the boom (e.g., Iran).

17. See the classic debate between Lev (1990) and Liddle (1990) over whether Indonesia's growing middle class would eventually support democratization and the rule of law.

18. Anderson (1983).

19. The restive provinces of Aceh and Irian Jaya (renamed West Papua after democratization) suffered terrible intermittent repression as well, though not on the magnitude of East Timor.

20. Slater (2010b).

21. B. Smith (2007) explores Indonesia's bureaucratic development in this pivotal period nationally, in an analysis deeply influenced by Schiller's (1996) analysis of such state-building dynamics at the local level.

22. Slater (2010a).

23. Tomsa (2008) and Harjanto (2010) provide excellent institutionalist analyses of Golkar as a party, both under and after Indonesia's authoritarian years.

24. For a treatment of the PDI and PPP as "semi-opposition" in the sense first used by Juan Linz, see Aspinall (2005).

25. MacIntyre (2001); Pepinsky (2009).

26. Slater (2010b).

27. Anderson (1978) offers a spectacular analysis from the time on why the crisis erupted; B. Smith (2007) provides the best analysis for how and why the regime survived it.

28. On the Islamic side of Indonesia's civil society under Suharto, see Hefner (2000). On the enormous contributions of the Nahdlatul Ulama and Muhammadiyah to Islamic organizational strength, see Bush (2010) and Menchik (2016).

29. Crouch (2011), 25, 207.

30. Crouch (2011), 9.

31. O'Donnell and Schmitter (1986); Geddes (1999).

32. Aspinall (2010) argues that this incorporation of old authoritarian elites simultaneously explains both the impressive stability and unimpressive quality of Indonesian democracy. Mietzner (2020) analogously demonstrates that the authoritarian-era Indonesian state fostered both democratic survival and democratic stagnation.

33. Slater (2004, 2018).

34. Crouch (2010).

35. Friedman and Wong (2008).

36. Mietzner (2012); Aspinall and Berenschot (2019); Power and Warburton (2020).

37. Haggard and Kaufman (1995) treat Thailand as a paradigmatic case of a "non-crisis" democratic transition in the 1980s, along with South Korea.

38. Of the many books that cover Thailand's populist shift under Thaksin, McCargo and Ukrist (2005) and Pasuk and Baker (2009) stand out. Sinpeng (2021) offers an excellent account of street protests and antidemocratic attitudes among conservatives in Thailand's democratic demise.

39. Larsson (2013) and Ferrara (2015) provide outstanding recent accounts of Thailand's political-economic development from a longue durée perspective. Ungpakorn (1997) offers a more critical and local Marxist account.

40. See Doner, Ritchie, and Slater (2005) and Doner (2009) on Thailand's intermediate and uneven state capacity to pursue industrial upgrading in comparative perspective.

41. Kuhonta (2011, 122). On Thailand's surprising relative success in health policy, see Selway (2015) and Harris (2017).

42. Walker (2012) explores the rise of Thailand's rural middle class under rapid capitalist development.

43. Chaloemtiarana (2007) provides a remarkable historical analysis of the Sarit era.

44. Huntington (1968).

45. Hicken (2009) offers the definitive comparative and theoretical account of Thai political parties' enduring fragmentation. Ockey (2004) expertly explores how parties' weak societal linkages helped shape Thailand's relatively low democratic quality.

46. Slater (2010b).

47. Bowie (1997).

48. McCargo (2005).

49. O'Donnell and Schmitter (1986).

50. Nishizaki (2011) provides a masterful ethnographic study of elitism and electoral clientelism in the Thai countryside.

51. Riedl et al. (2020).

52. Hicken (2006).

53. See McCargo (2008) on the politics of the Muslim insurgency in the Thai south, and Sinpeng (2021) on the pendular mobilization between "yellow shirts" and "red shirts" that culminated in military intervention.

54. For an analysis that zeroes in more on the geopolitical benefits accompanying political liberalization for Myanmar's military, see Slater (2014). M. Wong (2019) rightly stresses internal over external dynamics, however, when comparing Myanmar's democratic advances with Thailand's democratic breakdown during the 2010s. Egreteau and Jagan (2013) survey the military's foreign relations more broadly.

55. For expertly informed critiques of the shallowness of Myanmar's democratic experiment, Lintner (2013) and Morgenbesser (2016) are excellent examples.

56. Taylor (2001) offers a fine set of essays on Myanmar's political economy in the 1990s. On the rural political economy in this era, see Thawnghmung (2004). Khin (2012) provides a helpful assessment of the economy at the moment of political opening in 2011. McCarthy (2019) critiques both the NLD's weak welfare commitments during the decade of civil-military cohabitation and the parlous state of social welfare under pure military rule.

57. On the lack of "rule of law" as opposed to "law and order" in Myanmar, even after democratic reforms, see Cheesman (2015). Underdeveloped legal institutions are a common feature

of the developmental militarist cluster vis-à-vis the developmental Britannia cluster especially.

58. Callahan (2003); Slater (2010b); T. Lee (2015).

59. Callahan (2003) is the indispensable resource on how the Burmese military's early years paved its path to power. On the 1962–88 period, see Nakanishi (2013).

60. Public remarks at the Myanmar/Burma Update 2013, Australian National University, Canberra, March 2013.

61. Zin and Joseph (2012, 104).

62. Buchanan (2016) offers some of the best analysis of Myanmar's complex set of regional rebellions. Also see M. Smith (1991) and Staniland (2021).

63. On the link between Buddhist nationalist narratives and communal violence in Myanmar during its democratization period, see Walton and Hayward (2014).

Chapter 8

1. One need only pair India with Pakistan, however, to appreciate the limits of arguments stressing the democratic legacies of British colonialism, even in South Asia itself (Tudor 2013).

2. For a highly learned analysis that both appreciates Singapore's uniqueness and manages to cast it in comparative perspective with Malaysia, see Weiss (2021).

3. Given its small size, book-length treatments of Singapore tend to combine considerations of economic development and political control rather than focusing on one or the other. Major examples include Chua (1995), George (2000), Mauzy and Milne (2002), Trocki (2006), Calder (2016), Barr (2019), and Rahim and Barr (2019). See Khong (1995) for a more concise, chapter-length summary.

4. Slater and Smith (2016).

5. On Singapore's struggles to upgrade in the biotech sector—struggles it shares with other leading economies in developmental Asia—see J. Wong (2011).

6. Doner, Ritchie, and Slater (2005).

7. Ortmann (2011) sees this slippage in PAP electoral might during the 2000s as a gradual transition from a more closed to a more competitive authoritarian regime. For an argument that the PAP has become more deeply authoritarian rather than open since 2015, see Abdullah (2020). George (2012) focuses on restrictions of the media under the PAP.

8. Abdullah (2017) argues that Singapore's opposition poses much less of a threat to the ruling regime's legitimating ideology than does Malaysia's, only reinforcing our expectation that democratization in Singapore would be stabilizing more than destabilizing. On the comparability of Singapore and Malaysia as prospects for "strong-state democratization" despite such differences, see Slater (2012).

9. The data in this discussion draw from Chong and Lim (2015).

10. Ong (2022) explores opposition coordination in Singapore in comparative and theoretical perspective.

11. Oliver and Ostwald (2020).

12. For an argument that "conservative democratization" à la Japan or Taiwan would be truer to the PAP's ideological roots than its current path toward "welfarist authoritarianism" à la Malaysia or China, see Slater (2019).

13. Crouch (1995) provides a superb overview of Malaysia's political system at UMNO-BN's historical apex.

14. Gomez and Jomo (1999) is an excellent analytical primer on Malaysia's postcolonial economic development.

15. On the May 1969 riots themselves, see Goh (1971).

16. Jesudason (1989) surveys how ethnicity profoundly shapes Malaysia's political economy.

17. Even before the early 1970s, Malaysia's political system was always highly centralized, despite its de jure federalism, paving the way for the extreme interventionist turn after the 1969 riots (Tilman 1976).

18. Khoo (1995) wrote the definitive exposition of Mahathir and his ideology, in both the economic and political spheres. On how Mahathir personalized power over his two-plus decades of rule, see Hwang (2003) and Slater (2003).

19. Hatch and Yamamura (1996).

20. Slater (2003).

21. Case (1996, 2001) provides useful overviews of the Malaysian regime's durability up until and through the Asian financial crisis.

22. Pepinsky (2009) both establishes the severity and explores the coalitional politics of Malaysia's 1997–98 crash. The chapters in Jomo (2001) examine the crisis in Malaysia's financial sector, in particular, in great depth. On the lasting economic damage done by Mahathir's failures to accept reforms in response to the crisis, see Slater (2020).

23. Weiss (2006) is the consummate study of Malaysian protest during the early *reformasi* years. Heryanto and Mandal (2003) provide a useful comparative perspective on parallel patterns of antiauthoritarian contention in Malaysia and Indonesia.

24. Ooi (2007, 2009) offers sets of analytical essays on the Badawi years.

25. For those interested in Islam's ongoing influence on Malaysian politics and law, see Moustafa (2018). Funston (1980) provides a classic treatment of UMNO and the Partai Islam Se-Malaysia in the first decades of Malaysian independence. Hamayotsu (2002) offers a comparative treatment of Islam and nation-building in Malaysia and Indonesia.

26. On the "deformed" nature of democratization processes in Hong Kong as the British departed, see Baum (2000).

27. S. Yip and Yeung (2014) provide helpful details on Hong Kong's post-handover elections. Ho (1999), Tam (2001), and Lo and Wu (2002) offer earlier contributions in similar fashion.

28. Ma (2005) deftly explores the contentious politics of the 2003 security law. Also see J. Cheng (2005) for more on the Hong Kong democrats' early struggles under Chinese sovereignty.

29. Ortmann (2015) provides an excellent overview of Hong Kong's long political pathway to the explosion of the Umbrella movement.

30. For an interpretation of the Umbrella movement that emphasizes lingering historical identity conflicts between the mainland and Hong Kong, see E. Han (2014). In a similar vein, see Veg (2017). On the role of housing concerns in sparking localism and identity conflict, see S. Wong and Kin (2018).

31. More generally on Hong Kong's limited party institutionalization in recent decades, see Lam (2010).

Chapter 9

1. McAdams (2017) provides a sweeping global history of communist parties. The locus classicus on communist economies, by Kornai (1992), treats domination by such ruling parties as the defining trait of socialist systems, rather than their economic features, prefiguring the economic transformation of communist parties in China and Vietnam, especially after the Cold War.

2. The communist collapse gave way to new forms of authoritarianism rather than democratization in many countries, of course. Intriguingly, Mongolia provides a possible Asian example of democratization through strength in the wake of communism, although, as the country did not "join" developmental Asia through its economic policies in the process, it lies outside the scope of our analysis. Whether Mongolia's democratization since the early 1990s is better considered to have unfolded through strength or weakness is for others to judge.

3. There is a parallel here between the China–Vietnam relationship and the Japan–South Korea rivalry. In both dyads, the weaker party both emulates and resents the stronger.

4. On the Hun Sen regime's enduring personalism and recent descent from competitive to hegemonic authoritarian rule, see Morgenbesser (2018, 2019). Also see Un (2019) for an appropriately critical take.

5. Fewsmith (2001).

6. Naughton (1996); Y. Huang (2008).

7. Gallagher (2002).

8. Montinola, Qian, and Weingast (1995); Zhang (1999); Naughton (2014).

9. Zweig (2002); Hsueh (2011); Shambaugh (2013).

10. Shih (2004).

11. W. Yip and Hsiao (2008); Duckett (2010); Frazier (2010).

12. Shambaugh (2013).

13. Dickson (2003); Tsai (2007).

14. He and Thogersen (2010); He and Warren (2011); Fewsmith (2013); Manion (2015).

15. See Dickson (2016).

16. Wallace (2014).

17. Nathan (2003); Dickson (2016); Li (2016).

18. Pei (2006); Shambaugh (2013).

19. Shih (2009); Naughton (2014); Delisle and Goldstein (2019).

20. Lu and Chan (2016); Ding (2022).

21. Lynch (2015); Dickson (2016).

22. Dickson (2016), 303.

23. Slater and Wong (2013), 719.

24. Dickson (2016); Perry (2018).

25. Gilley (2008).

26. Li (2016); Roberts (2018).

27. Dickson (1997).

28. Fewsmith (2018); Ang (2020).

29. Levitsky and Way (2010).

30. Diamond (2015).

31. Gallagher (2017).

32. Dickson (2016).

33. Chen (2013).

34. Bell (2015).

35. Vu (2010).

36. Kerkvliet (1995).

37. Vu (2017).

38. Vu (2017), 245–46. On Vietnam's "bureaucratic socialism" both before and during doi moi, see Porter (1993).

39. Turley and Selden (1993).

40. Ninh (1990).

41. Elliott (2012), 191, 190.

42. Cima (1989).

43. Stern (1998).

44. Li (2016).

45. Malesky, Abrami, and Yu (2011).

46. Ding (2022), chap. 6.

47. Vasavakul (2019), chap. 4. On the struggles and limitations of building rule of law in reform-era Vietnam, see M. Sidel (2008).

48. At the heart of this literature sit Malesky and Schuler (2010) and Schuler (2021).

49. Kerkvliet (2005, 2019).

50. Nguyen (2016), 90; Kerkvliet (2019), 29.

51. Hellman (1998); Pei (2006); Malesky (2009).

52. Vuving (2013).

53. Heng (2001).

54. Grossman (2020), 9.

55. Grossman (2020), 9.

56. On Cambodia's tortuous path from civil war to UN oversight, see Kiernan (1993), Becker (1998), and Curtis (1998). Kiernan (2008) is a definitive account of the genocidal Khmer Rouge regime itself.

57. Strangio (2014), 55, 56.

58. Strangio (2014), 47.

59. Gottesman (2003), 70.

60. Chandler (2008), 279.

61. Strangio (2014), 156.

62. Ciorcari (2020), 127.

63. Ear (2013), 28.

64. Strangio (2014), 149.

65. Strangio (2014), 63.

66. Strangio (2014), 114.

67. Croissant (2018), 195–96.

68. Croissant (2019), 171.

69. Strangio (2020, chap. 4) expertly surveys China's outsize influence on Cambodia's recent political and economic development.

Conclusion

1. This is not to deny that "democracy" might be understood very differently in different contexts. Nor does "universal" equal "unanimous"—we simply mean that democracy as a value is not culturally bounded. Neither, of course, is authoritarianism. See Yu (2009) on how democracy may be understood differently in China than elsewhere, yet still be desirable.

2. This would be consistent with the Mansfield and Snyder (2007) position in the so-called sequencing debate. Our argument accords with their view that sequencing matters and that prior state-building enhances the stability of democratization, but we agree with Carothers's (2007) rejoinder that democratic elections can stabilize systems and strengthen states under certain conditions. See Slater (2008) for a discussion of mechanisms through which competitive elections can sometimes strengthen rather than weaken the state.

3. Authoritarian strength is necessary but insufficient for good governance. Strong authoritarian regimes might use their strong institutions to repress society rather than serve it.

4. For a compelling argument that new and fragile democracies are more likely to be belligerent overseas than to advance the "democratic peace," see Snyder (2000). Lyons (2005) argues that competitive elections can help stabilize fragile new democracies but that this largely depends on whether the transition also includes political demilitarization (as in Japan in our analysis, most obviously). Mann (2000) offers the grimmest take on what democracy can do: when "the people" is defined in ethnic terms, popular sovereignty can pave a path to genocide.

5. For analyses of the development of executive constraints and the rule of law under authoritarianism, see Meng (2020) and Y. Wang (2014), respectively.

6. Just because the cases in our book have only preemptively democratized under pressure does not mean that authoritarian regimes must wait until pressures arise to democratize preemptively. We see preemptive democratization absent pressures to be unlikely, yet not impossible, and as being faithful to the strategic logic of democracy through strength.

7. Leading works on political settlements include Jamal (2016), Barma (2017), and Khan (2018). For an application to Asia, see Jaffrey and Slater (2017).

8. Friedman and Wong (2008); Levitsky and Ziblatt (2018).

9. Ansell and Samuels (2014).

10. Przeworski (1991).

11. Riedl et al. (2020).

REFERENCES

Abdullah, Walid Jumblatt. 2017. "Bringing Ideology In: Differing Oppositional Challenges to Hegemony in Singapore and Malaysia." *Government and Opposition* 52, no. 3 (July): 483–510.

———. 2020. "'New Normal' No More: Democratic Backsliding in Singapore after 2015." *Democratization* 27, no. 7 (May): 1123–41.

Acemoglu, Daron, and James A. Robinson. 2006. *Economic Origins of Dictatorship and Democracy*. New York: Cambridge University Press.

Alagappa, Muthiah, ed. 2004. *Civil Society and Political Change in Asia: Expanding and Contracting Democratic Space*. Stanford, CA: Stanford University Press.

Albertus, Michael. 2015. *Autocracy and Redistribution: The Politics of Land Reform*. New York: Cambridge University Press.

Albertus, Michael, and Victor Menaldo. 2014. "Gaming Democracy: Elite Domination during Transition and the Prospects for Redistribution." *British Journal of Political Science* 44, no. 3 (July): 575–603.

———. 2018. *Authoritarianism and the Elite Origins of Democracy*. Cambridge: Cambridge University Press.

Amsden, Alice. 1985. "The State and Taiwan's Economic Development." In *Bringing the State Back In*, edited by Peter B. Evans, Dietrich Rueschemeyer, and Theda Skocpol, 78–106. Cambridge: Cambridge University Press.

———. 1989. *Asia's Next Giant: South Korea and Late Industrialization*. Oxford: Oxford University Press.

Anderson, Benedict R. O'G. 1978. "Last Days of Indonesia's Suharto?" *Southeast Asia Chronicle* 63 (July–August): 2–17.

———. "Old State, New Society: Indonesia's New Order in Comparative Historical Perspective." *Journal of Asian Studies* 42, no. 3 (May): 477–96.

Ang, Yuen Yuen. 2016. *How China Escaped the Poverty Trap*. Ithaca, NY: Cornell University Press.

———. 2020. *China's Gilded Age: The Paradox of Economic Boom and Vast Corruption*. Cambridge: Cambridge University Press.

Ansell, Ben W., and David J. Samuels. 2014. *Inequality and Democratization*. Cambridge: Cambridge University Press.

Arriola, Leonardo. 2013. *Multiethnic Coalitions in Africa: Business Financing of Opposition Election Campaigns*. New York: Cambridge University Press.

Aspinall, Edward. 2005. *Opposing Suharto: Compromise, Resistance and Regime Change in Indonesia*. Stanford, CA: Stanford University Press.

———. 2010. "Indonesia: The Irony of Success." *Journal of Democracy* 21, no. 2 (April): 20–34.

Aspinall, Edward, and Ward Berenschot. 2019. *Democracy for Sale: Elections, Clientelism, and the State in Indonesia*. Ithaca, NY: Cornell University Press.

Barma, Naazneen. 2017. *The Peacebuilding Puzzle: Political Order in Post-conflict Societies*. New York: Cambridge University Press.

Barr, Michael D. 2019. *Singapore: A Modern History*. London: I. B. Tauris.

Baum, Richard. 1996. *Burying Mao: Chinese Politics in the Age of Deng Xiaoping*. Princeton, NJ: Princeton University Press.

———. 2000. "Democracy Deformed: Hong Kong's 1998 Legislative Elections—and Beyond." *China Quarterly* 163: 439–64.

Becker, Elizabeth. 1998. *When the War Was Over: Cambodia and the Khmer Rouge Revolution*. New York: PublicAffairs.

Bell, Daniel. 2015. *The China Model: Political Meritocracy and the Limits of Democracy*. Princeton, NJ: Princeton University Press.

Bell, Daniel, and Chenyang Li, eds. 2013. *The East Asian Challenge for Democracy: Political Meritocracy in Comparative Perspective*. New York: Cambridge University Press.

Bellin, Eva. 2002. *Stalled Democracy: Capital, Labor, and the Paradox of State-Sponsored Development*. Ithaca, NY: Cornell University Press.

Boix, Charles. 2003. *Democracy and Redistribution*. Cambridge: Cambridge University Press.

Bowie, Katherine. 1997. *Rituals of National Loyalty: An Anthropology of the State and the Village Scout Movement in Thailand*. New York: Columbia University Press.

Breznitz, Dan. 2008. *Innovation and the State: Political Choice and Strategies for Growth in Israel, Taiwan and Ireland*. New Haven, CT: Yale University Press.

Brown, MacAlister, and Joseph J. Zasloff. 1998. *Cambodia Confounds the Peacemakers, 1979–1998*. Ithaca, NY: Cornell University Press.

Brown, Melissa. 2004. *Is Taiwan Chinese? The Impact of Power, Culture and Migration on Changing Identities*. Berkeley: University of California Press.

Brownlee, Jason. 2007. *Authoritarianism in an Age of Democratization*. New York: Cambridge University Press.

Buchanan, John. 2016. *Militias in Myanmar*. New York: Asia Foundation.

Bush, Robin. 2010. *Nahdlatul Ulama and the Struggle for Power within Islam and Politics in Indonesia*. Singapore: Institute of Southeast Asian Studies.

Calder, Kent E. 2016. *Singapore: Smart City, Smart State*. Washington, DC: Brookings Institution Press.

Callahan, Mary P. 2003. *Making Enemies: War and State Building in Burma*. Ithaca, NY: Cornell University Press.

Carothers, Thomas. 2007. "How Democracies Emerge: The 'Sequencing' Fallacy." *Journal of Democracy* 18, no. 1 (January): 12–27.

Case, William. 1996. "UMNO Paramountcy: A Report on Single-Party Dominance in Malaysia." *Party Politics* 2, no. 1 (January): 115–27.

———. 2001. "Malaysia's Resilient Pseudodemocracy." *Journal of Democracy* 12, no. 1 (January): 5–14.

Cha, Victor D. 2016. *Powerplay: The Origins of the American Alliance System in Asia*. Princeton, NJ: Princeton University Press.

Chaloemtiarana, Thak. 2007. *Thailand: The Politics of Despotic Paternalism*. Chiang Mai: Silkworm Books.

Chandler, David. 2008. *A History of Cambodia*. 4th ed. Boulder, CO: Westview Press.

Chao, Linda, and Ramon Myers. 1998. *The First Chinese Democracy: Political Life in the Republic of China on Taiwan*. Baltimore: Johns Hopkins University Press.

Cheesman, Nick. 2015. *Opposing the Rule of Law: How Myanmar's Courts Make Law and Order*. New York: Cambridge University Press.

Chen, Jie. 2013. *A Middle Class without Democracy: Economic Growth and the Prospects for Democratization in China*. New York: Oxford University Press.

Cheng, Joseph Y. S. 2005. "Hong Kong's Democrats Stumble." *Journal of Democracy* 16, no. 1 (January): 138–52.

Cheng, Tun-Jen. 1989. "Democratizing the Quasi-Leninist Regime in Taiwan." *World Politics* 41, no. 4 (July): 471–99.

———. 1990. "Political Regimes and Development Strategies: South Korea and Taiwan." In *Manufacturing Miracles: Paths of Industrialization in Latin America and East Asia*, edited by Gary Gereffi. Princeton, NJ: Princeton University Press.

———. 2008. "Embracing Defeat: The KMT and PRI after 2000." In *Political Transitions in Dominant Party Systems: Learning to Lose*, edited by Edward Friedman and Joseph Wong. New York: Routledge.

Cheng, Tun-Jen, and Eun-Mee Kim. 1994. "Making Democracy: Generalizing the South Korean Case." In *The Politics of Democratization: Generalizing East Asian Experiences*, edited by Edward Friedman. Boulder, CO: Westview Press.

Choi, Jang-Jip. 1993. "Political Cleavages in South Korea." In *State and Society in Contemporary Korea*, edited by Hagen Koo. Ithaca, NY: Cornell University Press.

Choi, Yearn H. 1978. "Failure of Democracy in Legislative Processes: The Case of South Korea, 1960." *World Affairs* 140, no. 4 (January): 331–40.

Chong, Zi Liang, and Lim Yan Liang. 2015. "'Shift towards PAP among the Better-Off.'" *Straits Times*, November 5.

Chu, Yun-Han. 1992. *Crafting Democracy in Taiwan*. Taipei: Institute for National Policy Research.

Chua, Beng Huat. 1995. *Communitarian Ideology and Democracy in Singapore*. New York: Routledge.

Cima, Ronald J. 1989. "Vietnam in 1988: The Brink of Renewal." *Asian Survey* 29, no. 1 (January): 64–72.

Ciorciari, John D. 2020. "Cambodia in 2019: Backing Further into a Corner." *Asian Survey* 60, no. 1: 125–31.

Coppedge, Michael, John Gerring, Carl Henrik Knutsen, Staffan I. Lindberg, Jan Teorell, David Altman, Michael Bernhard, et al. 2020. "V-Dem [Country–Year/Country–Date] Dataset v10." Varieties of Democracy (V-Dem) Project. https://doi.org/10.23696/vdemds20.

Cotton, James. 1989. "From Authoritarianism to Democracy in South Korea." *Political Studies* 37, no. 2 (June): 244–59.

———. 1997. "East Asian Democracy: Progress and Limits." In *Consolidating the Third Wave Democracies: Regional Challenges*, edited by Larry Diamond, Marc F. Plattner, Yun-han Chu, and Hung-mao Tien. Baltimore: Johns Hopkins University Press.

Croissant, Aurel. 2018. "Cambodia in 2017: Descending into Dictatorship?" *Asian Survey* 58, no. 1: 194–200.

———. 2019. "Cambodia in 2018: Requiem for Multiparty Politics." *Asian Survey* 59, no. 1: 170–76.

Croissant, Aurel, and Olli Hellman, eds. 2020. *Stateness and Democracy in East Asia*. New York: Cambridge University Press.

Crouch, Harold. 1995. *Government and Society in Malaysia*. Ithaca, NY: Cornell University Press.

———. 2011. *Political Reform in Post-Soeharto Indonesia*. Singapore: Institute of Southeast Asian Studies.

Curtis, Grant. 1998. *Cambodia Reborn? The Transition to Democracy and Development*. Washington, DC: Brookings Institution Press.

Dahl, Robert A. 1971. *Polyarchy: Participation and opposition*. New Haven, CT: Yale University Press.

Delisle, Jacques, and Avery Goldstein. 2019. "China's Economic Reform and Opening at Forty: Past Accomplishments and Emerging Challenges." In *To Get Rich Is Glorious: Challenges Facing China's Economic Reform and Opening at Forty*, edited by Jacques Delisle and Avery Goldstein. Washington, DC: Brookings Institution Press.

Diamond, Larry. 2015. "Facing Up to the Democratic Recession." *Journal of Democracy* 26, no. 1 (January): 141–55.

Diamond, Larry, Marc F. Plattner, and Yun-han Chu, eds. 2013. *Democracy in East Asia: A New Century*. Baltimore: Johns Hopkins University Press.

Dickson, Bruce. 1996. "The Kuomintang before Democratization: Organizational Change and the Role of Elections." In *Taiwan's Electoral Politics and Democratic Transition: Riding the Third Wave*, edited by Hung-mao Tien. Armonk, NY: M. E. Sharpe.

———. 1997. *Democratization in China and Taiwan: The Adaptability of Leninist Parties*. Oxford: Clarendon Press.

———. 2003. *Red Capitalists in China: The Party, Private Entrepreneurs, and Prospects for Political Change*. Cambridge: Cambridge University Press.

———. 2016. *The Dictator's Dilemma: The Chinese Community Party's Strategy for Survival*. New York: Oxford University Press.

Dikotter, Frank. 2010. *Mao's Great Famine: The History of China's Most Devastating Catastrophe, 1958–1962*. London: Bloomsbury.

———. 2013. *The Tragedy of Liberation: A History of the Chinese Revolution, 1945–1957*. London: Bloomsbury.

Dimitrov, Martin, ed. 2013. *Why Communism Didn't Collapse: Understanding Authoritarian Regime Resilience in Asia and Europe*. New York: Cambridge University Press.

Ding, Iza. 2022. *The Performative State: Public Scrutiny and Environmental Governance in China*. Ithaca, NY: Cornell University Press.

Dittmer, Lowell. 2001. Review of *The Tiananmen Papers*, compiled by Zhang Liang, edited by Andrew Nathan and Perry Link. *China Quarterly* 166 (June): 476–83.

Doner, Richard. 2009. *The Politics of Uneven Development: Thailand's Economic Growth in Comparative Perspective*. New York: Cambridge University Press.

Doner, Richard, Bryan Ritchie, and Dan Slater. 2005. "Systemic Vulnerability and the Origins of Developmental States: Northeast and Southeast Asia in Comparative Perspective." *International Organization* 59, no. 2 (Spring): 327–61.

Dower, John. 1999. *Embracing Defeat: Japan in the Wake of World War II*. New York: W. W. Norton.

Duckett, Jane. 2010. *The Chinese State's Retreat from Health: Policy and the Politics of Retrenchment*. London: Routledge.

Duus, Peter, and Daniel Okimoto. 1979. "Fascism and the History of Pre-war Japan: The Failure of a Concept." *Journal of Asian Studies* 39, no. 1 (November): 65–76.

Ear, Sophal. 2013. *Aid Dependence in Cambodia: How Foreign Assistance Undermines Democracy*. New York: Columbia University Press.

Egreteau, Renaud, and Larry Jagan. 2013. *Soldiers and Diplomacy in Burma: Understanding the Foreign Relations of the Burmese Praetorian State*. Singapore: NUS Press.

Eibl, Ferdinand, Steffen Hertog, and Dan Slater. 2021. "War Makes the Regime: Regional Rebellions and Political Militarization Worldwide." *British Journal of Political Science* 51, no. 3 (July): 1002–23.

Elliot, David W. P. 2012. *Changing Worlds: Vietnam's Transition from the Cold War to Globalization*. New York: Oxford University Press.

Elstrom, Manfred. 2021. *Workers and Change in China*. New York: Cambridge University Press.

Escriba-Folch, Abel, and Joseph Wright. 2015. *Foreign Pressure and the Politics of Autocratic Survival*. New York: Oxford University Press.

Evans, Peter, and James Rauch. 1999. "Bureaucracy and Growth: A Cross-National Analysis of the Effects of 'Weberian' State Structures on Economic Growth." *American Sociological Review* 64, no. 5 (October): 748–65.

Evans, Peter B. 1995. *Embedded Autonomy: States and Industrial Transformation*. Princeton, NJ: Princeton University Press.

Fearon, James D. 1995. "Rationalist Explanations for War." *International Organization* 49, no. 3 (Summer): 379–414.

Ferrara, Federico. 2015. *The Political Development of Modern Thailand*. New York: Cambridge University Press.

Fewsmith, Joseph. 2001. *China since Tiananmen: The Politics of Transition*. Cambridge: Cambridge University Press.

———. 2013. *The Logic and Limits of Political Reform in China*. New York: Cambridge University Press.

———. 2018. "Can Fighting Corruption Save the Party?" In *The China Questions: Critical Insights into a Rising Power*, edited by Jennifer Rudolph and Michael Szonyi. Cambridge, MA: Harvard University Press.

Fowler, James. 1999. "The United States and South Korean Democratization." *Political Science Quarterly* 114, no. 2 (August): 265–88.

Frazier, Mark. 2010. *Socialist Insecurity: Pensions and the Politics of Uneven Development*. Ithaca, NY: Cornell University Press.

Friedman, Edward, Paul Pickowicz, and Mark Selden. 1991. *Chinese Village, Socialist State*. New Haven, CT: Yale University Press.

Friedman, Edward, and Joseph Wong, eds. 2008. *Political Transitions in Dominant Party Systems: Learning to Lose*. New York: Routledge.

Funston, John. 1980. *Malay Politics in Malaysia: A Study of UMNO and PAS*. Kuala Lumpur: Heinemann.

Gallagher, Mary. 2002. "Reform and Openness: Why China's Reforms Have Delayed Democracy." *World Politics* 54, no. 3 (June): 338–72.

———. 2017. *Authoritarian Legality in China: Law, Workers, and the State*. New York: Cambridge University Press.

Gandhi, Jennifer. 2008. *Political Institutions under Dictatorship*. New York: Cambridge University Press.

Geddes, Barbara. 1999. "What Do We Know about Democratization after Twenty Years?" *Annual Review of Political Science* 2, no. 1: 115–44.

George, Cherian. 2000. *Singapore, the Air-Conditioned Nation: Essays on the Politics of Comfort and Control, 1990–2000*. Singapore: Landmark Books.

———. 2012. *Freedom from the Press: Journalism and State Power in Singapore*. Singapore: NUS Press.

Gilley, Bruce. 2008. "Taiwan's Democratic Transition: A Model for China?" In *Political Change in China: Comparisons with Taiwan*, edited by Bruce Gilley and Larry Diamond. Boulder, CO: Lynne Rienner.

Ginsburg, Tom, and Tamir Moustafa, eds. 2008. *Rule by Law: The Politics of Courts in Authoritarian Regimes*. New York: Cambridge University Press.

Goh Cheng Teik. 1971. *The May Thirteenth Incident and Democracy in Malaysia*. Singapore: Oxford University Press.

Gold, Thomas. 1986. *State and Society in the Taiwan Miracle*. Armonk, NY: M. E. Sharpe.

Gomez, Edmund Terence, and Jomo K. S. 1999. *Malaysia's Political Economy: Politics, Patronage, and Profits*. New York: Cambridge University Press.

Gordon, Andrew. 1991. *Labor and Imperial Democracy in Japan*. Berkeley: University of California Press.

———. 2014. *A Modern History of Japan: From Tokugawa Times to the Present*. 3rd ed. New York: Oxford University Press.

Gottesman, Evan. 2003. *Cambodia after the Khmer Rouge: Inside the Politics of Nation Building*. New Haven, CT: Yale University Press.

Greitens, Sheena Chestnut. 2016. *Dictators and Their Secret Police: Coercive Institutions and State Violence*. New York: Cambridge University Press.

Grossman, Derek. 2020. *Regional Responses to U.S.-China Competition in the Indo-Pacific: Vietnam*. Santa Monica, CA: RAND.

Grzymala-Busse, Anna. 2002. *Redeeming the Communist Past: The Regeneration of Communist Parties in East Central Europe*. New York: Cambridge University Press.

Gunitsky, Seva. 2017. *Aftershocks: Great Powers and Domestic Reforms in the Twentieth Century*. Princeton, NJ: Princeton University Press.

Haberkorn, Tyrell. 2018. *In Plain Sight: Impunity and Human Rights in Thailand*. Madison: University of Wisconsin Press.

Haddad, Mary A. 2012. *Building Democracy in Japan*. New York: Cambridge University Press.

Haggard, Stephan. 1990. *Pathways from the Periphery: The Politics of Growth in the Newly Indus-trializing Countries*. Ithaca, NY: Cornell University Press.

———. 2018. *Developmental States*. New York: Cambridge University Press.

Haggard, Stephan, and Robert Kaufman. 1995. *The Political Economy of Democratic Transitions*. Princeton, NJ: Princeton University Press.

———. 2008. *Development, Democracy and Welfare States: Latin America, East Asia and Eastern Europe*. Princeton, NJ: Princeton University Press.

———. 2012. "Inequality and Regime Change: Democratic Transitions and the Stability of Democratic Rule." *American Political Science Review* 106, no. 3 (August): 495–516.

———. 2016. *Dictators and Democrats: Masses, Elites, and Regime Change*. Princeton, NJ: Princeton University Press.

Hamayotsu, Kikue. 2002. "Islam and Nation Building in Southeast Asia: Malaysia and Indonesia in Comparative Perspective." *Pacific Affairs* 75, no. 3 (Fall): 353–75.

Hamilton-Hart, Natasha. 2002. *Asian States, Asian Bankers: Central Banking in Southeast Asia*. Ithaca, NY: Cornell University Press.

Han, Enze. 2014. "Hong Kong's Crisis Is One of Identity as Well as Democracy." *The Conversa-tion*, October 13. http://www.theworldweekly.com/reader/i/title/2494.

Han, Sung-Joo. 1974. *The Failure of Democracy in South Korea*. Berkeley: University of California Press.

———. 1988. "South Korea in 1987: The Politics of Democratization." *Asian Survey* 28, no. 1 (January): 52–61.

Harjanto, Nico. 2010. "Political Party Survival: The Golongan Karya Party and Electoral Politics in Indonesia." PhD diss., Northern Illinois University.

Harris, Joseph. 2017. *Achieving Access: Professional Movements and the Politics of Health Universal-ism*. Ithaca, NY: Cornell University Press.

Hassan, Mai. 2020. *Regime Threats and State Solutions: Bureaucratic Loyalty and Embeddedness in Kenya*. New York: Cambridge University Press.

Hatch, Walter. 2010. *Asia's Flying Geese: How Regionalization Shapes Japan*. Ithaca, NY: Cornell University Press.

Hatch, Walter, and Kozo Yamamura. 1996. *Asia in Japan's Embrace: Building a Regional Produc-tion Alliance*. New York: Cambridge University Press.

He, Baogang, and Stig Thogersen. 2010. "Giving the People a Voice? Experiments with Consultative Authoritarian Institutions in China." *Journal of Contemporary China* 16, no. 66 (July): 675–92.

He, Baogang, and Mark Warren. 2011. "Authoritarian Deliberation: The Deliberative Turn in Chinese Political Development." *Perspectives on Politics* 9, no. 2 (June): 269–89.

Hefner, Robert. 2000. *Civil Islam: Muslims and Democratization in Indonesia*. Princeton, NJ: Princeton University Press.

Hellman, Joel. 1998. "Winners Take All: The Politics of Partial Reform in Postcommunist Tran-sitions." *World Politics* 50, no. 2 (January): 203–34.

Heng, Russell Hiang-Khng. 2001. "Vietnam: Light at the End of the Economic Tunnel?" *South-east Asian Affairs* 2001: 357–68.

Heo, Uk, and Terrence Roehrig. 2018. *The Evolution of the South Korea-United States Alliance*. New York: Cambridge University Press.

Heryanto, Ariel, and Sumit K. Mandal. 2003. "Challenges to Authoritarianism in Indonesia and Malaysia." In *Challenging Authoritarianism in Southeast Asia: Comparing Indonesia and Malaysia*, edited by Ariel Haryanto and Sumit Mandal. New York: RoutledgeCurzon.

Hicken, Allen. 2006. "Party Fabrication: Constitutional Reform and the Rise of Thai Rak Thai." *Journal of East Asian Studies* 6, no. 3 (March): 381–407.

———. 2009. *Building Party Systems in Developing Democracies*. New York: Cambridge University Press.

Hicken, Allen, and Erik Martinez Kuhonta, eds. 2015. *Party System Institutionalization in Asia: Democracies, Autocracies, and the Shadows of the Past*. New York: Cambridge University Press.

Ho, Karl. 1999. "The Hong Kong Legislative Election of 1998." *Electoral Studies* 18, no. 3: 438–45.

Horowitz, Donald L. 2013. *Constitutional Change and Democracy in Indonesia*. New York: Cambridge University Press.

Hsueh, Roselyn. 2011. *China's Regulatory State: A New Strategy for Globalization*. Ithaca, NY: Cornell University Press.

Hu, Fu. 1993. "The Electoral Mechanism and Political Change in Taiwan." In *In the Shadow of China: Political Developments in Taiwan since 1949*, edited by Steve Tsang. Honolulu: University of Hawaii Press.

Huang, Teh-Fu. 1996. "Elections and the Evolution of the Kuomintang." In *Taiwan's Electoral Politics and Democratic Transition: Riding the Third Wave*, edited by Hung-mao Tien. Armonk, NY: M. E. Sharpe.

Huang, Yasheng. 2005. *Selling China: Foreign Direct Investment during the Reform Era*. Cambridge: Cambridge University Press.

———. 2008. *Capitalism with Chinese Characteristics: Entrepreneurship and the State*. New York: Cambridge University Press.

Huntington, Samuel. 1968. *Political Order in Changing Societies*. New Haven, CT: Yale University Press.

———. 1991a. "How Countries Democratize." *Political Science Quarterly* 106, no. 4: 579–616.

———. 1991b. *The Third Wave: Democratization in the Late Twentieth Century*. Norman: University of Oklahoma Press.

Hutchcroft, Paul D. 2000. "Colonial Masters, National Politicos, and Provincial Lords: Central Authority and Local Autonomy in the American Philippines, 1900–1913." *Journal of Asian Studies* 59, no. 2 (May): 277–306.

Hwang, In-Won. 2003. *Personalized Politics: The Malaysian State under Mahathir*. Singapore: Institute for Southeast Asian Studies.

Jacobs, Bruce. 2012. *Democratizing Taiwan*. Leiden: Brill Academic Publishers.

Jaffrey, Sana, and Dan Slater. 2017. "Violence and Regimes in Asia: Capable States and Durable Settlements." In *The State of Conflict and Violence in Asia*. New York: Asia Foundation.

Jamal, Manal. 2016. *Promoting Democracy: The Force of Political Settlements in Uncertain Times*. New York: New York University Press.

Jesudason, James V. 1989. *Ethnicity and the Economy: The State, Chinese Business, and Multinationals in Malaysia*. Singapore: Oxford University Press.

Johannen, Uwe, and James Gomez, eds. 2001. *Democratic Transitions in Asia*. Bangkok: Friedrich Naumann Foundation.

Johnson, Chalmers. 1982. *MITI and the Japanese Miracle: The Growth of Industrial Policy, 1925–1975*. Stanford, CA: Stanford University Press.

———. 1999. "The Developmental State: Odyssey of a Concept." In *The Developmental State*, edited by Merideth Woo-Cumings. Ithaca, NY: Cornell University Press.

Jomo, K. S., ed. 2001. *Malaysian Eclipse: Economic Crisis and Recovery*. London: Zed Books.

Kasza, Gregory. 2006. *One World of Welfare: Japan in Comparative Perspective*. Ithaca, NY: Cornell University Press.

Keohane, Robert. 1984. *After Hegemony: Cooperation and Discord and the World Political Economy*. Princeton, NJ: Princeton University Press.

Kerkvliet, Benedict J. Tria. 1995. "Village-State Relations in Vietnam: The Effect of Everyday Politics on Decollectivization." *Journal of Asian Studies* 54, no. 2 (March): 396–418.

———. 2005. *The Power of Everyday Politics: How Vietnamese Peasants Transformed National Policy*. Ithaca, NY: Cornell University Press.

———. 2019. *Speaking Out in Vietnam: Public Political Criticism in a Communist Party–Ruled Nation*. Ithaca, NY: Cornell University Press.

Khan, Mushtaq. 2018. "Political Settlements and the Analysis of Institutions." *African Affairs* 117, no. 469 (October): 636–55.

Khin, Maung Nyo. 2012. "Taking Stock of Myanmar's Economy in 2011." In *Myanmar's Transition: Openings, Obstacles, and Opportunities*, edited by Nick Cheesman, Monique Skidmore, and Trevor Wilson. Singapore: Institute for Southeast Asian Studies.

Khong, Cho-Oon. 1995. "Singapore: Political Legitimacy through Managing Conformity." In *Political Legitimacy in Southeast Asia: The Quest for Moral Authority*, edited by Muthiah Alagappa. Stanford, CA: Stanford University Press.

Khoo, Boo Teik. 1995. *Paradoxes of Mahathirism: An Intellectual Biography of Mahathir Mohamad*. New York: Oxford University Press.

Kiernan, Ben. 1993. "The Inclusion of the Khmer Rouge in the Cambodian Peace Process: Causes and Consequences." In *Genocide and Democracy in Cambodia: The Khmer Rouge, the United Nations and the International Community*, edited by Ben Kiernan, 191–272. New Haven, CT: Yale University Southeast Asia Studies.

———. 2008. *The Pol Pot Regime: Race, Power, and Genocide in Cambodia under the Khmer Rouge, 1975–79*. 3rd ed. New Haven, CT: Yale University Press.

Kim, Byung-Kook. 1998. "Korea's Crisis of Success." In *Democracy in East Asia*, edited by Larry Diamond and Marc F. Plattner. Baltimore: Johns Hopkins University Press.

———. 2008. "Defeat in Victory, Victory in Defeat: The Korean Conservatives in Democratic Consolidation." In *Political Transitions in Dominant Party Systems: Learning to Lose*, edited by Edward Friedman and Joseph Wong. New York: Routledge.

———. 2011. "The Leviathan: Economic Bureaucracy under Park." In *The Park Chung Hee Era: The Transformation of South Korea*, edited by Byung-Kook Kim and Ezra Vogel. Cambridge, MA: Harvard University Press.

Kim, Byung-Kook, and Ezra Vogel, eds. 2011. *The Park Chung Hee Era: The Transformation of South Korea*. Cambridge, MA: Harvard University Press.

Kim, Eugene C. I., and Ke-Soo Kim. 1964. "The April 1960 Korean Student Movement." *Western Political Quarterly* 17, no. 1 (March): 83–92.

Kim, Q.-Y. 1983. *The Fall of Syngman Rhee*. Berkeley: Institute of East Asian Studies, University of California.

Kim, Sang-Joon. 1994. "Characteristic Features of Korean Democratization." *Asian Perspective* 18, no. 2 (Fall/Winter): 181–96.

Kim, Sungmoon. 2014. *Confucian Democracy in East Asia: Theory and Practice*. New York: Cambridge University Press.

Kim, Sunhyuk. 2000. *The Politics of Democratization: The Role of Civil Society*. Pittsburgh: University of Pittsburgh Press.

Koh, B. C. 1985. "The 1985 Parliamentary Election in South Korea." *Asian Survey* 25, no. 9 (September): 883–97.

Kohli, Atul. 2004. *State-Directed Development: Political Power and Industrialization in the Global Periphery*. Cambridge: Cambridge University Press.

Kohno, Masaru. 1997. *Japan's Postwar Party Politics*. Princeton, NJ: Princeton University Press.

Koo, Hagen. 1993. "The State, Minjung, and the Working Class in South Korea." In *State and Society in Contemporary Korea*, edited by Hagen Koo. Ithaca, NY: Cornell University Press.

Kornai, Janos. 1992. *The Socialist System: The Political Economy of Communism*. Princeton, NJ: Princeton University Press.

Krauss, Ellis, and Robert Pekkanen. 2010. "The Rise and Fall of Japan's Liberal Democratic Party." *Journal of Asian Studies* 69, no. 1 (February): 5–15.

Ku, Yuen-Wen. 1997. *Welfare Capitalism in Taiwan: State, Economy and Social Policy*. New York: St. Martin's Press.

Kuhonta, Erik Martinez. 2011. *The Institutional Imperative: The Politics of Equitable Development in Southeast Asia*. Stanford, CA: Stanford University Press.

Lam, Jermain T. M. 2010. "Party Institutionalization in Hong Kong." *Asian Perspective* 34, no. 2 (June): 53–82.

Lange, Matthew. 2009. *Lineages of Despotism and Development: British Colonialism and State Power*. Chicago: University of Chicago Press.

Langston, Joy K. 2017. *Democratization and Authoritarian Party Survival: Mexico's PRI*. New York: Oxford University Press.

Laothamatas, Anek, ed. 1997. *Democratization in Southeast and East Asia*. Bangkok: Silkworm Books.

Larsson, Tomas. 2013. *Land and Loyalty: Security and the Development of Property Rights in Thailand*. Singapore: NUS Press.

Lee, Namhee. 2007. *The Making of Minjung: Democracy and the Politics of Representation in South Korea*. Ithaca, NY: Cornell University Press.

Lee, Sang-Chul, and Karlyn Kohrs Campbell. 1994. "Korean President Roh Tae-Woo's 1988 Inaugural Address: Campaigning for Investiture." *Quarterly Journal of Speech* 80, no. 1 (February): 37–52.

Lee, Terence. 2015. *Defect or Defend: Military Responses to Popular Protests in Authoritarian Asia*. Singapore: Institute for Southeast Asian Studies.

Lev, Daniel S. 1990. "Intermediate Classes and Change in Indonesia: Some Initial Reflections." In *The Politics of Middle Class Indonesia*, edited by Richard Tanter and Kenneth Young, 25–43. Clayton, Victoria, Australia: Monash University, Centre for Southeast Asian Studies.

Levitsky, Steven, and Lucan A. Way. 2010. *Competitive Authoritarianism: Hybrid Regimes after the Cold War*. New York: Cambridge University Press.

Levitsky, Steven, and Daniel Ziblatt. 2018. *How Democracies Die*. New York: Crown.

Li, Cheng. 2016. *Chinese Politics in the Xi Jinping Era: Reassessing Collective Leadership*. Washington, DC: Brookings Institution Press.

Liddle, William. 1990. "The Middle Class and New Order Legitimacy: A Response to Dan Lev." In *The Politics of Middle Class Indonesia*, edited by Richard Tanter and Kenneth Young, 49–58. Clayton, Victoria, Australia: Monash University, Centre for Southeast Asian Studies.

Lieberthal, Kenneth, and Michel Oksenberg. 1988. *Policy-Making in China: Leaders, Structures and Processes*. Princeton, NJ: Princeton University Press.

Lintner, Bertil. 2013. "The Military's Still in Charge: Why Reform in Burma Is Only Skin Deep." *Foreign Policy*, July 16.

Lo, Shiu-hing, and Wu Wing-yat. 2002. "The 2000 Legislative Council Elections in Hong Kong." *Representation* 38, no. 4 (July): 327–39.

Looney, Kristen. 2020. *Mobilizing for Development: The Modernization of Rural Asia*. Ithaca, NY: Cornell University Press.

Loxton, James. 2015. "Authoritarian Successor Parties." *Journal of Democracy* 26, no. 3 (July): 157–70.

Loxton, James, and Scott Mainwaring, eds. 2018. *Life after Dictatorship: Authoritarian Successor Parties Worldwide*. Cambridge: Cambridge University Press.

Lu, Jian, and Chris King-Chi Chan. 2016. "Collective Identity, Framing and Mobilization of Environmental Protests in Urban China: A Case Study of Qidong's Protest." *China: An International Journal* 14, no. 2 (May): 102–22.

Lynch, Daniel. 2015. *China's Futures: PRC Elites Debate Economics, Politics and Foreign Policy*. Stanford, CA: Stanford University Press.

Lyons, Terrence. 2005. *Demilitarizing Politics: Elections on the Uncertain Road to Peace*. Boulder, CO: Lynne Rienner.

Ma, Ngok. 2005. "Civil Society in Self-Defense: The Struggle against National Security Legislation in Hong Kong." *Journal of Contemporary China* 14, no. 44 (August): 465–82.

MacFarquhar, Roderick. 1974. *The Origins of the Cultural Revolution*. Vol. 1, *Contradictions among the People, 1956–1957*. New York: Columbia University Press.

———. 1983. *The Origins of the Cultural Revolution*. Vol. 2, *The Great Leap Forward*. New York: Columbia University Press.

———. 1999. *The Origins of the Cultural Revolution*. Vol. 3, *The Coming of the Cataclysm, 1961–1966*. New York: Columbia University Press.

MacIntyre, Andrew. 2001. "Institutions and Investors: The Politics of the Economic Crisis in Southeast Asia." *International Organization* 55, no. 1 (Winter): 81–122.

Magaloni, Beatriz. 2006. *Voting for Autocracy: Hegemonic Party Survival and Its Demise in Mexico*. New York: Cambridge University Press.

Malesky, Edmund. 2009. "Gerrymandering—Vietnamese Style: Escaping the Partial Reform Equilibrium in a Nondemocratic Regime." *Journal of Politics* 71, no. 1 (January): 132–59.

Malesky, Edmund, Regina Abrami, and Yu Zheng. 2011. "Institutions and Inequality in Single-Party Regimes: A Comparative Analysis of Vietnam and China." *Comparative Politics* 43, no. 4 (July): 401–19.

Malesky, Edmund, and Paul Schuler. 2010. "Nodding or Needling? Analyzing Delegate Responsiveness in an Authoritarian Parliament." *American Political Science Review* 104, no. 3: 482–502.

Manion, Melanie. 2015. *Information for Autocrats: Representation in Chinese Local Congresses.* New York: Cambridge University Press.

Mann, Michael. 2000. *The Dark Side of Democracy: Explaining Ethnic Conflict.* New York: Cambridge University Press.

Mansfield, Edward, and Jack Snyder. 2007. "The Sequencing 'Fallacy.'" *Journal of Democracy* 18, no. 3 (July): 5–9.

Marshall, T. H. 1950. *Citizenship and Social Class and Other Essays.* New York: Cambridge University Press.

Mattlin, Mikael. 2011. *Politicized Society: The Long Shadow of Taiwan's One-Party Legacy.* Copenhagen: Nordic Institute of Asian Studies Press.

Mauzy, Diane K., and R. S. Milne. 2002. *Singapore Politics under the People's Action Party.* New York: Routledge.

McAdams, A. James. 2017. *Vanguard of the Revolution: The Global Idea of the Communist Party.* Princeton, NJ: Princeton University Press.

McCargo, Duncan. 2005. "Network Monarchy and Legitimacy Crises in Thailand." *Pacific Review* 18, no. 4: 499–519.

———. 2008. *Tearing Apart the Land: Islam and Legitimacy in Southern Thailand.* Ithaca, NY: Cornell University Press.

McCargo, Duncan, and Ukrist Pathmanand. 2005. *The Thaksinization of Thailand.* Copenhagen: Nordic Institute of Asian Studies Press.

McCarthy, Gerard. 2019. "Regressive Democracy: Explaining Distributive Politics in Myanmar's Political Transition." PhD diss., Australia National University.

McKoy, Michael K., and Michael K. Miller. 2012. "The Patron's Dilemma: The Dynamics of Foreign-Supported Democratization." *Journal of Conflict Resolution* 56, no. 5 (April): 904–32.

Menchik, Jeremy. 2016. *Islam and Democracy in Indonesia: Tolerance without Liberalism.* New York: Cambridge University Press.

Meng, Anne. 2020. *Constraining Dictatorship: From Personalized Rule to Institutionalized Regimes.* New York: Cambridge University Press.

Mietzner, Marcus. 2012. "Indonesia's Democratic Stagnation: Anti-reformist Elites and Resilient Civil Society." *Democratization* 19, no. 2 (April): 209–29.

———. 2014. "Successful and Failed Democratic Transitions from Military Rule in Majority Muslim Societies: The Cases of Indonesia and Egypt." *Contemporary Politics* 20, no. 4 (October): 435–52.

———. 2020. "Stateness and State Capacity in Post-authoritarian Indonesia: Securing Democracy's Survival, Entrenching Its Low Quality." In *Stateness and Democracy in East Asia*, edited by Aurel Croissant and Olli Hellman. New York: Cambridge University Press.

Miller, Jennifer M. 2019. *Cold War Democracy: The United States and Japan.* Cambridge, MA: Harvard University Press.

Miller, Michael K. 2021a. "Don't Call It a Comeback: Autocratic Ruling Parties after Democratization." *British Journal of Political Science* 51, no. 2 (April): 559–83.

————. 2021b. *Shock to the System: Coups, Elections and War on the Road to Democratization.* Princeton, NJ: Princeton University Press.

Milly, Deborah. 1999. *Poverty, Equality and Growth: The Politics of Economic Need in Postwar Japan.* Cambridge, MA: Harvard University Press.

Montinola, Gabriella, Yingyi Qian, and Barry Weingast. 1995. "Federalism, Chinese Style: The Political Basis for Economic Success in China." *World Politics* 48, no. 1 (October): 50–81.

Moody, Peter. 1992. *Political Change on Taiwan: A Study of Ruling Party Adaptability.* New York: Praeger.

Moon, Chung-In, and Byung-Joon Jun. 2011. "Modernization Strategies: Ideas and Influences." In *The Park Chung Hee Era: The Transformation of South Korea,* edited by Byung-Kook Kim and Ezra Vogel. Cambridge, MA: Harvard University Press.

Moore, Barrington. 1966. *Social Origins of Democracy and Dictatorship.* Boston: Beacon Press.

Morgenbesser, Lee. 2016. *Behind the Façade: Elections under Authoritarianism in Southeast Asia.* Albany: State University of New York Press.

————. 2018. "Misclassification on the Mekong: The Origins of Hun Sen's Personalist Dictatorship." *Democratization* 25, no. 2 (February): 191–208.

————. 2019. "Cambodia's Transition to Hegemonic Authoritarianism." *Journal of Democracy* 30, no. 1 (January): 158–171.

Morley, James W., ed. 1993. *Driven by Growth: Political Change in the Asia-Pacific Region.* Armonk, NY: M. E. Sharpe.

Morse, Yonatan L. 2019. *How Autocrats Compete: Parties, Patrons, and Unfair Elections in Africa.* New York: Cambridge University Press.

Moustafa, Tamir. 2018. *Constituting Religion: Islam, Liberal Rights, and the Malaysian State.* New York: Cambridge University Press.

Nakamura, Masanori. 1994. "Democratization, Peace and Economic Development in Occupied Japan, 1945–1952." In *The Politics of Democratization: Generalizing East Asian Experiences,* edited by Edward Friedman. Boulder, CO: Westview Press.

Nakanishi, Yoshihiro. 2013. *Strong Soldiers, Failed Revolution: The State and Military in Burma, 1962–88.* Singapore: NUS Press.

Nalepa, Monika. 2010. *Skeletons in the Closet: Transitional Justice in Post-communist Europe.* New York: Cambridge University Press.

Nathan, Andrew. 2003. "Authoritarian Resilience." *Journal of Democracy* 14, no. 1 (January): 6–17.

————. 2019. "The New Tiananmen Papers: Inside the Secret Meeting That Changed China." *Foreign Affairs,* July 2019.

National Security Archive. 2001. "The US 'Tiananmen Papers.'" June 4. https://nsarchive2.gwu.edu/NSAEBB/NSAEBB47/index2.html.

Naughton, Barry. 1996. *Growing Out of the Plan: Chinese Economic Reform 1978–1993.* Cambridge: Cambridge University Press.

————. 2014. "China's Economy: Complacency, Crisis and the Challenge of Reform." *Daedalus* 143, no. 2 (Spring): 14–25.

Nguyen, Hai Hong. 2016. *Political Dynamics of Grassroots Democracy in Vietnam.* New York: Palgrave Macmillan.

Ninh, Kim. 1990. "Vietnam: Renovation in Transition?" *Southeast Asian Affairs* 1990: 383–95.

Nishizaki, Yoshinori. 2011. *Political Authority and Provincial Identity in Thailand: The Making of Banharn-buri*. Ithaca, NY: Cornell Southeast Asia Program.

Nolan, Peter. 1995. *China's Rise, Russia's Fall: Politics, Economics and Planning in the Transition from Stalinism*. London: Palgrave Macmillan.

Ockey, James. 2004. *Making Democracy: Leadership, Class, Gender, and Political Participation in Thailand*. Honolulu: University of Hawaii Press.

O'Donnell, Guillermo, and Philippe Schmitter. 1986. *Transitions from Authoritarian Rule: Tentative Conclusions from Uncertain Democracies*. Baltimore: Johns Hopkins University Press.

Ogden, Suzanne, Kathleen Hartford, Nancy Sullivan, and David Zweig, eds. 1992. *China's Search for Democracy: The Students and Mass Movement of 1989*. New York: Routledge Press.

Oh, John Kie-Chiang. 1999. *Korean Politics: The Quest for Democratization and Economic Development*. Ithaca, NY: Cornell University Press.

Oliver, Steven, and Kai Ostwald. 2020. "Singapore's Pandemic Election: Opposition Parties and Valence Politics in GE2020." *Pacific Affairs* 93, no. 4 (December): 759–80.

Ong, Elvin. 2022. *Opposing Power: Building Opposition Alliances in Electoral Autocracies*. Ann Arbor: University of Michigan Press.

Ooi, Kee Beng. 2007. *Lost in Translation: Malaysia under Abdullah*. Singapore: Institute for Southeast Asian Studies.

———. 2009. *Arrested Reform: The Undoing of Abdullah Badawi*. Kuala Lumpur: Research for Social Advancement.

Ortmann, Stephan. 2011. "Singapore: Authoritarian but Newly Competitive." *Journal of Democracy* 22, no. 4 (October): 153–64.

———. 2015. "The Umbrella Movement and Hong Kong's Protracted Democratization Process." *Asian Affairs* 46, no. 1 (February): 32–50.

Pasuk Phongpaichit and Chris Baker. 2009. *Thaksin*. Bangkok: Silkworm Books.

Pei, Minxin. 2006. *China's Trapped Transition: The Limits of Developmental Autocracy*. Cambridge, MA: Harvard University Press.

Pempel, T. J. 1990. *Uncommon Democracies*. Ithaca, NY: Cornell University Press.

———. 1992. "Bureaucracy in Japan." *Political Science and Politics* 25, no. 1 (March): 19–24.

———. 2005. *Remapping East Asia*. Ithaca, NY: Cornell University Press.

———. 2021. *A Region of Regimes: Prosperity and Plunder in the Asia-Pacific*. Ithaca, NY: Cornell University Press.

Peng, Ito, and Joseph Wong. 2008. "Institutions and Institutional Purpose: Continuity and Change in East Asian Social Policy." *Politics and Society* 36, no. 1 (March): 61–88.

Pepinsky, Thomas B. 2009. *Economic Crises and the Breakdown of Authoritarian Regimes: Indonesia and Malaysia in Comparative Perspective*. New York: Cambridge University Press.

Perry, Elizabeth. 2008. "Chinese Conceptions of 'Rights': From Mencius to Mao—and Now." *Perspectives on Politics* 6, no. 1 (March): 37–50.

———. 2018. "Is the Chinese Communist Regime Legitimate?" In *The China Questions: Critical Insights into a Rising Power*, edited by Jennifer Rudolph and Michael Szonyi. Cambridge, MA: Harvard University Press.

Porter, Gareth. 1993. *Vietnam: The Politics of Bureaucratic Socialism*. Ithaca, NY: Cornell University Press.

Power, Thomas, and Eve Warburton, eds. 2020. *Democracy in Indonesia: From Stagnation to Regression?* Singapore: Institute for Southeast Asian Studies.

Przeworski, Adam. 1991. *Democracy and the Market: Political and Economic Reforms in Eastern Europe and Latin America.* New York: Cambridge University Press.

Pye, Lucian. 1991. *China: An Introduction.* 4th ed. New York: HarperCollins.

Rahim, Lily, and Michael Barr, eds. 2019. *The Limits of Authoritarian Governance in Singapore's Developmental State.* New York: Palgrave Macmillan.

Riedl, Rachel. 2014. *Authoritarian Origins of Democratic Party Systems in Africa.* New York: Cambridge University Press.

Riedl, Rachel, Dan Slater, Joseph Wong, and Daniel Ziblatt. 2020. "Authoritarian-Led Democratization." *Annual Review of Political Science* 23 (May): 315–32.

Rigger, Shelley. 1999. *Politics in Taiwan: Voting for Democracy.* New York: Routledge.

———. 2001. *From Opposition to Power: Taiwan's Democratic Progressive Party.* Boulder, CO: Lynne Rienner.

Rinjiro, Sodei. 1983. "A Question of Paternity." In *Japan Examined: Perspectives on Modern Japanese History,* edited by Harry Wray and Hilary Conroy. Honolulu: University of Hawaii Press.

Roberts, Margaret. 2018. *Censored: Distraction and Diversion inside China's Great Firewall.* Princeton, NJ: Princeton University Press.

Rodan, Garry, and Caroline Hughes. 2014. *The Politics of Accountability in Southeast Asia: The Dominance of Moral Ideologies.* Oxford: Oxford University Press.

Roosa, John. 2006. *Pretext for Mass Murder: The September 30th Movement and Suharto's Coup d'État in Indonesia.* Madison: University of Wisconsin Press.

———. 2020. *Buried Histories: The Anticommunist Massacres of 1965–1966 in Indonesia.* Madison: University of Wisconsin Press.

Rosenfeld, Bryn. 2021. *The Autocratic Middle Class: How State Dependency Reduces the Demand for Democracy.* Princeton, NJ: Princeton University Press.

Sachsenroder, Wolfgang, and Ulrike E. Frings, eds. 1998. *Political Party Systems and Democratic Development in East and Southeast Asia.* Singapore: Ashgate.

Samuels, Richard J. 1996. *Rich Nation, Strong Army: National Security and the Technological Transformation of Japan.* Ithaca, NY: Cornell University Press.

Saxer, Carl. 2002. *From Transition to Power Alternation: Democracy in South Korea, 1987–1997.* New York: Routledge.

Scalapino, Robert, and Junnosuke Masumi. 1962. *Parties and Politics in Contemporary Japan.* Berkeley: University of California Press.

Schaffer, Frederic C. 1998. *Democracy in Translation: Understanding Politics in an Unfamiliar Culture.* Ithaca, NY: Cornell University Press.

Schedler, Andreas. 2013. *The Politics of Uncertainty: Sustaining and Subverting Electoral Authoritarianism.* Oxford: Oxford University Press.

Schiller, Jim. 1996. *Developing Jepara: State and Society in New Order Indonesia.* Clayton, Victoria, Australia: Monash University, Centre of Southeast Asian Studies.

Schuler, Paul. 2021. *United Front: Projecting Solidarity through Deliberation in Vietnam's Single-Party Legislature.* Stanford, CA: Stanford University Press.

Selway, Joel Sawat. 2015. *Coalitions of the Well-Being: How Electoral Rules and Ethnic Politics Shape Health Policy in Developing Countries*. New York: Cambridge University Press.

Shair-Rosenfield, Sarah. 2019. *Electoral Reform and the Fate of New Democracies: Lessons from the Indonesian Case*. Ann Arbor: University of Michigan Press.

Shambaugh, David. 2008. *China's Communist Party: Atrophy and Adaptation*. Berkeley: University of California Press.

———. 2013. *China Goes Global: The Partial Power*. New York: Oxford University Press.

———. 2015. "The Coming Chinese Crackup." *Wall Street Journal*, March 6.

Shih, Victor. 2004. "Development the Second Time Around: The Political Logic of Developing Western China." *Journal of East Asian Studies* 4, no. 3 (December): 427–51.

———. 2009. *Factions and Finance in China: Elite Conflict and Inflation*. New York: Cambridge University Press.

———, ed. 2020. *Economic Shocks and Authoritarian Stability: Duration, Financial Control, and Institutions*. Ann Arbor: University of Michigan Press.

Shorrock, Tim. 1986. "The Struggle for Democracy in South Korea in the 1980s and the Rise of Anti-Americanism." *Third World Quarterly* 8, no. 4 (October): 1195–218.

Sidel, John T. 1998. "*Macet Total*: Logics of Circulation and Accumulation in the Demise of Indonesia's New Order." *Indonesia* 66 (October): 159–94.

Sidel, Mark. 2008. *Law and Society in Vietnam*. New York: Cambridge University Press.

Silverstein, Gordon. 2008. "Singapore: The Exception That Proves Rules Matter." In *Rule by Law: The Politics of Courts in Authoritarian Regimes*, edited by Tom Ginsburg and Tamir Moustafa. New York: Cambridge University Press.

Sinpeng, Aim. 2021. *Opposing Democracy in the Digital Age: The Yellow Shirts in Thailand*. Ann Arbor: University of Michigan Press.

Slater, Dan. 2003. "Iron Cage in an Iron Fist: Authoritarian Institutions and the Personalization of Power in Malaysia." *Comparative Politics* 36, no. 1 (October): 81–101.

———. 2004. "Indonesia's Accountability Trap: Party Cartels and Presidential Power after Democratic Transition." *Indonesia*, no. 78 (October): 61–92.

———. 2008. "Can Leviathan Be Democratic? Competitive Elections, Robust Mass Politics, and State Infrastructural Power." *Studies in Comparative International Development* 43, no. 3 (Fall/Winter): 252–72.

———. 2010a. "Altering Authoritarianism: Institutional Complexity and Autocratic Agency in Indonesia." In *Explaining Institutional Change: Ambiguity, Agency, and Power*, edited by James Mahoney and Kathlene Thelen. New York: Cambridge University Press.

———. 2010b. *Ordering Power: Contentious Politics and Authoritarian Leviathans in Southeast Asia*. New York: Cambridge University Press.

———. 2012. "Strong-State Democratization in Malaysia and Singapore." *Journal of Democracy* 23, no. 2 (April): 19–33.

———. 2013. "Democratic Careening." *World Politics* 65, no. 4 (October): 729–63.

———. 2014. "The Elements of Surprise: Assessing Burma's Double-Edged Détente." *South East Asia Research* 22, no. 2 (June): 171–82.

———. 2018. "Party Cartelization, Indonesian-Style: Presidential Power-Sharing and the Contingency of Democratic Opposition." *Journal of East Asian Studies* 18, no. 1 (January): 23–46.

———. 2019. "Democratizing Singapore's Developmental State." In *The Limits of Authoritarian Governance in Singapore's Developmental State*, edited by Lily Rahim and Michael Barr, 305–19. New York: Palgrave Macmillan.

———. 2020. "Maladjustment: Economic Shock and Authoritarian Dynamics in Malaysia." In *Economic Shocks and Authoritarian Stability: Duration, Financial Control, and Institutions*, edited by Victor Shih, 167–88. Ann Arbor: University of Michigan Press.

Slater, Dan, and Sofia Fenner. 2011. "State Power and Staying Power: Infrastructural Mechanisms and Authoritarian Durability." *Journal of International Affairs* 65, no. 1 (Fall/Winter): 15–29.

Slater, Dan, Benjamin Smith, and Gautam Nair. 2014. "Economic Origins of Democratic Breakdown? The Redistributive Model and the Postcolonial State." *Perspectives on Politics* 12, no. 2 (June): 353–74.

Slater, Dan, and Nicholas Rush Smith. 2016. "The Power of Counterrevolution: Elitist Origins of Political Order in Postcolonial Asia and Africa." *American Journal of Sociology* 121, no. 5 (March): 1472–1516.

Slater, Dan, and Joseph Wong. 2013. "The Strength Concede: Ruling Parties and Democratization in Developmental Asia." *Perspectives on Politics* 11, no. 3 (September): 717–33.

———. 2018. "Game for Democracy." In *Life after Dictatorship: Authoritarian Successor Parties Worldwide*, edited by James Loxton and Scott Mainwaring, 284–313. Cambridge: Cambridge University Press.

Smith, Benjamin. 2007. *Hard Times in the Lands of Plenty: Oil Politics in Iran and Indonesia*. Ithaca, NY: Cornell University Press.

Smith, Martin. 1991. *Burma: Insurgency and the Politics of Ethnicity*. London: Zed Books.

Snyder, Jack. 2000. *From Voting to Violence: Democratization and Nationalist Conflict*. New York: W. W. Norton.

Spence, Jonathan. 1990. *The Search for Modern China*. New York: W. W. Norton.

Staniland, Paul. 2021. *Ordering Violence: Explaining Armed Group-State Relations from Conflict to Cooperation*. Ithaca, NY: Cornell University Press.

Stern, Lewis M. 1998. *The Vietnamese Communist Party's Agenda for Reform: A Study of the Eight National Party Congress*. Jefferson, NC: McFarland.

Strangio, Sebastian. 2014. *Hun Sen's Cambodia*. New Haven, CT: Yale University Press.

———. 2020. *In the Dragon's Shadow: Southeast Asia in the Chinese Century*. New Haven, CT: Yale University Press.

Sundhaussen, Ulf. 1995. "Indonesia's New Order: A Model for Myanmar?" *Asian Survey* 35, no. 8 (August): 768–80.

Takayoshi, Matsuo. 1966. "The Development of Democracy in Japan—Taisho Democracy: Its Flowering and Breakdown." *The Developing Economies* 4, no. 4 (December): 612–32.

Takenaka, Harukata. 2014. *Failed Democratization in Prewar Japan*. Stanford, CA: Stanford University Press.

Talmadge, Caitlin. 2015. *The Dictator's Army: Battlefield Effectiveness in Authoritarian Regimes*. Ithaca, NY: Cornell University Press.

Tam, Waikeung. 2001. "A Critical Analysis of Hong Kong's 2000 Legislative Council Election: Context and Implications." *American Asian Review* 19, no. 4 (Winter): 201–37.

———. 2013. *Legal Mobilization under Authoritarianism: The Case of Post-colonial Hong Kong*. New York: Cambridge University Press.

Tang, Wenfang. 2018. "The 'Surprise' of Authoritarian Resilience in China." *American Affairs* 11, no. 1 (Spring): 101–17.

Taylor, Robert. 2001. *Burma: Political Economy under Military Rule*. London: Hurst.

Thawnghmung, Ardeth. 2004. *Behind the Teak Curtain: Authoritarianism, Agricultural Policies, and Political Legitimacy in Rural Burma/Myanmar*. New York: Routledge.

Tien, Hung-mao. 1989. *The Great Transition: Political and Social Change in the Republic of China*. Stanford, CA: Hoover Institution Press.

Tilman, Robert O. 1976. *The Centralization Theme in Malaysian Federal-State Relations, 1957–75*. Singapore: Institute for Southeast Asian Studies.

Tocqueville, Alexis de. (1858) 1955. *The Old Regime and the French Revolution*. New York: Anchor Books.

Tomsa, Dirk. 2008. *Party Politics and Democratization in Indonesia: Golkar in the Post-Suharto Era*. New York: Routledge.

Treisman, Daniel. 2020. "Democracy by Mistake: How the Errors of Autocrats Trigger Transitions to Freer Government." *American Political Science Review* 114, no. 3 (August): 792–810.

Trimberger, Ellen Kay. 1978. *Revolution from Above: Military Bureaucrats and Development in Japan, Turkey, Egypt, and Peru*. New York: Transaction Publishers.

Trocki, Carl A. 2006. *Singapore: Wealth, Power, and the Culture of Control*. New York: Routledge.

Tsai, Kellee. 2007. *Capitalism without Democracy: The Private Sector in Contemporary China*. Ithaca, NY: Cornell University Press.

Tsang, Steve. 1999. "Transforming a Party State into a Democracy." In *Democratization in Taiwan: Implications for China*, edited by Steve Tsang and Hung-mao Tien. Houndmills, UK: Palgrave Macmillan.

Tudor, Maya. 2013. *The Promise of Power: The Origins of Democracy in India and Autocracy in Pakistan*. Cambridge: Cambridge University Press.

Turley, William S., and Mark Selden, eds. 1993. *Reinventing Vietnamese Socialism: Do Moi in Comparative Perspective*. Boulder, CO: Westview Press.

Un, Kheang. 2019. *Cambodia: Return to Authoritarianism*. New York: Cambridge University Press.

Unger, Jonathan, ed. 1991. *The Pro-democracy Protests in China: Reports from the Provinces*. Armonk, NY: M. E. Sharpe.

Ungpakorn, Ji. 1997. *The Struggle for Democracy and Social Justice in Thailand*. Bangkok: Arom Pongpangan Foundation.

Vasavakul, Thaveeporn. 2019. *Vietnam: A Pathway from State Socialism*. New York: Cambridge University Press.

Veg, Sebastian. 2017. "The Rise of 'Localism' and Civic Identity in Post-handover Hong Kong: Questioning the Chinese Nation-State." *China Quarterly*, no. 230 (April): 323–47.

Vu, Tuong. 2010. *Paths to Development in Asia: South Korea, Vietnam, China, and Indonesia*. New York: Cambridge University Press.

———. 2017. *Vietnam's Communist Revolution: The Power and Limits of Ideology*. New York: Cambridge University Press.

Vuving, Alexander L. 2013. "Vietnam in 2012." *Southeast Asian Affairs* 2013: 325–47.

Wachman, Alan. 1994. *Taiwan: National Identity and Democratization*. Armonk, NY: M. E. Sharpe.

Wade, Robert. 1990. *Governing the Market: Economic Theory and the Role of Government in East Asian Industrialization.* Princeton, NJ: Princeton University Press.

Wagner, Edward. 1961. "Failure in Korea." *Foreign Affairs* 40, no. 1 (October): 128–35.

Walker, Andrew. 2012. *Thailand's Political Peasants: Power in the Modern Rural Economy.* Madison: University of Wisconsin Press.

Wallace, Jeremy L. 2014. *Cities and Stability: Urbanization, Redistribution and Regime Survival in China.* New York: Oxford University Press.

Walton, Matthew, and Susan Hayward. 2014. *Contesting Buddhist Narratives: Democratization, Nationalism, and Communal Violence in Myanmar.* Honolulu: East-West Center.

Wang, Vincent Wei-Cheng. 1995. "Developing the Information Industry in Taiwan: Entrepreneurial State, Guerrilla Capitalists, and Accommodative Technologists." *Pacific Affairs* 68, no. 4 (Winter): 551–76.

Wang, Yuhua. 2014. *Tying the Autocrat's Hands: The Rise of the Rule of Law in China.* New York: Cambridge University Press.

Wedeman, Andrew. 2003. *From Mao to Markets: Rent-Seeking, Local Protectionism, and Marketization in China.* Cambridge: Cambridge University Press.

Weiss, Meredith L. 2006. *Protest and Possibilities: Civil Society and Coalitions for Political Change in Malaysia.* Stanford, CA: Stanford University Press.

———. 2021. *The Roots of Resilience: Party Machines and Grassroots Politics in Southeast Asia.* Ithaca, NY: Cornell University Press.

White, Gordon. 1993. *Riding the Tiger: The Politics of Economic Reform in Post-Mao China.* Stanford, CA: Stanford University Press.

Winckler, Edwin. 1984. "Institutionalization and Participation on Taiwan: From Hard to Soft Authoritarianism?" *China Quarterly* 99 (September): 481–99.

Wong, Joseph. 2004a. "Democratization and the Left: Comparing East Asia and Latin America." *Comparative Political Studies* 37, no. 11 (December): 1213–37.

———. 2004b. *Healthy Democracies: Welfare Politics in Taiwan and South Korea.* Ithaca, NY: Cornell University Press.

———. 2008. "Maintaining KMT Dominance: Party Adaptation in Authoritarian and Democratic Taiwan." In *Political Transitions in Dominant Party Systems: Learning to Lose,* edited by Edward Friedman and Joseph Wong. New York: Routledge.

———. 2011. *Betting on Biotech: Innovation and the Limits of Asia's Developmental State.* Ithaca, NY: Cornell University Press.

———. 2020. "Authoritarian Durability in East Asia's Developmental States." In *Economic Shocks and Authoritarian Stability: Duration, Financial Control, and Institutions,* edited by Victor Shih. Ann Arbor: University of Michigan Press.

Wong, Matthew Y. H. 2019. "Chinese Influence, U.S. Linkages, or Neither? Comparing Regime Changes in Myanmar and Thailand." *Democratization* 26, no. 3 (July): 359–81.

Wong, Stan Hok-Wui, and Kin Man Wan. 2018. "The Housing Boom and the Rise of Localism in Hong Kong: Evidence from the Legislative Council Election in 2016." *China Perspectives* 3, no. 114 (April): 31–40.

Woo, Jung-En. 1991. *Race to the Swift: State and Finance in Korean Industrialization.* New York: Columbia University Press.

World Bank. 1993. *The East Asian Miracle: Economic Growth and Public Policy*. Oxford: Oxford University Press.

Yang, Jisheng. 2012. *Tombstone: The Great Chinese Famine, 1958 1962*. New York: Farrar, Straus and Giroux.

Yip, Stan, and Ronald Yeung. 2014. "The 2012 Legislative Council Election in Hong Kong." *Electoral Studies* 35:366–70.

Yip, Winnie, and William Hsiao. 2008. "The Chinese Health System at a Crossroads." *Health Affairs* 27, no. 2 (March/April): 460–68.

Yu Keping. 2009. *Democracy Is a Good Thing: Essays on Politics, Society, and Culture in Contemporary China*. Washington, DC: Brookings Institution Press.

Zhang, Le-Yin. 1999. "Chinese Central-Provincial Fiscal Relationships, Budgetary Decline and the Impact of the 1994 Fiscal Reform: An Evaluation." *China Quarterly* 157 (March): 115–41.

Ziblatt, Daniel. 2017. *Conservative Parties and the Birth of Democracy in Modern Europe, 1848–1950*. New York: Cambridge University Press.

Zin, Min, and Brian Joseph. 2012. "The Democrats' Opportunity." *Journal of Democracy* 23, no. 4 (October): 104–19.

Zweig, David. 2002. *Internationalizing China: Domestic Interests and Global Linkages*. Ithaca, NY: Cornell University Press.

INDEX

Note: Page numbers in *italics* indicate figures and tables.

agriculture, 131, 162, 168

Akbar Tandjung, 194, 199

Anwar Ibrahim, 225, 240, 242, 244, 245, 246

apex of power, 121, 142, 195, 221, 230, 271, 272

Aquino, Corazon, 6, 7

Arakan Rohingya Salvation Army (Myanmar), 216–17

ASEAN (Association of Southeast Asian Nations), 287, 289

Ashida, Hitoshi, 72

Asian financial crisis (1997–1998), 5, 22; Indonesia and, 179, 181, 184, 187, 190; Malaysia and, 225, 226, 236, 237, 241; Thailand and, 180, 241; Vietnam and, 280, 284

Asian Infrastructure Investment Bank, 265

Aung San Suu Kyi, 181, 211, 212, 217

authoritarianism, embittered, 224, 234, 252, 255; "bittersweet spot" and, 221, 275; Malaysia and, 244–47, 286

authoritarian regimes/elites, 3, 10, 13, 17, 57, 301n4; conservative, 302–3n15; democratization as last resort, 8; durable, 21; electoral, 14, 45, 49, 86, 237, 303n21; institutions built by, 186; preemptive reform and, 300; regime confidence and, 4, 5, 18–20; signals received by, 21–23, 296, 304n33; strength and weakness of, 15–18, 298; tragedy of dominant-party politics and, 224, 234, 299–300

Badawi, Abdullah, 245–46

Bangladesh, 29, 34, 38

Bell, Daniel, 276

Bhumipol, king of Thailand, 180, 206

"bittersweet spot," 23, 31, 147, 175, 221; CCP and, 272; CPP and, 24, 285; DJP and, 141, 148; Golkar (Indonesia) and, 190, 195; KMT and, 111, 148; Malaysia, 300; PAP (Singapore) and, 224, 231, 232; UMNO, 245, 248; UMNO-BN and, 225, 240, 286

BN (Barisan Nasional/National Front, Malaysia), 225, 234, 235, 238, 239; tragedy of dominant-party politics in, 234. *See also* UMNO

bureaucracy, 3, 4; bureaucratic continuity, 76; in developmental socialist cluster, 17; "iron cage" of, 16; in Japan, 75–76, 82, 86; in Taiwan, 90, 94, 203

Cambodia, 2, 9, 16, 51, 256, 285–86; Asian geography and, 30; as "avoidance case," 12, 21, 26; "bittersweet spot" missed by, 24, 285, 300; bureaucracy of, 17; CNRP (Cambodian National Rescue Party), 291–92; democracy scores of, 46; democratization in, 48; economic development in, 45; economic strength gathered in, 288–90; as "embittered case," 12, 24; emergence from war and genocide, 286–88; French colonial rule in, 33; Funcinpec (royalist party), 288; history of revolutionary violence in, 55; Japan's developmentalism and, 34; Khmer Rouge, 55, 257, 279, 286, 287; tragedy of dominant-party

337

A NOTE ON THE TYPE

This book has been composed in Arno, an Old-style serif typeface in the classic Venetian tradition, designed by Robert Slimbach at Adobe.

Printed in the USA
CPSIA information can be obtained
at www.ICGtesting.com
JSHW021031020724
65750JS00002B/8